Model Equity Compensation Plans

Model Equity Compensation Plans

Edited by
Scott S. Rodrick

The National Center for Employee Ownership
Oakland, California

Model Equity Compensation Plans
Editing and book design by Scott S. Rodrick

The National Center for Employee Ownership
1736 Franklin St., 8th Floor
Oakland, CA 94612
(510) 208-1300
(510) 272-9510 (fax)
E-mail: *nceo@nceo.org*
Web: *http://www.nceo.org/*

First printed September 1998
Reprinted with minor changes, May 1999, January 2000, June 2000

ISBN: 092690237-7

Table of Contents

Preface

Model Equity Compensation Plans is published by the National Center for Employee Ownership (NCEO) as a companion to *The Stock Options Book* and other NCEO publications on stock options and related plans. Whereas *The Stock Options Book* and other NCEO publications discuss what the various plans are, how they work, what their practical applications are, and so on, this book provides examples of the actual plans themselves, together with section-by-section explanations of the main plan documents.

What Plans Are (and Are Not) Covered Here

This book generally covers each of the plans discussed in *The Stock Options Book:*

- Incentive stock option (ISO) plans

- Nonqualified stock option (NSO) plans

- Employee stock purchase plans ("423" or "ESPP" plans)

- Phantom stock plans

Note that as presented here, the ISO and NSO documents are not wholly independent documents but rather *agreements* under an overall "Equity Incentive Plan." Also fitting into the "Equity Incentive Plan" scheme are a "Summary Memorandum" addressed to plan participants and a "Restricted Stock Purchase Agreement" to be used in conjunction with the stock option plans. (David Johanson, the drafter of the Equity Incentive Plan documents, strongly recommends doing it that way—that is, to create a single stock option plan that provides for ISOs, NSOs, and restricted stock grants.) Thus, the model plans presented here consist of three "packages":

1. Equity Incentive Plan (under which ISOs and/or NSOs may be granted)

2. Employee Stock Purchase Plan

3. Phantom Stock Plan

See the table of contents for a listing of the individual components of these plans. The page numbers of the explanations are keyed to the page numbers of the plans they refer to; for example, the Incentive Stock Option Agreement is on pages B-1, B-2, etc., and the explanation for it is on pages Exp-B-1, Exp-B-2, etc.

A company may choose to use any one or a combination of the above plans, depending on its circumstances and goals. Note that the stock purchase plan characterizes the right to purchase stock under the plan as a "stock option." Do not be confused by this terminology; some people refer to employee stock purchase plans as stock option plans, while others reserve that term for "true" stock options, namely ISOs and NSOs.

This book does *not* address the employee stock ownership plan (ESOP), a retirement plan governed by the Employee Retirement Income Security Act of 1974, as amended (ERISA), because an ESOP is fundamentally different from the above plans. Many of the NCEO's other publications cover ESOPs in detail.

How to Use This Book

These documents are necessarily model plans, not prototypes. That is, these plans are examples of what can be done, but are not do-it-yourself, fill-in-the-blank "cookbook" examples. Nothing here constitutes legal or other professional advice on which any company, individual, or other entity should solely rely in setting up or administering a plan. Instead, this book should help you understand how the plans discussed here work so that, in conjunction with qualified professionals, you can make sure your plan is tailored to your specific needs. Among other things, your plan may need to take local state laws into consideration. (For example, the stock option and stock purchase plans were prepared for California corporations, and some of the language addresses that.) We have performed only minor editing to prepare the plans for publication; our intent is to provide you directly with the work product of top attorneys in this field.

The NCEO maintains a directory of consultants (the *Resource Guide*), which is distributed exclusively to its members; upon request, the NCEO also provides individual referrals to its members.

About the Authors

Most of the plans have been designed by David R. Johanson, who authored the chapter in *The Stock Options Book* on "Employee Stock Options and Related Equity Incentives." He is a partner in the law firm of Johanson Berenson LLP, which has offices in California; Washington, D.C.; and Virginia. Mr. Johanson's office is located in Napa, California. The explanations of these plans were co-written by Mr. Johanson together with Gregory M. Hansen and James M. Cribley of the law firm of Case Bigelow & Lombardi in Hawaii.

The phantom stock plan and its explanation are by Brian Snarr, a partner in the law firm of Morrison Cohen Singer & Weinstein LLP in New York. Mr. Snarr wrote the chapters in *The Stock Options Book* on "Equity Compensation in Closely Held Companies" and "The Phantom Stock Alternative."

What Is on the Diskette

At the back of this book you will find a 3.5-inch, 1.44 MB IBM-compatible formatted diskette. It contains copies of the plans (but not the section-by-section explanations of the plans) in ASCII format (plain text, with the filename extension .TXT) and RTF format (Rich Text Format, with the filename extension .RTF). Any word processing program should be able to open one or both of these formats. The documents are formatted in a relatively plain fashion so that their structure is still intelligible when converted to plain text (where all formatting such as bold, etc. is lost). Appendix A is a key to which files match which documents.

Copyright Restrictions

Preface

Part 1

Employee Stock Option Plans

___ 199_ *Equity Incentive Plan*

SECTION 1
PURPOSE

The purpose of the _____ 199_ Equity Incentive Plan is to provide a means whereby _____, Inc., a California corporation (the "Corporation"), may attract able persons to remain in or to enter the employ of the Corporation, a Parent Corporation, or a Subsidiary and to provide a means whereby those employees, directors, officers, and other individuals or entities upon whom the responsibilities of the successful administration, management, planning, and/or organization of the Corporation may rest, and whose present and potential contributions to the welfare of the Corporation, a Parent Corporation or a Subsidiary are of importance, can acquire and maintain stock ownership, thereby strengthening their concern for the long-term welfare of the Corporation. A further purpose of the Plan is to provide such employees and individuals or entities with additional incentive and reward opportunities designed to enhance the profitable growth of the Corporation over the long term. Accordingly, the Plan provides for granting Common Stock, Incentive Stock Options, options which do not constitute Incentive Stock Options, or any combination of the foregoing, as is best suited to the circumstances of the particular employees and individuals or entities as provided herein.

SECTION 2
DEFINITIONS

The following definitions shall be applicable during the term of the Plan unless specifically modified by any paragraph:

(a)   *Award* means, individually or collectively, any Option granted pursuant to the Plan.

(b)   *Board* means the board of directors of the Corporation.

(c)   *Change of Control Value* means the amount determined in Clause (i), (ii) or (iii), whichever is applicable, as follows: (i) the per share price offered to stockholders of the Corporation in any merger, consolidation, sale or assets or dissolution transaction, (ii) the price per share offered to stockholders of the corporation in any tender offer or exchange offer whereby a Corporate Change takes place or (iii) if a Corporate Change occurs other than as described in Clause (i) or Clause (ii), the fair market value per share determined by the Board as of the date determined by the Board to be the date of cancellation and surrender of an Option. If the consideration offered to stockholders of the Corporation in any transaction described in this Paragraph or Paragraphs (d) and (e) of Section 8 consists of anything other than cash, the Board shall determine the fair cash equivalent of the portion of the consideration offered which is other than cash.

(d)   *Code* means the Internal Revenue Code of 1986, as amended. Reference in the Plan to any Section of the Code shall be deemed to include any amendments or successor provisions to such Section and any regulations under such Section.

(e)   *Common Stock* means the common stock of the Corporation.

(f)   *Corporation* means _____, Inc.

(g)   *Corporate Change* means one of the following events: (i) the merger, consolidation or other reorganization of the Corporation in which the outstanding Common Stock is converted into or exchanged for a different class of securities of the Corporation, a class of securities of any other issuer (except a Subsidiary or Parent Corporation), cash or other property other than (a) a merger, consolidation or reorganization of the Corporation which would result in the voting stock of the Corporation outstanding immediately prior thereto continuing to represent (either by remaining outstanding or by being converted into voting securities of the surviving entity), in combination with the ownership of any trustee or other fiduciary holding securities under an employee benefit plan of the Corporation, at least sixty percent (60%) of the combined voting power of the voting stock of the Corporation or such surviving entity outstanding immediately after such merger, consolidation or reorganization of the Corporation, or (b) merger, consolidation or reorganization of the Corporation effected to implement a recapitalization of the Corporation (or similar transaction) in which no person acquires more than forty-nine percent (49%) of the combined voting power of the Corporation's then outstanding stock; (ii) the sale, lease or exchange of all or substantially all of the assets of the Corporation to any other corporation or entity (except a Subsidiary or Parent Corporation); (iii) the adoption by the stockholders of the Corporation of a plan of liquidation and dissolution; (iv) the acquisition (other than acquisition pursuant to any other clause of this definition) by any person or entity, including without limitation a "group" as contemplated by Section 13(d)(3) of the Exchange Act, of beneficial ownership, as contemplated by such Section, of more than twenty-five percent (25%) (based on voting power) of the Corporation's outstanding capital stock or acquisition by a person or entity who currently has beneficial ownership which increases such person's or entity's beneficial ownership to fifty percent (50%) or more (based on voting power) of the Corporation's outstanding capital stock; or (v) as a result of or in connection with a

*Equity
Incentive
Plan*

contested election of directors, the persons who were directors of the Corporation before such election shall cease to constitute a majority of the Board. Notwithstanding the provisions of clause (iv) above, a Corporate Change shall not be considered to have occurred upon the acquisition (other than acquisition pursuant to any other clause of the preceding sentence) by any person or entity, including without limitation a "group" as contemplated by Section 13(d)(3) of the Exchange Act, of beneficial ownership, as contemplated by such Section, of more than twenty-five percent (25%) (based on voting power) of the Corporation's outstanding capital stock or the requisite percentage to increase their ownership to fifty percent (50%) resulting from a public offering of securities of the Corporation under the Securities Act of 1933, as amended.

(h)   *Designated Officer* means an officer of the Corporation, such as the President or Chief Operating Officer, who is given authority by the Board to grant options or make stock grants under the Plan.

(i)   *Exchange Act* means the Securities Exchange Act of 1934, as amended.

(j)   *Fair Market Value* means, as of any specified date, the closing price of the Common Stock on the NASDAQ (or, if the Common Stock is not listed on such exchange, such other national securities exchange on which the Common Stock is then listed) on that date, or if no prices are reported on that date, on the last preceding date on which such prices of the Common Stock are so reported. If the Common Stock is not then listed on any national securities exchange but is traded over the counter at the time determination of its Fair Market Value is required to be made hereunder, its Fair Market Value shall be deemed to be equal to the average between the reported high and low sales prices of Common Stock on the most recent date on which Common Stock was publicly traded. If the Common Stock is not publicly traded at the time a determination of its value is required to be made hereunder, the determination of its Fair Market Value shall be made by the Board in such manner as it deems appropriate (such determination will be made in good-faith as required by Section 422(c)(1) of the Code and may be based on the advice of an independent investment banker or appraiser recognized to be expert in making such valuations). Fair Market Value also shall satisfy the requirements under Section 260.140 of the California Code of Regulations, as necessary to qualify for an exemption from the provisions of Section 25110 of the California Corporations Code.

Equity Incentive Plan

(k)   *Grant* means individually or collectively, any Common Stock granted pursuant to the Plan.

(l)   *Grantee* means an employee, director, officer, other individual or entity who has been granted Common Stock pursuant to the Plan.

(m)   *Holder* means an individual or entity who has been granted an Award.

(n)   *Incentive Stock Option* means an Option within the meaning of Section 422 of the Code.

(o)   *Option* means an Award granted under Section 7 of the Plan and includes both Incentive Stock Options to purchase Common Stock and Options which do not constitute Incentive Stock Options to purchase Common Stock.

(p)   *Option Agreement* means a written agreement between the Corporation and an employee with respect to an Option.

(q)   *Optionee* means an employee, director, officer, entity or individual who has been granted an Option.

(r)   *Parent Corporation* shall have the meaning set forth in Section 424(e) of the Code.

(s)   *Plan* means the _____ 199_ Equity Incentive Plan.

(t)   *Rule 16b-3* means Rule 16b-3 of the General Rules and Regulations of the Securities and Exchange Commission under the Exchange Act, as such rule is currently in effect or as hereafter modified or amended.

(u)   *Subsidiary* means a company (whether a corporation, partnership, joint venture or other form of entity) in which the Corporation, or a corporation in which the Corporation owns a majority of the shares of capital stock, directly or indirectly, owns an equity interest of fifty percent (50%) or more, except solely with respect to the issuance of Incentive Stock Options the term "Subsidiary" shall have the same meaning as the term "subsidiary corporation" as defined in Section 424(f) of the Code.

Equity
Incentive
Plan

SECTION 3
EFFECTIVE DATE AND DURATION OF THE PLAN

The Plan shall be effective as of _____, 199_, the date of its adoption by the Board, provided that the Plan is approved by the stockholders of the Corporation within twelve (12) months before or thereafter and on or prior to the date of the first annual meeting of stockholders of the Corporation held subsequent to the acquisition of an equity security by a Holder hereunder for which exemption is claimed under Rule 16b-3. Notwithstanding any provision of the Plan or of any Option Agreement, no Option shall be exercisable and no Common Stock may be granted prior to such stockholder approval. The Plan shall be terminated and no further Awards or Common Stock may be granted under the Plan after ten (10) years from the date the Plan is adopted by the Board or the date the Plan is approved by the Corporation's shareholders, whichever is earlier. Subject to the provisions of Section 9, the Plan shall remain in effect until all Options granted under the Plan have been exercised or have expired by reason of lapse of time and all restrictions imposed upon restricted stock awards have lapsed. Any option exercised before shareholder approval is obtained must be rescinded if shareholder approval is not obtained within twelve (12) months before or after the Plan is adopted. Such shares shall not be counted in determining whether such approval is granted.

SECTION 4
ADMINISTRATION

(a)   *Administration of Plan by Board.* The Plan shall be administered by the Board in compliance with Rule 16b-3. Members of the Board shall abstain from participating in and deciding matters which directly affect their individual ownership interests under the Plan.

(b)   *Powers.* Subject to the terms of the Plan, the Board shall elect one or several Designated Officers who shall have sole authority, in their discretion, to determine which employees, officers, directors, individuals or entities shall receive an Award or Grant, the time or times when such Award or Grant shall be made, whether Common Stock, an Incentive Stock Option or nonqualified Option shall be granted and the number of shares of Common Stock which may be issued under each Option. In making such determinations, the Designated Officer may take into account the nature of the services rendered by these individuals, their present and potential contribution to the success of the Corporation, a Parent Corporation or a Subsidiary, and such other factors as the Board in its discretion shall deem relevant.

*Equity
Incentive
Plan*

(c)   *Additional Powers.* The Board shall have such additional powers as are delegated to it by the other provisions of the Plan. Subject to the express provisions of the Plan, the Board is authorized in its sole discretion, exercised in a nondiscriminatory manner, to construe and interpret the Plan and the respective agreements executed thereunder, to prescribe such rules and regulations relating to the Plan as it may deem advisable to carry out the Plan, and to determine the terms, restrictions and provisions of each Award or Grant, including such terms, restrictions and provisions as shall be requisite in the judgment of the Board to cause designated Options to qualify as Incentive Stock Options, and to make all other determinations necessary or advisable for administering the Plan. The Board may correct any defect or supply any omission or reconcile any inconsistency in any agreement relating to an Award or Grant in the manner and to the extent it shall deem expedient to carry it into effect. The determination of the Board on the matters referred to in this Section 4 shall be conclusive.

(d) *Compliance With Code Section 162(m).* In the event the Corporation, a Parent Corporation or a Subsidiary becomes a "publicly-held corporation" as defined in Section 162(m)(2) of the Code, the Corporation may establish a committee of outside directors meeting the requirements of Code Section 162(m) to (i) approve the grant of Options which might reasonably be anticipated to result in the payment of employee remuneration that would otherwise exceed the limit on employee remuneration deductible for income tax purposes by the Corporation pursuant to Code Section 162(m) and (ii) administer the Plan. In such event, the powers reserved to the Board in the Plan shall be exercised by such compensation committee. In addition, Options under the Plan shall be granted upon satisfaction of the conditions to such grants provided pursuant to Code Section 162(m) and any Treasury Regulations promulgated thereunder.

SECTION 5
GRANT OF OPTIONS AND STOCK SUBJECT TO THE PLAN

*Equity
Incentive
Plan*

(a) *Award Limits.* A Designated Officer may from time to time grant Awards and/or make Grants to one or more employees, directors, officers, individuals or entities determined by him or her to be eligible for participation in the Plan in accordance with the provisions of Section 6 of the Plan. The aggregate number of shares of Common Stock that may be issued under the Plan shall not exceed _____ shares. The aggregate number of shares of Common Stock that may be issued to any Holder and/or granted to any Grantee under the Plan shall not exceed [_____ percent (__%)] of the aggregate number of shares referred to in the preceding sentence. The total number of shares issuable upon exercise of all outstanding Options shall not exceed a number of shares which is equal to thirty percent (30%) of the then outstanding shares of the Corporation. Any of such shares which remain unissued and which are not subject to outstanding Options and/or Grants at the termination of the Plan shall cease to be subject to the Plan but, until termination of the Plan, the Corporation shall at all times reserve a sufficient number of shares to meet the requirements of the Plan. Shares shall be deemed to have been issued under the Plan only to the extent actually issued and delivered pursuant to an Award or Grant. To the extent that an Award or Grant lapses or the rights of its Holder or Grantee terminate, any shares of Common Stock subject to such Award or Grant shall again be available for the grant of an Award or making of a Grant. The aggregate number of shares which may be issued under the Plan shall be subject to adjustment in the same manner as provided in Section 8 of the Plan with respect to shares of Common Stock subject to Options then outstanding. Separate stock certificates shall be issued by the Corporation for those shares acquired pursuant to a Grant, the exercise of an Incentive Stock Option and for those shares acquired pursuant to the exercise of any Option which does not constitute an Incentive Stock Option.

(b)   *Stock Offered.* The stock to be offered pursuant to an Award or Grant may be authorized but unissued Common Stock or Common Stock previously issued and outstanding and reacquired by the Corporation.

SECTION 6
ELIGIBILITY

An Incentive Stock Option Award made pursuant to the Plan may be granted only to an individual who, at the time of grant, is an employee of the Corporation, a Parent Corporation or a Subsidiary. An Award of an Option which is not an Incentive Stock Option or a Grant of Common Stock may be made to an individual who, at the time of Award or Grant, is an employee of the Corporation, a Parent Corporation or a Subsidiary, or to an individual who has been identified by the Board or Designated Officer to receive an Award or Grant due to their contribution or service to the Corporation, including members of the Board of Directors of the Corporation, a Parent Corporation or a Subsidiary. An Award or Grant made pursuant to the Plan may be made on more than one occasion to the same person, and such Award or Grant may include a Common Stock Grant, an Incentive Stock Option, an Option which is not an Incentive Stock Option, or any combination thereof. Each Award or Grant shall be evidenced by a written instrument duly executed by or on behalf of the Corporation.

*Equity
Incentive
Plan*

SECTION 7
STOCK OPTIONS/GRANTS

(a)   *Stock Option Agreement.* Each Option shall be evidenced by an Option Agreement between the Corporation and the Optionee which shall contain such terms and conditions as may be approved by the Board and agreed upon by the Holder. The terms and conditions of the respective Option Agreements need not be identical. Each Option Agreement shall specify the effect of termination of employment, total and permanent disability, retirement or death on the exercisability of the Option. Under each Option Agreement, a Holder shall have the right to appoint any individual or legal entity in writing as his or her beneficiary under the Plan in the event of his death. Such designation may be revoked in writing by the Holder at any time and a new beneficiary may be appointed in writing on the form provided by the Board for such purpose. In the absence of such appointment, the beneficiary shall be the legal representative of the Holder's estate.

(b)   *Option Period.* The term of each Option shall be as specified by the Board at the date of grant and shall be stated in the Option Agreement; provided, however, that an option may not be exercised more than one hundred twenty (120) months from the date it is granted.

(c)   *Limitations on Exercise of Option.* Any Option granted hereunder shall be exercisable at such times and under such conditions as determined by the Board and as shall be permissible under the terms of the Plan, which shall be specified in the Option Agreement evidencing the Option; provided, however, that an option shall be exercised at the rate of at least twenty percent (20%) per year over five (5) years from the date it is granted. An Option may not be exercised for fractional shares.

(d)   *Special Limitations on Incentive Stock Options.* To the extent that the aggregate Fair Market Value (determined at the time the respective Incentive Stock Option is granted) of Common Stock with respect to which Incentive Stock Options are exercisable for the first time by an individual during any calendar year under all incentive stock option plans of the Corporation (and any Parent Corporation or Subsidiary) exceeds One Hundred Thousand Dollars ($100,000) (within the meaning of Section 422 of the Code), such excess Incentive Stock Options shall be treated as Options which do not constitute Incentive Stock Options. The Board shall determine, in accordance with applicable provisions of the Code, Treasury Regulations and other administrative pronouncements, which of an Optionee's Incentive Stock Options will not constitute Incentive Stock Options because of such limitation and shall notify the Optionee of such determination as soon as practicable after such determination. No Incentive Stock Option shall be granted to an individual if, at the time the Option is granted, such individual owns stock possessing more than ten percent (10%) of the total combined voting power of all classes of stock of the Corporation or of its Parent Corporation or a Subsidiary, within the meaning of Section 422(b)(6) of the Code, unless (i) at the time such Option is granted the Option price is at least one hundred ten percent (110%) of the Fair Market Value of the Common Stock subject to the Option and (ii) such Option by its terms is not exercisable after the expiration of five years from the date of grant.

(e)   *Option Price.* The purchase price of Common Stock issued under each Option shall be determined by the Board and shall be stated in the Option Agreement, but such purchase price shall, in the case of Incentive Stock Options, not be less than the Fair Market Value of Common Stock subject to the Option on the date the Option is granted, and, in the case of Options which do not constitute Incentive

Equity
Incentive
Plan

Stock Options, not be less than eighty-five percent (85%) of the fair value of the stock at the time the option is granted, except that the price shall be one hundred ten percent (110%) of the fair value in the case of any person or entity who owns stock comprising more than ten percent (10%) of the total combined voting power of all classes of stock of the Corporation or its Parent Corporation or Subsidiary. Fair value in the case of options that do not constitute Incentive Stock Options shall have the same meaning as set forth in Section 260.140.50 of the California Code of Regulations.

(f)   *Options and Rights in Substitution for Stock Options Made by Other Corporations.* Options may be granted under the Plan from time to time in substitution for stock options held by employees of corporations who become, or who became prior to the effective date of the Plan, employees of the Corporation, of any Parent Corporation or of any Subsidiary as a result of a merger or consolidation of the employing corporation with the Corporation, such Parent Corporation or such Subsidiary, or the acquisition by the Corporation, a Parent Corporation or a Subsidiary of all or a portion of the assets of the employing corporation, or the acquisition by the Corporation, a Parent Corporation or a Subsidiary of stock of the employing corporation with the result that such employing corporation becomes a Subsidiary.

(g)   *Restricted Stock Option Purchase Agreement.* Notwithstanding the foregoing, at the election of the Holder, the Option can be exercised provided that the Holder shall, as a condition of such exercise, execute and deliver the Restricted Stock Option Purchase Agreement (the "Purchase Agreement"), pursuant to which the Corporation shall be granted a "Repurchase Option" and "Right of First Refusal" as to all "Shares" (as such terms are defined in the Purchase Agreement).

Equity Incentive Plan

(h)   *Restricted Stock Grant Agreement.* Each Grant shall be evidenced by the execution and delivery of a Restricted Stock Grant Agreement (the "Grant Agreement"), pursuant to which the Corporation shall be granted a "Repurchase Option" and "Right of First Refusal" as to all "Shares" (as such terms are defined in the Grant Agreement).

SECTION 8
RECAPITALIZATION OR REORGANIZATION

(a)   Except as hereinafter otherwise provided, Awards or Grants shall be subject to adjustment by the Board at its discretion as to the number and price of shares of Common Stock in the event of changes in the outstanding Common Stock by reason of stock dividends, stock splits, reverse stock splits, reclassifications, recapitalizations, reorganizations, mergers, consolidations, combinations, exchanges or other relevant changes in capitalization occurring after the date of the grant of any such Options or Common Stock.

(b)   The existence of the Plan and the Awards and/or Grants made hereunder shall not affect in any way the right or power of the Board or the stockholders of the Corporation to make or authorize any adjustment, recapitalization, reorganization or other change in the capital structure of the Corporation, a Parent Corporation or a Subsidiary or their business, any merger or consolidation of the Corporation, a Parent Corporation or a Subsidiary, any issue of debt or equity securities having any priority or preference with respect to or affecting Common Stock or the rights thereof, the dissolution or liquidation of the Corporation, a Parent Corporation or a Subsidiary, or any sale, lease, exchange or other disposition of all or any part of their assets or business or any other corporate act or proceeding.

Equity
Incentive
Plan

(c)   The shares with respect to which Options may be granted are shares of Common Stock as presently constituted but if and whenever, prior to the expiration of an Option theretofore granted, the Corporation shall effect a subdivision or consolidation of shares of Common Stock or the payment of a stock dividend on Common Stock without receipt of consideration by the Corporation, the number of shares of Common Stock with respect to which such Option may thereafter be exercised (i) in the event of an increase in the number of outstanding shares shall be proportionately increased, and the purchase price per share shall be proportionately reduced, and (ii) in the event of a reduction in the number of outstanding shares shall be proportionately reduced, and the purchase price per share shall be proportionately increased.

(d)   If the Corporation recapitalizes or otherwise changes its capital structure, thereafter upon any exercise of an Option theretofore granted, the Optionee shall be entitled to purchase under such Option, in lieu of the number of shares of Common Stock as to which such Option shall then be exercisable, the number and class of shares of stock and securities, and the cash and other property to which the Optionee would have been entitled pursuant to the terms of the recapitalization if, immediately prior to such recapitalization, the Optionee had been the holder of such record of the number of shares of Common Stock then covered by such Option.

(e)   In the event of a Corporate Change, unless otherwise deemed to be impractical by the Board, then no later than (i) two business days prior to any Corporate Change referenced in Clause (i), (ii), (iii) and (v) of the definition thereof or (ii) ten business days after any Corporate Change referenced in Clause (iv) of the definition thereof, the Board, acting in its sole discretion without the consent or approval of any Optionee or Grantee, shall act to effect the following alternatives with respect to outstanding Options which acts may vary among in-dividual Optionees and, with respect to acts taken pursuant to Clause (i) above, may be contingent upon effectuation of the Corpo-rate Change: (A) in the event of a Corporate Change referenced in Clauses (i) and (ii) acceleration of exercise for all Options then out-standing so that such Options may be exercised in full for a limited period of time on or before a specified date (before or after such Cor-porate Change) fixed by the Board, after which specified date all un-exercised Options and all rights of Optionees thereunder shall termi-nate; (B) in the event of a Corporate Change referenced in Clauses (iii), (iv) and (v) require the mandatory surrender to the Corporation by selected Optionees of some or all of the outstanding Options held by such Optionees (irrespective of whether such Options are then ex-ercisable under the provisions of the Plan) as of a date (before or after such Corporate Change) specified by the Board, in which event the Board shall thereupon cancel such Options and pay to each Optionee an amount of cash per share equal to the excess, if any, of the Change of Control Value of the shares subject to such Option over the exer-cise price(s) under such Options for such shares; (C) in the event of a Corporate Change referenced in Clauses (iii), (iv) and (v), make such adjustments to Options then outstanding as the Board deems appro-priate to reflect such Corporate Change (provided, however, that the Board may determine in its sole discretion that no adjustment is nec-essary to Options then outstanding); (D) in the event of a Corporate Change referenced in Clauses (iii), (iv) and (v), provide that thereaf-ter upon any exercise of an Option theretofore granted the Optionee shall be entitled to purchase under such Option, in lieu of the num-ber of shares of Common Stock as to which such Option shall then be exercisable, the number and class of shares of stock or other securities or property (including, without limitation, cash) to which the Op-tionee would have been entitled pursuant to the terms of the agree-ment of merger, consolidation or sale of assets or plan of liquidation and dissolution if, immediately prior to such merger, consolidation or sale of assets or any distribution in liquidation and dissolution of the Corporation, the Optionee had been the holder of record of the num-ber of shares of Common Stock then covered by such Option; or (E) in the event of a Corporate Change referenced in Clauses (iii), (iv) and (v), cancel the Options granted if the Fair Market Value of the Common Stock underlying the Options is below the Option exercise price.

Equity Incentive Plan

(f)   Except as hereinbefore expressly provided, issuance by the Corpora-tion of shares of stock of any class or securities convertible into shares of stock of any class, for cash, property, labor or services, upon direct sale, upon the exercise of rights or warranty to subscribe there-fore, or upon conversion of shares or obligations of the Corporation convertible into such shares or other securities, and in any case whether or not for fair value, shall not affect, and no adjustment by reason thereof shall be made with respect to, the number of shares of Common Stock subject to Options theretofore granted, or the purchase price per share of Common Stock subject to Options.

SECTION 9
AMENDMENT OR TERMINATION OF THE PLAN

The Board in its discretion may terminate the Plan or any Option or Grant or alter or amend the Plan or any part thereof or any Option from time to time; provided that no change in any Award or Grant previously made may be made which would impair the rights of the Holder or Grantee without the consent of the Holder or Grantee, and provided further, that the Board may not, without approval of the stockholders, amend the Plan:

(a)   to increase the aggregate number of shares which may be issued pursuant to the provisions of the Plan on exercise or surrender of Options or upon Grants;

(b)   to change the minimum Option exercise price;

(c)   to change the class of employees eligible to receive Awards and/or Grants or increase materially the benefits accruing to employees under the Plan;

(d)   to extend the maximum period during which Awards may be granted or Grants may be made under the Plan;

(e)   to modify materially the requirements as to eligibility for participation in the Plan; or

(f)   to decrease any authority granted to the Board hereunder in contravention of Rule 16b-3.

SECTION 10
OTHER

(a)   *No Right to an Award or Grant.* Neither the adoption of the Plan nor any action of the Board or Designated Officer shall be deemed to give an employee any right to be granted an Option to purchase Common Stock, to receive a Grant or to any other rights hereunder except as may be evidenced by an Option Agreement duly executed on behalf of the Corporation, and then only to the extent of and on the terms and conditions expressly set forth therein. The Plan shall be unfunded. The Corporation shall not be required to establish any special or separate fund or to make any other segregation of funds or assets to assure the payment of any Award or Grant.

*Equity
Incentive
Plan*

(b)   *No Employment Rights Conferred.* Nothing contained in the Plan or in any Award or Grant made hereunder shall (i) confer upon any employee any right with respect to continuation of employment with the Corporation or any Parent Corporation or Subsidiary, or (ii) interfere in any way with the right of the Corporation or any Parent Corporation or Subsidiary to terminate his or her employment at any time.

(c)   *Other Laws; Withholding.* The Corporation shall not be obligated to issue any Common Stock pursuant to any Award granted or any Grant made under the Plan at any time when the offering of the shares covered by such Award has not been registered (or exempted) under the Securities Act of 1933 and such other state and federal laws, rules or regulations as the Corporation or the Board deems applicable and, in the opinion of legal counsel for the Corporation, there is no exemption from the registration requirements of such laws, rules or regulations available for the issuance and sale of such shares. No fractional shares of Common Stock shall be delivered, nor shall any cash in lieu of fractional shares be paid. The Corporation shall have the right to deduct in connection with all Awards or Grants any taxes required by law to be withheld and to require any payments necessary to enable it to satisfy its withholding obligations. The Board may permit the Holder of an Award or Grant to elect to surrender, or authorize the Corporation to withhold shares of Common Stock (valued at their Fair Market Value on the date of surrender or withholding of such shares) in satisfaction of the Corporation's withholding obligation, subject to such restrictions as the Board deems necessary to satisfy the requirements of Rule 16b-3.

Equity Incentive Plan

(d)   *No Restriction of Corporate Action.* Nothing contained in the Plan shall be construed to prevent the Corporation or any Parent Corporation or Subsidiary from taking any corporate action which is deemed by the Corporation or such Parent Corporation or Subsidiary to be appropriate or in its best interest, whether or not such action would have an adverse effect on the Plan or any Award made under the Plan. No employee, beneficiary or other person shall have any claim against the Corporation or any Parent Corporation or Subsidiary as a result of such action.

(e)   *Restrictions on Transfer.* An Award shall not be transferable otherwise than by will or the laws of descent and distribution and shall be exercisable during the lifetime of the Holder only by such Holder or the Holder's guardian or legal representative.

(f)   *Effect of Death, Disability or Termination of Employment.* The Option Agreement or other written instrument evidencing an Award shall specify the effect of the death, disability or termination of employment of the Holder on the Award; provided, however that an Optionee shall be entitled to exercise (i) at least six (6) months from the date of termination of employment with the Corporation if such termination is caused by death or disability or (ii) at least thirty (30) days from the date of termination of employment with the Corporation if such termination is caused by reasons other than death or disability.

All outstanding Incentive Stock Options will automatically be converted to a nonqualified stock option if the Optionee does not exercise the Incentive Stock Option (i) within three (3) months of the date of termination caused by reasons other than death or disability; or (ii) within twelve (12) months of the date of termination caused by disability.

(g)   *Information to Employees.* Optionees and Grantees under the Plan shall receive financial statements annually regarding the Corporation during the period the options are outstanding. The financial statements provided need not comply with Section 260.613 of the California Code of Regulations.

*Equity
Incentive
Plan*

(h)   *Rule 16b-3.* It is intended that the Plan and any grant of an Award made to a person subject to Section 16 of the Exchange Act meet all of the requirements of Rule 16b-3. If any provisions of the Plan or any such Award would disqualify the Plan or such Award hereunder, or would otherwise not comply with Rule 16b-3, such provision or Award shall be construed or deemed amended to conform to Rule 16b-3.

(i)   *Governing Law.* The Plan shall by construed in accordance with the laws of the State of California and all applicable federal law. The securities issued hereunder shall be governed by and in accordance with the Corporate Securities Laws of the State of California.

ADOPTED BY _____'S BOARD OF DIRECTORS AS OF _____ __, 199_.

APPROVED BY THE SHAREHOLDERS AS OF _____ __, 199__.

Incentive Stock Option Agreement

Pursuant to the __ 199_ Equity Incentive Plan

This INCENTIVE STOCK OPTION AGREEMENT (this "Agreement") is made as of the _____ day of _____, 199_, by and between _____, Inc., a California corporation (the "Corporation"), and _____ ("Employee").

WITNESSETH:

The Corporation has determined that it is in the best interests of the Corporation and its shareholders to encourage ownership in the Corporation by qualified employees, officers, and members of the Board of Directors of the Corporation or individuals as may be determined, thereby providing additional incentive for them to continue in the employ of the Corporation or its affiliates. To that end, an incentive stock option is granted by the Board to Employee pursuant, and subject to, the _____ 199_ Equity Incentive Plan (the "Plan") on the following terms and conditions:

SECTION I
DEFINED TERMS

Unless otherwise defined herein or, unless the context requires a different definition, capitalized terms used herein shall have the meanings assigned to them in the Plan.

SECTION II
SHARES OPTIONED, OPTION PRICE, AND TIME OF EXERCISE

Effective as of _____, 199__, the Corporation grants to Employee, subject to the terms and provisions set forth hereinafter and in the Plan, the right and option to purchase all or any part of the number of shares set forth in Exhibit A of the presently authorized but unissued common stock ("Common Stock") of the Corporation at the purchase price per share set forth as the Option Price in Exhibit A (the option hereby granted being hereinafter referred to as the "Option").

The Option shall not be considered granted (as of the effective date described above) or become exercisable unless and until Employee delivers to the Corporation a fully executed counterpart hereof. Thereafter, the Option shall be exercisable in accordance with the Exercise Schedule set forth on Exhibit A, subject to any termination, acceleration or change in such Exercise Schedule set forth in this Agreement apart from Exhibit A.

Neither the Option nor any other rights granted under this Agreement may be exercised after the Expiration Date set forth on Exhibit A and, before that time, the Option may be terminated as hereinafter provided. If Employee does not purchase the full number of shares to which he is entitled in any one year, he may purchase such shares in the next year specified in the Exercise Schedule hereto, in addition to the shares which he is otherwise entitled to purchase in the next year.

SECTION III
EXERCISE PROCEDURE

Incentive Stock Option Agreement

Employee shall exercise the Option by notifying the Corporation of the number of shares that he desires to purchase and by delivering with such notice the full payment for the purchase price of the shares being purchased. Such purchase price shall be payable in cash, in Common Stock or in a combination of cash and Common Stock. For purposes of determining the amount, if any, of the purchase price satisfied by payment in Common Stock, such Common Stock shall be valued at its Fair Market Value on the date of exercise, as determined by the Board at the time of exercise. In no event shall the purchase price be less than one hundred percent (100%) of the Fair Market Value of such stock at the time the Option is granted; except that the purchase price shall be one hundred ten percent (110%) of the fair value in the case of any person who owns stock possessing more than ten percent (10%) of the total combined voting power of all classes of stock of the Corporation. Fair value shall have the meaning as set forth in Section 260.140.50 of the California Code of Regulations. Any Common Stock delivered in satisfaction of all or a portion of the purchase price shall be appropriately endorsed for transfer and assignment to the Corporation.

Notwithstanding the foregoing, at the election of the Employee the Option can be exercised, provided that the Employee shall, as a condition of such exercise, execute and deliver the Restricted Stock Option Purchase Agreement in the form of Exhibit B hereto (the "Purchase Agreement"), pursuant to which the Corporation shall be granted a "Repurchase Option" and "Right of First Refusal" as to all "Shares" (as such terms are defined in the Purchase Agreement).

SECTION IV
TERMINATION OF EMPLOYMENT

If an optionee's employment (or other service) with the Company terminates either (i) for Cause or (ii) voluntary on the part of the optionee and without Good Reason (as determined by the Board, in its sole discretion), the options, to the extent not previously exercised, will terminate on the date of such termination of employment (or service). If an optionee's employment or other service with the Company terminates for reasons other than (a) termination that is either (i) for Cause, (ii) voluntary on the part of the optionee and without Good Reason, (b) termination by reason of disability and (c) death, options under the Plan may be exercised not later than three (3) months after such termination, but may be exercised only to the extent the options were exercisable on the date of termination, and in no event after ten (10) years from the date of granting thereof. Except as may be otherwise provided in this Agreement, the Option granted hereunder shall not be affected by any change of employment so long as Employee continues to be employed by the Corporation, a Parent Corporation or a Subsidiary.

"Cause" shall mean, as determined by the Board, in its sole discretion exercised in a nondiscriminatory manner, (i) the continued failure of the Employee to substantially perform his duties to the Corporation, a Parent Corporation or a Subsidiary (other than any such failure resulting from disability as defined above), (ii) the engaging by the Employee in willful, reckless or grossly negligent misconduct which is determined by the Board to be materially injurious to the Corporation or any of its affiliates, monetarily or otherwise, or (iii) the Employee's pleading guilty to or conviction of a felony.

Incentive Stock Option Agreement

"Good Reason" shall mean, as determined by the Board, in its sole discretion exercised in a nondiscriminatory manner, the occurrence of any of the following events without Employee's express written consent:

(i)   a substantial and adverse change in the Employee's duties, control, authority or status or position, or the assignment to the Employee or any duties or responsibilities which are inconsistent with such status or position, or a reduction in the duties and responsibilities previously exercised by the Employee, or a loss of title, loss of office, loss of significant authority, power or control, or any removal of him or her from or any failure to reappoint or reelect him to such positions, except in connection with the termination of his employment for Cause or disability (as defined above), or as a result of his death;

(ii)   a reduction in the Employee's base salary or a material reduction in the Employee's total compensation (i.e., a reduction in such total compensation of ten (10) percent or more); or

(iii)   any material breach by the Corporation of any provisions of any agreement with the Employee.

SECTION V
ACCELERATION OF EXERCISE

(a)   *Retirement and Total and Permanent Disability*. If an optionee should become permanently and totally disabled while an employee, non-employee director or officer of the Company or while providing other services to the Company, options shall become fully exercisable as to all shares subject to them and may be exercised at any time within one (1) year following the date of disability. If an optionee should retire with the written consent of the Company, options shall become fully exercisable as to all shares subject to them and may be exercised at any time with three (3) months of such retirement, but in no event after the Expiration Date set forth on Exhibit A. If such option is exercised after three months on or before the Expiration Date set forth in Exhibit A, such Option shall not receive favorable tax treatment under Code Section 421(a).

(b)   *Death*. If an optionee should die while an employee, non-employee director or officer of the Company or while providing other services to the Company, options may be exercised at any time within one (1) year following the date of death. Such Option may be exercised by the beneficiary designated by the Employee on Exhibit C hereto, in accordance with Section X hereto, or, if no beneficiary is designated on Exhibit C, by the executor or administrator of the Employee's estate, but in no event after the earlier of (i) the date one year following the Employee's date of death, or (ii) the Expiration Date set forth on Exhibit A hereto.

(c)   *Corporate Change*. Upon the occurrence of a Corporate Change, the Option (to the extent not previously terminated or forfeited) may, at the discretion of the Board, become fully exercisable as to all shares subject to it.

SECTION VI
NON-ASSIGNABILITY AND TERM OF OPTION

The Option shall not be transferrable or assignable by the Employee, otherwise than by will or the laws of descent and distribution and the Option shall be exercisable, during the Employee's lifetime, only by him or, during periods of legal disability, by his legal representative. No Option shall be subject to execution, attachment or similar process.

In no event may the Option be exercisable to any extent by anyone after the Expiration Date specified in Exhibit A. It is expressly agreed that, anything contained herein to the contrary notwithstanding, this Agreement shall not constitute, or be evidence of, any agreement or understanding, express or implied, that the Corporation, a Parent Corporation or a Subsidiary will employ Employee for any period of time or in any position or for any particular compensation.

SECTION VII
RIGHTS OF EMPLOYEE IN STOCK

Neither Employee, nor his successor in interest, shall have any of the rights of a shareholder of the Corporation with respect to the shares for which the Option is exercised until such shares are issued by the Corporation.

SECTION VIII
NOTICES

Any notice to be given hereunder shall be in writing and shall be addressed to the Corporation, in care of the Chief Financial Officer, at _____ Street, Suite ___, _____, California _____, and any notice to be given to Employee shall be addressed to the address designated below the signature appearing hereinafter, or at such other address as either party may hereafter designate in writing to the other. Any such notice shall have been deemed duly given upon three (3) days of sending such notice enclosed in a properly sealed envelope, addressed as aforesaid, registered or certified and deposited (with the proper postage and registration or certificate fee prepaid) in the United States mail.

Incentive Stock Option Agreement

SECTION IX
SUCCESSORS OR ASSIGNS OF THE CORPORATION

The Option shall be binding upon and shall inure to the benefit of any successor of the Corporation.

SECTION X
MISCELLANEOUS

(a)   *Designation of Beneficiary.* The Employee shall have the right to appoint any individual or legal entity in writing, on Exhibit C hereto, as his beneficiary to receive any Option (to the extent not previously terminated or forfeited) under this Agreement upon the Employee's death. Such designation under this Agreement may be revoked by the Employee at any time and a new beneficiary may be appointed by the Employee by execution and submission to the Board of a revised Exhibit C to this Agreement. In order to be effective, a designation of beneficiary must be completed by the Employee on Exhibit C and received to the Board, or its designee, prior to the date of the Employee's death. In the absence of such designation, the Employee's beneficiary shall be the legal representative of the Employee's estate.

(b)   *Incapacity of Employee or Beneficiary.* If any person entitled to a distribution under this Agreement is deemed by the Board to be incapable of making an election hereunder or of personally receiving and giving a valid receipt for such distribution hereunder, then, unless and until an election or claim therefore shall have been made by a duly appointed guardian or other legal representative of such person, the Board may provide for such election or distribution or any part thereof to be made to any other person or institution then contributing toward or providing for the care and maintenance of such person. Any such distribution shall be a distribution for the account of such person and a complete discharge of any liability of the Board, the Corporation and the Plan therefore.

*Incentive
Stock
Option
Agreement*

(c)   *Incorporation of the Plan.* The terms and provisions of the Plan are hereby incorporated in this Agreement. Unless otherwise specifically stated herein, such terms and provisions shall control in the event of any inconsistency between the Plan and this Agreement.

(d)   *Governing Law.* THIS AGREEMENT SHALL BE GOVERNED BY THE LAWS OF THE STATE OF CALIFORNIA AND ALL APPLICABLE FEDERAL LAWS. THE SECURITIES ISSUED HEREUNDER SHALL BE GOVERNED BY AND IN ACCORDANCE WITH THE CORPORATE SECURITY LAWS OF THE STATE OF CALIFORNIA.

(e)   *Gender.* Reference to the masculine herein shall be deemed to include the feminine, wherever appropriate.

(f)   *Counterparts.* This Agreement may be executed in one or more counterparts, which shall together constitute a valid and binding agreement.

IN WITNESS WHEREOF, this Agreement has been executed by the Corporation and the Employee as of the date and year first written above.

Employee___   _____, Inc., a California corporation

Address:_____   By:_____
_____   Title:_____

EXHIBIT A
INCENTIVE STOCK OPTION AGREEMENT PURSUANT TO THE __
199_ EQUITY INCENTIVE PLAN

1.   Date of Grant: _____, 199_ (Date of Offering)

2.   Employee: _____

3.   Number of Shares: _____ (_____) shares of Common Stock

4.   Option Price per Share: _____ ($_____) (not less than Fair
        Market Value)

5.   Exercise Schedule: _____ percent (__%) of the Options subject
        to this Agreement shall first be exercisable on _____ (the date
        one (1) year after the Date of Grant specified above).

        _____ percent (__%) of the Options subject to this
        Agreement shall thereafter be exercisable on each anniversary date of
        the Date of Grant specified above until the Options are fully exercis-
        able.

6.   Expiration Date: _____ (not more than ten (10) years
        from Date of Grant; (5) years from Date of Grant for 10 percent or
        more shareholders).

To qualify for Incentive Stock Option tax treatment, the Employee must not
dispose of shares obtained on exercise of an Option until at least two years
after the date of grant and one year after the date of exercise of the Option. If
these holding periods are not met, the sale or other disposition of shares will
be a disqualifying disposition pursuant to Code Section 422(c).

Incentive
Stock
Option
Agreement

EXHIBIT B
RESTRICTED STOCK OPTION PURCHASE AGREEMENT FOR THE INCENTIVE STOCK OPTION AGREEMENT PURSUANT TO THE __ 199_ EQUITY INCENTIVE PLAN

[Users of the Model Equity Compensation Plans book: See the separate restricted stock agreement that can be adapted for both the ISO plan and the NSO plan.]

*Incentive
Stock
Option
Agreement*

EXHIBIT C
DESIGNATION OF BENEFICIARY FOR THE INCENTIVE STOCK OPTION AGREEMENT PURSUANT TO THE __ 199_ EQUITY INCENTIVE PLAN

Name of Employee: _____

Original Date of Agreement: _____

If I shall cease to be an Employee of the Corporation, a Parent Corporation or a Subsidiary by reason of my death, or if I shall die after I have terminated my employment with the Corporation, the Parent Corporation or a Subsidiary, but, prior to the expiration of the Option (as provided in the Agreement), then all rights to the Option granted under this Agreement that I hereby hold upon my death, to the extent not previously terminated or forfeited, shall be transferred to _____ (insert name of beneficiary) in the manner provided for in the Plan and the Agreement.

_____

_____
Date

Receipt acknowledged on behalf of _____ by:

_____

_____
Date

Incentive Stock Option Agreement

*Incentive
Stock
Option
Agreement*

Nonqualified Stock Option Agreement

Pursuant to the __ 199_ Equity Incentive Plan

This NONQUALIFIED STOCK OPTION AGREEMENT (this "Agreement") is made as of the _____ day of _____, 199_, by _____, Inc, a California corporation (the "Corporation"), and _____ ("Holder").

WITNESSETH:

The Corporation has determined that it is in the best interests of the Corporation and its shareholders to encourage ownership in the Corporation by qualified employees, officers, and members of the Board of Directors of the Corporation or individuals as may be determined, thereby providing additional incentive for them to continue in the employ of or provide services to the Corporation or its affiliates. To that end, a nonqualified stock option is granted by the Board to Holder pursuant, and subject to, the _____ 199_ Equity Incentive Plan (the "Plan") on the following terms and conditions:

SECTION I
DEFINED TERMS

Unless otherwise defined herein or, unless the context requires a different definition, capitalized terms used herein shall have the meanings assigned to them in the Plan.

SECTION II
SHARES OPTIONED, OPTION PRICE, AND TIME OF EXERCISE

Effective as of _____, 199__, the Corporation grants to Holder, subject to the terms and provisions set forth hereinafter and in the Plan, the right and option to purchase all or any part of the number of shares set forth in Exhibit A of the presently authorized but unissued common stock ("Common Stock"), of the Corporation at the purchase price per share set forth as the Option Price in Exhibit A (the option hereby granted being hereinafter referred to as the "Option").

The Option shall not be considered granted (as of the effective date described above) or become exercisable unless and until Holder delivers to the Corporation a fully executed counterpart hereof. Thereafter, the Option shall be exercisable in accordance with the Exercise Schedule set forth on Exhibit A, subject to any termination, acceleration or change in such Exercise Schedule set forth in this Agreement apart from Exhibit A.

Neither the Option nor any other rights granted under this Agreement may be exercised after the Expiration Date set forth on Exhibit A and, before that time, the Option may be terminated as hereinafter provided. If Holder does not purchase the full number of shares to which he is entitled in any one year, he may purchase such shares in the next year specified in the Exercise Schedule hereto, in addition to the shares which he is otherwise entitled to purchase in the next year.

SECTION III
EXERCISE PROCEDURE WITHHOLDING

Nonqualified Stock Option Agreement

Holder shall exercise the Option by notifying the Corporation of the number of shares that he desires to purchase and by delivering with such notice the full payment for the purchase price of the shares being purchased. Such purchase price shall be payable in cash, in Common Stock or in a combination of cash and Common Stock. For purposes of determining the amount, if any, of the purchase price satisfied by payment in Common Stock, such Common Stock shall be valued at its Fair Market Value on the date of exercise, as determined by the Board at the time of exercise. In no event, shall the purchase price be less than eighty-five percent (85%) of the fair value of such stock at the time the Option is granted; except that the purchase price shall be one hundred ten percent (110%) of the fair value in the case of any person who owns stock possessing more than ten percent (10%) of the total combined voting power of all classes of stock of the Corporation. Fair value shall have the meaning as set forth in Section 260.140.50 of the California Code of Regulations. Any Common Stock delivered in satisfaction of all or a portion of the purchase price shall be appropriately endorsed for transfer and assignment to the Corporation.

Notwithstanding the foregoing, at the election of the Holder, the Option can be exercised provided that the Holder shall, as a condition of such exercise, execute and deliver the Restricted Stock Option Purchase Agreement in the form of Exhibit B hereto (the "Purchase Agreement"), pursuant to which the Corporation shall be granted a "Repurchase Option" and a "Right of First Refusal" as to all "Shares" (as such terms are defined in the Purchase Agreement).

The Corporation will, as soon as is reasonably possible, notify the Holder of the amount of withholding tax, if any, that must be paid under federal, state and local law due to exercise of the Option. The Corporation shall have no obligation to deliver certificates for the shares purchased until Holder pays to the Corporation the amount of withholding specified in the Corporation's notice in cash or in Common Stock. Alternatively, Holder may direct the Corporation to withhold that number of shares of Common Stock (valued according to the procedures set forth in this section on the date of withholding) sufficient to satisfy such obligation, subject to such restrictions or procedures as the Board deems necessary to satisfy Rule 16b-3.

SECTION IV
TERMINATION OF EMPLOYMENT/SERVICE

If an optionee's employment (or other service) with the Company terminates either (i) for Cause or (ii) voluntary on the part of the optionee and without Good Reason (as determined by the Board, in its sole discretion), the options, to the extent not previously exercised, will terminate on the date of such termination of employment (or service). If an optionee's employment or other service with the Company terminates for reasons other than (a) termination that is either (i) for Cause, (ii) voluntary on the part of the optionee and without Good Reason, (b) termination by reason of disability and (c) death, options under the Plan may be exercised not later than three (3) months after such termination, but may be exercised only to the extent the options were exercisable on the date of termination, and in no event after ten (10) years from the date of granting thereof. Except as may be otherwise provided in this Agreement, the Option granted hereunder shall not be affected by any change of employment so long as Employee continues to be employed by the Corporation, a Parent Corporation, or a Subsidiary.

Nonqualified Stock Option Agreement

"Cause" shall mean, as determined by the Board, in its sole discretion exercised in a nondiscriminatory manner, (i) the continued failure of the Holder to substantially perform his duties to the Corporation, a Parent Corporation or a Subsidiary (other than any such failure resulting from disability as defined above), (ii) the engaging by the Holder in willful, reckless or grossly negligent misconduct which is determined by the Board to be materially injurious to the Corporation or any of its affiliates, monetarily or otherwise, or (iii) the Holder's pleading guilty to or conviction of a felony.

"Good Reason" shall mean, as determined by the Board, in its sole discretion exercised in a nondiscriminatory manner, the occurrence of any of the following events without Holder's express written consent:

(i)   a substantial and adverse change in the Holder's duties, control, authority or status or position, or the assignment to the Holder or any duties or responsibilities which are inconsistent with such status or position, or a reduction in the duties and responsibilities previously exercised by the Holder, or a loss of title, loss of office, loss of significant authority, power or control, or any removal of him or her from or any failure to reappoint or reelect him to such positions, except in connection with the termination of his employment for Cause or disability (as defined above), or as a result of his death;

(ii)   a reduction in the Holder's base salary or a material reduction in the Holder's total compensation (i.e., a reduction in such total compensation of ten (10) percent or more); or

(iii)   any material breach by the Corporation of any provisions of any agreement with the Holder.

SECTION V
ACCELERATION OF EXERCISE

(a)   RETIREMENT AND TOTAL AND PERMANENT DISABILITY. If an optionee should become permanently and totally disabled while an employee, non-employee director or officer of the Company or while providing other services to the Company, options shall become fully exercisable as to all shares subject to them and may be exercised at any time within one (1) year following the date of disability. If an optionee should retire with the written consent of the Company, options shall become fully exercisable as to all shares subject to them and may be exercised at any time with three (3) months of such retirement, but in no event after the Expiration Date set forth on Exhibit A.

Nonqualified Stock Option Agreement

(b)   DEATH. If an optionee should die while an employee, non-employee director or officer of the Company or while providing other services to the Company, options may be exercised at any time within one (1) year following the date of death. Such Option may be exercised by the beneficiary designated by the Employee on Exhibit C hereto, in accordance with Section X hereto, or, if no beneficiary is designated on Exhibit C, by the executor or administrator of the Employee's estate, but in no event after the earlier of (i) the date one year following the Employee's date of death, or (ii) the Expiration Date set forth on Exhibit A hereto.

(c)   CORPORATE CHANGE. Upon the occurrence of a Corporate Change, the Option (to the extent not previously terminated or forfeited) may, at the discretion of the Board, become fully exercisable as to all shares subject to it.

SECTION VI
NON-ASSIGNABILITY AND TERM OF OPTION

The Option shall not be transferrable or assignable by the Holder, otherwise than by will or the laws of descent and distribution and the Option shall be exercisable, during the Holder's lifetime, only by him or, during periods of legal disability, by his legal representative. No Option shall be subject to execution, attachment, or similar process.

In no event may the Option be exercisable to any extent by anyone after the Expiration Date specified in Exhibit A. It is expressly agreed that, anything contained herein to the contrary notwithstanding, this Agreement shall not constitute, or be evidence of, any agreement or understanding, express or implied, that the Corporation, a Parent Corporation or a Subsidiary will employ Holder for any period of time or in any position or for any particular compensation.

SECTION VII
RIGHTS OF HOLDER IN STOCK

Neither Holder, nor his successor in interest, shall have any of the rights of a shareholder of the Corporation with respect to the shares for which the Option is issued until such shares are exercised by the Corporation.

SECTION VIII
NOTICES

Any notice to be given hereunder shall be in writing and shall be addressed to the Corporation, in care of the Chief Financial Officer, at _____, Suite __, _____, California _____, and any notice to be given to the Holder shall be addressed to the address designated below the signature appearing hereinafter, or at such other address as either party may hereafter designate in writing to the other. Any such notice shall have been deemed duly given upon three (3) days of sending such notice enclosed in a properly sealed envelope, addressed as aforesaid, registered or certified and deposited (with the proper postage and registration or certificate fee prepaid) in the United States mail.

Nonqualified Stock Option Agreement

SECTION IX
SUCCESSORS OR ASSIGNS OF THE CORPORATION

The Option shall be binding upon and shall inure to the benefit of any successor of the Corporation.

SECTION X
MISCELLANEOUS

(a)   *Designation of Beneficiary.* The Holder shall have the right to appoint any individual or legal entity in writing, on Exhibit C hereto, as his beneficiary to receive any Option (to the extent not previously terminated or forfeited) under this Agreement upon the Holder's death. Such designation under this Agreement may be revoked by the Holder at any time and a new beneficiary may be appointed by the Holder by execution and submission to the Board of a revised Exhibit C to this Agreement. In order to be effective, a designation of beneficiary must be completed by the Holder on Exhibit C and received to the Board, or its designee, prior to the date of the Holder's death. In the absence of such designation, the Holder's beneficiary shall be the legal representative of the Holder's estate.

(b)   *Incapacity of Holder or Beneficiary.* If any person entitled to a distribution under this Agreement is deemed by the Board to be incapable of making an election hereunder or of personally receiving and giving a valid receipt for such distribution hereunder, then, unless and until an election or claim therefore shall have been made by a duly appointed guardian or other legal representative of such person, the Board may provide for such election or distribution or any part thereof to be made to any other person or institution then contributing toward or providing for the care and maintenance of such person. Any such distribution shall be a distribution for the account of such person and a complete discharge of any liability of the Board, the Corporation and the Plan therefore.

Nonqualified Stock Option Agreement

(c)   *Incorporation of the Plan.* The terms and provisions of the Plan are hereby incorporated in this Agreement. Unless otherwise specifically stated herein, such terms and provisions shall control in the event of any inconsistency between the Plan and this Agreement.

(d)   *Governing Law.* THIS AGREEMENT SHALL BE GOVERNED BY THE LAWS OF THE STATE OF CALIFORNIA AND ALL APPLICABLE FEDERAL LAWS. THE SECURITIES ISSUED HEREUNDER SHALL BE GOVERNED BY AND IN ACCORDANCE WITH THE CORPORATE SECURITIES LAWS OF THE STATE OF CALIFORNIA.

(e)   *Gender.* Reference to the masculine herein shall be deemed to include the feminine, wherever appropriate.

(f)   *Counterparts.* This Agreement may be executed in one or more counterparts, which shall together constitute a valid and binding agreement.

IN WITNESS WHEREOF, this Agreement has been executed by the Corporation and the Holder as of the date and year first written above.

Employee_____   _____, Inc., a California corporation

Address:_____   By:_____

_____   Title:_____

EXHIBIT A
NONQUALIFIED STOCK OPTION AGREEMENT PURSUANT TO THE
_____ 199_ EQUITY INCENTIVE PLAN

1.   Date of Grant: _____, 199__ (Date of Offering)

2.   Holder: _____

3.   Number of Shares: _____ (_____) shares of
Common Stock

4.   Option Price Per Share: _____ ($_____) (not less
than 85% of fair value if less than 10% is held and not less than 110% of fair
value if more than 10% is held by Holder).

5.   Exercise Schedule: _____ percent (__%) of the Options
subject to this Agreement shall first be exercisable on _____ (the date
one (1) year after the Date of Grant specified above).

_____ percent (__%) of the Options subject to this Agreement shall
thereafter be exercisable on each anniversary date of the Date of Grant specified above until the Options are fully exercisable.

6.   Expiration Date: _____ (not more than ten (10) years
from Date of Grant).

*Nonqualified
Stock Option
Agreement*

EXHIBIT B
RESTRICTED STOCK OPTION PURCHASE AGREEMENT FOR THE
NONQUALIFIED STOCK OPTION AGREEMENT PURSUANT TO THE
_____ 199_ EQUITY INCENTIVE PLAN

[Users of the Model Equity Compensation Plans publication: See the separate restricted stock agreement that can be adapted for both the ISO plan and the NSO plan.]

Nonqualified
Stock Option
Agreement

EXHIBIT C
DESIGNATION OF BENEFICIARY FOR THE NONQUALIFIED STOCK OPTION AGREEMENT PURSUANT TO THE _____ 199_ EQUITY INCENTIVE PLAN

Name of Holder: _____

Original Date of Agreement: _____

If I shall cease to be employed or engaged by the Corporation, a Parent Corporation or a Subsidiary by reason of my death, or if I shall die after I have terminated my employment or engagement with the Corporation, the Parent Corporation or a Subsidiary, but, prior to the expiration of the Option (as provided in the Agreement), then all rights to the Option granted under this Agreement that I hereby hold upon my death, to the extent not previously terminated or forfeited, shall be transferred to _____ (insert name of beneficiary) in the manner provided for in the Plan and the Agreement.

Nonqualified Stock Option Agreement

_____

_____
Date

Receipt acknowledged on behalf of _____by:

_____

_____
Date

Restricted Stock Option Purchase Agreement

THIS AGREEMENT is made and entered into as of _____, 19___, between _____, Inc., a California corporation (the "Corporation"), and _____ (the "Purchaser"), the holder of a stock option granted under the _____ 199_ Equity Incentive Plan.

RECITALS:

A.   Pursuant to the exercise of a stock option granted to the Purchaser by the Corporation under an [Incentive/Nonqualified] Stock Option Agreement dated _____, 199_ (the "Option Agreement"), the Purchaser has elected to purchase _____ shares of the Corporation's Common Stock for an aggregate purchase price of $_____.

B.   As provided in the Option Agreement, the Purchaser has agreed to grant the Corporation the option to repurchase such shares under certain circumstances.

NOW, THEREFORE, in consideration of the mutual covenants exchanged, the parties agree as follows:

1.   *Exercise of Option.*

    (a)   *Exercise.* The Purchaser hereby agrees to purchase _____ shares of the Corporation's Common Stock (the "Shares") pursuant to an exercise of the option granted in the Option Agreement, at an option exercise price of $_____ per share (the "Option Price").

    (b)   *Payment.* Concurrently with the delivery of this Agreement to the Corporation, the Purchaser shall pay the consideration for the Shares purchased hereunder and shall deliver any additional documents that may be required by the Option Agreement as a condition to such exercise.

2.   *Repurchase Option.*

    (a)   *Shares Subject to Repurchase.* The Purchaser hereby grants to the Corporation the option (the "Repurchase Option") to repurchase all or part of the Shares, upon the occurrences set forth in subsection (b).

(b)   *Occurrences Permitting Exercise.* The Corporation may exercise the Repurchase Option upon the Purchaser's purchase of the Corporation's Common Stock pursuant to the exercise of stock options granted in the Option Agreement ("Offering Event").

(c)   *Exercise of Repurchase Option.* Upon the occurrence of an Offering Event, the Corporation may exercise the Repurchase Option by delivering a notice pursuant to Section 15 of this Agreement to the Purchaser (or his permitted transferee or legal representative, as the case may be), within ninety (90) days after the date of the Offering Event (the "90-Day Period"). The Corporation's notice to the Purchaser shall indicate the Corporation's election to exercise its Repurchase Option and the number of Shares to be purchased by the Corporation or the Corporation's designee, who shall be identified in such notice, and the notice shall set forth a date for closing not later than thirty (30) days from the date of the giving of such notice.

(d)   *Closing for Repurchase of Shares.* The closing for the repurchase of the Shares pursuant to the exercise of the Repurchase Option shall take place at the Corporation's principal offices. At the closing, the holder of the certificate(s) representing the Shares being transferred shall deliver such certificate or certificates evidencing the Shares to the Corporation, duly endorsed for transfer, and the Corporation (or its designee) shall tender payment of the purchase price for the Shares being purchased. The purchase price for the Shares shall be payable in full in cash, or by certified check or cashier's check; provided, however, that the Corporation may elect to offset against and deduct from any payment of the purchase price any indebtedness then owed by the Purchaser to the Corporation.

3.   **Restrictions on Transfer; Right of First Refusal.**

(a)   *Right of First Refusal.* Except as provided in this Section 3, the Purchaser shall not sell, assign, transfer, pledge or otherwise dispose of any of the Shares, or any right or interest therein, either voluntarily or involuntarily, without first delivering a written notice (the "Transfer Notice") to the Corporation, which shall have the option to purchase such Shares as provided herein (the "Right of First Refusal"). The Transfer Notice must specify: (i) the name and address of the proposed transferee; (ii) the number of Shares, or interest therein, proposed to be sold or transferred; (iii) the price or amount to be paid for the proposed transfer (including the amount of any debt to be paid, cancelled or forgiven upon foreclosure of a security interest in the Shares or upon any other transfer to the Purchaser's creditors); and (iv) all other material terms and conditions of the proposed transfer.

(b) *Election to Purchase Shares.* Within thirty (30) days after receipt of the Transfer Notice, the Corporation or its designee (as the case may be) may elect to purchase all, but not less than all, of the Shares to which the Transfer Notice refers at the per share price specified in the Transfer Notice. If no price is specified in the Transfer Notice, the purchase price shall be the fair market value of the Shares on the date the Corporation receives the Transfer Notice, as determined in good faith by the Board of Directors of the Corporation. Such Right of First Refusal shall be exercised by delivery to the Purchaser by the Corporation or its designee of a written election to exercise such Right of First Refusal, specifying the number of Shares to be purchased by the Corporation or its designee (as the case may be). Notwithstanding the foregoing, the Corporation may elect to offset against and deduct from any payment of the purchase price any indebtedness then owed by the Purchaser to the Corporation.

Restricted Stock Option Purchase Agreement

(c) *Closing for Purchase of Shares.* In the event the Corporation elects to acquire Shares of the Purchaser as specified in the Transfer Notice, the Secretary of the Corporation shall so notify the Purchaser and settlement thereof shall be made in cash within thirty (30) days after the Corporation receives the Transfer Notice; provided, however, that if the terms of payment set forth in the Transfer Notice were other than cash against delivery, the Corporation shall pay for such Shares on the same terms and conditions set forth in the Transfer Notice.

(d) *Transfer Free of Right of First Refusal.* If the Shares referred to in the Transfer Notice are not purchased by the Corporation, or its designee(s), the Purchaser, within a period of ninety (90) days from the date of delivery of the Transfer Notice to the Corporation, may sell such Shares to the person or persons named in the Transfer Notice at the price and on the terms specified in the Transfer Notice, provided that such sale or transfer is consummated within ninety (90) days following the date of delivery of the Transfer Notice to the Corporation and, provided further, that such sale is in accordance with all the terms and conditions hereof. The transferee will hold all Shares transferred hereunder subject to the provisions of this Agreement.

(e)   *Gift of Shares.* Notwithstanding any other term of this Section 3, the Purchaser may make a gift of all or part of the Shares to any of his parents, brothers or sisters, spouse or issue, or to a trust for his or their exclusive benefit. The donee or donees shall hold such Shares subject to all provisions of this Agreement.

(f)   *Nullification of Improper Transfer.* Any transfer by the Purchaser in violation of this Section shall be null and void and of no effect.

4.   *Adjustments.* If, from time to time during the term of this Agreement: (i) there is any stock dividend, distribution or dividend of cash or property, stock split, or other change in the character or amount of any of the outstanding securities of the Corporation; or (ii) there is any consolidation, merger or sale of all, or substantially all, of the assets of the Corporation; or (iii) the Shares are converted into any other class of securities by capital reorganization or recapitalization; then, in such event, any and all new, substituted or additional securities, cash or other property to which the Purchaser is entitled by reason of his ownership of the Shares shall be immediately subject to the Repurchase Option, the Right of First Refusal and the other terms of this Agreement. While the total Option Price shall remain the same after any such event, the Option Price per share shall be appropriately adjusted.

Restricted Stock Option Purchase Agreement

5.   **Termination of Restrictions.**

(a)   *Termination of Repurchase Option and Right of First Refusal.* The Repurchase Option and Right of First Refusal shall terminate:

(i)   on the termination of this Agreement pursuant to written agreement of the parties;

(ii)   at such time as the Corporation consummates an underwritten public offering of its common stock.

6.   *Legends.*

(a)   *Endorsement on Certificates.* The certificates representing the Shares subject to this Agreement shall be endorsed with a legend substantially in the following form:

"THE SHARES REPRESENTED BY THIS
CERTIFICATE MAY BE TRANSFERRED
ONLY IN ACCORDANCE WITH THE TERMS
OF A RESTRICTED STOCK OPTION
PURCHASE AGREEMENT BETWEEN THE
CORPORATION AND THE REGISTERED
HOLDER OR HIS PREDECESSOR IN
INTEREST, A COPY OF WHICH MAY BE
OBTAINED UPON WRITTEN REQUEST TO
THE SECRETARY OF THE CORPORATION.
THE AGREEMENT MAY BE INSPECTED AT
THE PRINCIPAL OFFICE OF THE
CORPORATION DURING NORMAL
BUSINESS HOURS."

(b)   *Termination of All Restrictions.* In the event the restrictions imposed by this Agreement shall be terminated as herein provided, a new certificate or certificates representing the Shares shall be issued, on request, without the legend referred to in Section 7(a).

(c)   *Securities Law Legends.* Any transfer or sale of the Shares is further subject to all restrictions on transfer imposed by state or Federal securities laws. Accordingly, it is understood and agreed that the certificates representing the Shares shall bear any legends required by such state or Federal securities laws.

Restricted Stock Option Purchase Agreement

7.   *Dissolution of Marriage.*

(a)   *Purchase of Shares from Former Spouse.* In the event of the dissolution of the Purchaser's marriage, including a decree of divorce or judgment of dissolution or separate maintenance, or under a property settlement or separation agreement, the Purchaser shall have the right and option to purchase from his or her spouse all of the Shares (i) awarded to the spouse pursuant to a decree of dissolution of marriage or any other order by any court of competent jurisdiction and/or any property settlement agreement (whether or not incorporated by reference in any such decree), or (ii) gifted to the spouse by the Purchaser prior to the dissolution, at the fair market value of such Shares on the date such shares are transferred to the spouse as determined by the Corporation's Board of Directors, upon the terms set forth below. The Purchaser shall exercise his or her right, if at all, within thirty (30) days following the entry of any such decree or property settlement agreement by delivery to the Purchaser's former spouse of written notice of exercise, specifying the number of Shares the Purchaser elects to purchase. The purchase price for the Shares shall be paid by delivery of a promissory note for the purchase price bearing interest at the rate of ten percent (10%) per annum payable in four (4) equal annual installments of principal and interest, commencing on the anniversary date of the exercise of the option; *provided, however,* that if, subsequent to the date any or all of the Shares is awarded to the Purchaser's former spouse as provided above, the Corporation exercises its Repurchase Option with respect to any or all of the Shares so awarded, the amount remaining due under such promissory note shall be reduced by the difference between the fair market value of such Shares determined as set forth above and the amount received by the Purchaser for such Shares upon exercise by the Corporation of the Repurchase Option.

(b)   *Transfer of Rights to Corporation.* In the event the Purchaser does not exercise his or her right to purchase all of the Shares awarded to the Purchaser's former spouse, the Purchaser shall provide written notice to the Corporation of the number of Shares available for purchase and the purchase price of such Shares determined in accordance with Section 7(a) within thirty (30) days of the entry of the decree or property settlement agreement. The Corporation shall then have the right to purchase any of the Shares not acquired by the Purchaser directly from the Purchaser's former spouse in the manner provided in Sections 3(b)-3(e) above at the same price and on the same terms that were available to the Purchaser.

(c)   *Shares Subject to Repurchase by Corporation.* Notwithstanding any other provisions of this Agreement, all Shares held by the Purchaser's spouse or former spouse will be subject to the Repurchase Option as such term is defined in Section 2, the Right of First Refusal by the Corporation as such term is defined in Section 3, and all other provisions of this Agreement.

8.   **Consent of Spouse.** If the Purchaser is married on the date of this Agreement, the Purchaser's spouse shall execute a Consent of Spouse in the form attached hereto, effective on the date hereof. Such consent shall not be deemed to confer or convey to the spouse any rights in the Shares that do not otherwise exist by operation of law or the agreement of the parties. If the Purchaser should marry or remarry subsequent to the date of this Agreement, the Purchaser shall within thirty (30) days thereafter obtain his or her new spouse's acknowledgment of and consent to the existence and binding effect of all restrictions contained in this Agreement by signing a Consent of Spouse in the form attached hereto.

Restricted
Stock
Option
Purchase
Agreement

9. *Compliance with Income Tax Laws.*

    (a)   *Withholding Tax.* The Purchaser authorizes the Corporation to withhold in accordance with applicable law from any compensation payable to him or her any taxes required to be withheld by Federal, state or local laws as a result of the purchase of the Shares. Furthermore, in the event of any determination that the Corporation has failed to withhold a sum sufficient to pay all withholding taxes due in connection with the purchase of the Shares, the Purchaser agrees to pay the Corporation the amount of such deficiency in cash within five (5) days after receiving a written demand from the Corporation to do so, whether or not the Purchaser is an employee of the Corporation at that time. The Purchaser agrees to notify the Corporation of any sale or other disposition (within the meaning of Section 421(b) of the Internal Revenue Code of 1986, as amended (the "Code"), by the Purchaser of any of the Shares within one (1) year of the date hereof or within two (2) years from the date of grant of any incentive stock option by the Corporation pursuant to the exercise of which such Shares were acquired hereunder.

10. *Purchaser's Representations.* In connection with the purchase of the Shares, the Purchaser hereby represents and warrants to the Corporation as follows:

    (a)   *Investment Intent; Capacity to Protect Interests.* The Purchaser is purchasing the Shares solely for his or her own account for investment and not with a view to or for sale in connection with any distribution of the Shares or any portion thereof and not with any present intention of selling, offering to sell or otherwise disposing of or distributing the Shares or any portion thereof in any transaction other than a transaction exempt from registration under the Securities Act of 1933, as amended (the "Act"). The Purchaser also represents that the entire legal and beneficial interest of the Shares is being purchased, and will be held, for the Purchaser's account only, and neither in whole or in part for any other person. The Purchaser either (i) has a pre-existing business or personal relationship with the Corporation or any of its officers, directors or controlling persons, or (ii) by reason of the Purchaser's business or financial experience or the business or financial experience of the Purchaser's professional advisors who are unaffiliated with and who are not compensated by the Corporation or any affiliate or selling agent of the Corporation, directly or indirectly, could be reasonably assumed to have the capacity to evaluate the merits and risks of an investment in

Restricted Stock Option Purchase Agreement

the Corporation and to protect the Purchaser's own interests in connection with this transaction.

(b)   *Information Concerning Corporation.* The Purchaser has heretofore discussed the Corporation and its plans, operations and financial condition with the Corporation's officers and has heretofore received all such information as the Purchaser has deemed necessary and appropriate to enable the Purchaser to evaluate the financial risk inherent in making an investment in the Shares, and the Purchaser has received satisfactory and complete information concerning the business and financial condition of the Corporation in response to all inquiries in respect thereof.

(c)   *Economic Risk.* The Purchaser realizes that the purchase of the Shares will be a highly speculative investment and involves a high degree of risk, and the Purchaser is able, without impairing his or her financial condition, to hold the Shares for an indefinite period of time and to suffer a complete loss on the Purchaser's investment.

*Restricted
Stock
Option
Purchase
Agreement*

(d)   *Restricted Securities.* The Purchaser understands and acknowledges that:

(i)   the sale of the Shares has not been registered under the Act, and the Shares must be held indefinitely unless subsequently registered under the Act or an exemption from such registration is available and the Corporation is under no obligation to register the Shares;

(ii)   the share certificate representing the Shares will be stamped with the legends specified in Section 6 hereof; and

(iii)   the Corporation will make a notation in its records of the aforementioned restrictions on transfer and legends.

(e)   *Disposition under Rule 144.* The Purchaser understands that the Shares are restricted securities within the meaning of Rule 144 promulgated under the Act; that unless the Shares have been issued pursuant to Rule 701 promulgated under the Act the exemption from registration under Rule 144 will not be available in any event for at least one year from the date of purchase and payment of the Shares (AND THAT PAYMENT BY A NOTE IS NOT DEEMED PAYMENT UNLESS IT IS SECURED BY ASSETS OTHER THAN THE SHARES), and even then will not be available unless: (i) a public trading market then exists for the Common Stock of the Corporation; (ii) adequate information concerning the Corporation is then available to the public; and (iii) other terms and conditions of Rule 144 are complied with; and that any sale of the Shares may be made only in limited amounts in accordance with such terms and conditions.

(f)   *Further Limitations on Disposition*. Without in any way limiting his representations set forth above, the Purchaser further agrees that he or she shall in no event make any disposition of all or any portion of the Shares unless and until:

(i)   (A) There is then in effect a Registration Statement under the Act covering such proposed disposition and such disposition is made in accordance with said Registration Statement; *or*, (B)(1) the Purchaser shall have notified the Corporation of the proposed disposition and shall have furnished the Corporation with a detailed statement of the circumstances surrounding the proposed disposition, (2) the Purchaser shall have furnished the Corporation with an opinion of the Purchaser's counsel to the effect that such disposition will not require registration of such shares under the Act, *and* (3) such opinion of the Purchaser's counsel shall have been concurred in by counsel for the Corporation and the Corporation shall have advised the Purchaser of such concurrence; *and*,

Restricted Stock Option Purchase Agreement

(ii)   The Shares proposed to be transferred are not subject to the Repurchase Option set forth in Section 2 hereof and the Purchaser shall have complied with the Right of First Refusal set forth in Section 3 hereof.

11.   *"Market Stand-Off" Agreement.* The Purchaser hereby agrees that he or she shall not, to the extent reasonably requested by the Corporation and an underwriter of Common Stock (or other securities) of the Corporation, sell or otherwise transfer or dispose (other than to donees who agree to be similarly bound) of any Shares during the one hundred eighty (180)-day period following the effective date of a registration statement of the Corporation filed under the Securities Act; provided, however, that: (a) all officers and directors of the Corporation and all other persons with registration rights enter into similar agreements; and (b) such agreement shall be applicable only to the first such registration statement of the Corporation which covers shares (or securities) to be sold on its behalf to the public in an underwritten public offering. Such agreement shall be in writing in a form satisfactory to the Corporation and such underwriter. In order

to enforce the foregoing covenant, the Corporation may impose stop-transfer instructions with respect to the Shares of each Shareholder (and the shares or securities of every other person subject to the foregoing restriction) until the end of such one hundred eighty (180)-day period.

12. *Enforcement.* The Purchaser agrees that a violation on his or her part of any of the terms of this Agreement (other than those contained in Section 10 above) may cause irreparable damage to the Corporation, the exact amount of which is impossible to ascertain, and for that reason agrees that the Corporation shall be entitled to a decree of specific performance of the terms hereof or an injunction restraining further violation, such right to be in addition to any other remedies of said parties.

13. *Controlling Provisions.* To the extent that there may be any conflict between the provisions of this Agreement and the provisions contained in the Corporation's By-Laws on the transfer or restriction on transfer of Shares, the terms of this Agreement shall be controlling.

14. *Ownership, Voting Rights, Duties.* This Agreement shall not affect in any way the ownership, voting rights or other rights or duties of the Purchaser, except as specifically provided herein.

Restricted Stock Option Purchase Agreement

15. *Notices.* All notices and other communications required or permitted hereunder shall be in writing and shall be deemed effectively given upon personal delivery or within 72 hours after mailing, if mailed by first-class mail, registered or certified, postage prepaid and properly addressed. Notice to be given to the Corporation shall be delivered or addressed to the Corporation at its principal place of business; notice to be given to a holder of Shares shall be delivered or addressed to such holder at his or her or its address set forth on the signature page of this Agreement or at another address if given to the Secretary of the Corporation for the purpose of notice or, if no address is given, in care of the Corporation at its principal place of business.

16. *Binding Effect.* This Agreement shall inure to the benefit of the Corporation and its successors and assigns and, subject to the restrictions on transfer set forth herein, be binding upon the Purchaser, his permitted transferees, heirs, legatees, executors, administrators and legal successors, who shall hold the Shares subject to the terms hereof. The Corporation may assign its rights under the terms of this Agreement without the consent of the Purchaser.

17. *Entire Agreement.* This Agreement supersedes all previous written or oral agreements between the parties regarding the subject matter hereof, and constitutes the entire agreement of the parties regarding

such subject matter. This Agreement may not be modified or terminated except by a writing executed by all of the parties hereto.

18.　　*Not Employment Contract.* Nothing in this Agreement shall affect in any manner whatsoever the right or power of the Purchaser or the Corporation to terminate the Purchaser's employment, for any reason or for no reason, with or without cause, subject to the provisions of applicable law. This Agreement is not an employment contract.

19.　　*Counterparts.* This Agreement may be executed in counterparts, each of which shall be deemed to be an original, but all of which together shall constitute one and the same instrument.

20.　　*Governing Law.* This Agreement, together with the exhibits hereto, shall be governed by and construed under the laws of the State of California, as such laws are applied to contracts entered into by residents of such state and performed in such state.

21.　　*Attorneys' Fees.* In the event of litigation brought by either party to enforce the provisions of this Agreement or for damages based upon the breach thereof, the prevailing party shall be entitled to recover his costs and reasonable attorneys' fees, as determined by the court.

22.　　*Severability.* If any provision of this Agreement is held by a court of competent jurisdiction to be invalid, void or unenforceable, the remaining provisions shall nevertheless continue in full force and effect without being impaired or invalidated in any way and shall be construed in accordance with the purposes and tenor and effect of this Agreement.

Restricted Stock Option Purchase Agreement

IN WITNESS WHEREOF, the parties have executed this Agreement on the date first above written.

_____, INC.,_____　　　　PURCHASER
a California corporation

By:_____　　　　By:_____

Title:_____　　　　Address: _____

　　　　　　　　　　　　　　　　　_____

CONSENT OF SPOUSE

I, _____, spouse of _____, acknowledge that I have read the Restricted Stock Option Purchase Agreement dated as of _____, 199__, to which this Consent is attached (the "Agreement") and that I know its contents. I am aware that by its provisions (a) my spouse and _____, Inc. (the "Corporation") have the option to purchase all the Shares of the Corporation of which I may become possessed as a result of a gift from my spouse or a court decree and/or any property settlement in any domestic litigation, (b) the Corporation has the option to purchase certain Shares of the Corporation which my spouse owns pursuant to the Agreement, including any interest I might have therein, upon termination of his or her employment under circumstances set forth in the Agreement, and (c) certain other restrictions are imposed upon the sale or other disposition of the Shares.

I hereby agree that my interest, if any, in the Shares subject to the Agreement shall be irrevocably bound by the Agreement and further understand and agree that any community property interest I may have in the Shares shall be similarly bound by the Agreement.

Restricted Stock Option Purchase Agreement

I agree to the sale and purchase described in Section 8 of the Agreement and I hereby consent to the sale of the Shares by my spouse or his legal representative in accordance with the provisions of the Agreement. Further, as part of the consideration for the Agreement, I agree that at my death, if I have not disposed of any interest of mine in the Shares by an outright bequest of such Shares to my spouse, then my spouse and the Corporation shall have the same rights against my legal representative to purchase any interest of mine in the Shares as they would have had pursuant to Section 8 of the Agreement if I had acquired the Shares pursuant to a court decree in domestic litigation.

I am aware that the legal, financial and related matters contained in the Agreement are complex and that I am free to seek independent professional guidance or counsel with respect to this Consent. I have either sought such guidance or counsel or determined after reviewing the Agreement carefully that I will waive such right.

Dated as of the _____ of _____, 199__.

_____

Action by Unanimous Written Consent of the _____, Inc., Shareholders

The undersigned, constituting all of the shareholders of _____, Inc., a California corporation (the "Company"), and desiring to take action by unanimous written consent as authorized by the bylaws of the Company and Section 603 of the California General Corporation Law, as applicable, do hereby adopt the following resolutions:

WHEREAS, the shareholders deem it to be in the best interests of the Company to adopt the _____ 199_ Equity Incentive Plan (the "Plan") for the purpose of providing certain incentives to the employees of the Company.

NOW, THEREFORE, IT IS

RESOLVED, that the Plan is approved, authorized and adopted by the shareholders in the form attached hereto as Exhibit "A."

FURTHER RESOLVED, that the President and the Secretary of the Company are hereby authorized and directed to perform any and all acts as they shall deem necessary or appropriate to carry out the purposes and intent of the foregoing resolutions.

IN WITNESS WHEREOF, the undersigned have executed this Action by Unanimous Written Consent as of _____ __, 199_.

Dated: _____ __, 199_

Signatures continued on next page

Action by
Unanimous
Written
Consent

Summary Memorandum

__ 199_ Equity Incentive Plan

TO: Holders of Options to Purchase Common Stock

SUBJECT: Employee Stock Options/Grants

The purpose of this memorandum is to clarify some of the procedures and consequences relating to the grant of shares of Common Stock as well as options to purchase shares of Common Stock of _____, Inc., a California corporation (the "Corporation"), under the _____ 199_ Equity Incentive Plan (the "Plan"), and the purchase and subsequent disposition of shares of the Corporation's Common Stock received upon the exercise of such options. The exact terms and conditions of the options, including the exercise price of the shares of Common Stock, are governed by the provisions of the Plan and the agreements thereunder between the Corporation and the participating employees, directors, officers or other individuals.

> THIS MEMORANDUM IS FOR GENERAL INFORMATION ONLY AND SHOULD NOT BE CONSTRUED AS AN OFFER FOR THE SALE OF SECURITIES. EACH INDIVIDUAL IS ENCOURAGED TO CONSULT WITH INDEPENDENT COUNSEL AS TO THE APPLICABILITY OF THE TAX AND SECURITIES LAWS AND OTHER MATTERS DISCUSSED HEREIN TO HIS OR HER SPECIFIC SITUATION.

GENERAL

The Corporation's Board of Directors adopted the Plan as of _____, 199_. The Corporation's shareholders adopted the plan as of _____, 199_. A total of _____ shares of Common Stock have been reserved for issuance upon the exercise of options and stock grants under the Plan.

The Plan allows for the grant of stock options intended to qualify as "incentive stock options" under Section 422 of the Internal Revenue Code of 1986, as amended (the "Code"), as well as nonstatutory stock options. See "Federal Income Tax Consequences" below for information concerning the tax treatment of incentive stock options and nonstatutory stock options. The Plan also allows for the grant of Common Stock as a bonus for services actually rendered to the Corporation.

SUMMARY OF THE PLAN

Set forth below is a summary of the principal features of the Plan.

Administration

The Plan is currently being administered by the Corporation's Board of Directors (the "Board"). The interpretation and construction of any provision of the Plan by the Board shall be final and conclusive.

Eligibility

The Plan provides that options and/or stock may be granted to the Corporation's employees, directors, officers or other individuals or entities involved with the Corporation. One or several Corporation officers designated by the Board, such as the President and/or Chief Operating Officer will select the participants and determine the number of shares to be subject to each option and/or grant. However, incentive stock options can only be granted to employees.

Summary Memorandum

The Plan provides for a maximum number of shares of the Corporation's Common Stock which may be granted, either directly or under an option, to any one employee or other eligible participant. In addition, the value of the shares subject to all incentive stock options of an optionee that become exercisable for the first time during any calendar year cannot exceed $100,000 (determined as of the date of grant). See "Federal Income Tax Consequences" below.

Terms of Options

Each option is evidenced by a stock option agreement between the Corporation and the person to whom such option is granted, which sets forth the terms and conditions of the option. The following terms and conditions generally apply to all options, unless the stock option agreement provides otherwise:

(a)   *Exercise of the Option.* The optionee must earn the right to exercise his or her option by continuing to work for the Corporation. The Board determines when options granted under the Plan may be exercisable, but in no event shall an option be exercised more than ten (10) years after the date of grant. An option is exercised by giving written notice of exercise to the Corporation specifying the number of full shares of Common Stock to be purchased, and by tendering payment to the Corporation for the purchase price. Unless otherwise provided in the stock option agreement, the purchase price of shares purchased upon exercise of an option shall be paid by any of the following means, or by any combination thereof: (i) cash; (ii) certified or bank's cashier's check; or (iii) surrender to the Corporation of shares of the Corporation's Common Stock, provided a public market then exists for such Common Stock.

(b) *Exercise Price.* The exercise price of options granted under the Plan is determined by the Board and must not be less than: (i) the fair market value of the Common Stock on the date the option is granted in the case of incentive stock options; or (ii) 85% percent of such fair market value in the case of nonstatutory stock options. Where the participant owns stock representing more than ten percent (10%) of the total combined voting power of the Corporation's issued and outstanding capital stock, the exercise price for options must not be less than 110% of such fair market value. Until such time as there has been a registered public offering of the Corporation's Common Stock and a public trading market for the Corporation's Common Stock exists, the fair market value of Common Stock will be determined by the Board. In making its determination, the Board will take into account such relevant factors as recent transactions (if any) in shares of the Corporation's Common Stock and the Corporation's past financial performance and prospects for future earnings.

(c) *Restricted Stock Option Purchase Agreement.* As a condition to the exercise of any option granted under the Plan, the optionee must sign and deliver a Restricted Stock Option Purchase Agreement in a form approved by the Board pursuant to which the Corporation is granted: (1) a repurchase option when the optionee exercises his/her Option; and (2) a right of first refusal if the optionee sells stock received under the Plan. See "Terms of Restricted Stock Option Purchase Agreement" below.

Summary Memorandum

(d) *Termination of Employment.* If an optionee's employment (or other service) with the Corporation terminates either (i) for cause or (ii) voluntary on the part of the optionee and without good reason (as determined by the Board, in its sole discretion), the options, to the extent not previously exercised, will terminate on the date of such termination of employment (or service). If an optionee's employment or other service with the Corporation terminates for reasons other than (a) termination that is either (i) for cause, (ii) voluntary on the part of the optionee and without good reason, (b) termination by reason of disability and (c) death, options under the Plan may be exercised not later than three (3) months after such termination, but may be exercised only to the extent the options were exercisable on the date of termination.

(e) *Retirement and Total and Permanent Disability.* If an optionee should become permanently and totally disabled while an employee, non-employee director or officer of the Corporation or while providing other services to the Corporation, options shall become fully exercisable as to all shares subject to them and may be exercised at any time within one (1) year following the date of disability. If an optionee should retire with the written consent of the Corporation, options shall become fully exercisable as to all shares subject to them and may be exercised at any time within three (3) months of such retirement. Incentive stock options that are not exercised within one (1) year of such termination will automatically be converted to non-statutory stock options, and will lose special tax treatment. (Please see discussion on Federal Income Tax Consequences below.)

(f)   *Death.* If an optionee should die while an employee, non-employee director or officer of the Corporation or while providing other services to the Corporation, options may be exercised at any time within one (1) year following the date of death.

(g)   *Termination of Options.* All options granted under the Plan expire on the date specified in the option agreement, but in no event shall the term of incentive stock options exceed ten (10) years. However, all incentive stock options granted under the Plan to any participant who owns stock possessing more than ten percent (10%) of the total combined voting power of the Corporation's outstanding capital stock must expire not later than five (5) years from the date of grant.

(h)   *Nontransferability of Options.* An option is nontransferable by the optionee otherwise than by will or the laws of descent and distribution, and is exercisable during his or her lifetime only by him, or in the event of his or her death, by a person who acquires the right to exercise the option by bequest or inheritance or by reason of the death of the optionee.

(i)   *Other Provisions.* The option agreement may contain such other terms, provisions and conditions not inconsistent with the Plan as may be determined by the Board.

Adjustments Upon Changes in Capitalization

In the event of any change in the Corporation's capital structure, appropriate adjustments shall be made by the Board in the number of shares subject to each option and the per share exercise price thereof. Upon the occurrence of the following events which constitute a "Corporate Change:" (1) certain mergers or consolidations, (2) sale, lease or exchange of substantially all of the assets of the Corporation, (3) liquidation or dissolution, (4) acquisition by any person or entity of more than twenty-five percent (25%) (based on voting power) of the Corporation's outstanding capital stock or acquisition by a person or entity who currently has beneficial ownership in the Corporation which increases such ownership to fifty percent (50%) or more, (5) as a result of a contested election, persons who were directors cease to constitute a majority of the Board, the Board also may make provisions for proportionately adjusting the number or class of stock covered by any option, as well as the option exercise price. The Board may take any of the following actions in connection with the occurrence of a Corporate Change: (1) accelerate the exercisability for the options to be exercised, (2) require the mandatory surrender of outstanding options to the Corporation in exchange for cash for the bargain element the optionee would have realized upon the occurrence of the Corporate Change, if any, (3) make adjustments to the options to reflect such Corporate Change, (4) provide that upon exercise of the option, the optionee will be entitled to purchase other securities or property, or (5) cancel the options if the fair market value of the Common Stock of the Corporation which underlies the options is below the option exercise price.

Amendment and Termination of the Plan

The Board may amend the Plan at any time or from time to time or may terminate it without the approval of the Corporation's shareholders; provided, however, that the approval of the holders of a majority of the outstanding shares of the Corporation entitled to vote is required for any amendment which increases the maximum number of shares for which options may be granted, changes the minimum option exercise price or the standards of eligibility, materially increases the benefits which may accrue to participants under the Plan or decreases any authority granted to the Board in contravention of Rule 16b-3 of the General Rules and Regulations of the Securities and Exchange Commission under the Exchange Act ("Exchange Act"). However, no such action by the Board or shareholders may alter or impair any option previously granted under the Plan. In any event, the Plan shall terminate on _____ ___, 20__.

Summary Memorandum

Terms of Restricted Stock Option Purchase Agreement

All optionees must execute and deliver to the Corporation a form of Restricted Stock Option Purchase Agreement (the "Purchase Agreement") approved by the Board in connection with the exercise of options granted under the Plan. The Purchase Agreement provides, among other things, that the Corporation shall have a repurchase option and a right of first refusal to purchase any shares which are subject to a bona fide purchase offer from a third party. The Corporation will repurchase shares received by an optionee upon exercise of his or her options from the optionee.

An optionee may not sell or transfer (including transfer by operation of law) the shares received upon exercise of his or her option unless he or she first gives written notice to the Corporation of his or her intention to do so and first offers the shares to the Corporation. Such written notice must include: (i) the name and address of the person or firm to whom such shares are to be sold; (ii) the number of shares, or interest therein, to be sold or transferred; (iii) the price or amount to be paid for the proposed transfer (including the amount of any debt to be paid, canceled or forgiven upon foreclosure of a security interest in the shares or upon any other transfer to the optionee's creditors); and (iv) all other terms of the proposed transfer. Within thirty (30) days after receipt of the notice, the Corporation or its designee may elect to purchase all (but not less than all) such shares so offered at the purchase price set forth in the optionee's notice, which purchase must be consummated no later than thirty (30) days following the date of delivery of optionee's notice to the Corporation.

If none or only part of the shares referred to in the optionee's notice to the Corporation is bid for purchase by the Corporation, or its designee or designees, the optionee may dispose of any or all shares referred to in the notice to the Corporation to any person or persons, but only within a period of ninety (90) days from the date of delivery of the notice to the Corporation, and provided further that any such sale is in accordance with all the terms and conditions set forth in the Purchase Agreement.

The optionee may make a gift of all or part of his or her shares to any of his or her parents, spouse or issue or to a trust for his or their exclusive benefit; provided, however, that the gift shall be held subject to the above-described repurchase option and right of first refusal.

Terms of Restricted Stock Grant Agreement

Summary Memorandum

All grantees must execute and deliver to the Corporation a form of Restricted Stock Grant Agreement (the "Grant Agreement"), approved by the Board in connection with the granting of Common Stock under the Plan. The Grant Agreement provides, among other things, that the Corporation shall have a repurchase option to purchase any shares if during the term of the Grant Agreement the grantee ceases to be employed or contracted by the Corporation on a full-time basis for any reason, or no reason, with or without cause, including involuntary termination, death or disability. The grantee may not sell or transfer any of the shares without first delivering a Transfer Notice to the Corporation, which shall have the option to purchase such shares. The Transfer Notice must specify: (i) the name and address of the proposed transferee; (ii) the number of shares, or interest therein, proposed to be sold or transferred; (iii) the price or amount to be paid for the proposed transfer (including the amount of any debt to be paid, canceled or forgiven upon foreclosure of a security interest in the shares or upon any other transfer to the grantee's creditors); and (iv) all other material terms and conditions of the proposed transfer.

Within thirty (30) days after receipt of the Transfer Notice, the Corporation may elect to purchase all, but not less than all, of the shares to which the Transfer Notice refers at the per share price specified in the Transfer Notice. If no price is specified in the Transfer Notice, the purchase price shall be the fair market value of the shares on the date the Corporation receives the Transfer Notice, as determined in good faith by the Board of Directors of the Corporation.

In the event the Corporation elects to acquire shares from the grantee as specified in the Transfer Notice, the Secretary of the Corporation shall so notify the Grantee and settlement thereof shall be made in cash within thirty (30) days after the Corporation receives the Transfer Notice, provided that if the terms of payment set forth in the Transfer Notice were other than cash against delivery, the Corporation shall pay for such shares on the same terms and conditions set forth in the Transfer Notice.

If the shares referred to in the Transfer Notice are not purchased by the Corporation, the grantee, within a period of ninety (90) days from the date of delivery of the Transfer Notice to the Corporation, may sell such shares to the person or persons named in the Transfer Notice at the price and on the terms specified in the Transfer Notice, provided that such sale or transfer is consummated within ninety (90) days following the date of delivery of the Transfer Notice to the Corporation and, provided further, that such sale is in accordance with all the terms and conditions hereof. The transferee will hold all shares transferred hereunder subject to the provisions of this Agreement.

The grantee may make a gift of all or part of the shares to any of his parents, brothers or sisters, spouse or issue, or to a trust for his or their exclusive benefit. The donee or donees shall hold such shares subject to all provisions of this Agreement.

Federal Income Tax Consequences

Summary Memorandum

    (a)   *Incentive Stock Options.*

Section 422 of the Internal Revenue Code of 1986, as amended (the "Code"), provides favorable federal income tax treatment for stock options which qualify as "incentive stock options." When an option granted under an option plan qualifies as an incentive stock option, the optionee does not recognize income for federal income tax purposes upon the grant or exercise of the incentive stock option (unless the alternative minimum tax applies as discussed below). Upon a sale of the shares (assuming that the sale occurs no sooner than two years after the grant of the option and one year after the receipt of the shares by the optionee), any gain or loss will be treated as long-term capital gain or loss for federal income tax purposes.

In order for an option to qualify as an "incentive stock option," it must be exercised while the optionee is an employee of the Corporation or of a parent or subsidiary of the Corporation, or within ninety (90) days after the optionee ceases to be an employee for any reason other than death, in which case there is no statutory limitation, or permanent and total disability, in which case the exercise may occur within one year after termination of employment. See "Terms of Options" above.

Other conditions which must be satisfied include the following: (i) the option cannot be exercisable more than ten (10) years from the date of grant;

(ii) the exercise price of the option must not be less than the fair market value of the shares at the time the option is granted; (iii) the Plan must have been approved by the shareholders of the Corporation; (iv) the option must be nontransferable other than upon death and must be exercisable during the optionee's lifetime by him or her only; (v) the optionee may not own more than 10% of the voting power or value of all classes of the Corporation's capital stock immediately before the option is granted, unless the exercise price is at least 110% of the fair market value of the shares on the date of grant and the option is exercisable only within five years of the date of grant; and (vi) the value of the shares subject to one or more incentive stock options that are exercisable for the first time during any calendar year (under all stock option plans of the Corporation and its parents and subsidiaries) cannot exceed $100,000 (determined as of the date of grant).

The favorable federal income tax consequences described above will not apply to the extent the optionee disposes of the shares acquired within one year of the date of exercise or within two years of the date of grant of the option (hereinafter a "disqualifying disposition"). A disqualifying disposition does not include the disposition of shares acquired upon exercise of an option after the employee's death and, under certain circumstances, the disposition of shares (acquired by exercising an incentive stock option) by an insolvent individual to a trustee, receiver or other similar fiduciary in an insolvency proceeding.

Summary
Memorandum

In the event of a disqualifying disposition, the optionee generally will recognize ordinary income in the year of disposition equal to the amount by which the fair market value of the stock at the date of exercise exceeds the option exercise price. Any additional gain will be long-term or short-term gain, depending on how long the optionee has held the stock. The income recognized on a disqualifying disposition will be added to the optionee's tax basis for determining gain or loss with respect to a subsequent sale of his or her stock.

The Corporation is obligated to provide optionees with a statement regarding the transfer of shares of the Corporation's Common Stock pursuant to the exercise of an incentive stock option on or before January 31 of the year following the year of the transfer. Generally, this statement identifies the Corporation and the optionee and describes the transaction.

(b)   *Alternative Minimum Tax.*

The excess of the stock's fair market value over the option exercise price of an incentive stock option, which is generally not subject to tax at the time of exercise, is treated as an item of income in determining an individual taxpayer's alternative minimum tax liability. The alternative minimum tax is defined under the Code as the excess of the "tentative minimum tax" over the "regular tax." The "tentative minimum tax" is the amount of tax due on the individual's alternative minimum taxable income ("AMTI") at the applicable alternative minimum tax rate. Under the Omnibus Budget Reconciliation Act of 1993 ("OBRA 1993"), the alternative minimum tax rates were increased to 26% of excess tentative minimum tax up to $175,000 and 28% of so much of the taxable excess as exceeds $175,000.

It is advisable for all optionees holding incentive stock options to attempt to forecast their income tax liabilities before deciding when to exercise incentive stock options, or even whether to receive stock compensation in the form of incentive stock options. Despite the potential advantages for capital gains income after OBRA 1993 (as discussed below), the alternative minimum tax risk can make incentive stock options unappealing if the potential spread on exercise of the option in any particular year will be substantial (e.g., greater than $50,000). Moreover, the Internal Revenue Service (the "IRS") takes the position that an optionee owes alternative minimum tax and is not entitled to a refund in the event of a disqualifying disposition of the stock in a subsequent year, notwithstanding the loss of the original tax benefit, in determining his or her regular tax liability for the year of the disqualifying disposition. In determining alternative minimum tax liability in subsequent years, however, the optionee will be entitled to increase the basis of the stock by the amount of this income adjustment. Furthermore, if there is a disqualifying disposition of the stock in the year of exercise, the alternative minimum taxable income adjustment will be limited to the gain on the sale.

*Summary
Memorandum*

   (c)   *Nonstatutory Stock Options.*

Options granted under the Plan that do not qualify as incentive stock options are considered "nonstatutory" stock options and do not qualify for any special tax benefits to the optionee. Under the Code, such stock options are not deemed to have a readily ascertainable value, so the optionee generally does not recognize any taxable income at the time he or she is granted a nonstatutory stock option. However, upon exercise of a nonstatutory stock option, the optionee will generally recognize taxable compensation measured by the excess of the fair market value of the shares on the date of exercise over the option exercise price unless such shares are subject to a substantial risk of forfeiture and are not freely transferable at such time, in which case the tax is generally deferred until one of such restrictions lapse.

The income recognized by the optionee will be treated as wage compensation and will be subject to federal income tax and F.I.C.A. withholding by the Corporation out of the current earnings paid to the optionee up to 28% of such income. There may be additional state income tax withholding. If wage withholdings are insufficient to pay the tax, the optionee will be required to make direct payment to the Corporation for the tax liability. Upon a resale of such shares by the optionee, any difference between the sale price and the fair market value of the shares on the date of exercise of the option will be treated as capital gain or loss.

The IRS takes the position that under Treasury Regulation Section 1.61-15(c)(1), an optionee must report the grant of a nonstatutory stock option by attaching a statement concerning the option grant to his or her federal income tax return for the taxable year in which he or she acquired the option. Accordingly, the Corporation advises all recipients of nonstatutory stock options under the Plan to file such a statement.

(d)   *Capital Gains.*

The Code provides a special tax rate of 20% for capital gains (10% for taxpayers in the 15% bracket). This can be compared to the lowest ordinary income tax rate of 15% and the maximum rate on such income of over 40% (with adjustments). In addition, while ordinary compensation income is subject to certain payroll and Medicare taxes, capital gains are not; this increases the effective tax rate advantage of capital gains. Capital losses may generally be offset only against capital gains. Shares acquired upon exercise of an option must generally be held for more than 12 months for gain or loss from the sale of such shares to qualify for long-term capital gain or loss treatment.

(e)   *Use of Stock to Exercise Options.*

Summary
Memorandum

Under certain circumstances, the Board may permit the exercise of options using shares of the Corporation's stock already owned by the optionee through appropriate provisions in the stock option agreement. This allows the optionee to exercise additional options and, under certain circumstances, provide for payment of his or her withholding taxes, without the payment of cash. The federal income tax treatment of such exchanges depends upon the nature of the stock option and the shares exchanged. Generally, incentive stock options can be exercised using shares previously owned by the optionee in payment of the exercise price (based on the value of the surrendered shares) without triggering the recognition of income by the optionee (provided the exchange does not constitute a disqualifying disposition of shares previously acquired upon exercise of an incentive stock option). Also no gain will generally be recognized upon the exercise of a nonstatutory stock option in this manner to the extent that the fair market value of all of the surrendered shares does not exceed the aggregate option exercise price of the acquired shares. Any excess will generally be treated as ordinary income. Finally, the tax basis of the surrendered stock is generally carried over to the newly acquired shares.

(f)   *Stock Grants*

For restricted stock grants that are nontransferable and subject to a substantial risk of forfeiture pursuant to the Grant Agreement, grantees will recognize ordinary income in the amount of the fair market value of the stock on the date of lapse of either restriction less any amount paid for the stock. Any increase in value after such taxable event generally will be taxed as capital gain upon disposition.

An individual or entity receiving restricted stock pursuant to the Plan may elect to have the ordinary income element of the restricted property close at the time the property is transferred. Closing the taxable event under Code § 83(b) gives the employee the opportunity to limit his/her ordinary income from the transaction to any spread on the date the property is transferred between the fair market value and the amount paid for the property. Any appreciation in property after the date of the transfer is then potential capital gain income which will be recognized when the property is disposed of by the employee. The Code § 83(b) election must be made within 30 days after the transfer of the property; and once the election is made, it is irrevocable, unless the Internal Revenue Service agrees to the revocation. The election is not without risk. If an individual or entity makes the election and recognizes ordinary income and the property is thereafter forfeited pursuant to the restrictions, no deduction is available to the individual or entity.

      (g)   *Qualified Small Business Stock.*

A provision of OBRA 1993 provides, in certain circumstances, for a reduction in the capital gains tax rate for individuals or certain other taxpayers who acquire "qualified small business stock" at its original issue and hold it for more than five years. One-half of the gain (up to certain limits) on such stock is generally excluded from taxable income for regular tax purposes and 25% of such gain (up to certain limits) is generally excluded for alternative minimum tax purposes.

Summary Memorandum

The new law has many limitations, only two of which are described here. In order to qualify, the issuer must not have more than $50,000,000 in gross assets, including amounts received on issuance of the stock. Gross assets generally means cash and the adjusted tax basis of other property. In addition, the issuer must use at least 80% of its assets in the "active conduct" of one or more qualified trades or businesses for substantially all of the holding period of the stock. For issuers who have been in existence for more than two years, up to 50% of the issuer's assets may qualify as used in the "active conduct" of a business by being held for reasonably required working capital needs or held for investment and reasonably expected to be used within two years to finance research and development. The Corporation must meet this test for substantially all of the taxpayer's holding period for the stock. If the Corporation meets this test, it must also submit periodic reports to the IRS and to the Corporation's shareholders detailing its compliance with the law's requirements.

*   *   *

The foregoing summary of the effect of current federal income taxation upon grantees and optionees with respect to the grant of options for, and the purchase and subsequent disposition of, shares under the Plan does not purport to be complete, and reference is made to the applicable provisions of the Code. The laws, court decisions and administrative rulings applicable to federal income taxation change frequently, and the discussion in this summary is based only on such laws, court decisions and administrative rulings as of the date hereof.

The foregoing summary also does not reflect provisions of the income tax laws of any state or foreign jurisdiction in which grantees or optionees may reside, and does not address prospective estate, gift and other tax consequences of acquiring stock under the Plan. In particular, the income tax laws of some states do not presently contain provisions comparable to the incentive stock option provisions of the Code. All grantees and optionees are urged to consult their own tax and financial advisers regarding the current and prospective tax consequences of acquiring options and shares under the Plan.

Restrictions on Transfer and Absence of Public Market

Summary Memorandum

The shares of Common Stock issuable under the Plan either upon grant or upon the exercise of options granted under the Plan are "restricted securities" within the meaning of Rule 144 under the Securities Act of 1933, as amended (the "Act"), insofar as such securities have not been registered thereunder and must be held indefinitely unless they are subsequently registered or an exemption from such registration is available; provided, however, that, in any event, the exemption from registration under Rule 144 will not be available for at least one (1) year after the purchase and payment for the shares, unless the options and the shares were issued pursuant to Rule 701, and even then will not be available unless: (i) a public trading market then exists for the Common Stock; (ii) adequate information concerning the Corporation is then available to the public; and (iii) other terms and conditions of Rule 144 are complied with, including, among other things, the sale being made through a broker in an unsolicited "broker's transaction" or in transactions directly with a "market maker" and the number of shares being sold in any three-month period not exceeding specified limitations. There is not now a public market for shares of the Corporation's Common Stock and there can be no assurance that a public market will ever exist. Accordingly, optionees should be prepared to hold the shares of Common Stock received upon exercise of their options for an indefinite period of time.

The shares of Common Stock granted under the Plan or options granted under the Plan and the shares of Common Stock issuable upon exercise of such options have not been qualified under the securities laws of any state and are being issued in reliance upon available exemptions from such qualification. Shares of Common Stock granted under the Plan or acquired upon the exercise of any option granted under the Plan may be transferred only in accordance with the provisions of applicable state securities or "blue sky" laws. To make sure that another exemption from registration under the Act would be available for the original grant of options and the issuance of shares upon exercise thereof, you will be required to make certain "investment representations" to the Corporation at the time you exercise the option. (See Exhibit A to this Summary Memorandum for the form of such representations.) These representations relate to your investment intent and your acknowledgment of disclosure by the Corporation of, and your access to, financial and other information concerning the Corporation. A restrictive legend will be placed on the stock certificate stating that no sale or other disposition of the stock may be made without meeting certain conditions, which include registration of the stock by the Corporation or an opinion to the Corporation by an attorney that an exemption is available under the Act for a resale of the stock. You are advised that because the Corporation's securities have not been registered under the Act, any shares purchased upon exercise of an option must be held indefinitely unless they are subsequently registered for sale under the Act or an exception from such registration is available.

In the event the Corporation has a class of stock which is subject to the registration and reporting provisions of the Exchange Act, officers, directors and holders of at least 10% of the Corporation's stock will be subject to the "short-swing" profits provisions of Section 16 of the Exchange Act, which would require them to forfeit the profits from any sale of stock within six months of any stock acquisition date. Option grants constitute an acquisition of stock for this purpose unless they are granted pursuant to a plan which satisfies the requirements of Rule 16b-3 promulgated under the Exchange Act. The Corporation intends to maintain the Plan in conformity with the provisions of Rule 16b-3 as in effect from time to time.

Summary Memorandum

Information About the Corporation

The Corporation agrees to provide to all optionees and grantees during the term of the option copies of all annual reports and other information which are provided to all shareholders of the Corporation.

EXHIBIT A
INVESTMENT REPRESENTATION STATEMENT

PURCHASER :

Corporation   :   _____, Inc. (the "Corporation")

SECURITY   :   COMMON STOCK

AMOUNT   :

DATE   :

In connection with the purchase or grant of the above-listed Securities, I, the Purchaser, represent to the Corporation the following:

(a)   I am aware of the Corporation's business affairs and financial condition, and have acquired sufficient information about the Corporation to reach an informed and knowledgeable decision to acquire the Securities. I am purchasing or receiving these Securities for my own account for investment purposes only and not with a view to, or for the resale in connection with, any "distribution" thereof for purposes of the Securities Act of 1933, as amended (the "Securities Act").

(b)   I understand that the Securities have not been registered under the Securities Act in reliance upon a specific exemption therefrom, which exemption depends upon, among other things, the bona fide nature of my investment intent as expressed herein. In this connection, I understand that, in the view of the Securities and Exchange Commission (the "SEC"), the statutory basis for such exemption may be unavailable if my representation was predicated solely upon a present intention to hold these Securities for the minimum capital gains period specified under tax statutes, for a deferred sale, for or until an increase or decrease in the market price of the Securities, or for a period of one year or any other fixed period in the future.

(c)   I further understand that the Securities must be held indefinitely unless subsequently registered under the Securities Act or unless an exemption from registration is otherwise available. Moreover, I understand that the Corporation is under no obligation to register the Securities. In addition, I understand that the certificate evidencing the Securities will be imprinted with a legend which prohibits the transfer of the Securities unless they are registered or such registration is not required in the opinion of counsel for the Corporation.

(d)   I am familiar with the provisions of Rule 701 and Rule 144, each promulgated under the Securities Act, which, in substance, permit limited public resale of "restricted securities" acquired, directly or indirectly, from the issuer thereof, in a non-public offering subject to the satisfaction of certain conditions. Rule 701 provides that if the issuer qualified under Rule 701 at the time of issuance of the Securities, such issuance will be exempt from registration under the Securities Act. In the event the Corporation later becomes subject to the reporting requirements of Sections 13 or 15(d) of the Securities Exchange Act of 1934, ninety (90) days thereafter the securities exempt under Rule 701 may be resold, subject to the satisfaction of certain of the conditions specified by Rule 144, including among other things: (1) the sale being made through a broker in an unsolicited "broker's transaction" or in transactions directly with a market maker (as such term is defined under the Securities Exchange Act of 1934); and, in the case of an affiliate, (2) the availability of certain public information about the Corporation, and the amount of securities being sold during any three-month period not exceeding the limitations specified in Rule 144(e), if applicable. Notwithstanding this paragraph (d), I acknowledge and agree to the restrictions set forth in paragraph (e) hereof.

In the event that the Corporation does not qualify under Rule 701 at the time of issuance of the Securities, then the Securities may be resold in certain limited circumstances subject to the provisions of Rule 144, which requires among other things: (1) the availability of certain public information about the Corporation, (2) the resale occurring not less than one year after the party has purchased, and made full payment for, within the meaning of Rule 144, the securities to be sold; and, in the case of an affiliate, or of a non-affiliate who has held the securities less than two years, (3) the sale being made through a broker in an unsolicited "broker's transaction" or in transactions directly with a market maker (as said term is defined under the Securities Exchange Act of 1934) and the amount of securities being sold during any three month period not exceeding the specified limitations stated therein, if applicable.

Summary
Memorandum

(e)   I agree, in connection with any initial underwritten public offering of the Corporation's securities, (1) not to sell, make short sale of, loan, grant any options for the purchase of, or otherwise dispose of any shares of Common Stock of the Corporation held by me (other than those shares included in the registration) without the prior written consent of the Corporation or the underwriters managing such initial underwritten public offering of the Corporation's securities for one hundred eighty (180) days from the effective date of such registration, and (2) I further agree to execute any agreement reflecting (1) above as may be requested by the underwriters at the time of the public offering; *provided, however,* that the officers and directors of the Corporation who own the stock of the Corporation also agree to such restrictions.

(f)   I further understand that in the event all of the applicable requirements of Rule 144 or Rule 701 are not satisfied, registration under the
Securities Act, compliance with Regulation A, or some other registration exemption will be required; and that, notwithstanding the fact
that Rule 144 and Rule 701 are not exclusive, the Staff of the SEC has
expressed its opinion that persons proposing to sell private place-
ment securities other than in a registered offering and otherwise than
pursuant to Rule 144 or Rule 701 will have a substantial burden of
proof in establishing that an exemption from registration is available
for such offers or sales, and that such persons and their respective
brokers who participate in such transactions do so at their own risk.

Signature of Purchaser:

Dated: _____, 199_

*Summary
Memorandum*

Explanation of Equity Incentive Plan

Section 1: "Purpose"

This section lays out the general purposes and applications of the Model Equity Incentive Plan (the "Plan"). It is largely self-explanatory.

Certain terms are capitalized to signify that they have the meanings defined in the Plan. This manner of capitalization is generally carried over into this explanation to avoid ambiguity.

The final sentence of the section describes the Plan's flexibility, explaining that the Corporation may select from a range of items as best suits the individual circumstances, including: (1) granting restricted stock, (2) awarding Incentive Stock Options, (3) awarding options which do not constitute Incentive Stock Options, or (4) any combination of the foregoing. This section should be tailored to each corporation's circumstances.

Section 2: "Definitions"

The definitions used throughout the Plan are gathered in this section and are mostly self-explanatory.

The distinction between the terms "Award" and "Grant" as used in the Plan should be noted. The Awards are of the stock Options whereas the Grants are of the Corporation's stock itself, either (1) by way of a direct Grant of restricted stock or (2) a Grant of restricted stock in fulfillment of an exercised stock Option.

The defined term "Change of Control Value" refers to actions the Board of Directors takes upon a Corporate Change—for example, as described in section 8 of the Plan.

The defined term "Corporate Change" also concerns alternatives available to the Board of Directors as to acceleration, surrender or adjustment of the Options as detailed in section 8(e) of the Plan. The Corporate Change definition is quite technical, but in general involves (1) a merger (with some limitations), (2) the sale of substantially all the assets of the Corporation, (3) a plan of liquidation or dissolution, (4) the acquisition of 25% of the voting power of the Corporation's stock or the increase of the voting power held by a prior shareholder to more than 50%, or (5) a contested election of directors in which prior directors cease to be a majority. This is a typical definition but may, of course, be modified to reflect particular circumstances or needs.

The "Designated Officer" is the person to whom the Board of Directors delegates the authority and duty to Award Options or make Grants of restricted stock.

An "Incentive Stock Option" is one that qualifies for the favorable tax treatment under Section 422 of the Internal Revenue Code of 1986, as amended (the "Code"). When an option awarded under the Plan qualifies as an Incentive Stock Option, the Optionee does not recognize income for federal income tax purposes upon the Award or the exercise of the Incentive Stock Option (unless the alternative minimum tax applies). Upon a sale of the stock (assuming that the sale occurs no sooner than two years after the Grant of the Option and one year after the receipt of the stock by the Optionee), any gain or loss will be treated as long-term capital gain or loss for federal income tax purposes.

An "Option Agreement" is an agreement between the Corporation and the employee. It can take the form either of (1) an Incentive Stock Option Agreement, or (2) a Non-qualified Stock Option Agreement.

Section 3: "Effective Date and Duration of the Plan"

A specific date is established for the effective date of the Plan.

Because the Plan includes Incentive Stock Options and is designed to satisfy Section 25102(o) of the California Corporations Code (and Sections 260.140.42, 260.140.45 and 260.140.46 of Title 10 of the California Code of Regulations), the Corporation's shareholders must approve the Plan within one year of the effective date (this can be either before or after the effective date). No Option can be exercised until the Corporation's shareholders have approved the Plan.

Explanation of Equity Incentive Plan

The Plan terminates 10 years after the earlier of the date of approval of the Plan by the Corporation's (1) Board of Directors or (2) its shareholders. Despite the "termination," Options which were Awarded during the life of the Plan can still be exercised after termination until the period for their exercise expires.

Section 4: "Administration"

This section outlines the administration of the Plan. The ultimate power lies with the Corporation's Board of Directors. The Corporation's Board of Directors is authorized to delegate and usually does delegate the authority and duty to make individual Awards of Options and/or Grants of restricted stock to one or more Designated Officers.

Members of the Board of Directors must abstain from the decisions on matters that affect their individual interests in the Plan.

Special rules apply if the Corporation, its Parent Corporation, or any Subsidiary is a publicly-held corporation. A publicly-held corporation is one that issues a class of securities that is required to be registered under Section 12 of the Securities Act of 1934. A committee of outside directors must in that case be established to administer the Plan and to make Awards where the limit on deductible employee remuneration under Section 162(m) of the Code might be exceeded. Section 162(m) deals with compensation in excess of specific limits for top corporate officers.

Section 5: "Grant of Options and Stock Subject to the Plan"

This section establishes the maximum number of shares a Corporation's stock which may be Awarded or Granted under the Plan. It also establishes a percentage limitation on Awards and Grants to any one person. Finally, it fixes an outside limit to the number of shares of stock that may be Awarded or Granted under the Plan, specifically 30% of the outstanding shares of the Corporation. This percentage is only for illustrative purposes; you can set it at any level desired or leave it out. Most shareholders would prefer to see an established limit, however.

Section 6: "Eligibility"

Incentive Stock Options may be awarded only to employees of (1) the Corporation, (2) its Parent Corporation, or (3) a Subsidiary.

Options that do not qualify as Incentive Stock Options may be Awarded to employees of (1) the Corporation, (2) its Parent Corporation, or (3) a Subsidiary and they may also be Awarded to non-employee individuals who have been identified by the Corporation's Board of Directors or Designated Officer to receive an Award or Grant due to their contribution or service to the Corporation, including members of the Board of Directors of the Corporation, a Parent Corporation or a Subsidiary.

Grants of restricted stock may be made to employees of (1) the Corporation, (2) its Parent Corporation, or (3) a Subsidiary and they may also be Awarded to non-employee individuals who have been identified by the Corporation's Board of Directors or Designated Officer to receive an Award or Grant due to their contribution or service to the Corporation, including members of the Board of Directors of the Corporation, a Parent Corporation or a Subsidiary.

Explanation of Equity Incentive Plan

An individual may be the recipient of Awards or Grants on more than one occasion.

Section 7: "Stock Options/Grants"

(a) *Stock Option Agreement*

A separate Stock Option Agreement is made for each Award of an Option. The terms can be varied as between the various Optionees who receive Awards and such Awards may tied to the attainment of performance objectives that differ among Optionees. The Holder of an Option may designate a beneficiary in the event of death. This is accomplished by the exhibit attached to the Stock Option Agreement.

(b) *Option Period*

The Option Period is fixed at the time of the Award of the Option but it can not be longer than 10 years. Technically, it could be longer for Options that do not qualify as Incentive Stock Options.

(c) *Limitations on Exercise of Option*

The terms of exercise are also fixed at the time of the Award of the Option but the Option must be exercisable at no slower than the rate of 20% per year over 5 years. This requirement is added to comply with Section

25102(o) of the California Corporations Code and may not be applicable in other jurisdictions. The exercise may not be for less than full shares.

(d) Special Limitations on Incentive Stock Options
To the extent the aggregate Fair Market Value of stock with respect to which Incentive Stock Options are exercisable for the first time during any calendar year exceeds $100,000, such Options are not treated as Incentive Stock Options. An Award of an Incentive Stock Option to a 10% or greater shareholder may only be made where (1) the price is at least 110% of the Fair Market Value ("fair value" as defined in Section 260.140.50 of Title 10 of the California Code of Regulations) and (2) exercise may not be made until after five years.

(e) Option Price
The Option price is another item fixed at the time of the Award. The Option price for Incentive Stock Options may not be less than the Fair Market Value on the date of the Award. The Option price for Options that do not meet the requirements to be Incentive Stock Options may not be less than 85% of the "fair value" on the date of the Award (except for those awards to 10% or greater shareholders where the minimum Option price is 110% of the "fair value" on the date of the Award). Again, this requirement is necessary to comply with the broad-based options exemption from qualification set forth in Section 25102(o) of the California Corporation's Code.

Explanation of Equity Incentive Plan

(f) Options and Rights in Substitution for Stock Options Made by Other Corporations
If the Corporation acquires or is acquired by another corporation, Options may be Awarded to the new employees in substitution for prior Awards of the newly related corporation.

(g) Restricted Stock Purchase Agreement
The execution of the Restricted Stock Purchase Agreement is a precondition to the Grant of stock pursuant to the exercise of an Option. The Restricted Stock Purchase Agreement provides a repurchase option and a right of first refusal in favor of the Corporation. Certain requirements apply to such repurchase rights under many state laws, including California.

(h) Restricted Stock Grant Agreement
The execution of the Restricted Stock Grant Agreement is a precondition to the Grant of restricted stock pursuant to the exercise of a direct restricted stock Grant as well. Again, the Restricted Stock Grant Agreement provides a repurchase option and a right of first refusal in favor of the Corporation that must meet certain requirements in many states.

Section 8: "Recapitalization or Reorganizations"

Awards or Grants may be adjusted by the Corporation's Board of Directors in the event of changes in the number of shares of stock or changes in the character of the shares of stock.

The power of the Corporation's Board of Directors and its shareholders to change the capital structure of the Corporation is not affected by the Plan.

Where an Option is outstanding before a stock split or consolidation, the shares of the Corporation's·stock subject to the Option are similarly adjusted. A similar adjustment is made in the event of a recapitalization or other change in the capital structure.

For Corporate Changes other than a contested election situation, the Corporation's Board of Directors must select from among the available alternatives two days prior to the Corporate Change. In the contested election situation, the Corporation's Board of Directors has ten days after the Corporate Change within which to select the alternatives. The available alternatives tie back to the Corporate Change definition in section 2. The Corporate Change definition involves: (1) a merger (with some limitations), (2) the sale of substantially all the assets of the Corporation, (3) a plan of liquidation or dissolution, (4) the acquisition of 25% of the voting power of the Corporations stock or the increase of the voting power held by a prior shareholder to more than 50%, or (5) a contested election of directors in which prior directors cease to be a majority. In the merger, sale or stock acquisition situations, the Corporation's Board of Directors has the alternative of accelerating the time for exercise of the Options. In the liquidation, stock acquisition and contested election situations, the Corporation's Board of Directors has the alternatives of (1) requiring a mandatory surrender of the options, (2) adjusting the Options, (3) offering other securities, or (4) canceling the Options if the Fair Market Value of the stock is less than the Option price.

Explanation of Equity Incentive Plan

Section 9: "Amendment or Termination of the Plan"

The Corporation's Board of Directors may terminate the Plan or any Option or Grant or alter or amend the Plan or any part thereof or any Option from time to time, but it may not unilaterally impair the rights of Option Holders or restricted stock Grantees. In the specific circumstances listed in this section, the Corporation's shareholders must approve certain changes to the Plan.

Section 10: "Other"

The Plan does not in and of itself confer any rights to any employee to purchase stock, to receive an Award of an Option or to receive a Grant of restricted stock. The Plan is unfunded.

The Plan also does not confer any right to continued employment.

Unless there is an available exemption from securities registration requirements, no stock is obligated to be issued under any Award or Grant. Only whole shares will be issued. The Corporation is authorized to make required tax withholdings.

The Corporation may take any action in its interest even if the action has an adverse affect upon the Plan.

Awards of Options are not transferable, although in the event of the disability or death of the Holder they may be exercised by the legal representative in certain limited circumstances.

To the extent the Corporation is issuing Options under the exemption set forth in Section 25102(o) of the California Corporations Code, financial statements must be provided to Optionees on an annual basis.

*Explanation
of Equity
Incentive
Plan*

Explanation of Incentive Stock Option Agreement

Section I: "Definitions"

This section notes that certain terms are capitalized to signify that they have the meanings defined in the Equity Incentive Plan unless the context requires or specifies a different definition. This manner of capitalization is generally carried over into this explanation to avoid ambiguity.

Regarding who is awarded the options, note the following: Various sections in the Incentive Stock Option (ISO) Agreement refer to the Employee as the grantee; other sections refer to any person who owns the Option; and the preamble provides that the ISO may be granted to employees, officers, and members of the Board of Directors. The Equity Incentive Plan provides for the grant of ISOs (as in this document), which may only go to employees; nonqualified stock options (NSOs), which may go to anyone, including outside directors or consultants, venture capitalists, etc.; and restricted stock, which may go to anyone.

Section II: "Option Shares, Option Exercise Price, and Time of Exercise"

This section sets forth the effective date of the granting of ISOs and the requirement that the Options may not be exercisable by an Optionee until the Optionee executes a Restricted Stock Option Purchase Agreement and returns a copy to the Corporation. It also describes the expiration date of the ISOs and the circumstances under which the Corporation may terminate the ISOs.

Section III: "Exercise Procedure"

An Employee may exercise an Option by delivering to the Corporation a notice and full payment for the shares, either in cash or in Common Stock of the Corporation, based upon the fair market value of the Common Stock as determined by the Board of Directors at the time of grant. Note: In order to ensure that the option exercise price is not less than the fair market value of the Option stock on the date of grant, the Corporation's Board of Directors may want to retain an independent financial advisor to confirm the fair market value of the Option stock on the date of grant. In no event shall the purchase price paid by the Employee be less than 100% of the fair market value of the stock at the time the Option was granted to the Employee, with one exception. The purchase price shall be 110% of the fair market value at the time the Option was granted to the Employee if the Employee owns, at the time the Option is granted, more than 10% of the stock of the Corporation.

The second paragraph of this section provides that notwithstanding the above, the Holder of the Option can exercise it by executing and delivering the Restricted Stock Purchase Agreement.

Section IV: "Termination of Employment"

If an Optionee's employment or contractual relationship is terminated voluntarily, without good reason, or for cause, any Options held will terminate on the date of termination of employment or contractual relationship. The terms "for cause" and "good reason" are defined in this section. If an Optionee's employment or contractual relationship is terminated for any other reason, excepting retirement, disability, or death, any unexercised Options may be exercised not later than three months after such termination, but in no event after ten years from the date of the awarding of such Options.

A change in the status of employment, so long as the Employee continues to be employed by the Corporation, a Parent Corporation or a Subsidiary, shall not affect the Options held by an Employee.

Section V: "Acceleration of Exercise"

Explanation of Incentive Stock Option Agreement

In the event of the Retirement, Total and Permanent Disability, or Death of an Optionee while an Employee, director or officer of the Company, the ability to exercise the Options is accelerated, and the Options may become subject to certain deadlines. These rules are self explanatory in the ISO Agreement.

In the event of a substantial change in ownership or structure of the Corporation, the Option may, at the discretion of the Corporation's Board of Directors, become full exercisable as to all shares subject to it.

Section VI: "Non-Assignability and Term of Option"

The Options may not be transferred or assigned by the Optionee, except by transfer to heirs at death, and the Option may only be exercised by the Optionee during his or her lifetime, or after death, by the Optionee's legal representative.

The Options cannot be exercised after the Expiration Date stated in the ISO Agreement. Further, the ISO Agreement shall not constitute a right to employment to any Optionee.

Section VII: "Rights of Employee in Stock"

Neither an Employee nor his or her successor in interest shall have any of the rights of a shareholder of the Corporation with respect to the shares for which the Option may be exercised until such shares are issued by the Corporation.

Section VIII: "Notices"

Any notice to be given must be in writing and must be addressed to the Corporation, in care of the Corporation's President or Chief Financial Officer, as determined in the Equity Incentive Plan and the ISO Agreement, and any notice to be given to an Employee must be addressed to the address designated by the Corporation for the Employee in the ISO Agreement.

Section IX: "Successors or Assigns of the Corporation"

The Option shall be binding upon, and the benefit of the Option shall apply to, any successor of the Corporation.

Section X: "Miscellaneous"

This section contains a variety of provisions that are self-explanatory. A few comments may be helpful:

- *Designation of Beneficiary:* The Employee shall have the right to appoint any individual or legal entity in writing as his or her beneficiary to receive any Option upon the Employee's death.

- *Incapacity of Employee or Beneficiary:* If any person entitled to receive an Option or shares under the ISO Agreement is deemed by the Corporation's Board of Directors to be incapable of making any election required under the ISO Agreement, then the Board of Directors shall have the power to choose the person or institution entitled to make such an election.

*Explanation
of Incentive
Stock
Option
Agreement*

*Explanation
of Incentive
Stock
Option
Agreement*

Explanation of Nonqualified Stock Option Agreement

Section I: "Definitions"

This section notes that certain terms are capitalized to signify that they have the meanings defined in the Equity Incentive Plan unless the context requires or specifies a different definition. This manner of capitalization is generally carried over into this explanation to avoid ambiguity.

The Equity Incentive Plan provides for the grant of Incentive Stock Options (ISOs), which may only go to employees; nonqualified stock options (NSOs), which may go to anyone, including outside directors or consultants, venture capitalists, etc.; and restricted stock, which may go to anyone. In addition, the Equity Incentive Plan refers to Awards of Options and Grants of restricted stock.

Section II: "Option Shares, Option Exercise Price, and Time of Exercise"

This section sets forth the effective date of the granting of NSOs, and the requirement that the Options may not be exercisable by an Optionee until the Optionee executes a Restricted Stock Option Purchase Agreement and returns a copy to the Corporation. It also describes the expiration date of the NSOs and the circumstances under which the Corporation may terminate the NSOs.

Section III: " Exercise Procedure"

An Employee or other Optionee may exercise an Option by delivering to the Corporation a notice and full payment for the shares, either in cash or in Common Stock of the Corporation, based upon the fair market value of the Common Stock as determined by the Board of Directors at the time of grant. Note: In order to ensure that the option exercise price is not less than 85% of the "fair value" (as defined in the California Corporations Code) of the Option stock on the date of grant (as required by the California Corporations Code if the Options are broad-based [i.e., awarded to all Employees]), the Corporation's Board of Directors may want to retain an independent financial advisor to confirm the fair market value of the Option stock on the date of grant. In the event of broad-based Options awarded to Employees or others in California, in no event shall the purchase price paid by the Employee be less than 85% of the fair value of the stock at the time the Option was granted to the Employee or other Optionee, with one exception. The purchase price shall be 110% of the fair value at the time the Option was granted to the Employee or other Optionee if the Employee or other Optionee owns, at the time the Option is granted, more than 10% of the stock of the Corporation. In the event this restriction related to minimum Option exercise price does not apply, the primary practical issue for the Employer to consider in awarding the Option is that the difference between the Option exercise price and the underlying stock's fair market value will constitute ordinary income to the Optionee at the time of award unless the stock is not freely transferable and is subject to a substantial risk of forfeiture at such time.

The second paragraph of this section provides that notwithstanding the above, the Holder of the Option can exercise it by executing and delivering the Restricted Stock Purchase Agreement.

The Corporation shall notify the Holder of the amount of withholding tax due that must be paid under state and federal law. The Corporation shall have no obligation to deliver the certificates until it receives either the amount of the withholding or the Holder authorizes the Corporation to withhold a number of shares sufficient to satisfy such obligation.

Section IV: "Termination of Employment"

Explanation of Nonqualified Stock Option Agreement

If an Optionee's employment or contractual relationship is terminated voluntarily, without good reason, or for cause, any Options held will terminate on the date of termination of employment or contractual relationship. The terms "for cause" and "good reason" are defined in this section. If an Optionee's employment or contractual relationship is terminated for any other reason, excepting retirement, disability, or death, any unexercised Options may be exercised not later than three months after such termination, but in no event after ten years from the date of the awarding of such Options.

A change in the status of employment, so long as the Employee continues to be employed by the Corporation, a Parent Corporation or a Subsidiary, shall not affect the Options held by an Employee.

Section V: "Acceleration of Exercise"

In the event of the Retirement, Total and Permanent Disability, or Death of an Optionee while an Employee, director or officer of the Company, the ability to exercise the Options is accelerated, and the Options may become subject to certain deadlines. These rules are self-explanatory in the NSO Agreement.

In the event of a substantial change in ownership or structure of the Corporation, the Option may, at the discretion of the Corporation's Board of Directors, become fully exercisable as to all shares subject to it.

Section VI: "Non-Assignability and Term of Option"

The Options may not be transferred or assigned by the Optionee, except by transfer to heirs at death, and the Option may only be exercised by the Optionee during his or her lifetime, or after death, by the Optionee's legal representative.

The Options cannot be exercised after the Expiration Date stated in the NSO Agreement. Further, the NSO Agreement shall not constitute a right to employment to any Optionee.

Section VII: "Rights of Employee in Stock"

Neither an Employee or other Optionee, nor his/her successor in interest, shall have any of the rights of a shareholder of the Corporation with respect to the shares for which the Option may be exercised until such shares are issued by the Corporation.

Section VIII: "Notices"

Any notice to be given must be in writing and must be addressed to the Corporation, in care of the Corporation's President or Chief Financial Officer, as determined in the Equity Incentive Plan and the NSO Agreement, and any notice to be given to an Employee must be addressed to the address designated by the Corporation for the Employee in the NSO Agreement.

Section IX: "Successors or Assigns of the Corporation"

The Option shall be binding upon, and the benefit of the Option shall apply to, any successor of the Corporation.

Section X: "Miscellaneous"

This section contains a variety of provisions that are self-explanatory. A few comments may be helpful:

(a) *Designation of Beneficiary.* The Employee or other Optionee shall have the right to appoint any individual or legal entity in writing as his/her beneficiary to receive any Option upon the Employee's or other Optionee's death.

Explanation of Nonqualified Stock Option Agreement

(b) *Incapacity of Employee or Beneficiary.* If any person entitled to receive an Option or shares under the NSO Agreement is deemed by the Corporation's Board of Directors to be incapable of making any election required under the NSO Agreement, then the Board of Directors shall have the power to choose the person or institution entitled to make such an election.

Exhibits

The last few pages of the NSO Agreement contain the actual award document for NSOs, which may be modified to reflect specific terms for a particular Optionee (i.e., the number of options, the time of exercise, the option exercise price, limits on exercisability, etc.), the Restricted Stock Option Purchase Agreement (which is explained separately in this publication), and the Designation of Beneficiary form.

*Explanation of
Nonqualified
Stock Option
Agreement*

Explanation of Restricted Stock Option Purchase Agreement

The Restricted Stock Option Purchase Agreement is entered into between the Corporation and the Holder of an Option under either an Incentive Stock Option Agreement or a Nonqualified Stock Option Agreement. The Agreement grants the Corporation the option to repurchase such shares under certain circumstances.

Section 1: "Exercise of Option"

(a) *Exercise:* The Purchaser agrees to purchase the specified number of shares pursuant to an exercise of the option granted in the Option Agreement, at the Option Price.

(b) *Payment:* The Purchaser shall pay for the Shares purchased at the time of the delivery of the Agreement and shall deliver any additional documents that may be required by the Option Agreement.

Section 2: "Repurchase Option"

This section grants the Repurchase Option in reference to the terms of the Incentive Stock Option Agreement or the Nonqualified Stock Option Agreement.

The section also specifies the manner of exercise of the Repurchase Option and the method of the closing of that repurchase transaction.

Section 3: "Restrictions on Transfer; Right of First Refusal"

This section grants a right of first refusal to the Corporation to purchase the shares in the event of any transfer of the shares or any interest therein, whether voluntary or involuntary. It specifies the method of notice for such a transfer and the method of closing the corporation purchase. In the event that the Corporation does not purchase the shares within 90 days, then a sale or transfer of the interest to the outside party is permitted. The exception to this right of first refusal is where the shares are being given as a gift to listed close relatives or placed in a similar trust.

Section 4: "Adjustments"

If there is any stock division or consolidation or if the shares are converted to other securities, then the replacement shares are subject to the Repurchase Option.

Section 5: "Termination of Restrictions"

The Repurchase Option and Right of First Refusal terminate on the termination of the Agreement by written agreement of the parties or at such time as the Corporation consummates an underwritten public offering of its common stock.

Section 6: "Legends"

The stock certificates will bear the legend specified in this section, unless and until the restrictions are terminated. The stock certificates will also bear any legends required by State or Federal securities laws.

Section 7: "Dissolution of Marriage"

This section deals with the circumstances of a divorce by the Purchaser of Shares. The Purchaser is given an option to repurchase any shares awarded to the former spouse or shares previously gifted to that spouse. In the event the Purchase does not exercise that purchase option, then the Corporation is able to do so.

Section 8: "Consent of Spouse"

The Purchaser current spouse or any subsequent spouse is required to execute a Consent of Spouse in the form attached to the Agreement.

*Explanation
of Restricted
Stock Option
Purchase
Agreement*

Section 9: "Compliance With Income Tax Laws"

The Purchaser authorizes the Corporation to withhold in accordance with applicable law from any compensation payable to him or her any taxes required to be withheld by federal, state, or local laws as a result of the purchase of the Shares, and if any additional sums should have been withheld, the Purchaser agrees to pay those sums over to the Corporation.

Section 10: "Purchaser's Representations"

This section provides specific representations to the Corporation to establish that the Shares are exempt from registration and that the Purchaser will sell the Shares only in accordance with the rules that permit the transfer of unregistered securities.

Section 11: "'Market Stand-Off' Agreement"

In the event of a stock registration of the Shares, the Purchaser will comply with stock sale restrictions applicable to such registration.

Section 12: "Enforcement"

The Corporation can enforce its rights including by obtaining a decree of specific performance or an injunction in addition to any other remedies.

Section 13: "Controlling Provisions"

The Agreement supersedes other transfer restriction provisions.

Section 14: "Ownership, Voting Rights, Duties"

The ownership, voting rights or other rights or duties of the Purchaser are not affected by the Agreement, except as specifically provided in the Agreement.

Section 15: "Notices"

This section specifies the manner of giving notices.

Section 16: "Binding Effect"

The Agreement is for the benefit of and binds the parties and their successors and assigns, permitted transferees, heirs, legatees, executors, administrators, and legal successors.

Section 17: "Entire Agreement"

This is the final Agreement and supersedes all previous written or oral agreements. The Agreement may only be amended in writing signed by all parties.

Explanation of Restricted Stock Option Purchase Agreement

Section 18: "Not Employment Contract"

The Agreement is not an employment contract, and either the Corporation or the Purchaser of Stock may terminate the Purchaser's employment.

Section 19: "Counterparts"

The parties may sign separate copies of the Agreement.

Section 20: "Governing Law"

California laws govern the Agreement.

Section 21: "Attorneys' Fees"

In the event of litigation the prevailing party is entitled to recover his or her costs and reasonable attorneys' fees.

Section 22: "Severability"

If any provision of the Agreement is determined to be invalid, void, or unenforceable, the remaining provisions continue to be effective.

*Explanation
of Restricted
Stock Option
Purchase
Agreement*

Part 2

Employee Stock Purchase Plan

__, Inc., 199_ Employee Stock Purchase Plan

SECTION 1
PURPOSE

The purpose of the _____ 199_ Employee Stock Purchase Plan is to provide a means whereby _____, Inc., a California corporation (the "Corporation"), may attract able persons to remain in or to enter the employ of the Corporation, the Parent Corporation or a Subsidiary and to provide a means whereby those employees upon whom the responsibilities of the successful administration and management rest, and whose present and potential contributions to the welfare of the Corporation, the Parent Corporation or a Subsidiary are of importance, can acquire and maintain stock ownership, thereby strengthening their concern for the long-term welfare of the Corporation. A further purpose of the Plan is to provide such employees with additional incentive and reward opportunities designed to enhance the profitable growth of the Corporation over the long term. Accordingly, the Plan provides for granting purchase plan options as is best suited to the circumstances of the particular employees as provided herein.

SECTION 2
DEFINITIONS

The following definitions shall be applicable during the term of the Plan unless specifically modified by any paragraph:

(a)   *Award* means, individually or collectively, any Option granted pursuant to the Plan.

(b)   *Board* means the board of directors of the Corporation.

(c)   *Change of Control Value* means the amount determined in Clause (i), (ii) or (iii), whichever is applicable, as follows: (i) the per share price offered to stockholders of the Corporation in any merger, consolidation, sale or assets or dissolution transaction, (ii) the price per share offered to stockholders of the corporation in any tender offer or exchange offer whereby a Corporate Change takes place or (iii) if a Corporate Change occurs other than as described in Clause (i) or Clause (ii), the fair market value per share determined by the Board as of the date determined by the Board to be the date of cancellation and surrender of an Option. If the consideration offered to stockholders of the Corporation in any transaction described in this Paragraph or Paragraphs (d) and (e) of Section 8 consists of anything other than cash, the Board shall determine the fair cash equivalent of the portion of the consideration offered which is other than cash.

(d)   *Code* means the Internal Revenue Code of 1986, as amended. Reference in the Plan to any Section of the Code shall be deemed to include any amendments or successor provisions to such Section and any regulations under such Section.

(e)   *Common Stock* means the common stock of the Corporation.

(f)   *Corporation* means _____, Inc.

(g)   *Corporate Change* means one of the following events: (i) the merger, consolidation or other reorganization of the Corporation in which the outstanding Common Stock is converted into or exchanged for a different class of securities of the Corporation, a class of securities of any other issuer (except a Subsidiary or Parent Corporation), cash or other property other than (a) a merger, consolidation or reorganization of the Corporation which would result in the voting stock of the Corporation outstanding immediately prior thereto continuing to represent (either by remaining outstanding or by being converted into voting securities of the surviving entity), in combination with the ownership of any trustee or other fiduciary holding securities under an employee benefit plan of the Corporation, at least sixty percent (60%) of the combined voting power of the voting stock of the Corporation or such surviving entity outstanding immediately after such merger, consolidation or reorganization of the Corporation, or (b) merger, consolidation or reorganization of the Corporation effected to implement a recapitalization of the Corporation (or similar transaction) in which no person acquires more than forty-nine percent (49%) of the combined voting power of the Corporation's then outstanding stock; (ii) the sale, lease or exchange of all or substantially all of the assets of the Corporation to any other corporation or entity (except a Subsidiary or Parent Corporation); (iii) the adoption by the stockholders of the Corporation of a plan of liquidation and dissolution; (iv) the acquisition (other than acquisition pursuant to any other clause of this definition) by any person or entity, including without limitation a "group" as contemplated by Section 13(d)(3) of the Exchange Act, of beneficial ownership, as contemplated by such Section, of more than twenty-five percent (25%) (based on voting power) of the Corporation's outstanding capital stock or acquisition by a person or entity who currently has beneficial ownership which increases such person's or entity's beneficial ownership to fifty percent (50%) or more (based on voting power) of the Corporation's outstanding capital stock; or (v) as a result of or in connection with a contested election of directors, the persons who were directors of the

Employee Stock Purchase Plan

Corporation before such election shall cease to constitute a majority of the Board. Notwithstanding the provisions of clause (iv) above, a Corporate Change shall not be considered to have occurred upon the acquisition (other than acquisition pursuant to any other clause of the preceding sentence) by any person or entity, including without limitation a "group" as contemplated by Section 13(d)(3) of the Exchange Act, of beneficial ownership, as contemplated by such Section, of more than twenty-five percent (25%) (based on voting power) of the Corporation's outstanding capital stock or the requisite percentage to increase their ownership to fifty percent (50%) resulting from a public offering of securities of the Corporation under the Securities Act of 1933, as amended.

(h)   *Employee* means any person who renders actual service for the benefit of the Corporation under any agreement, appointment or contract of hire.

(i)   *Exchange Act* means the Securities Exchange Act of 1934, as amended.

(j)   *Fair Market Value* means, as of any specified date, the closing price of the Common Stock on the NASDAQ (or, if the Common Stock is not listed on such exchange, such other national securities exchange on which the Common Stock is then listed) on that date, or if no prices are reported on that date, on the last preceding date on which such prices of the Common Stock are so reported. If the Common Stock is not then listed on any national securities exchange but is traded over the counter at the time determination of its Fair Market Value is required to be made hereunder, its Fair Market Value shall be deemed to be equal to the average between the reported high and low sales prices of Common Stock on the most recent date on which Common Stock was publicly traded. If the Common Stock is not publicly traded at the time a determination of its value is required to be made hereunder, the determination of its Fair Market Value shall be made by the Board in such manner as it deems appropriate (such determination may be based on the advice of an independent investment banker or appraiser recognized to be expert in making such valuations). Fair Market Value also shall satisfy the requirements under Section 260.140 of the California Code of Regulations, as necessary to qualify for an exemption from the provisions of Section 25110 of the California Corporations Code.

Employee Stock Purchase Plan

(k)   *Holder* means an individual who has been granted an Award.

(l)   *Option* means an Award granted under Section 7 of the Plan and is an Option within the meaning of Section 423 of the Code.

(m)   *Option Agreement* means a written agreement between the Corporation and an Employee with respect to an Option.

(n)   *Optionee* means an Employee who has been granted an Option.

(o)   *Parent Corporation* shall have the meaning set forth in Section 424(e) of the Code.

(p)   *Plan* means the _____ 199_ Employee Stock Purchase Plan.

(q)   *Rule 16b-3* means Rule 16b-3 of the General Rules and Regulations of the Securities and Exchange Commission under the Exchange Act, as such rule is currently in effect or as hereafter modified or amended.

(r)   *Subsidiary* means a company (whether a corporation, partnership, joint venture or other form of entity) in which the Corporation, or a corporation in which the Corporation owns a majority of the shares of capital stock directly or indirectly, owns an equity interest of fifty percent (50%) or more, except solely with respect to the issuance of Incentive Stock Options the term "Subsidiary" shall have the same meaning as the term "subsidiary corporation" as defined in Section 424(f) of the Code.

SECTION 3
EFFECTIVE DATE AND DURATION OF THE PLAN

Employee Stock Purchase Plan

The Plan shall be effective as of 199_, the date of its adoption by the Board, provided that the Plan is approved by the stockholders of the Corporation within twelve (12) months before or after the date of adoption by the Board, and on or prior to the date of the first annual meeting of stockholders of the Corporation held subsequent to the acquisition of an equity security by a Holder hereunder for which exemption is claimed under Rule 16b-3. Notwithstanding any provision of the Plan or of any Option Agreement, no Option shall be exercisable prior to such stockholder approval. No further Awards may be granted under the Plan after ten (10) years from the date the Plan is adopted by the Board or the date the Plan is approved by the Corporation's shareholders, whichever is earlier. Subject to the provisions of Section 9, the Plan shall remain in effect until all Options granted under the Plan have been exercised or have expired by reason of lapse of time and all restrictions imposed upon restricted stock awards have lapsed. Any option exercised before shareholder approval is obtained must be rescinded if shareholder approval is not obtained within twelve (12) months before or after the Plan is adopted. Such shares shall not be counted in determining whether such approval is granted.

SECTION 4
ADMINISTRATION

(a)   *Administration of Plan by Board.* The Plan shall be administered by the Board in compliance with Rule 16b-3. Members of the Board shall abstain from participating in and deciding matters which directly affect their individual ownership interests under the Plan.

(b)   *Powers.* Subject to the terms of the Plan, the Board shall have sole authority, in its discretion, to determine which Employees shall receive an Award, the time or times when such Award shall be made and the number of shares of Common Stock which may be issued under each Option. In making such determinations, the Board may take into account the nature of the services rendered by these Employees, their present and potential contribution to the success of the Corporation, a Parent Corporation or a Subsidiary, and such other factors as the Board in its discretion shall deem relevant.

(c)   *Additional Powers.* The Board shall have such additional powers as are delegated to it by the other provisions of the Plan. Subject to the express provisions of the Plan, the Board is authorized in its sole discretion, exercised in a nondiscriminatory manner, to construe and interpret the Plan and the respective agreements executed thereunder, to prescribe such rules and regulations relating to the Plan as it may deem advisable to carry out the Plan, and to determine the terms, restrictions and provisions of each Award, including such terms, restrictions and provisions as shall be requisite in the judgment of the Board and to make all other determinations necessary or advisable for administering the Plan. The Board may correct any defect or supply any omission or reconcile any inconsistency in any agreement relating to an Award in the manner and to the extent it shall deem expedient to carry it into effect. The determination of the Board on the matters referred to in this Section 4 shall be conclusive.

*Employee
Stock
Purchase
Plan*

(d)   *Compliance With Code §162(m).* In the event the Corporation, a Parent Corporation or a Subsidiary becomes a "publicly-held corporation" as defined in of Section 162(m)(2) of the Code, the Corporation may establish a committee of outside directors meeting the requirements of Code §162(m) to (i) approve the grant of Options which might reasonably be anticipated to result in the payment of employee remuneration that would otherwise exceed the limit on employee remuneration deductible for income tax purposes by the Corporation pursuant to Code §162(m) and (ii) administer the Plan. In such event, the powers reserved to the Board in the Plan shall be exercised by such compensation committee. In addition, Options under the Plan shall be granted upon satisfaction of the conditions to such grants provided pursuant to Code §162(m) and any Treasury Regulations promulgated thereunder.

SECTION 5
GRANT OF OPTIONS SUBJECT TO THE PLAN

(a)   *Award Limits.* The Board may from time to time grant Awards to one
       or more Employees determined by it to be eligible for participation in
       the Plan in accordance with the provisions of Section 6 of the Plan.
       The aggregate number of shares of Common Stock that may be is-
       sued under the Plan shall not exceed [_____] shares. Any of such
       shares which remain unissued and which are not subject to out-
       standing Options at the termination of the Plan shall cease to be sub-
       ject to the Plan but, until termination of the Plan, the Corporation
       shall at all times reserve a sufficient number of shares to meet the re-
       quirements of the Plan. Shares shall be deemed to have been issued
       under the Plan only to the extent actually issued and delivered pur-
       suant to an Award. To the extent that an Award lapses or the rights of
       its Holder terminate, any shares of Common Stock subject to such
       Award shall again be available for the grant of an Award. The aggre-
       gate number of shares which may be issued under the Plan shall be
       subject to adjustment in the same manner as provided in Section 8 of
       the Plan with respect to shares of Common Stock subject to Options
       then outstanding.

*Employee
Stock
Purchase
Plan*

(b)   *Stock Offered.* The stock to be offered pursuant to the grant of an
       Award may be authorized but unissued Common Stock or Common
       Stock previously issued and outstanding and reacquired by the Cor-
       poration.

SECTION 6
ELIGIBILITY

An Option Award made pursuant to the Plan may be granted only to an individual who, at the time of grant, is an Employee of the Corporation, a Parent Corporation or a Subsidiary. An Award made pursuant to the Plan may
be granted on more than one occasion to the same person. Each Award shall
be evidenced by a written instrument duly executed by or on behalf of the
Corporation. Notwithstanding the foregoing, no Employee of the Corporation, a Parent Corporation or a Subsidiary shall be granted an Option under
the Plan if such Employee, immediately after the Option is granted, owns
stock possessing five percent (5%) or more of the total combined voting
power or five percent (5%) or more of the value of all classes of stock of the
Corporation, or its Parent Corporation or Subsidiary. For purposes of determining stock ownership, the rules of Section 424(d) of the Code shall apply.
In addition, the stock which the Holder may purchase under outstanding
Options shall be treated as stock owned by the Holder.

The Board may exclude the following Employees from recovering Options
under the Plan:

1.   Employees who have been employed by the Corporation, a Parent Corporation, or a Subsidiary less than two (2) years;

2.   Employees whose customary employment with the Corporation, a Parent or a Subsidiary is twenty (20) hours or less per week;

3.   Employees whose customary employment with the Corporation, a Parent or Subsidiary is not for more than five (5) months in any calendar year; and

4.   Highly compensated employees within the meaning of Section 414(q) of the Code.

SECTION 7
STOCK OPTIONS

(a)   *Stock Option Agreement.* Each Option shall be evidenced by an Option Agreement between the Corporation and the Optionee which shall contain such terms and conditions as may be approved by the Board and agreed upon by the Holder and are consistent with Section 423 of the Code. The terms and conditions of the respective Option Agreements need not be identical. Each Option Agreement shall specify the effect of termination of employment, total and permanent disability, retirement or death on the exercisability of the Option. Under each Option Agreement, a Holder shall have the right to appoint any individual or legal entity in writing as his or her beneficiary under the Plan in the event of his death. Such designation may be revoked in writing by the Holder at any time and a new beneficiary may be appointed in writing on the form provided by the Board for such purpose. In the absence of such appointment, the beneficiary shall be the legal representative of the Holder's estate.

Employee Stock Purchase Plan

(b)   *Option Period.* The term of each Option shall be as specified by the Board at the date of grant and shall be stated in the Option Agreement; provided, however, that an Option may not be exercised after the expiration of:

(1)   Five (5) years from the date such Option is granted if the Plan requires that the Option Price must be not less than eighty-five percent (85%) of the Fair Market Value of the Corporation's stock at the time the Option is exercised; or

(2)   Twenty-Seven (27) months from the date such Option is granted if the Option provides for an Option Price in some other permissible manner under Section 423 of the Code (such as a flat dollar amount).

(c)   *Limitations on Exercise of Option.* An Option may be exercisable in whole or in such installments and at such times as determined by the Board and the applicable term relating to the exercise of the option shall be stated in the Option Agreement and must be uniform for all Employees with the following exceptions: (1) the Board may limit the maximum number Options that can be exercised under the Plan, as it has done under Section 5, and (2) the Board may limit the amount of Options that all Employees may be granted to a specified relationship to total compensation or the base or regular rate of compensation; and provided, however, that an Option may be exercised at the rate of at least twenty percent (20%) per year over five (5) years from the date it is granted.

(d)   *Special Limitations Regarding Exercise of Option.* No Employee may be granted an Option which permits his or her rights to exercise Options under all employee stock purchase plans of the Corporation, Parent Corporation and Subsidiaries to accrue at a rate that exceeds $25,000 of the Fair Market Value of such stock (determined at the time of grant) for each calendar year in which such Option is outstanding at any time. For the purposes of this rule:

Employee Stock Purchase Plan

(1)   The right to purchase Common Stock under an Option accrues when the Option (or any portion thereof) first becomes exercisable during the calendar year;

(2)   The right to purchase Common Stock under an Option accrues at the rate provided in the Option, but in no case may such rate exceed $25,000 of Fair Market Value of such stock (determined at the time of grant) for any one calendar year; and

(3)   A right to purchase Common Stock which has accrued under one Option granted pursuant to the Plan may not be carried over to any other Option.

The Board shall determine, in accordance with applicable provisions of the Code, Treasury Regulations, and other administrative pronouncements which Options will not constitute Options under Section 423 of the Code because of such limitations and shall notify the Optionee of such determination as soon as practicable after such determination.

(e) *Option Price.* The purchase price of Common Stock issued under each Option shall be determined by the Board and shall be stated in the Option Agreement, but such purchase price shall not be less than the lesser of:

    (A) An amount equal to eighty-five percent (85%) of the Fair Market Value of the Common Stock at the time the Option is granted; or

    (B) An amount which under the terms of the Option may not be less than eighty-five percent (85%) of the Fair Market Value of such Common Stock at the time of the exercise of the Option.

Fair Market Value shall have the same meaning as Fair Value as set forth in Section 260.140.50 of the California Code of Regulations.

(f) *Options and Rights in Substitution for Stock Options Granted by Other Corporations.* Options may be granted under the Plan from time to time in substitution for stock options held by Employees of corporations who become, or who became prior to the effective date of the Plan, Employees of the Corporation, of any Parent Corporation or of any Subsidiary as a result of a merger or consolidation of the employing corporation with the Corporation, such Parent Corporation or such Subsidiary, or the acquisition by the Corporation, a Parent Corporation or a Subsidiary of all or a portion of the assets of the employing corporation, or the acquisition by the Corporation, a Parent Corporation or a Subsidiary of stock of the employing corporation with the result that such employing corporation becomes a Subsidiary.

(g) *Restricted Stock Purchase Agreement.* Notwithstanding the foregoing, a Holder and the Corporation shall, as a condition of exercise of an Option, execute and deliver a Restricted Stock Purchase Agreement (the "Purchase Agreement"), pursuant to which the Corporation shall be granted a "Repurchase Option" and a "Right of First Refusal" as to all "Shares" (as such terms are defined in the Purchase Agreement).

Employee Stock Purchase Plan

SECTION 8
RECAPITALIZATION OR REORGANIZATION

(a)   Except as hereinafter otherwise provided, Awards shall be subject to adjustment by the Board at its discretion as to the number and price of shares of Common Stock in the event of changes in the outstanding Common Stock by reason of stock dividends, stock splits, reverse stock splits, reclassifications, recapitalizations, reorganizations, mergers, consolidations, combinations, exchanges or other relevant changes in capitalization occurring after the date of the grant of any such Options.

(b)   The existence of the Plan and the Awards granted hereunder shall not affect in any way the right or power of the Board or the stockholders of the Corporation to make or authorize any adjustment, recapitalization, reorganization or other change in the capital structure of the Corporation, a Parent Corporation or a Subsidiary or their business, any merger or consolidation of the Corporation, a Parent Corporation or a Subsidiary, any issue of debt or equity securities having any priority or preference with respect to or affecting Common Stock or the rights thereof, the dissolution or liquidation of the Corporation, a Parent Corporation or a Subsidiary, or any sale, lease, exchange or other disposition of all or any part of their assets or business or any other corporate act or proceeding.

Employee Stock Purchase Plan

(c)   The shares with respect to which Options may be granted are shares of Common Stock as presently constituted but if and whenever, prior to the expiration of an Option theretofore granted, the Corporation shall effect a subdivision or consolidation of shares of Common Stock or the payment of a stock dividend on Common Stock without receipt of consideration by the Corporation, the number of shares of Common Stock with respect to which such Option may thereafter be exercised (i) in the event of an increase in the number of outstanding shares shall be proportionately increased, and the purchase price per share shall be proportionately reduced, and (ii) in the event of a reduction in the number of outstanding shares shall be proportionately reduced, and the purchase price per share shall be proportionately increased.

(d)   If the Corporation recapitalizes or otherwise changes its capital structure, thereafter upon any exercise of an Option theretofore granted, the Optionee shall be entitled to purchase under such Option, in lieu of the number of shares of Common Stock as to which such Option shall then be exercisable, the number and class of shares of stock and securities, and the cash and other property to which the Optionee would have been entitled pursuant to the terms of the recapitalization if, immediately prior to such recapitalization, the Optionee had been the holder of such record of the number of shares of Common Stock then covered by such Option.

(e) In the event of a Corporate Change, unless otherwise deemed to be impractical by the Board, then no later than (i) two business days prior to any Corporate Change referenced in Clause (i), (ii), (iii) or (v) of the definition thereof or (ii) ten business days after any Corporate Change referenced in Clause (iv) of the definition thereof, the Board, acting in its sole discretion without the consent or approval of any Optionee, shall act to effect one or more of the following alternatives with respect to outstanding Options which acts may vary among individual Optionees and, with respect to acts taken pursuant to Clause (i) above, may be contingent upon effectuation of the Corporate change: (A) accelerate the time at which Options then outstanding may be exercised so that such Options may be exercised in full for a limited period of time on or before a specified date (before or after such Corporate Change) fixed by the Board, after which specified date all unexercised Options and all rights of Optionees thereunder shall terminate; (B) require the mandatory surrender to the Corporation by selected Optionees of some or all of the outstanding Options held by such Optionees (irrespective of whether such Options are then exercisable under the provisions of the Plan) as of a date (before or after such Corporate Change) specified by the Board, in which event the Board shall thereupon cancel such options and pay to each Optionee an amount of cash per share equal to the excess, if any, of the Change of Control Value of the shares subject to such Option over the exercise price(s) under such Options for such shares; (C) make such adjustments to Options then outstanding as the Board deems appropriate to reflect such Corporate Change (provided, however, that the Board may determine in its sole discretion that no adjustment is necessary to Options then outstanding); (D) provide that thereafter upon any exercise of an Option theretofore granted the Optionee shall be entitled to purchase under such Option, in lieu of the number of shares of Common Stock as to which such Option shall then be exercisable, the number and class of shares of stock or other securities or property (including, without limitation, cash) to which the Optionee would have been entitled pursuant to the terms of the agreement of merger, consolidation or sale of assets or plan of liquidation and dissolution if, immediately prior to such merger, consolidation or sale of assets or any distribution in liquidation and dissolution of the Corporation, the Optionee had been the holder of record of the number of shares of Common Stock then covered by such Option; or (E) cancel the Options granted if the Fair Market Value of the Common Stock underlying the Options is below the Option exercise price.

(f) Except as hereinbefore expressly provided, issuance by the Corporation of shares of stock of any class or securities convertible into

*Employee
Stock
Purchase
Plan*

shares of stock of any class, for cash, property, labor or services, upon direct sale, upon the exercise of rights or warranty to subscribe therefore, or upon conversion of shares or obligations of the Corporation convertible into such shares or other securities, and in any case whether or not for fair value, shall not affect, and no adjustment by reason thereof shall be made with respect to, the number of shares of Common Stock subject to Options theretofore granted, or the purchase price per share of Common Stock subject to Options.

SECTION 9
AMENDMENT OR TERMINATION OF THE PLAN

The Board in its discretion may terminate the Plan or any Option or alter or amend the Plan or any part thereof or any Option from time to time; provided, however, that no change in any Award previously granted may be made which would impair the rights of the Holder without the consent of the Holder, and provided further, that the Board may not, without approval of the stockholders, amend the Plan:

Employee Stock Purchase Plan

(a)   to increase the aggregate number of shares of Common Stock which may be issued pursuant to the provisions of the Plan on exercise or surrender of Options;

(b)   to change the minimum Option Price;

(c)   to change the class of employees eligible to receive Awards or increase materially the benefits accruing to Employees under the Plan;

(d)   to extend the maximum period during which Awards may be granted under the Plan;

(e)   to modify materially the requirements as to eligibility for participation in the Plan; or

(f)   to decrease any authority granted to the Board hereunder in contravention of Rule 16b-3.

SECTION 10
OTHER

(a)   *No Right to Award.* Neither the adaption of the Plan nor any action of the Board shall be deemed to give an Employee any right to be granted an Option to purchase Common Stock or any other rights hereunder except as may be evidenced by an Option Agreement duly executed on behalf of the Corporation, and then only to the extent of and on the terms and conditions expressly set forth therein. The Plan shall be unfunded. The Corporation shall not be required to establish any special or separate fund or to make any other segregation of funds or assets to assure the payment of any Award.

(b) *No Employment Rights Conferred.* Nothing contained in the Plan or in any Award made hereunder shall (i) confer upon any Employee any right with respect to continuation of employment with the Corporation or any Parent Corporation or Subsidiary, or (ii) interfere in any way with the right of the Corporation or any Parent Corporation or Subsidiary to terminate his or her employment at any time.

(c) *Other Laws: Withholding.* The Corporation shall not be obligated to issue any Common Stock pursuant to any Award granted under the Plan at any time when the offering of the shares covered by such Award has not been registered (or exempted) under the Securities Act of 1933 and such other state and federal laws, rules or regulations as the Corporation or the Board deems applicable and, in the opinion of legal counsel for the Corporation, there is no exemption from the registration requirements of such laws, rules or regulations available for the issuance and sale of such shares. No fractional shares of Common Stock shall be delivered, nor shall any cash in lieu of fractional shares be paid. The Corporation shall have the right to deduct in connection with all Awards any taxes required by law to be withheld and to require any payments necessary to enable it to satisfy its withholding obligations. The Board may permit the Holder of an Award to elect to surrender, or authorize the Corporation to withhold shares of Common Stock (valued at their Fair Market Value on the date of surrender or withholding of such shares) in satisfaction of the Corporation's withholding obligation, subject to such restrictions as the Board deems necessary to satisfy the requirements of Rule 16b-3.

Employee Stock Purchase Plan

(d) *No Restriction of Corporate Action.* Nothing contained in the Plan shall be construed to prevent the Corporation or any Parent Corporation or Subsidiary from taking any corporate action which is deemed by the Corporation or such Parent Corporation or Subsidiary to be appropriate or in its best interest, whether or not such action would have an adverse effect on the Plan or any Award made under the Plan. No Employee, beneficiary or other person shall have any claim against the Corporation or any Parent Corporation or Subsidiary as a result of such action.

(e) *Restrictions on Transfer.* An Award shall not be transferable otherwise than by will or the laws of descent and distribution and shall be exercisable during the lifetime of the Holder only by such 'Holder or the Holder's guardian or legal representative. The Option Agreement or other written instrument evidencing an Award shall specify the effect of the death, disability or retirement of the Holder on the Award; provided, however that an Optionee shall be entitled to exercise (i) at least six (6) months from the date of termination of employment with the Corporation if such termination is caused by death or disability or (ii) at least thirty (30) days from the date of termination of employment with the Corporation if such termination is caused by other than death or disability.

(f)   *Information to Employees.* Optionees under the Plan shall receive financial statements annually regarding the corporation during the period the options are outstanding. The financial statements provided need not comply with Section 260.613 of the California Code of Regulations.

(g)   *Rule 16b-3.* It is intended that the Plan and any grant of an Award made to a person subject to Section 16 of the Exchange Act meet all of the requirements of Rule 16b-3. If any provisions of the plan or any such Award would disqualify the Plan or such Award hereunder, or would otherwise not comply with Rule 16b-3, such provision or Award shall be construed or deemed amended to conform to Rule 16b-3.

(h)   *Governing Law.* The Plan shall by construed in accordance with the laws of the State of California and all applicable federal law. The securities issued hereunder shall be governed by and in accordance with the Corporate Securities Laws of the State of California.

*Employee
Stock
Purchase
Plan*

ADOPTED BY THE BOARD AS OF 199_

APPROVED BY THE SHAREHOLDERS AS OF 199_

Stock Option Agreement

Pursuant to the __ 199_ Employee Stock Purchase Plan

This STOCK OPTION AGREEMENT (this "Agreement") is made as of the _____ day of _____, 199__, by and between _____, INC., a California corporation (the "Corporation"), and _____ ("Employee").

WITNESSETH:

The Corporation has determined that it is in the best interests of the Corporation and its shareholders to encourage ownership in the Corporation by employees of the Corporation and its affiliates, thereby providing additional incentive for them to continue in the employ of the Corporation or its affiliates. To that end, a stock option is granted by the Board to Employee pursuant, and subject to, the _____ 199_ Employee Stock Purchase Plan (the "Plan") on the following terms and conditions:

SECTION I
DEFINED TERMS

Unless otherwise defined herein or, unless the context requires a different definition, capitalized terms used herein shall have the meanings assigned to them in the Plan.

SECTION II
SHARES OPTIONED, OPTION PRICE, AND TIME OF EXERCISE

Effective as of _____, 19___, the Corporation grants to Employee, subject to the terms and provisions set forth hereinafter and in the Plan, the right and option to purchase all or any part of the number of shares set forth in Exhibit A of the presently authorized but unissued common stock ("Common Stock") of the Corporation at the purchase price per share set forth as the Option Price in Exhibit A (the option hereby granted being hereinafter referred to as the "Option").

The Option shall not be considered granted (as of the effective date described above) or become exercisable unless and until Employee delivers to the Corporation a fully executed counterpart hereof. Thereafter, the Option shall be exercisable in accordance with the Exercise Schedule set forth on Exhibit A, subject to any termination, acceleration or change in such Exercise Schedule set forth in this Agreement apart from Exhibit A.

Neither the Option nor any other rights granted under this Agreement may be exercised after the Expiration Date set forth on Exhibit A and, before that time, the Option may be terminated as hereinafter provided.

SECTION III
EXERCISE PROCEDURE

*Stock
Option
Agreement*

Employee shall exercise the Option by notifying the Corporation of the number of shares that he desires to purchase and by delivering with such notice the full payment for the purchase price of the shares being purchased or a promissory note with adequate security in the amount of the purchase price, payable by payroll deduction over a period not exceeding two years at an interest rate of the Prime Rate plus three (3) percent points; provided, however, that the monetary limit on such purchase price shall be $5,000 when it is paid in this manner. "Prime Rate" shall mean the money rate published in the Wall Street Journal (Western Edition) as of the date of exercise. For purposes of determining the amount, if any, of the purchase price satisfied by payment in Common Stock, such Common Stock shall be valued at its Fair Market Value on the date of exercise, as determined by the Board at the time of exercise. In no event shall the purchase price be less than the lesser of: (A) An amount equal to eighty-five (85%) of the Fair Market Value of the Common Stock at the time the Option is granted; or (B) An amount which under the terms of the Option may not be less than eighty-five (85%) of the Fair Market Value of such stock at the time of the exercise of the Option. Any Common Stock delivered in satisfaction of all or a portion of the purchase price shall be appropriately endorsed for transfer and assignment to the Corporation.

Notwithstanding the foregoing, at the election of the Holder, the Option can be exercised provided that the Holder shall, as a condition of such exercise, execute and deliver the Restricted Stock Purchase Agreement in the form of Exhibit B hereto (the "Purchase Agreement"), pursuant to which the Corporation shall be granted a "Repurchase Option" and "Right of First Refusal" as to all "Shares" (as such terms are defined in the Purchase Agreement).

SECTION IV
TERMINATION OF EMPLOYMENT

In the event of the termination of the employment of the Employee, including a termination that is voluntary on the part of the Employee and with Good Reason, other than (a) a termination that is either (i) for Cause or (ii) voluntary on the part of the Employee and without Good Reason, (b) a termination by reason of retirement or disability within the meaning of the then existing long-term disability plan maintained by the Corporation, or (c) death, the Employee may exercise the Option at any time within three (3) months of such termination of employment, but in no event after ten (10) years from the date of granting thereof, but only to the extent of the number of shares for which the Option is exercisable by him at the date of the termination of employment. In the event of a termination of the employment of the Employee that is either (i) for Cause or (ii) voluntary on the part of the Employee and without Good Reason, the Option, to the extent not previously exercised, shall forthwith terminate on the date of such termination of employment. Except as may be otherwise provided in this Agreement, the Option granted hereunder shall not be affected by any change of employment so long as Employee continues to be employed by the Corporation, a Parent Corporation or a Subsidiary.

"Cause" shall mean, as determined by the Board, in its sole discretion exercised in a nondiscriminatory manner, (i) the continued failure of the Employee to substantially perform his duties to the Corporation, a Parent Corporation or a Subsidiary (other than any such failure resulting from disability as defined above), (ii) the engaging by the Employee in willful, reckless or grossly negligent misconduct which is determined by the Board to be materially injurious to the Corporation or any of its affiliates, monetarily or otherwise, or (iii) the Employee's pleading guilty to or conviction of a felony.

Stock Option Agreement

"Good Reason" shall mean, as determined by the Board, in its sole discretion exercised in a nondiscriminatory manner, the occurrence of any of the following events without Employee's express written consent:

(i)   a substantial and adverse change in the Employee's duties, control, authority or status or position, or the assignment to the Employee of any duties or responsibilities which are inconsistent with such status or position, or a reduction in the duties and responsibilities previously exercised by the Employee, or a loss of title, loss of office, loss of significant authority, power or control, or any removal of him or her from or any failure to reappoint or reelect him to such positions, except in connection with the termination of his employment for Cause or disability (as defined above), or as a result of his death;

(ii)   a reduction in the Employee's base salary or a material reduction in the Employee's total compensation (i.e., a reduction in such total compensation of ten (10) percent or more); or

(iii)   any material breach by the Corporation of any provisions of any agreement with the Employee.

SECTION V
ACCELERATION OF EXERCISE

(a)   *Retirement and Total and Permanent Disability.* In the event of the Employee's retirement (with the written consent of the Corporation) or termination by reason of total and permanent disability (within the meaning of the then existing long-term disability plan maintained by the Corporation), the Option (to the extent not previously terminated or forfeited) shall become fully exercisable as to all shares subject to it and the Employee may exercise the Option at any time within (3) months of such retirement (or within one year after termination of employment due to disability as defined above), but in no event after the Expiration Date set forth on Exhibit A. If such option is exercised after the Expiration Date set forth in Exhibit A, such Option shall not receive favorable tax treatment under Code Section 421(a).

(b)   *Death.* In the event the Employee dies during his employment by the Corporation or a Subsidiary or Parent Corporation, the Option (to the extent not previously terminated or forfeited) shall become fully exercisable as to all shares subject to it. Such Option may be exercised by the beneficiary designated by the Employee on Exhibit C hereto, in accordance with Section X hereto, or, if no beneficiary is designated on Exhibit C, by the executor or administrator of the Employee's estate, but in no event after the earlier of (i) the date one year following the Employee's date of death, or (ii) the Expiration Date set forth on Exhibit A hereto.

Stock
Option
Agreement

(c)   *Corporate Change.* Upon the occurrence of a Corporate Change, the Option (to the extent not previously terminated or forfeited) may, at the discretion of the Board, become fully exercisable as to all shares subject to it.

SECTION VI
NON-ASSIGNABILITY AND TERM OF OPTION

The Option shall not be transferable or assignable by the Employee, otherwise than by will or the laws of descent and distribution and the Option shall be exercisable, during the Employee's lifetime, only by him or, during periods of legal disability, by his legal representative. No Option shall be subject to execution, attachment, or similar process.

In no event may the Option be exercisable to any extent by anyone after the Expiration Date specified in Exhibit A. It is expressly agreed that, anything contained herein to the contrary notwithstanding, this Agreement shall not constitute, or be evidence of, any agreement or understanding, express or implied, that the Corporation will employ Employee for any period of time or in any position or for any particular compensation.

SECTION VII
RIGHTS OF EMPLOYEE IN STOCK

Neither Employee, nor his successor in interest, shall have any of the rights of a shareholder of the Corporation with respect to the shares for which the Option is exercised until such shares are issued by the Corporation.

SECTION VIII
NOTICES

Any notice to be given hereunder shall be in writing and shall be addressed to the Corporation, in care of the Board, at _____ Street, Suite __, ____, California ____, and any notice to be given to the Employee shall be addressed to the address designated below the signature appearing hereinafter, or at such other address as either party may hereafter designate in writing to the other. Any such notice shall have been deemed duly given upon three (3) days of sending such notice enclosed in a properly sealed envelope, addressed as aforesaid, registered or certified and deposited (with the proper postage and registration or certificate fee prepaid) in the United States mail.

SECTION IX
SUCCESSORS OR ASSIGNS OF THE CORPORATION

The Option shall be binding upon and shall inure to the benefit of any successor of the Corporation.

Stock
Option
Agreement

SECTION X
MISCELLANEOUS

(a)   *Designation of Beneficiary.* The Employee shall have the right to appoint any individual or legal entity in writing, on Exhibit C hereto, as his beneficiary to receive any Option (to the extent not previously terminated or forfeited) under this Agreement upon the Employee's death. Such designation under this Agreement may be revoked by the Employee at any time and a new beneficiary may be appointed by the Employee by execution and submission to the Board of a revised Exhibit C to this Agreement. In order to be effective, a designation of beneficiary must be completed by the Employee on Exhibit C and received by the Board, or its designee, prior to the date of the Employee's death. In the absence of such designation, the Employee's beneficiary shall be the legal representative of the Employee's estate.

(b)   *Incapacity of Employee or Beneficiary.* If any person entitled to a distribution under this Agreement is deemed by the Board to be incapable of making an election hereunder or of personally receiving and giving a valid receipt for such distribution hereunder, then, unless and until an election or claim therefore shall have been made by a duly appointed guardian or other legal representative of such person, the Board may provide for such election or distribution or any part thereof to be made to any other person or institution then contributing toward or providing for the care and maintenance of such person. Any such distribution shall be a distribution for the account of such person and a complete discharge of any liability of the Board, the Corporation and the Plan therefore.

(c)   *Incorporation of the Plan.* The terms and provisions of the Plan are hereby incorporated in this Agreement. Unless otherwise specifically stated herein, such terms and provisions shall control in the event of any inconsistency between the Plan and this Agreement.

(d)   *Governing Law.* THIS AGREEMENT SHALL BE GOVERNED BY THE LAWS OF THE STATE OF CALIFORNIA AND ALL APPLICABLE FEDERAL LAWS. THE SECURITIES ISSUED HEREUNDER SHALL BE GOVERNED BY AND IN ACCORDANCE WITH THE CORPORATE SECURITY LAWS OF THE STATE OF CALIFORNIA.

Stock
Option
Agreement

(e)   *Gender.* Reference to the masculine herein shall be deemed to include the feminine, wherever appropriate.

(f)   *Counterparts.* This Agreement may be executed in one or more counterparts, which shall together constitute a valid and binding agreement.

IN WITNESS WHEREOF, this Agreement has been executed by the Corporation and the Employee as of the date and year first written above.

Employee: _____   _____, Inc.

Address: _____   By: _____

_____   Title: _____

EXHIBIT A
STOCK OPTION AGREEMENT PURSUANT TO _____, INC.
199_ EMPLOYEE STOCK PURCHASE PLAN

1. Date of Grant:_____ , 199_ (Date of Offering)

2. Employee: _____

3. Number of Shares: Not less than _____ and not more than
    _____ (__ to _____) shares of Common Stock

4. Option Price per Share: Dollars ($) (not less than 85% of Fair Market
    Value on date of _____)

5. Exercise Schedule: One hundred percent (100%) vested on the fourth an-
    niversary of the Date of Grant

6. Expiration Date: Five (5) years from Date of Grant

Stock
Option
Agreement

EXHIBIT B
RESTRICTED STOCK PURCHASE AGREEMENT PURSUANT TO THE
_____ 199_ EMPLOYEE STOCK PURCHASE PLAN

[Users of the Model Equity Plans publication: See the restricted stock agreement provided separately here.]

Stock
Option
Agreement

EXHIBIT C
DESIGNATION OF BENEFICIARY PURSUANT TO THE
_____ 199_ EMPLOYEE STOCK PURCHASE PLAN

Name of Employee: _____

Original Date of Agreement: _____

If I shall cease to be an Employee of the Corporation, a Parent Corporation, or a Subsidiary by reason of my death, or if I shall die after I have terminated my employment with the Corporation, the Parent Corporation or a Subsidiary, but, prior to the expiration of the Option (as provided in the Agreement), then all rights to the Option granted under this Agreement that I hereby hold upon my death, to the extent not previously terminated or forfeited, shall be transferred to _____ (insert name of beneficiary) in the manner provided for in the Plan and the Agreement.

_____

_____
Date

Receipt acknowledged on behalf of _____, Inc., by:

_____

_____
Date

Stock
Option
Agreement

Stock
Option
Agreement

Action by Unanimous Written Consent of the ___, Inc., Board of Directors

The undersigned, constituting all of the members of the Board of Directors (the "Board") of _____, Inc., a California corporation (the "Company"), and desiring to take action by unanimous written consent as authorized by the bylaws of the Company and sections 307 and 311 of the California General Corporation Law, as applicable, do hereby adopt the following resolutions:

WHEREAS, the Board deems it to be in the best interests of the Company and its shareholders to adopt the _____ 199_ Employee Stock Purchase Plan (the "Plan") for the purpose of providing certain incentives to the employees of the Company.

NOW, THEREFORE, IT IS

RESOLVED, that the Plan is approved, authorized and adopted by the Board in the form attached hereto as Exhibit "A."

FURTHER RESOLVED, that the Board will grant options ranging from _____ (__) to _____ (_____) shares of the Company's common stock to each of the Company's current employees who are participants in the _____, Inc. Employee Stock Ownership Plan, at an exercise price of $_____.

FURTHER RESOLVED, that the President and the Secretary of the Company are hereby authorized and directed to perform any and all acts as they shall deem necessary or appropriate to carry out the purposes and intent of the foregoing resolutions.

IN WITNESS WHEREOF, the undersigned have executed this Action by Unanimous Written Consent as of _____, 199_.

Dated: _____, 199_   _____, INC.

By:

_____, Director

_____, Director

_____, Director

Action by Unanimous Written Consent of the __, Inc., Shareholders

The undersigned, constituting all of the shareholders of _____, Inc., a California corporation (the "Company"), and desiring to take action by unanimous written consent as authorized by the bylaws of the Company and Section 603 of the California General Corporation Law, as applicable, do hereby adopt the following resolutions:

WHEREAS, the shareholders deem it to be in the best interests of the Company to adopt the _____ 199_ Employee Stock Purchase Plan (the "Plan") for the purpose of providing certain incentives to the employees of the Company.

NOW, THEREFORE, IT IS

RESOLVED, that the Plan is approved, authorized and adopted by the shareholders in the form attached hereto as Exhibit "A."

FURTHER RESOLVED, that the President and the Secretary of the Company are hereby authorized and directed to perform any and all acts as they shall deem necessary or appropriate to carry out the purposes and intent of the foregoing resolutions.

IN WITNESS WHEREOF, the undersigned have executed this Action by Unanimous Written Consent as of _____ __, 199_.

Dated: _____ __, 199_

Signatures continued on next page

*Action by
Unanimous
Written
Consent of
the
Shareholders*

Memorandum

TO: _____, Inc.

FROM: _____

RE: Procedures for Stock Sale/Grant and Exercise of Employee Stock Purchase Plan Options

DATE: _____ __, 199_

The following outlines the procedures relating to (1) the stock sale of _____, Inc. (the "Company") to certain key employees, (2) grant and exercise of employee stock purchase plan options under the _____ 199_ Employee Stock Purchase Plan (the "Plan"), and (3) the Company's right of repurchase and right of first refusal under the Restricted Stock Purchase Agreement.

A. Stock Sale

1. Set the number of shares to be sold.

2. Currently, there is _____ authorized shares. The following are outstanding:

   _____

   _____

3. Dilution Issues: The Company will need to think the post-transaction capital structure. (The Articles do not provide for preemptive rights so that the Board can issue new stock without first offering it to other shareholders.)

4. Execution of the Restricted Stock Purchase Agreement.

5. Preparation of Stock Certificates which has a legend restriction stating the restrictions under the Restricted Stock Purchase Agreement.

6. Drafting of a promissory note, if necessary. (Please note that such promissory note has to be adequately secured by collateral other than the shares acquired.) Future services by the employee cannot constitute payment or part payment for shares of the Company. California General Corporation Law

Section 409(a)(1). The way to avoid this problem is to have a Employee Stock Purchase Plan implemented.

7.   Filing of Notice of Transaction under Section 25012(f) of the California Corporations Code. The purchasers have to meet the requirements of this section.

B.   Employee Stock Purchase Plan

The following outlines the procedures relating to the Plan. Capitalized terms not defined in this memorandum have the meanings assigned to them in the Plan, the Stock Option Agreement, and the Restricted Stock Purchase Agreement and their exhibits.

Memorandum

1.   *Grants of Stock Options.*

a.   Board resolutions approving the grant is required. At the Board meeting the fair market value of the stock underlying the stock options must be determined.

b.   Stock Option Agreement must be signed by optionee and the Company.

c.   Exhibit A and C of Stock Option Agreement must be completed. (Exhibit A must provide for immediate vesting.)

d.   Summary Memorandum must be distributed to the optionee.

e.   Financial statements need to be distributed at least annually to the optionee.

2.   *Optionee's Exercise of Stock Options.*

a.   The Restricted Stock Purchase Agreement must be signed by the optionee and the Company.

b.   The Investment Representation Statement needs to be signed by the optionee.

C.   Repurchase Right/Right of First Refusal

1.   *Repurchase Rights of the Company.*

a.   Upon termination of employment of the optionee with the Company for any reason, the Company may exercise its right to repurchase the stock underlying the options within three months of the date of termination. The Company must give notice to the optionee within this three month period.

b. The closing for such repurchase must take place within 30 days of giving notice to the optionee. The purchase price must be the higher of the Option Price or the fair market value of the Shares on the date of the Offering Event, as determined in good faith by the Board of Directors of the Company.

2. *Right of First Refusal of the Company.*

a. If the optionee wishes to transfer the stock acquired by exercising its options, he or she must first deliver a transfer notice to the Company.

b. Within 30 days of the date of receipt of the transfer notice, the Company may elect to purchase such stock from the optionee at the price specified in the transfer notice.

Memorandum

Memorandum

Security Pledge Agreement

Pursuant to the _____, Inc., Restricted Stock Purchase Agreement

This AGREEMENT is made and entered into on _____, by and between _____, Inc, a California corporation (the "Pledgee"), and _____ (the "Pledgor"), the holder of a stock option granted under _____ 199_ Employee Stock Purchase Plan (the "Plan").

Recitals

At the time of the execution of this Agreement the Pledgee lent the Debtor the amount of $_____ (the "Loan"), based upon an option price of $_____ per share, as evidenced by the Promissory Note of the Pledgor dated _____.

To induce the Pledgee to make the Loan, the Pledgor has agreed to pledge certain stock to the Pledgee as security for the repayment of the Loan.

IT IS THEREFORE AGREED:

Pledge

1. In consideration of the sum of $_____ lent to the Pledgor by the Pledgee, receipt of which is acknowledged, the Pledgor grants a security interest to the Pledgee that includes all instruments held by the Pledgor that give him or her any and all rights in shares received as a result of exercise of stock options under the Plan, duly endorsed in blank and delivered to the Pledgee with this Agreement. The Pledgor appoints the Pledgee his attorney-in-fact to arrange for the transfer of the pledged shares on the books of the issuer to the name of the Pledgee. The Pledgee shall hold the pledged shares as security for the repayment of the Loan, and shall not encumber or dispose of the shares except in accordance with the provisions of Paragraph 8 of this Agreement.

Dividends

2. During the term of this pledge, all dividends and other amounts received by the Pledgee as a result of the Pledgee's record ownership of the pledged shares shall be applied to the payment of the principal and interest on the Loan.

Voting Rights

3.   During the term of this pledge, and as long as the Pledgor is not in default in the performance of any of the terms of this Agreement or in the payment of the principal or interest of the Loan, the Pledgor shall have the right to vote the pledged shares on all corporate questions. The Pledgee shall execute due and timely proxies in favor of the Pledgor to this end.

Representations

4.   The Pledgor warrants and represents that there are no restrictions on the transfer of any of the pledged shares, other than may appear on the face of the certificates, and that the Pledgor has the right to transfer the shares without obtaining the consents of the other shareholders; provided, however, that the terms of the Restricted Stock Purchase Agreement executed by the Pledgor on _____ are followed at all times.

Adjustments

Security
Pledge
Agreement

5.   In the event that, during the term of this pledge, any share dividend, reclassification, readjustment, or other change is declared or made in the capital structure of the company that has issued the pledged shares, all new, substituted, and additional shares or other securities issued by reason of any change shall be held by the Pledgee in the same manner as the shares originally pledged under this Agreement.

Warrants and Rights

6.   In the event that during the term of this pledge, subscription warrants or any other rights or options shall be issued in connection with the pledged shares, the warrants, rights, and options shall be immediately assigned by the Pledgee to the Pledgor, and if exercised by the Pledgor, all new shares or other securities so acquired by the Pledgor shall be immediately assigned to the Pledgee to be held in the same manner as the shares originally pledged under this Agreement.

Payment of Loan

7.   On payment at maturity of the principal and interest of the Loan, less amounts received and applied by the Pledgee in reduction of the Loan, the Pledgee shall transfer to the Pledgor all the pledged shares and all rights received by the Pledgee as a result of the Pledgee's record ownership of the pledged shares.

Default

8. In the event that the Pledgor defaults in the performance of any of the terms of this Agreement, or in the payment at maturity of the principal or interest of the Loan, the Pledgee shall have the rights and remedies provided in the California Commercial Code. In this connection, the Pledgee may, on five days' written notice to the Pledgor, and without liability for any diminution in price that may have occurred, sell all the pledged shares in the manner and for the price that the Pledgee may determine. At any bona fide public sale the Pledgee shall be free to purchase all or any part of the pledged shares. Out of the proceeds of any sale the Pledgee may retain an amount equal to the principal and interest then due on the Loan, plus the amount of the expenses of the sale, and shall pay any balance of the proceeds of any sale to the Pledgor. If the proceeds of the sale are insufficient to cover the principal and interest of the Loan plus expenses of the sale, the Pledger shall remain liable to the Pledgee for any deficiency, in accordance with the provisions set forth under California Commercial Code Section 9504.

PLEDGEE _____, INC.

By: _____

Title: _____

*Security
Pledge
Agreement*

PLEDGOR

By: _____

Address: _____

_____

_____

Security
Pledge
Agreement

Promissory Note
Pursuant to the ___, Inc.,
Restricted Stock Purchase Agreement

_____[City]
_____County, State of California

1.   FOR VALUE RECEIVED, the undersigned promises to pay to the or-
      der of _____, Inc., a California corporation (the "Company") at
      _____, Suite ___, ____, California, ____, or at any other place in the
      State of California that any holder of this note may designate in
      writing, the amount of $_____ [not to exceed $5,000], based upon
      an option price of $ _____ per share (the "Option Price"), such
      amount to be repaid in equal installments by monthly or weekly pay-
      roll deductions over _____ months not exceeding twenty-four (24)
      months at an interest rate at the Prime Rate plus three (3) percentage
      points, from the date written above until paid. "Prime Rate" shall
      mean the money rate published in the Wall Street Journal (Western
      Edition) as of the date of exercise.

2.   The payment of this note is secured by a Security Pledge Agreement
      (the "Agreement") of this date from _____
      ("Purchaser"), the holder of a stock option granted under the _____
      199_ Employee Stock Purchase Plan, to the Company granting a se-
      curity interest in and to the shares purchased by the Purchaser under
      the Agreement.

3.   If this note is placed in an attorney's hands for collection, or collected
      by a lawsuit or through a bankruptcy, or probate, or any other court,
      either before or after maturity, there shall be paid to the holder of this
      note reasonable attorneys' fees, costs, and other expenses incurred by
      the holder in enforcing the terms of this note.

4.   Failure to pay any part of the option price or interest of this note
      when due, or failure to carry out any of the terms, covenants, or con-
      ditions of the Agreement, shall authorize the holder of this note to
      declare as immediately due and payable the then-unpaid principal
      and to exercise any and all of the rights and remedies provided by
      the California Commercial Code as well as all other rights and reme-
      dies either at law or in equity possessed by the holder of this note.

5.   The makers, signers, and endorsers of this note jointly and severally
      waive presentment, notice of dishonor, and protest.

_____, INC.

By: _____

Title: _____

PURCHASER

By: _____

Address: _____

_____

_____

*Promissory
Note*

__, Inc., Restricted Stock Purchase Agreement

THIS AGREEMENT is made and entered into as of _____, 19___, between _____, Inc., a California corporation (the "Company"), and _____ (the "Purchaser"), the holder of a stock option granted under _____ 199_ Employee Stock Purchase Plan.

RECITALS:

A.   Pursuant to the exercise of a stock option granted to the Purchaser by the Company under a Stock Option Agreement dated _____, 19__ (the "Option Agreement"), the Purchaser has elected to purchase _____ shares of the Company's Common Stock for a total purchase price of $_____.

B.   As provided in the Option Agreement, the Purchaser has agreed to grant the Company the option to repurchase such shares in certain circumstances.

NOW, THEREFORE, in consideration of the mutual covenants exchanged, the parties agree as follows:

1.   *Exercise of Option.*

   (a)   *Exercise.* The Purchaser hereby agrees to purchase _____ shares of the Company's Common Stock (the "Shares") pursuant to an exercise of the option granted in the Option Agreement, at an option price of $_____ per share (the "Option Price").

   (b)   *Payment.* Concurrently with the delivery of this Agreement to the Company, the Purchaser shall pay the consideration for the Shares purchased hereunder or shall deliver a promissory note with adequate security provided in the amount of the Option Price to the Company, such amount to be repaid by payroll deduction over a period not exceeding two years at an interest rate of the Prime Rate plus three (3) percentage points. "Prime Rate" shall mean the money rate published in the Wall Street Journal (Western Edition) as of the date of exercise. The Purchaser shall deliver any additional documents that may be required by the Option Agreement as a condition to such exercise.

2.   *Repurchase Option.*

(a)   *Shares Subject to Repurchase.* The Purchaser hereby grants to the Company the option (the "Repurchase Option") to repurchase all or part of the Shares, upon the occurrences set forth in subsection (b).

(b)   *Occurrences Permitting Exercise.* The Company may exercise the Repurchase Option if during the term of this Agreement the Purchaser shall cease to be employed by the Company (including a parent or subsidiary of the Company) at least five hundred hours each year (an "Offering Event").

(c)   *Exercise of Repurchase Option.* Upon the occurrence of an Offering Event, the Company may exercise the Repurchase Option by delivering a notice pursuant to Section 15 of this Agreement to the Purchaser (or his permitted transferee or legal representative, as the case may be), within three (3) months after the date the Company receives notice of the Offering Event. Such notice shall indicate the Company's election to exercise its Repurchase Option and the number of Shares to be purchased by the Company or the Company's designee, who shall be identified in such notice, and the notice shall set forth a date for closing not later than thirty (30) days from the date of the giving of such notice.

Restricted Stock Purchase Agreement

(d)   *Closing for Repurchase of Shares.* The closing for the repurchase of the Shares pursuant to the exercise of the Repurchase Option shall take place at the Company's principal offices. At the closing, the holder of the certificate(s) representing the Shares being transferred shall deliver such certificate or certificates evidencing the Shares to the Company, duly endorsed for transfer, and the Company (or its designee) shall tender payment of the purchase price for the Shares being purchased. The purchase price for the Shares shall be the higher of fair value (as defined in Sections 260.140.41 and 260.140.42 of the California Code of Regulations) of the Shares at the date of termination of employment as determined in good faith by the Board of Directors of the Company or the original Option Price (the "Repurchase Option Price") and shall be payable in full in cash, or by certified check or cashier's check, provided that the Company may elect to offset against and deduct from any payment of the purchase price any indebtedness then owed by the Purchaser to the Company.

3.　　*Restrictions on Transfer; Right of First Refusal.*

(a)　　*Right of First Refusal.* Except as provided in this Section 3, the Purchaser shall not sell, assign, transfer, pledge or otherwise dispose of any of the Shares, or any right or interest therein, either voluntarily or involuntarily, without first receiving a bona fide written offer from an independent prospective buyer delivering a written notice (the "Transfer Notice") to the Company, and then to the shareholders of the Company, which shall have the option to purchase such Shares as provided herein (the "Right of First Refusal"). The Transfer Notice must specify, among other things, (i) a copy of the written offer to purchase from a bona fide third party; (ii) the name and address of the proposed transferee; (iii) the number of Shares, or interest therein, proposed to be sold or transferred; (iv) the price or amount to be paid for the proposed transfer (including the amount of any debt to be paid, canceled or forgiven upon foreclosure of a security interest in the Shares or upon any other transfer to the Purchaser's creditors); and (v) all other material terms and conditions of the proposed transfer.

(b)　　*Election to Purchase Shares.* Within sixty (60) days after receipt of the Transfer Notice, the Company or its designee (as the case may be), or the other shareholders of the Company, as the case may be, may elect to purchase all, but not less than all, of the Shares to which the Transfer Notice refers at the per share price specified in the Transfer Notice. If no price is specified in the Transfer Notice, the purchase price shall be the fair market value of the Shares, as determined in good faith by the Board of Directors of the Company. Such Right of First Refusal shall be exercised by delivery to the Purchaser by the Company or its designee, of a written election to exercise such Right of First Refusal, specifying the number of Shares to be purchased by the Company or its designee (as the case may be). Notwithstanding the foregoing, the Company may elect to offset against and deduct from any payment of the purchase price any indebtedness then owed by the Purchaser to the Company.

Restricted Stock Purchase Agreement

(c)　　*Closing for Purchase of Shares.* In the event the Company elects to acquire Shares of the Purchaser as specified in the Transfer Notice, the Secretary of the Company shall so notify the Purchaser and settlement thereof shall be made in cash within thirty (30) days after the Company receives the Transfer Notice, provided that if the terms of payment set forth in the Transfer Notice were other than cash against delivery, the

Company shall pay for such Shares on the same terms and conditions set forth in the Transfer Notice.

(d) *Transfer Free of Right of First Refusal.* If the Shares referred to in the Transfer Notice are not purchased as indicated above by the Company, or its designee(s), the Purchaser, within a period of one hundred twenty (120) days from the date of delivery of the Transfer Notice to the Company, may sell such Shares to the person or persons named in the Transfer Notice at the price and on the terms specified in the Transfer Notice, provided that such sale or transfer is consummated within one hundred twenty (120) days following the date of delivery of the Transfer Notice to the Company and, provided further, that such sale is in accordance with all the terms and conditions hereof. The transferee will hold all Shares transferred hereunder subject to the provisions of this Agreement.

(e) *Gift of Shares.* Notwithstanding any other term of this Section 3, the Purchaser may make a gift of all or part of the Shares to his spouse or any of his issue, or to a trust for his or their exclusive benefit. The donee or donees shall hold such Shares subject to all provisions of this Agreement.

(f) *Nullification of Improper Transfer.* Any transfer by the Purchaser in violation of this Section shall be null and void and of no effect.

4. *Adjustments.* If, from time to time during the term of this Agreement: (i) there is any stock dividend, distribution or dividend of cash or property, stock split, or other change in the character or amount of any of the outstanding securities of the Company; or (ii) there is any consolidation, merger or sale of all, or substantially all, of the assets of the Company; or (iii) the Shares are converted into any other class of securities by capital reorganization or recapitalization; then in such event, any and all new, substituted or additional securities, cash, or other property to which the Purchaser is entitled by reason of his ownership of the Shares shall be immediately subject to the Repurchase Option, the Right of First Refusal and the other terms of this Agreement. While the total Repurchase Option Price shall remain the same after any such event, the Repurchase Option Price per share shall be appropriately adjusted.

5. *Termination of Restrictions.*

(a) *Termination of Repurchase Option and Right of First Refusal.* The Repurchase Option and Right of First Refusal shall terminate:

(i)   on the termination of this Agreement pursuant to written agreement of the parties;

(ii)   at such time as the Company consummates an underwritten public offering of its common stock; or

(iii)   if the Company dissolves, or if more than fifty percent (50%) of the outstanding shares of the Company's capital stock entitled to vote are sold, redeemed or exchanged in any (i) merger, consolidation, or reorganization involving the Company and one or more unaffiliated corporations, (ii) exchange of capital stock of the Company for stock of any unaffiliated corporation, provided that the security holders of the Company receive in exchange for the Company's capital stock securities for which a public market exists, or (iii) sale of all or substantially all of the assets of the Company to an unaffiliated corporation. For purposes of this subsection, an "unaffiliated corporation" means any corporation that is not controlled by or under common control with, directly or indirectly, the Company or any or all of its shareholders. Notwithstanding anything to the contrary herein, sale to the _____, Inc. Employee Stock Ownership Plan and Trust will not terminate the Repurchase Option and the Right of First Refusal.

Restricted Stock Purchase Agreement

6.   *Legends.*

(a)   *Endorsement on Certificates.* The certificates representing the Shares subject to this Agreement shall be endorsed with a legend substantially in the following form:

"THE SHARES REPRESENTED BY THIS CERTIFICATE MAY BE TRANSFERRED ONLY IN ACCORDANCE WITH THE TERMS OF A RESTRICTED STOCK PURCHASE AGREEMENT BETWEEN THE COMPANY AND THE REGISTERED HOLDER OR HIS PREDECESSOR IN INTEREST, A COPY OF WHICH MAY BE OBTAINED UPON WRITTEN REQUEST TO THE SECRETARY OF THE COMPANY. THE AGREEMENT MAY BE INSPECTED AT THE PRINCIPAL OFFICE OF THE COMPANY DURING NORMAL BUSINESS HOURS."

(b)   *Termination of All Restrictions.* In the event the restrictions imposed by this Agreement shall be terminated as herein provided, a new certificate or certificates representing the Shares shall be issued, on request, without the legend referred to in Section 6(a) of this Agreement.

(c)   *Securities Law Legends.* Any transfer or sale of the Shares is further subject to all restrictions on transfer imposed by state or Federal securities laws. Accordingly, it is understood and agreed that the certificates representing the Shares shall bear any legends required by such state or Federal securities laws.

7.   *Dissolution of Marriage.*

Restricted Stock Purchase Agreement

(a)   *Purchase of Shares from Former Spouse.* In the event of the dissolution of the Purchaser's marriage, including a decree of divorce or judgment of dissolution or separate maintenance, or under a property settlement or separation agreement, the Purchaser shall have the right and option to purchase from his or her spouse all of the Shares (i) awarded to the spouse pursuant to a decree of dissolution of marriage or any other order by any court of competent jurisdiction and/or any property settlement agreement (whether or not incorporated by reference in any such decree), or (ii) gifted to the spouse by the Purchaser prior to the dissolution, at the fair market value of such Shares as determined by the Company's Board of Directors, upon the terms set forth below. The Purchaser shall exercise his or her right, if at all, within thirty (30) days following the entry of any such decree or property settlement agreement by delivery to the Purchaser's former spouse of written notice of exercise, specifying the number of Shares the Purchaser elects to Purchase. The purchase price for the Shares shall be paid by delivery of a promissory note for the purchase price bearing interest at the rate of ten percent (10%) per annum payable in four (4) equal annual installments of principal and interest, commencing on the anniversary date of the exercise of the option; *provided, however,* that if, subsequent to the date any or all of the Shares are awarded to the Purchaser's former spouse as provided above, the Company exercises its Repurchase Option with respect to any or all of the Shares so awarded, the amount remaining due under such promissory note shall be reduced by the difference between the fair market value of such Shares determined as set forth above and the amount received by the Purchaser for such Shares upon exercise by the Company of the Repurchase Option.

(b) *Transfer of Rights to Company.* In the event the Purchaser does not exercise his or her right to purchase all of the Shares awarded to the Purchaser's former spouse, the Purchaser shall provide written notice to the Company of the number of Shares available for purchase within thirty (30) days of the entry of the decree or property settlement agreement. The Company shall then have the right to purchase any of the Shares not acquired by the Purchaser directly from the Purchaser's former spouse in the manner provided in Sections 3(b)-3(e) above at the same price and on the same terms that were available to the Purchaser.

8. *Consent of Spouse.* If the Purchaser is married on the date of this Agreement, the Purchaser's spouse shall execute a Consent of Spouse in the form attached hereto, effective on the date hereof. Such consent shall not be deemed to confer or convey to the spouse any rights in the Shares that do not otherwise exist by operation of law or the agreement of the parties. If the Purchaser should marry or remarry subsequent to the date of this Agreement, the Purchaser shall within thirty (30) days thereafter obtain his or her new spouse's acknowledgment of and consent to the existence and binding effect of all restrictions contained in this Agreement by signing a Consent of Spouse in the form attached hereto.

9. *Compliance with Income Tax Laws.*

(a) *Withholding Tax.* The Purchaser authorizes the Company to withhold in accordance with applicable law from any compensation payable to him or her any taxes required to be withheld by Federal, state or local laws as a result of the purchase of the Shares. Furthermore, in the event of any determination that the Company has failed to withhold a sum sufficient to pay all withholding taxes due in connection with the purchase of the Shares, the Purchaser agrees to pay the Company the amount of such deficiency in cash within five (5) days after receiving a written demand from the Company to do so, whether or not the Purchaser is an employee of the Company at that time. The Purchaser agrees to notify the Company of any sale or other disposition (within the meaning of Section 421(b) of the Internal Revenue Code of 1986, as amended (the "Code"), by the Purchaser of any of the Shares within one (1) year of the date hereof or within two (2) years from the date of grant of any incentive stock option by the Company pursuant to the exercise of which such Shares were acquired hereunder.

Restricted Stock Purchase Agreement

10.   *Purchaser's Representations.* In connection with the purchase of the Shares, the Purchaser hereby represents and warrants to the Company as follows:

    (a)   *Investment Intent; Capacity to Protect Interests.* The Purchaser is purchasing the Shares solely for his or her own account for investment and not with a view to or for sale in connection with any distribution of the Shares or any portion thereof and not with any present intention of selling, offering to sell or otherwise disposing of or distributing the Shares or any portion thereof in any transaction other than a transaction exempt from registration under the Securities Act of 1933, as amended (the "Act"). The Purchaser also represents that the entire legal and beneficial interest of the Shares is being purchased, and will be held, for the Purchaser's account only, and neither in whole or in part for any other person. The Purchaser further represents either that he or she (i) has a pre-existing business or personal relationship with the Company or any of its officers, directors or controlling persons, or (ii) by reason of the Purchaser's business or financial experience or the business or financial experience of the Purchaser's professional advisors who are unaffiliated with and who are not compensated by the Company or any affiliate or selling agent of the Company, directly or indirectly, could be reasonably assumed to have the capacity to evaluate the merits and risks of an investment in the Company and to protect the Purchaser's own interests in connection with this transaction.

    (b)   *Information Concerning Company.* The Purchaser has heretofore discussed the Company and its plans, operations and financial condition with the Company's officers and has heretofore received all such information as the Purchaser has deemed necessary and appropriate to enable the Purchaser to evaluate the financial risk inherent in making an investment in the Shares, and the Purchaser has received satisfactory and complete information concerning the business and financial condition of the Company in response to all inquiries in respect thereof.

    (c)   *Economic Risk.* The Purchaser realizes that the purchase of the Shares will be a highly speculative investment and involves a high degree of risk, and the Purchaser is able, without impairing his or her financial condition, to hold the Shares for an indefinite period of time and to suffer a complete loss on the Purchaser's investment.

    (d)   *Restricted Securities.* The Purchaser understands and acknowledges that:

Restricted Stock Purchase Agreement

(i)   the sale of the Shares has not been registered under the Act, and the Shares must be held indefinitely unless subsequently registered under the Act or an exemption from such registration is available and the Company is under no obligation to register the Shares;

(ii)   the share certificate representing the Shares will be stamped with the legends specified in Section 6 hereof; and

(iii)   the Company will make a notation in its records of the aforementioned restrictions on transfer and legends.

(e)   *Disposition Under Rule 144.* The Purchaser understands that the Shares are restricted securities within the meaning of Rule 144 promulgated under the Act; that unless the Shares have been issued pursuant to Rule 701 promulgated under the Act the exemption from registration under Rule 144 will not be available in any event for at least one year from the date of purchase and payment of the Shares (AND, FOR PURPOSES OF THIS EXEMPTION, PAYMENT BY A NOTE IS NOT DEEMED PAYMENT UNLESS IT IS SECURED BY ASSETS OTHER THAN THE SHARES, AND IF IT IS NOT SO SECURED, THE ABOVE TWO-YEAR RESTRICTION ON TRANSFER DOES NOT BEGIN TO RUN UNTIL THE NOTE IS PAID IN FULL), and even then will not be available unless: (i) a public trading market then exists for the Common Stock of the Company; (ii) adequate information concerning the Company is then available to the public; and (iii) other terms and conditions of Rule 144 are complied with; and that any sale of the Shares may be made only in limited amounts in accordance with such terms and conditions.

Restricted Stock Purchase Agreement

(f)   *Further Limitations on Disposition.* Without in any way limiting his representations set forth above, the Purchaser further agrees that he shall in no event make any disposition of all or any portion of the Shares unless and until:

(i)   (A) There is then in effect a Registration Statement under the Act covering such proposed disposition and such disposition is made in accordance with such Registration Statement; *or*, (B)(1) the Purchaser shall have notified the Company of the proposed disposition and shall have furnished the Company with a detailed statement of the circumstances surrounding the proposed disposition, (2) the Purchaser shall have furnished the Company with an opinion of the Purchaser's counsel to the effect that such disposition will not require registration of such shares under the Act, *and* (3) such opinion of the Purchaser's counsel shall have been concurred in by counsel for the Company and the Company shall have advised the Purchaser of such concurrence; *and,*

(ii)   The Shares proposed to be transferred are not subject to the Repurchase Option set forth in Section 2 hereof and the Purchaser shall have complied with the Right of First Refusal set forth in Section 3 hereof.

Restricted Stock Purchase Agreement

11.   *Initial Public Offering "Market Stand-Off" Agreement.* The Purchaser hereby agrees that he or she shall not, to the extent reasonably requested by the Company and an underwriter of Common Stock (or other securities) of the Company, sell or otherwise transfer or dispose (other than to donees who agree to be similarly bound) of any Shares during the one hundred eighty (180)-day period following the effective date of a registration statement of the Company filed under the Securities Act; provided, however, that: (a) all officers and directors of the Company and all other persons with registration rights enter into similar agreements; and (b) such agreement shall be applicable only to the first such registration statement of the Company which covers shares (or securities) to be sold on its behalf to the public in an underwritten offering. Such agreement shall be in writing in a form satisfactory to the Company and such underwriter. In order to enforce the foregoing covenant, the Company may impose stop-transfer instructions with respect to the Shares of each Shareholder (and the shares or securities of every other person subject to the foregoing restriction) until the end of such one hundred eighty (180)-day period.

12.   *Enforcement.* The Purchaser agrees that a violation on his or her part of any of the terms of this Agreement (other than those contained in Section 10 above) may cause irreparable damage to the Company, the exact amount of which is impossible to ascertain, and for that reason agrees that the Company shall be entitled to a decree of specific performance of the terms hereof or an injunction restraining further violation, such right to be in addition to any other remedies of such parties.

13.   *Controlling Provisions.* To the extent that there may be any conflict between the provisions of this Agreement and the provisions contained in the Company's bylaws on the transfer or restriction on transfer of Shares, the terms of this Agreement shall be controlling. This Agreement may not be modified except by a writing signed by the party to be bound.

14.   *Ownership, Voting Rights, Duties.* This Agreement shall not affect in any way the ownership, voting rights or other rights or duties of the Purchaser, except as specifically provided herein.

15.   *Notices.* All notices and other communications required or permitted hereunder shall be in writing and shall be deemed effectively given upon personal delivery or within 72 hours after mailing, if mailed by first-class mail, registered or certified, postage prepaid and properly addressed. Notice to be given to the Company shall be delivered or addressed to the Company at its principal place of business; notice to be given to a holder of Shares shall be delivered or addressed to such holder at its address set forth on the signature page of this Agreement or at another address if given to the Secretary of the Company for the purpose of notice or, if no address is given, in care of the Company at its principal place of business.

16.   *Binding Effect.* This Agreement shall inure to the benefit of the Company and its successors and assigns and, subject to the restrictions on transfer set forth herein, be binding upon the Purchaser, his permitted transferees, heirs, legatees, executors, administrators and legal successors, who shall hold the Shares subject to the terms hereof. The Company may assign its rights under the terms of this Agreement without the consent of the Purchaser.

17.   *Entire Agreement.* This Agreement supersedes all previous written or oral agreements between the parties regarding the subject matter hereof, and constitutes the entire agreement of the parties regarding such subject matter. This Agreement may not be modified or terminated except by a writing executed by all of the parties hereto.

18.   *Not Employment Contract.* Nothing in this Agreement shall affect in any manner whatsoever the right or power of the Purchaser or the Company to terminate the Purchaser's employment, for any reason or for no reason, with or without cause, subject to the provisions of applicable law. This Agreement is not an employment contract.

19.   *Counterparts.* This Agreement may be executed in counterparts, each of which shall be deemed to be an original, but all of which together shall constitute one and the same instrument.

20.   *Governing Law.* THIS AGREEMENT, TOGETHER WITH THE EXHIBITS HERETO, SHALL BE GOVERNED BY AND CONSTRUED UNDER THE LAWS OF THE STATE OF CALIFORNIA AS SUCH LAWS ARE APPLIED TO CONTRACTS ENTERED INTO BY RESIDENTS OF SUCH STATE AND PERFORMED IN SUCH STATE. THE SECURITIES SOLD AND PURCHASED HEREUNDER SHALL BE GOVERNED BY AND IN

Restricted Stock Purchase Agreement

ACCORDANCE WITH THE CORPORATE SECURITIES LAWS OF THE STATE OF CALIFORNIA.

21.   *Attorneys' Fees.* In the event of litigation brought by either party to enforce the provisions of this Agreement or for damages based upon the breach thereof, the prevailing party shall be entitled to recover his costs and reasonable attorneys' fees, as determined by the court.

22.   *Severability.* If any provision of this Agreement is held by a court of competent jurisdiction to be invalid, void or unenforceable, the remaining provisions shall nevertheless continue in full force and effect without being impaired or invalidated in any way and shall be construed in accordance with the purposes and tenor and effect of this Agreement.

IN WITNESS WHEREOF, the parties have executed this Agreement on the date first above written.

_____, INC.

*Restricted
Stock
Purchase
Agreement*

By: _____

Title: _____

PURCHASER

By: _____

Address: _____
                 _____
                 _____

CONSENT OF SPOUSE

I, _____, spouse of _____, acknowledge that I have read the Restricted Stock Purchase Agreement dated as of _____, 19__ to which this Consent is attached (the "Agreement") and that I know its contents. I am aware that by its provisions (a) my spouse and _____, Inc. (the "Company") have the option to purchase all the Shares of the Company of which I may become possessed as a result of a gift from my spouse or a court decree and/or any property settlement in any domestic litigation, (b) the Company has the option to purchase certain Shares of the Company which my spouse owns pursuant to the Agreement including any interest I might have therein, upon termination of his employment under circumstances set forth in the Agreement, and (c) certain other restrictions are imposed upon the sale or other disposition of the Shares.

I hereby agree that my interest, if any, in the Shares subject to the Agreement shall be irrevocably bound by the Agreement and further understand and agree that any community property interest I may have in the Shares shall be similarly bound by the Agreement.

I agree to the sale and purchase described in Section 7 of the Agreement and I hereby consent to the sale of the Shares by my spouse or his [her] legal representative in accordance with the provisions of the Agreement. Further, as part of the consideration for the Agreement, I agree that at my death, if I have not disposed of any interest of mine in the Shares by an outright bequest of said Shares to my spouse, then my spouse and the Company shall have the same rights against my legal representative to purchase any interest of mine in the Shares as they would have had pursuant to Section 7 of the Agreement if I had acquired the Shares pursuant to a court decree in domestic litigation.

Restricted Stock Purchase Agreement

I am aware that the legal, financial, and related matters contained in the Agreement are complex and that I am free to seek independent professional guidance or counsel with respect to this Consent. I have either sought such guidance or counsel or determined after reviewing the Agreement carefully that I will waive such right.

Dated as of the _____ of _____, 19__.

_____

*Restricted
Stock
Purchase
Agreement*

Summary Memorandum

__ 199_ Employee Stock Purchase Plan

TO: Holders of Options to Purchase Common Stock

SUBJECT: Purchase Plan Options

The purpose of this memorandum is to clarify some of the procedures and consequences relating to the grant of options to purchase shares of Common Stock of _____, Inc., a California corporation (the "Company"), under the _____, Inc. 199_ Employee Stock Purchase Plan (the "Plan"), and the purchase and subsequent disposition of shares of the Company's Common Stock received upon the exercise of such options. The exact terms and conditions of the options, including the exercise price of the shares of Common Stock, are governed by the provisions of the Plan and the agreements thereunder between the Company and the participating employees.

> THIS MEMORANDUM IS FOR GENERAL INFORMATION ONLY AND SHOULD NOT BE CONSTRUED AS AN OFFER FOR THE SALE OF SECURITIES. EACH INDIVIDUAL IS ENCOURAGED TO CONSULT WITH INDEPENDENT COUNSEL AS TO THE APPLICABILITY OF THE TAX AND SECURITIES LAW AND OTHER MATTERS DISCUSSED HEREIN TO HIS OR HER SPECIFIC SITUATION.

GENERAL

The Plan was adopted by the Company's Board of Directors and shareholders as of _____, 199_. A total of _____ shares of Common Stock have been reserved for issuance upon the exercise of options granted under the Plan.

The Plan allows for the grant of stock options intended to qualify as employee stock purchase plan options under Section 423 of the Internal Revenue Code of 1986, as amended (the "Code"). See "Federal Income Tax Consequences" below for information concerning the tax treatment of employee purchase plan options and nonstatutory stock.

SUMMARY OF THE PLAN

Set forth below is a summary of the principal features of the Plan.

Administration

The Plan is currently being administered by the Company's Board of Directors (the "Board"). The interpretation and construction of any provision of the Plan by the Board shall be final and conclusive.

Eligibility

The Plan provides that options may be granted only to the Company's employees. The Board selects the participants and determines the number of shares to be subject to each option; provided, however, that such selection satisfies the requirements of Section 423 of the Code. The Plan provides for a maximum number of shares of the Company's common stock which may be granted under an option to any one eligible employee.

Terms of Options

Each option is evidenced by a stock option agreement between the Company and the person to whom such option is granted, which sets forth the terms and conditions of the option. The following terms and conditions generally apply to all options, unless the stock option agreement provides otherwise:

*Summary
Memorandum*

1.   *Exercise of the Option.* The optionee must earn the right to exercise his or her option by continuing to work for the Company. The Board determines when options granted under the Plan may be exercisable. An option is exercised by giving written notice of exercise to the Company specifying the number of full shares of Common Stock to be purchased and by tendering payment to the Company for the purchase price. Unless otherwise provided in the stock option agreement, the purchase price of shares purchased upon exercise of an option shall be paid by any of the following means, or by any combination thereof: (i) cash; (ii) by certified or bank's cashier's check; or (iii) by payroll deduction over a period not exceeding two (2) years at an interest rate of Prime Rate plus three (3) percentage points; provided, however, that the monetary limit on such purchase price shall be $5,000 when it is paid in this manner. "Prime Rate" shall mean the money rate published in the Wall Street Journal (Western Edition) as of the date of grant. The Board may modify the terms of (iii) in a non-discriminatory manner from year to year.

2.   *Exercise Price.* The exercise price of options granted under the Plan is determined by the Board and must not be less than the lesser of: (i) eighty-five percent (85%) of the fair market value of the Common Stock on the date the option is granted; or (ii) 85% percent of such fair market value on the date of exercise. Until such time as there has been a registered public offering of the Company's Common Stock and a public trading market for the Company's Common Stock exists, the fair market value of Common Stock will be determined by

the Board. In making its determination, the Board will take into account such relevant factors as recent transactions (if any) in shares of the Company's Common Stock and the Company's past financial performance and prospects for future earnings.

3.   *Restricted Stock Purchase Agreement.* As a condition to the exercise of any option granted under the Plan, the optionee must sign and deliver a Restricted Stock Purchase Agreement in a form approved by the Board pursuant to which the Company is granted: (1) a repurchase option when the optionee terminates employment or other services with the Company; and (2) a right of first refusal if the optionee sells stock received under the Plan. See "Terms of Restricted Stock Purchase Agreement" below.

4.   *Termination of Employment.* If an optionee's employment (or other service) with the Company terminates either (i) for cause or (ii) voluntary on the part of the optionee and without good reason (as determined by the Board, in its sole discretion), the options, to the extent not previously exercised or expired, will terminate on the date of such termination of employment (or service). If an optionee's employment or other service with the Company terminates for reasons other than (a) termination that is either (i) for cause, (ii) voluntary on the part of the optionee and without good reason, (b) termination by reason of disability and (c) death, options under the Plan may be exercised not later than three (3) months after such termination, but may be exercised only to the extent the options were exercisable on the date of termination.

Summary Memorandum

5.   *Retirement and Total and Permanent Disability.* If an optionee should become permanently and totally disabled while an employee, non-employee director or officer of the Company or while providing other services to the Company, options shall become fully exercisable as to all shares subject to them and may be exercised at any time within one (1) year following the date of disability to the extent not previously exercised or expired. If an optionee should retire with the written consent of the Company, options shall become fully exercisable as to all shares subject to them and may be exercised at any time with three (3) months of such retirement.

6.   *Death.* If an optionee should die while an employee, non-employee director or officer of the Company or while providing other services to the Company, options may be exercised at any time within one (1) year following the date of death to the extent not previously exercised or expired.

7.   *Termination of Options.* All options granted under the Plan expire on the date specified in the option agreement.

8. *Nontransferability of Options.* An option is nontransferable by the optionee otherwise than by will or the laws of descent and distribution, and is exercisable during his or her lifetime only by him, or in the event of his or her death, by a person who acquires the right to exercise the option by bequest or inheritance or by reason of the death of the optionee.

9. *Other Provisions.* The option agreement may contain such other terms, provisions and conditions not inconsistent with the Plan as may be determined by the Board.

Adjustments Upon Changes in Capitalization

In the event of any change in the Company's capital structure, appropriate adjustments shall be made by the Board in the number of shares subject to each option and the per share exercise price thereof. Upon the occurrence of the following events which constitute a "Corporate Change:" (1) certain mergers or consolidations, (2) sale, lease or exchange of substantially all of the assets of the Company, (3) liquidation or dissolution, (4) acquisition by any person or entity of more than twenty-five percent (25%) (based on voting power) of the Company's outstanding capital stock or acquisition by a person or entity who currently has beneficial ownership in the Company which increases such ownership to fifty percent (50%) or more, or (5) as a result of a contested election, persons who were directors cease to constitute a majority of the Board, the Board also may make provisions for proportionately adjusting the number or class of stock covered by any option, as well as the option exercise price. In addition, the Board may take any of the following actions in connection with the occurrence of a Corporate Change: (1) accelerate the time in which the options may be exercised, (2) require the mandatory surrender of outstanding options to the Company in exchange for cash for the bargain element the optionee would have realized upon the occurrence of the Corporate Change, if any, (3) make adjustments to the options to reflect such Corporate Change, (4) provide that upon exercise of the option, the optionee will be entitled to purchase other securities or property, or (5) cancel the options if the fair market value of the Common Stock of the Company which underlies the options is below the option exercise price.

Amendment and Termination of the Plan

The Company's Board of Directors may amend the Plan at any time or from time to time or may terminate it without the approval of the Company's shareholders; provided, however, that the approval of the holders of a majority of the outstanding shares of the Company entitled to vote is required for any amendment which increases the maximum number of shares for which options may be granted, changes the minimum option price or the standards of eligibility, materially increases the benefits which may accrue to participants under the Plan, or decreases any authority granted to the Board in contravention of Rule 16b-3 of the Securities Exchange Act of 1934, as amended ("Exchange Act"). However, no such action by the Board or share-holders may alter or impair any option previously granted under the Plan. In any event, the Plan shall terminate on ____ __, 20__.

Terms of Restricted Stock Purchase Agreement

All optionees must execute and deliver to the Company a form of Restricted Stock Purchase Agreement (the "Purchase Agreement") approved by the Board in connection with the exercise of options granted under the Plan. The Purchase Agreement provides, among other things, that the Company shall have a repurchase option and a right of first refusal to purchase any shares which are subject to a bona fide written purchase offer from a third party. An optionee may not sell or transfer (including transfer by operation of law) the shares received upon exercise of his or her option unless he or she first gives written notice to the Company of his or her intention to do so and first offers the shares to the Company. Such written notice must include, among other things: (i) a copy of the written offer to purchase from a bona fide third party; (ii) the name and address of the person or firm to whom such shares are to be sold; (iii) the number of shares, or interest therein, to be sold or transferred; (iv) the price or amount to be paid for the proposed transfer (including the amount of any debt to be paid, canceled or forgiven upon foreclosure of a security interest in the shares or upon any other transfer to the optionee's creditors); and (v) all other terms of the proposed transfer. Within sixty (60) days after receipt of the notice, the Company or its designee or the Company's other shareholders may elect to purchase all (but not less than all) such shares so offered at the purchase price set forth in the op-tionee's notice, which purchase must be consummated no later than sixty (60) days following the date of delivery of optionee's notice to the Company.

Summary Memorandum

If none or only part of the shares referred to in the optionee's notice to the Company is bid for purchase by the Company, or its designee or designees, or the Company's other shareholders, the optionee may dispose of any or all shares referred to in the notice to the Company to any person or persons, but only within a period of one hundred twenty (120) days from the date of de-livery of the notice to the Company, and provided, further, that any such sale is in accordance with all the terms and conditions set forth in the Purchase Agreement.

Any gift by an optionee of all or part of his or her shares to any of his or her spouse or issue, or to a trust for his or their exclusive benefit will not be subject to the above-described repurchase option and right of first refusal; provided, however, that any Common Stock received upon exercise of an option by such transferee shall be subject to the above-described repurchase option and right of first refusal.

Federal Income Tax Consequences

A.   Employee Stock Purchase Plan Options.

Section 423 of the Internal Revenue Code of 1986, as amended (the "Code"), provides favorable federal income tax treatment for stock options which qualify as "purchase plan options." When an option granted under an option plan qualifies as a purchase plan option, the optionee does not recognize income for federal income tax purposes upon the grant or exercise of the purchase plan option. Upon a sale of the shares (assuming that the sale occurs no sooner than two years after the grant of the option and one year after the receipt of the shares by the optionee), any gain or loss will be treated as long-term capital gain or loss for federal income tax purposes.

In order for an option to qualify as an "purchase plan option," it must be exercised while the optionee is an employee of the Company or of a subsidiary of the Company, or within ninety (90) days after the optionee ceases to be an employee for any reason. See "Terms of Options" above.

*Summary
Memorandum*

Other conditions which must be satisfied include the following: (i) the option cannot be exercisable more than (A) five years from the date such option is granted, if under the terms of the Plan, the option price is not to be less than eighty-five percent (85%) of the fair market value of such shares at the time of the exercise of the option; or (B) twenty-seven (27) months from the date such option is granted, if the option price is not determinable in the manner described in (A); (ii) the exercise price of the option must not be less than the lesser of eighty-five percent (85%) of the fair market value of the shares at the date of grant or exercise; (iii) the Plan must have been approved by the shareholders of the Company; (iv) the option must be nontransferable other than upon death and must be exercisable during the optionee's lifetime by him or her only; (v) the optionee may not own more than 5% of the voting power or value of all classes of the Company's shares immediately after the option is granted; and (vi) options are granted to all employees except for certain statutory exceptions; (vii) under the terms of the Plan, all employees shall have basically the same rights and privileges; and (viii) no employee may be granted an option which permits his or her rights to purchase stock which exceeds $25,000 of fair market value of such stock as of the date of grant for each calendar year in which such stock is outstanding at any time.

The favorable federal income tax consequences described above will not apply to the extent the optionee disposes of the shares acquired within one year of the date of exercise or two years of the date of grant of the option (hereinafter a "disqualifying disposition"). A disqualifying disposition does not include the disposition of shares acquired upon exercise of an option after the employee's death and, under certain circumstances, the disposition of shares (acquired by exercising an incentive stock option) by an insolvent individual to a trustee, receiver or other similar fiduciary in an insolvency proceeding.

In the event of a disqualifying disposition, the optionee generally will recognize ordinary income in the year of disposition equal to the amount by which the fair market value of the stock at the date of exercise exceeds the exercise price. Any additional gain will be long-term or short-term gain, depending on how long the optionee has held the stock. The income recognized on a disqualifying disposition will be added to the optionee's tax basis for determining gain or loss with respect to a subsequent sale of his or her stock.

The Company must furnish a statement to employees who exercise options which have an exercise price of between 85% and 100% of fair market value at the time of exercise on or before January 31st of the year following the year of the option exercise. This statement must provide the following information:

1. The name, address and federal identification number of the transferor;

2. The date of the transfer;

3. The number of shares transferred; and

4. That the transfer is pursuant to a Code § 423 plan.

*Summary
Memorandum*

The statement is required only with respect to the first transfer of such shares by the person who exercises the option.

B.   *Capital Gains.*

The Code provides a special tax rate of 20% for capital gains (10% for taxpayers in the 15% bracket). This can be compared to the lowest ordinary income rate of 15% and the maximum rate on such income of over 40%. In addition, while ordinary compensation income is subject to certain payroll and medicare taxes, capital gains are not; this increases the effective tax rate advantage of capital gains. Capital losses may generally be offset only against capital gains. Shares acquired upon exercise of an option must generally be held for more than 12 months for gain or loss from the sale of such shares to qualify for long-term capital gain or loss treatment.

*   *   *

The foregoing summary of the effect of current federal income taxation upon optionees with respect to the grant of options for, and the purchase and subsequent disposition of, shares under the Plan does not purport to be complete, and reference is made to the applicable provisions of the Code. The laws, court decisions and administrative rulings applicable to federal income taxation change frequently, and the discussion in this summary is based only on such laws, court decisions and administrative rulings as of the date hereof.

The foregoing summary also does not reflect provisions of the income tax laws of any state or foreign jurisdiction in which optionees may reside, and does not address prospective estate, gift and other tax consequences of acquiring stock under the Plan. In particular, the income tax laws of some states do not presently contain provisions comparable to the purchase plan option provisions of the Code. All optionees are urged to consult their own tax and financial advisers regarding the current and prospective tax consequences of acquiring options and shares under the Plan.

Restrictions on Transfer and Absence of Public Market

The shares of Common Stock issuable upon the exercise of options granted under the Plan are "restricted securities" within the meaning of Rule 144 under the Securities Act of 1933, as amended (the "Act"), insofar as such securities have not been registered thereunder and must be held indefinitely unless they are subsequently registered or an exemption from such registration is available; provided that, in any event, the exemption from registration under Rule 144 will not be available for at least one (1) year after the purchase and payment for the shares, unless the options and the shares were issued pursuant to Rule 701, and even then will not be available unless: (i) a public trading market then exists for the Common Stock; (ii) adequate information concerning the Company is then available to the public; and (iii) other terms and conditions of Rule 144 are complied with, including, among other things, the sale being made through a broker in an unsolicited "broker's transaction" or in transactions directly with a "market maker" and the number of shares being sold in any three-month period not exceeding specified limitations. There is not now a public market for shares of the Company's Common Stock and there can be no assurance that a public market will ever exist. Accordingly, optionees should be prepared to hold the shares of Common Stock received upon exercise of their options for an indefinite period of time.

The options granted under the Plan and the shares of Common Stock issuable upon exercise of such options have not been qualified under the securities laws of any state and are being issued in reliance upon available exemptions from such qualification. Shares of Common Stock acquired upon the exercise of any option granted under the Plan may be transferred only in accordance with the provisions of applicable state securities or "blue sky" laws. To make sure that another exemption from registration under the Act would be available for the original grant of options and the issuance of shares upon exercise thereof, you will be required to make certain "investment representations" to the Company at the time you exercise the option. (See Exhibit A to this Summary Memorandum for the form of such representations.) These representations relate to your investment intent and your acknowledgment of disclosure by the Company of, and your access to, financial and other information concerning the Company. A restrictive legend will be placed on the stock certificate stating that no sale or other disposition of the stock may be made without meeting certain conditions, which include registration of the stock by the Company or an opinion to the Company by an attorney that an exemption is available under the Act for a resale of the stock. You are advised that because the Company's securities have not been registered under the Act, any shares purchased upon exercise of an option must be held indefinitely unless they are subsequently registered for sale under the Act or an exception from such registration is available.

In the event the Company has a class of stock which is subject to the registration and reporting provisions of the Exchange Act, officers, directors and holders of at least 10 percent of the Company's stock will be subject to the "short-swing" profits provisions of Section 16 of the Exchange Act, which would require them to forfeit the profits from any sale of stock within six months of any stock acquisition date. Option grants constitute an acquisition of stock for this purpose unless they are granted pursuant to a plan which satisfies the requirements of Rule 16b-3 promulgated under the Exchange Act. The Company intends to maintain the Plan in conformity with the provisions of Rule 16b-3 as in effect from time to time.

Information About the Company

The Company will distribute to all optionees copies of the annual financial statements of the Company during the term of the option.

*Summary
Memorandum*

EXHIBIT A
INVESTMENT REPRESENTATION STATEMENT

PURCHASER :

COMPANY   :   _____, Inc. (the "Company")

SECURITY   :   COMMON STOCK

AMOUNT   :

DATE   :

In connection with the purchase of the above-listed Securities, I, the Purchaser, represent to the Company the following:

1.   I am aware of the Company's business affairs and financial condition, and have acquired sufficient information about the Company to reach an informed and knowledgeable decision to acquire the Securities. I am purchasing these Securities for my own account for investment purposes only and not with a view to, or for the resale in connection with, any "distribution" thereof for purposes of the Securities Act of 1933, as amended (the "Securities Act").

Summary
Memorandum

2.   I understand that the Securities have not been registered under the Securities Act in reliance upon a specific exemption therefrom, which exemption depends upon, among other things, the bona fide nature of my investment intent as expressed herein. In this connection, I understand that, in the view of the Securities and Exchange Commission (the "SEC"), the statutory basis for such exemption may be unavailable if my representation was predicated solely upon a present intention to hold these Securities for the minimum capital gains period specified under tax statutes, for a deferred sale, for or until an increase or decrease in the market price of the Securities, or for a period of one year or any other fixed period in the future.

3.   I further understand that the Securities must be held indefinitely unless subsequently registered under the Securities Act or unless an exemption from registration is otherwise available. Moreover, I understand that the Company is under no obligation to register the Securities. In addition, I understand that the certificate evidencing the Securities will be imprinted with a legend which prohibits the transfer of the Securities unless they are registered or such registration is not required in the opinion of counsel for the Company.

4.   After having read the Section regarding Restrictions on Transfer and Absence of Public Market on page eight of the attached Summary Memorandum, I am familiar with the provisions of Rule 701 and

Rule 144, each promulgated under the Securities Act, which, in substance, permit limited public resale of "restricted securities" acquired, directly or indirectly, from the issuer thereof, in a non-public offering subject to the satisfaction of certain conditions. Rule 701 provides that if the issuer qualified under Rule 701 at the time of issuance of the Securities, such issuance will be exempt from registration under the Securities Act. In the event the Company later becomes subject to the reporting requirements of Section 13 or 15(d) of the Securities Exchange Act of 1934, ninety (90) days thereafter the securities exempt under Rule 701 may be resold, subject to the satisfaction of certain of the conditions specified by Rule 144, including among other things: (1) the sale being made through a broker in an unsolicited "broker's transaction" or in transactions directly with a market maker (as said term is defined under the Securities Exchange Act of 1934); and, in the case of an affiliate, (2) the availability of certain public information about the Company, and the amount of securities being sold during any three-month period not exceeding the limitations specified in Rule 144(e), if applicable. Notwithstanding this paragraph (d), I acknowledge and agree to the restrictions set forth in paragraph (e) hereof.

5.   In the event that the Company does not qualify under Rule 701 at the time of issuance of the Securities, then the Securities may be resold in certain limited circumstances subject to the provisions of Rule 144, which requires among other things: (1) the availability of certain public information about the Company, (2) the resale occurring not less than one year after the party has purchased, and made full payment for, within the meaning of Rule 144, the securities to be sold; and, in the case of an affiliate, or of a non-affiliate who has held the securities less than two years, (3) the sale being made through a broker in an unsolicited "broker's transaction" or in transactions directly with a market maker (as said term is defined under the Securities Exchange Act of 1934) and the amount of securities being sold during any three month period not exceeding the specified limitations stated therein, if applicable.

Summary Memorandum

6.   I agree, in connection with any initial underwritten public offering of the Company's securities, (1) not to sell, make short sale of, loan, grant any options for the purchase of, or otherwise dispose of any shares of Common Stock of the Company held by me (other than those shares included in the registration) without the prior written consent of the Company or the underwriters managing such initial underwritten public offering of the Company's securities for one hundred eighty (180) days from the effective date of such registration, and (2) I further agree to execute any agreement reflecting (1) above as may be requested by the underwriters at the time of the public offering; provided however that the officers and directors of

the Company who own the stock of the Company also agree to such restrictions.

7.   I further understand that in the event all of the applicable require-ments of Rule 144 or Rule 701 are not satisfied, registration under the Securities Act, compliance with Regulation A, or some other registra-tion exemption will be required; and that, notwithstanding the fact that Rule 144 and Rule 701 are not exclusive, the Staff of the SEC has expressed its opinion that persons proposing to sell private place-ment securities other than in a registered offering and otherwise than pursuant to Rule 144 or Rule 701 will have a substantial burden of proof in establishing that an exemption from registration is available for such offers or sales, and that such persons and their respective brokers who participate in such transactions do so at their own risk.

Signature of Purchaser:

Dated: , 199_

Summary
Memorandum

List of Financial Consultants

Mr. _____
Vice President
_____
_____
_____
_____, CA _____
Tel: (___) ___-___
Fax: (___) ___-___

Mr. _____
_____, Inc.
_____
_____
_____, CA _____
Tel: (___) ___-___
Fax: (___) ___-___

Mr. _____
_____
_____
_____
_____, CA _____
Tel: (___) ___-___
Fax: (___) ___-___

Mr. _____
_____
_____
_____
_____, CA _____
Tel: (___) ___-___
Fax: (___) ___-___

List of
Financial
Consultants

Explanation of Employee Stock Purchase Plan

Section 1: "Purpose"

This section lays out the purposes of the Plan. It is largely self-explanatory.

Section 2: "Definitions"

The definitions used throughout the Plan are gathered in this section and are mostly self-explanatory.

The "Awards" are of the Stock Options.

The defined terms "Change of Control Value" and "Corporate Change" tie in with alternatives available to the Board as to acceleration, surrender or adjustment of the Options as detailed in Section 8 (d) and (e). The Corporate Change definition is quite technical, but in general involves (1) a merger (with some limitations), (2) the sale of substantially all the assets of the Corporation, (3) a plan of liquidation or dissolution, (4) the acquisition of 25% of the voting power of the Corporations stock or the increase of the voting power held by a prior shareholder to more than 50%, or (5) a contested election of directors in which prior directors cease to be a majority.

A "Parent Corporation" means any corporation (other than the employer corporation) in an unbroken chain of corporations ending with the employer corporation if, at the time of the granting of the option, each of the corporations other than the employer corporation owns stock possessing 50 percent or more of the total combined voting power of all classes of stock in one of the other corporations in such chain.

A "Subsidiary Corporation" means any corporation (other than the employer corporation) in an unbroken chain of corporations beginning with the employer corporation if, at the time of the granting of the option, each of the corporations other than the last corporation in the unbroken chain owns stock possessing 50 percent or more of the total combined voting power of all classes of stock in one of the other corporations in such chain.

Section 3: "Effective Date and Duration of the Plan"

A specific date is established for the effective date of the Plan.

The Shareholders of the Corporation must approve the plan within one year of the effective date (this can be either before or after the effective date). No Option can be exercised until the Stockholders have approved the Plan.

The Plan terminates 10 years after the earlier of the date of approval of the Plan by (1) the Board, or (2) the Shareholders. Despite the "termination," Options which were Awarded during the life of the Plan can still be exercised after termination until the period for their exercise shall expire.

Section 4: "Administration"

This section outlines the administration of the Plan. The ultimate power lies with the Board of Directors.

The Board Members must abstain from the decisions on matters that affect their individual interests in the Plan.

Special rules apply if the Corporation, its Parent Corporation, or any Subsidiary is a publicly-held corporation. A publicly-held corporation is one that issues a class of securities that is required to be registered under Section 12 of the Securities Act of 1934. A committee of outside directors must in that case be established to administer the Plan and to make Awards where the limit on deductible employee remuneration might be exceeded.

Section 5: "Grant of Options Subject to the Plan"

This section establishes the maximum number of shares which may be issued under the Plan.

In the event of a recapitalization or reorganization of the Corporation, the number of shares which may be issued under the Plan are proportionately adjusted.

Section 6: "Eligibility"

*Explanation
of Employee
Stock
Purchase
Plan*

Options may only be Awarded to persons who are at the time of the award employees of (1) the Corporation, (2) its Parent Corporation, or (3) a Subsidiary. Subsequent awards may be made to the same person.

Awards may not be made under the Plan where the Employee owns 5% or more of the voting power of the Corporation, its Parent, or a Subsidiary.

There are certain employees which the Board may exclude from the Plan. The listing is mandated by Section 423(b)(4). The excludable employees include new employees (less than 2 years), part time employees, seasonal employees, and highly compensated employees.

Section 7: "Stock Options"

(a) *Stock Option Agreement*

A separate Stock Option Agreement is made for each Award of an Option. The terms can be varied as between the various awardees.
The Holder of an Option may designate a beneficiary in the event of death. This is accomplished by the exhibit attached to the Stock Option Agreement.

(b) *Option Period*

The Option Period is fixed at the time of the Award of the Option but it can not be longer than (1) 5 years if the Option Price is not less than 85% of the Fair Market Value at the time of exercise, or (2) 27 months if some other method, such as a fixed price, is used to determine the Option Price.

(c) *Limitations on Exercise of Option*
The terms of exercise are also fixed at the time of the Award of the Option but the option must be exercisable at no slower than the rate of 20% per year over 5 years. The exercise can not be for less than full shares.

(d) *Special Limitations*
The Special Limitation is mandated by Section 423(b)(8) and limits the accrual of options to $25,000 per person per year. The $25,000 is measured by the Fair Market Value of the stock determined at the time of the award of the Option.

(e) *Option Price*
The Option price is another item fixed at the time of the Award. The Option price can not be less than the lower of (1) 85% of the Fair Market Value on the date of the Award, or (2) 85% of the Fair Market Value on the date of exercise.

(f) *Options and Rights in Substitution for Stock Options Made by Other Corporations*
If the Corporation acquires or is acquired by another corporation, Options may be Awarded to the new employees in substitution for prior Awards of the newly related corporation.

Explanation of Employee Stock Purchase Plan

(g) *Restricted Stock Option Purchase Agreement*
The execution of the Restricted Stock Purchase Agreement is a precondition to the Grant of Stock pursuant to the exercise of a Stock option. The Restricted Stock Purchase Agreement provides a repurchase option and a right of first refusal in favor of the Corporation.

Section 8: "Recapitalization or Reorganization"

Awards or Grants may be adjusted by the in the event of changes in the number of shares or changes in the character of the shares.

The power of the Board and Shareholders to change the capital structure of the Corporation is not affected by the Plan.

Where on Option is outstanding before a stock split or consolidation the shares subject to the Option are similarly adjusted. A similar adjustment is made in the event of a recapitalization or other change in the capital structure.

For Corporate Changes other than the control acquisition situation the Board must select the available alternatives two days prior to the Corporate Change. In the control acquisition situation the Board has ten days after the Corporate Change within which to select the alternatives. The available alternatives tie back to the Corporate Change definition in Section 2. The Corporate Change definition involves (1) a merger (with some limitations), (2) the sale of substantially all the assets of the Corporation, (3) a plan of liquidation or dissolution, (4) the acquisition of 25% of the voting power of the Corporations stock or the increase of the voting power held by a prior shareholder to more than 50%, or (5) a contested election of directors in which prior directors cease to be a majority. In the merger, sale or stock acquisition situations the Board has the alternative of accelerating the time for exercise of the Options. In the liquidation, stock acquisition, and contested election situations the Board has the alternatives of (1) requiring a mandatory surrender of the options, (2) adjusting the Options, (3) offering other securities, or (4) canceling the Options if the fair market value of the stock is less than the Option Price.

Section 9: "Amendment or Termination of the Plan"

The Board can terminate or the Plan, but is can not unilaterally impair the rights of Option Holders or Stock Grantees. In the specific circumstances listed in this section, Shareholder approval is also required.

Section 10: "Other"

The Plan does not in itself confer any rights to any employee to purchase Stock, to receive an Award of an Option or to receive a Grant of Stock. The Plan is unfunded.

The Plan does not confer any right to continued employment.

Unless there is an available exemption from securities registration requirements, no stock is obligated to be issued under any Award or Grant. Only whole shares will be issued. The Corporation is authorized to make required tax withholdings.

The Corporation can take any action in its interest even if the action has an adverse affect upon the Plan.

Awards of Options are not transferable, although in the event of the disability or death of the Holder they may be exercised by the legal representative in certain limited circumstances.

*Explanation
of Employee
Stock
Purchase
Plan*

Part 3

Phantom Stock Plan

Employer Inc. Phantom Stock Plan

SECTIONS TO FILL IN OR CHANGE ACCORDING TO YOUR NEEDS ARE ENCLOSED IN ANGLE BRACKETS (<<>>); BLANKS TO FILL IN ARE UNDERSCORED (_____).

Section 1. *Establishment of Plan; Definitions.*

(a)   Employer, a _____ corporation ("Employer") hereby establishes the Employer, Inc. Phantom Stock Plan (the "Plan") effective as of _____.

(b)   For purposes of this Plan, the following terms have the following meanings:

"1934 Act" means the Securities Exchange Act of 1934. (References to specific provisions of law shall be deemed to include references to amendments or supplements thereto or subsequent provisions of law of similar import.)

"Phantom Units" means the phantom units granted pursuant to the Plan.

"Book Value" shall mean the book value of a share of Employer Stock determined by the Employer's independent auditors in accordance with generally accepted accounting principles consistently applied in accordance with past practice with respect to the Employer; which determination shall, absent manifest error, be final and binding.

"Cause" means: (i) any action by a Participant involving willful malfeasance or a willful breach of such Participant's fiduciary duties in connection with such Participant's employment by the Employer; (ii) the conviction of a Participant of a felony or of a fraud; (iii) substantial and continuing refusal or neglect by a Participant to perform the duties requested of him or her provided such are duties ordinarily performed by a person employed in a similar capacity (other than as a result of death, illness or other objective incapacity) which refusal or neglect continues for a period of ten (10) days after written notice thereof to the Participant from the Committee; or (iv) termination of a Participant's employment for cause in accordance with provisions of his or her employment agreement, if any, with the Employer.

"Change of Control" means, with respect to the Employer or Employer, as the case may be, any (i) issuance, sale, assignment, transfer or other disposition of equity interests, (ii) exercise or conversion of equity interests which entitles the registered owner thereof to vote in an election of Directors of the subject company ("Voting Stock"), or (iii) issuance, sale, assignment, transfer or other disposition of any other security, right, option, warrant or agreement, convertible or exercisable into equity interests or Voting Stock (collectively "Voting Securities"), or any series of such transactions described in Clause (i), (ii), and/or (iii), which, in the aggregate, results in a Person (or a group of Persons under Rule 13d promulgated under the 1934 Act other than Employer or any of its affiliates being the record owner or "beneficial owner" (as such term is defined for purposes of Rule 13d-3 promulgated under the 1934 Act) of Voting Securities and/or Voting Stock entitled to elect more than fifty percent (50%) of the Directors of the subject company or of the surviving entity in a merger between the such company and such surviving entity, or such other Person (or group) in fact elects or appoints a majority of the Directors of such company or such surviving entity.

"Code" means the Internal Revenue Code of 1986, as amended.

*Phantom
Stock
Plan*

"Committee" means the committee (appointed by the Board of Directors Employer) consisting of three or more members who shall administer the Plan and serve at the pleasure of the Board of Directors of Employer. Initially, the Committee shall consist of ____, ____ and ____. If at any time Employer shall have a class of common stock required to be registered under the 1934 Act, the Committee, (to the extent it is not already in compliance with this provision) shall be dissolved and reappointed by the Board of Directors of Employer and shall thereafter consist solely of two or more persons, each of whom shall qualify as (i) a "Non-Employee Director", as that term is defined in subparagraph (b)(3)(i) of Rule 16b-3 (*"Rule 16b-3"*) promulgated under 1934 Act, and (ii) an "outside director", within the meaning of Section 162(m) of the Code.

"Competitive Activity" means (i) the participation in, engagement by, possession of a financial or other interest in or filling a position directly or indirectly, whether individually or as an employee, agent, partner, shareholder, consultant, or otherwise by the Participant in any enterprise or business if such enterprise or business competes with the business of the Employer, or any of its subsidiaries, in any state in which the Employer or any such subsidiary conducts its business; (ii) the solicitation by the Participant of any other Person to engage in any of the foregoing activities; (iii) the solicitation of any employee of the Employer or any of its subsidiaries to leave the Employer or any of its subsidiaries, or to do business with any enterprise or business which competes with the business of the Employer

or any of its subsidiaries; or (iv) the solicitation of any customer, vendor or supplier of the Employer or any of its subsidiaries. The ownership of an interest constituting not more than two percent of the outstanding debt or equity in a company whose securities are traded on a recognized stock exchange or traded on the over-the-counter market shall not be deemed financial participation in a competitor even though that company may be a competitor of the Employer or any of its subsidiaries.

"Date of Grant" means the effective date of the grant of a Phantom Unit by the Committee.

"EBITDA" means, with respect to the relevant fiscal year of the Employer, the earnings before interest, taxes, depreciation and amortization of the Employer <<calculated on a consolidated basis>> for such period, as determined in accordance with generally accepted accounting principles applied on a consistent basis with the Employer's past practice, adjusted by excluding (i) any net extraordinary gains or net extraordinary losses, as the case may be; (ii) any net gains or losses in respect of dispositions of assets (including, without limitation, pursuant to sale and leaseback transactions and sales of capital stock in subsidiaries) other than in the ordinary course of business; and (iii) the net income of any entity acquired prior to the date (A) such entity becomes a direct or indirect subsidiary of the Employer, (B) such entity is merged or consolidated with the Employer or any of its subsidiaries or (C) such entity's assets are acquired by the Employer or any of its subsidiaries. EBITDA shall be computed before state and federal taxes but after non-income taxes such as, but not limited to, sales taxes, excise taxes, and franchise taxes in each case attributable to the Employer <<and all of its consolidated subsidiaries as if the Employer was a stand alone taxable "C" corporation>>.

"Employer" means Employer, Inc., a ____ corporation.

"Employer Stock" means the ____ par value common stock of Employer.

"Exercise Period" means, with respect to a vested shares of Phantom Stock,

(i)   in the case of a Participant who is employed by the employer at the time of exercise, the period commencing on the first to occur of (A) the first anniversary of the date on which all shares of Phantom Stock granted on the Date of Grant of the subject shares of Phantom Stock became fully vested (the "First Full Vesting Anniversary") and (B) the time immediately prior to the occurrence of a Triggering Event, and expiring (x) on the 90th day after the occurrence of a Triggering Effect or (y) if no Triggering Event occurs before _____, then on such date;

(ii)   in the case of a Participant whose employment relationship with the employer has been terminated (for any reason other than for Cause), the period commencing with the date of such termination (but not before the First Full Vesting Anniversary) and ending 180 days following such date.

"Fair Market Value" means

(i)   if Employer Stock is Publicly Traded in a market in which actual transactions are reported, the mean of the high and low prices at which the are reported to have traded on the relevant date in all markets on which trading in the Employer Stock is reported, or if there is no reported sale of the Employer Stock on the relevant date, the mean of the highest reported bid price and lowest reported asked price for the Employer Stock on the relevant date,

(ii)   if the Employer Stock is Publicly Traded but only in markets in which there is no reporting of actual transactions, the mean of the highest reported bid price and lowest reported asked price for the Employer Stock on the relevant date, or

Phantom Stock Plan

(iii)   if the Employer Stock is not Publicly Traded, the value of Employer Stock as determined by the Committee in good faith, which, in the absence of evidence which in the discretion of the Committee would indicate a lower Fair Market Value, shall equal the quotient obtained by dividing

(A)   the average obtained by dividing by two the sum of (1) the sales (less returns, allowances and reserves for warranty work) of the Employer for the full fiscal year immediately preceding the date Fair Market Value is being determined and (2) the product obtained by multiplying <<five>> by the Employer's EBITDA for the full fiscal year immediately preceding the date Fair Market Value is being determined,

by

(B)   the number of outstanding shares of Employer Stock <<adjusted as necessary for other classes of Employer Stock that may be outstanding>> on a fully diluted basis as at the end of such fiscal year, *provided* that in the event that a share of Phantom Stock is being exercised concurrently with or after the occurrence of a Triggering Event, the Fair Market Value shall be (I) if the Triggering Event resulted from a Sale of Stock or a Sale of Assets, the aggregate consideration paid in connection with such transaction (less the aggregate amount payable under this Plan to Participants), divided by the number of then outstanding shares of Employer Stock <<adjusted as necessary for other classes of Employer Stock that may be outstanding>> on a fully diluted basis, but treating shares of Phantom Stock as not being outstanding or (II) if the Triggering Event resulted from a Public Offering, the public offering price per share of Employer Stock in such Public Offering.

Notwithstanding the foregoing in the event that one or more shares of Phantom Stock are being exercised by a Participant who resigned his employment with the Employer and engaged in a Competitive Activity at any time during his employ at the Employer or during his employment with the Employer or during the six-month period commencing with such resignation, the Fair Market Value shall be the Book Value as at the end of the Employer's fiscal year immediately preceding such resignation.

For purposes of measuring the Fair Market Value in connection with a Triggering Event, the date as of which Fair Market Value shall be determined shall be the effective date of the transaction giving rise to the Triggering Event; provided that in the event that a Public Offering causes the Triggering Event; the effective date of such transaction shall be the date that the Employer and/or the selling security holders (as the case may be) receive the net proceeds of such Public Offering.

Phantom Stock Plan

"*Measurement Value*" means, in respect of a share of Phantom Stock, the <<value>> <<Fair Market Value>>, as determined by the Committee, of a share of Employer Stock on the Date of Grant of such share of Phantom Stock .

"*Participants*" has the meaning set forth in Section 4 below.

"*Person*" means and includes a natural person, corporation, limited partnership, general partnership, joint stock company, business trust or other organization or entity, whether or not a legal entity.

"Publicly Traded" means that a class of stock (or equity interest) is required to be registered under Section 12 of the Securities Exchange Act of 1934, as amended or that stock (or equity interest) of that class has been sold within the preceding twelve months in an underwritten public offering.

"Phantom Dividends" means the cumulative amount of dividends declared and paid with respect to one share of Employer Stock during the period beginning on the date of <<vesting>> <<grant>> of a share of Phantom Stock and ending on the date of exercise of such share, but excluding any extraordinary dividends, if so determined by the Committee in the exercise of its sole discretion.

"Phantom Stock" means the rights to payment from Employer granted to Participants pursuant to the terms of the Plan.

"Public Offering" means the consummation of the sale of Employer Stock pursuant to a registration statement declared effective under the Securities Act of 1933, as amended.

"Sale of Assets" means, the sale, transfer or the disposition by the Employer of all or substantially all of its assets.

Phantom Stock Plan

"Sale of Stock" means with respect to Employer, the sale, transfer or disposition for value by the equity owners to an unaffiliated third party of an amount of equity interests such that, after giving effect to such sale, transfer or other disposition, a Change of Control results (regardless of the form of the transaction, including without limitation, a cash-out merger or a merger, recapitalization or consolidation).

"Triggering Event" means the first to occur of a Sale of Stock, Public Offering or a Sale of Assets.

Section 2. *Purposes of the Plan.* The purpose of the Plan is to build and retain a capable, experienced long-term management team and to retain the best personnel of the Employer by providing incentive and reward to a limited group of key executives, management employees and personnel to promote the success of the Employer and its stockholders. Employer expects that it will benefit from the added flexible incentive which these persons will have in the welfare of the Employer as a result of their benefits under this Plan being determined by reference to the appreciation in the value of the Employer Stock.

Section 3. *Administration of the Plan.* The Committee will hold its meetings at such times and places as it may determine and will maintain written minutes of its meetings. A majority of the members of the Committee will constitute a quorum at any meeting of the Committee. All determinations of the Committee will be made by the vote of a majority of the committee members who participate in a meeting. The members of the Committee may participate in a meeting of the Committee in person or by conference telephone or similar communications equipment by means of which all members can hear each other. Any decision or determination by written consent of all of the members of the Committee will be as effective as if it had been made by a vote of a majority of the members who participate in a meeting. The Committee shall have full power and authority, subject to the provisions of the Plan: (a) to designate the individuals who may participate in the Plan, (b) to determine the terms of their participation in the Plan, (c) to determine the terms, timing and conditions of the granting of shares of Phantom Stock under the Plan, (d) to interpret and construe the provisions of the Plan, (e) to supervise the administration of the Plan, (f) to promulgate, amend and rescind rules and regulations relating to the Plan, (g) to determine whether a Triggering Event has occurred and (h) to take all actions in connection with or relating to or interpreting the Plan as the Committee deems to be necessary or appropriate. All decisions, interpretations and designations of the Committee shall be conclusive and binding on all persons. No members of the Committee shall be liable for any act or omission in connection with the administration of the Plan unless it resulted from the Committee member's willful misconduct.

Phantom Stock Plan

Section 4. *Eligibility.* Key employees <<directors and independent contractors>> of the Employer, including officers (each such individual participating in the Plan, a "Participant" and collectively, the "Participants"), who are responsible for the management, growth and protection of the business of the Employer <<and its subsidiaries>> as determined by the Committee are eligible to be granted awards of shares of Phantom Stock under the Plan. It is intended that this plan qualify as an unfunded "top hat" plan for the benefit of a select group of management or highly compensated employees, as described in Section 201(2) of the Employee Retirement Security Act of 1974, and that the Committee limit participation in the Plan accordingly.

Section 5. *Shares of Phantom Stock.*

5.1   *In General.* Each share of Phantom Stock granted under the Plan shall, except as provided in Section 6.2 hereof, constitute a right to receive in cash the appreciation in the Fair Market Value of one share of Employer Stock, as determined as of the date of the exercise of such share of Phantom Stock, over the Measurement Value of such share of Phantom Stock, <<plus the cumulative value of Phantom Dividends applicable to such share>>. The Measurement Value shall be stated in the grant as described in Section 5.4 below and shall be subject to adjustment as provided in Section 8 below.

5.2   *Number of Shares of Phantom Stock Subject to Grant.* The total number of shares of Phantom Stock that may be granted under the Plan is ___, provided that if any shares of Phantom Stock shall be forfeited or otherwise expire without being exercised or be retired by Employer, such shares of Phantom Stock shall not again be granted under the Plan.

5.3   *Grant of Phantom Stock .* The Committee, in its sole discretion, shall from time to time prior to the termination of the Plan, determine which individuals, from among those eligible, shall be granted shares of Phantom Stock under the Plan. As promptly as practicable after an employee is granted shares of Phantom Stock, the Committee shall send the Participant a document setting forth the terms of the grant, including the Date of Grant. The Committee shall establish or cause to be established a bookkeeping account for each Participant and shall record or cause to be recorded the number of shares of Phantom Stock granted to each Participant pursuant to each grant, the Date of Grant, the Measurement Value of such shares of Phantom Stock <<and the cumulative amount of Phantom Dividends applicable to such shares.>>

5.4   *Vesting.* Subject to the immediately succeeding two sentences and Section 8(c) below, a Participant's right to payment for any shares of Phantom Stock granted to him or her shall vest in the following percentages of shares of Phantom Stock awarded to such Participant on the following anniversaries of the Date of Grant of such shares of Phantom Stock, provided that such Participant is actively employed by the Employer on each such anniversary:

Percentage of Phantom Stock Awarded to Participant which are Vested	Anniversary of Date of Grant
20%	First
40%	Second
60%	Third
80%	Fourth
100%	Fifth

<<Notwithstanding the foregoing, for vesting purposes alone, the shares of Phantom Stock initially granted under this Plan as set forth in Schedule 1 hereto shall be deemed to have been granted on (and the Date of Grant with respect thereto shall be) ____. [*Note: the possible effect of Regs. Section 1.162-27(e)(2)(i) on grants of prior service credit if Code Section 162(m) ($1,000,000 compensation deduction cap for public companies) may apply.*]>> All shares of Phantom Stock, including vested shares of Phantom Stock, shall be subject to termination in accordance with the provisions of this Plan.

Section 6. *Exercise: Payments, Etc.*

6.1   *Exercise, etc.*

    (a)   Each Participant may exercise any or all vested shares of Phantom Stock awarded to him or her by causing the Employer to redeem same at any time and from time to time during the Exercise Period applicable to such grant in the manner hereinafter provided, subject to the limitations set forth in Section 6.1 (a) or 6.2 below.

    (b)   Whenever a Participant desires to exercise any or all of his or her vested shares of Phantom Stock as provided above in Section 6.1(a) above, such Participant shall give written notice during the Exercise Period to the Employer of his or her election to do so, which notice shall be irrevocable, shall specify the number of vested shares of Phantom Stock being exercised and, if applicable, be accompanied by the statement required by Section 6.2(c) below. The amount to which such Participant is entitled by virtue of such exercise shall promptly be paid by the Employer by check; <<provided, that in the event that such exercise occurs prior to the occurrence of a Triggering Event, the Participant's aggregate entitlement to receive payments under this Plan shall be limited so that such Participant shall not receive any amount in respect of exercised shares of Phantom Stock to the extent such payments in any 12-month period would in the aggregate exceed ____ of such Participant's base compensation from the Employer as at the time of exercise of the shares of Phantom Stock (or, in respect of payment for shares of Phantom Stock exercised after the Participant's employment relationship with the Employer has terminated, the Participant's base compensation as in effect immediately preceding such termination). If, as a result of the application of the immediately preceding sentence, a portion of the Participant entitlement to payment resulting from the exercise of shares of Phantom Stock is deferred until subsequent years, such Participant shall not be entitled to receive interest on any such deferred amounts.>> Exercise notices shall be addressed to:

    Employer, Inc.
    Phantom Stock Plan Committee

    _____
    _____
    _____
    _____

*Phantom
Stock
Plan*

6.2 *Termination of Employment; Option of Employer to Purchase.*

(a) In the event a Participant shall cease to be employed by the Employer, Employer shall have the right (but not the obligation) ("Call Right") to purchase (and the Participant shall have the obligation to sell) all of such Participant's shares of Phantom Stock at an aggregate purchase price equal to the aggregate Fair Market Value of the shares of Phantom Stock which were exercisable as at the date of such cessation of employment, less the aggregate Measurement Value of such vested shares of Phantom Stock <<plus the aggregate amount of Phantom Dividends applicable to such shares of Phantom Stock.>> Such Call Right shall be exercised by written notice to the Participant, which notice shall fix the settlement of the payment of the shares of Phantom Stock (the "Closing") at not less than <<5>> nor more than <<30>> days after the date such notice is given. The purchase price to be paid for the subject shares of Phantom Stock shall be paid <<in cash or by certified check or wire transfer>> at the Closing. The Closing shall take place at the offices of Employer at 1:00 p.m. on the date fixed in the exercise notice. Such shares of Phantom Stock shall be canceled on the books of Employer upon the delivery of the purchase price therefor.

(b) Shares of Phantom Stock shall cease to vest after any cessation of employment, and, if a Participant's employment or association with the Employer is terminated at the request of the Employer for Cause, the Participant's right to exercise vested shares of Phantom Stock shall terminate immediately upon such termination and all of such Participant's shares of Phantom Stock shall be forfeited without any payment being due.

(c) In connection with any exercise by a Participant after such Participant's resignation of employment with the Employer, the exercising Participant shall be required to tender a sworn statement to the Employer stating whether such Participant has engaged in a Competitive Activity at any time during Participant's employment with the Employer or during the six-month period commencing with such resignation.

(d) The shares of Phantom Stock shall terminate upon the expiration of the applicable Exercise Period thereof.

(e) The time of cessation of employment and application of the definition of "Exercise Period" shall be determined by the Committee.

6.3 *Withholding and Other Tax Matters.* The Employer shall include all payments made pursuant to the Plan in determining each Participant's compensation for services rendered and shall reflect such amount in such Participant's Form W-2 or 1099, as applicable. From all such payments, the Employer shall withhold all taxes as required by Federal, state and local income tax laws.

6.4 *Source of Payments.* All payments under the Plan shall be from the general assets of the Employer, and no special or separate fund shall be established or segregated to assure or otherwise guaranty such payments hereunder. Participants shall have no rights greater than those of an unsecured creditor of the Company with respect to any vested Phantom Stock granted hereunder.

Section 7. *Beneficiaries.* Designation of beneficiaries to receive any amounts payable under the Plan subsequent to the death of a Participant shall be made in writing and filed with the Employer in such form and manner as the Committee may from time to time prescribe. Beneficiary designations may be changed by a Participant or former Participant in the same manner at any time prior to death, and may thereafter, with respect to the interest of a surviving beneficiary eligible to receive a payment, be designated or changed by such surviving beneficiary unless a successor beneficiary to such surviving beneficiary has been designated by the Participant, former Participant or prior beneficiary. If a Participant, former Participant or beneficiary eligible to receive any payment under the Plan dies without a surviving beneficiary having been designated, or with his or her estate or a trust designated as beneficiary, his or her shares of Phantom Stock, which shall remain subject to the exercise and vesting limitations set forth in this Plan, shall be distributed to the legal representative of his or her estate, or to the trustee of any such trust, in the manner provided for in Section 6.1 as soon as practicable after his or her death.

*Phantom
Stock
Plan*

Section 8. *Changes in Capitalization; Adjustments to Measurement Value.*

(a)   In the event there is a change in the number of shares of Employer Stock as a result of a distribution, split, reverse split, subdivision, recapitalization, merger, consolidation (whether or not the Employer is a surviving entity), combination or exchange of equity interests, separation, reorganization or liquidation or similar event, the maximum aggregate number of shares of Phantom Stock which may be granted under the Plan, the number of notional units of Employer Stock underlying outstanding shares of Phantom Stock, and the determination of Fair Market Value, Book Value and the Measurement Value of any shares of Phantom Stock shall be appropriately adjusted to give effect to such change; provided, however, no adjustment to (i) the number of shares of Employer Stock with respect to which shares of Phantom Stock may be granted under the Plan or, (ii) the number of shares of Employer Stock underlying outstanding shares of Phantom Stock (as well as the Measurement Value thereof) shall be made unless, and then only to the extent that, such adjustment, together with all respective prior adjustments which were not made as a result of this proviso, involves a net change of more than ____ percent, as determined by the Committee in good faith..

(b)   The Employer shall, to the extent possible, give each Participant holding unexercised shares of Phantom Stock granted pursuant to this Plan at least thirty (30) days prior written notice of any Triggering Event. Unless the Employer cancels the shares of Phantom Stock as provided in Section 8(c) below, such shares of Phantom Stock shall continue to be exercisable in accordance with the terms of this Plan, and, subject to the vesting limitations set forth in Section 5.4 above, the Participant shall be entitled to receive upon exercise the same amounts the Participant would have been entitled to receive upon exercise immediately prior to the occurrence of the Triggering Event.

Phantom Stock Plan

(c)   At the option of the Employer, in the event a Triggering Event occurs, the Employer may cancel all unexercised vested or unvested shares of Phantom Stock issued pursuant to this Plan as of the effective date of any such Triggering Event, in which event the Employer shall pay to each Participant, in respect of each such vested shares of Phantom Stock, the excess of the Fair Market Value thereof over the Measurement Value thereof, whether or not exercised, as set forth in this Plan *plus* the value of any Phantom Dividends, and shall not be required to make any payment in respect of unvested shares of Phantom Stock canceled as of such effective date.

(d)   In the case of liquidation (other than a liquidation in which the holders of Employer Stock receive equity interests of an entity which is the successor in interest to the Employer as a part of a merger, consolidation or recapitalization) or upon dissolution of the Employer (each of which shall not be deemed a "Triggering Event" under this Plan), each shares of Phantom Stock outstanding hereunder shall terminate; provided, however each Participant shall, to the extent practicable, be given 30 days prior written notice of such event, during which time he or she shall have a right to exercise his or her partly or wholly unexercised shares of Phantom Stock (in each case, subject to the exercise and vesting limitations set forth in this Plan).

(e)   The Committee shall make all determinations under this Section 8, and all such determinations, absent manifest error, shall be conclusive and binding.

Section 9. *Amendment and Termination of Plan.* No further grants of shares of Phantom Stock may be made after ____. Prior to such date, the Committee, in its sole discretion and at any time, may terminate the Plan or adopt such written amendments or modifications of the Plan and any award of shares of Phantom Stock under the Plan as it may deem advisable, effective at any date the Committee determines; provided, however, that no such termination, amendment or modification shall, without the consent of the affected Participants, deprive any Participant of any right or benefit to which he or she has previously become entitled under the Plan. After ____ payments shall be permitted to be made with respect to shares of Phantom Stock granted prior to such date.

Section 10. *Miscellaneous Provisions.*

(a)   *Limitation of Rights.* No employee or any other person shall have any claim or right to be granted any shares of Phantom Stock under the Plan. Nothing herein is intended or shall be interpreted to give any employee or other person participating in the Plan the right to be employed, reemployed or continued to be employed by the Employer or any of its subsidiaries or will interfere with or restrict in any way the rights of the Employer or any of its subsidiaries to discharge any employee at any time for any reason whatsoever, with or without Cause. Nothing herein shall confer any right or benefit or any entitlement to any benefit on any Participant unless and until a benefit is actually vested pursuant to the Plan. The adoption and maintenance of the Plan shall not be deemed to constitute a contract of employment or otherwise between the Employer or any of its subsidiaries and any employee, or to be a consideration for or an inducement or condition of any employment.

(b)   *No Trust Created.* Neither the provisions of the Plan nor any action taken by the Employer or the Committee pursuant to the provisions of the Plan shall be deemed to create any trust, express or implied, or any fiduciary relationship between or among the Employer, the Committee, any member of the Committee, or any Participant, former Participant or beneficiary of either.

(c)   *Voting and Distribution Rights.* No Participant, former Participant or beneficiary of either shall be entitled to any voting rights, any rights to receive any distributions in respect of Employer Stock, or any right to any other attribute of equity ownership provided for by applicable state law.

(d)   *Non-Alienation of Benefits.* No right or benefits under this Plan shall be subject to alienation, transfer, sale, assignment, pledge, encumbrance, charge, security interest, hypothecation, levy, attachment or execution of a judgment of any kind, otherwise than by will or the laws of

*Phantom
Stock
Plan*

descent and distribution to the extent provided herein. No right or benefit under the Plan shall in any manner be liable for or subject to the debts, contract liabilities or torts of any Participant, former Participant or beneficiary of either.

(e)   *Applicable State Law.* All questions pertaining to the Plan shall be determined under the laws of the State of ____ without regard to such State's conflicts of law principles.

*Phantom
Stock
Plan*

Letter to Participant in Phantom Stock Plan

<<date>>

<<name>>
<<location>>

Dear _____ :

I am pleased to inform you that Employer Corporation. ("Employer") has recently established the Employer Inc. Phantom Stock Plan (the "Plan") and that, effective _____, you have been conditionally granted _____ shares of Phantom Stock under the Plan with a Measurement Value equal to $_____ per share, subject to adjustment as provided in Section 8(d) of the Plan. Each share of Phantom Stock constitutes a right to receive in cash the appreciation in the Fair Market Value (as defined under the Plan) of one share of Company common stock, as determined on the date of exercise of such share of Phantom Stock, over the Measurement Value <<plus the value of cumulative Phantom Dividends>>, unless you are terminated from your employment with Employer for Cause (as defined under the Plan) or engage in a Competitive Activity (as defined under the Plan) following any resignation of employment.

Enclosed for your reference is a copy of the Plan. You are urged to read it carefully. In accordance with Section 5.4 of the Plan, << percent>> (%) of your shares of Phantom Stock are vested as of the date hereof. With respect to the remaining shares of Phantom Stock (_____ % of today's grant, the "Unvested Shares of Phantom Stock "), if you remain in the active employ of the Employer on the following dates, you will vest in the following percentage of your Unvested Shares of Phantom Stock granted to you which corresponds to such date:

DATE   PERCENTAGE

____   ____%
____   ____%
____   ____%

Subject to the provisions of the Plan, you may cash-out your vested shares of Phantom Stock (including Unvested Shares of Phantom Stock which become vested in accordance with the Plan) as follows:

(a)   in the event that you desire to exercise your vested shares of Phantom Stock while you are still employed by the Employer, your vested shares of Phantom Stock may be exercised only during the period commencing with the first to occur of (i) the time immediately prior to the occurrence of a Triggering Event (as defined in the Plan) and (ii) ____ and ending (x) on the 90th day after the occurrence of a Triggering Event or (y) if no Triggering Event occurs prior to ____, then on that date;

(b)   in the event that you desire to exercise your vested shares of Phantom Stock after your employment with the Employer has been terminated (other than as a result of your dismissal for Cause or your resignation from your employment for any reason other than as a result of your death or disability), your vested shares of Phantom Stock may be exercised only during the 90 day period commencing with the date of such termination; and

(c)   in the event that you desire to exercise your vested shares of Phantom Stock after your employment with the Employer has been terminated as a result of your resignation for any reason (other than as a result of your death or disability), your vested shares of Phantom Stock may be exercised only during the 30 day period commencing with the later to occur of (i) ____ and (ii) the six-month anniversary of such termination.

If you are terminated for Cause, your shares of Phantom Stock are forfeited.

The Plan contains other important provisions with respect to the vesting and exercise of shares of Phantom Stock, and you should review it carefully.

Sincerely,

EMPLOYER, INC.
PHANTOM STOCK
PLAN COMMITTEE

Encl.

Letter to Participant in Phantom Stock Plan

Explanation of Phantom Stock Plan

Section 1. "Establishment of Plan"

The Plan is prepared for adoption by an employer that is a corporation. It could also be adopted by a partnership or limited liability company. If an entity other than a corporation were to adopt the Plan, the definition of "Employer Stock" would have to be changed and the appointment of the "Committee" would have to be adjusted to correspond to the governing body of the employer entity among other changes.

Some of the definitions are optional and do not need to be included unless certain Plan provisions are present, as noted below:

- *"Cause"*: This Plan is drafted so that vested phantom units are forfeited by an employee who is terminated from employment for cause. This is a typical feature in phantom plans, but is optional.

- *"Change of Control"*: The definition of a Change of Control is used to define a "Sale of Stock," which is in turn part of the definition of a "Triggering Event," which is a payout event under Section 8 of the Plan. This is an optional feature.

- *"Competitive Activity"*: This term is used in conjunction with Section 6.2(c), concerning exercise of phantom units after an employee's termination of employment. The Plan provides that an employee who engages in competitive activity after leaving the employer cannot exercise his or her right to phantom units under the Plan.

- *"EBITDA"*: This refers to the employer's earnings before interest, tax, depreciation, and amortization. This definition is useful for an employer that is not publicly traded and wishes to provide a means to value the underlying employer stock on which the phantom units are based. EBITDA is a measure of value frequently used in venture capital and private equity transactions. There are other ways of measuring employer value, including the book value of employer assets and a set value periodically established by the Committee without reference to external financial factors.

- *"Exercise Period"*: An Exercise Period is the time during which an employee is permitted to cash out his or her vested shares of phantom stock.

   Paragraph (i) of the definition of "Exercise Period" applies to exercise while a Participant is currently employed (versus exercise after termination of employment.) It provides that the Exercise Period begins on the

earlier of (1) one year after all shares of phantom stock become fully
vested or (2) upon the occurrence of a Triggering Event. A Plan Participant can thus exercise a right as to partially vested shares of phantom
stock only if there is a Triggering Event. The Plan is drafted so that the
Exercise Period ends ninety (90) days after the Triggering Event or on a
specified termination date. No specific termination date needs to be provided. If no termination date is provided, the phantom shares remain exercisable during the entire term of a Plan Participant's employment.

  Paragraph (ii) provides that a Plan Participant has six (6) months after termination (other than for cause) to exercise his or her rights under
the Plan. This would apply to an exercise either by a former employee or
by his or her estate, in the event the former employee is deceased. If a
provision concerning competitive activity is included, the Exercise Period can be modified so that exercisability is suspended until completion
of the non-compete period.

Section 2: "Purpose of Plan"

Section 2 states that the basic intent of the Plan is to provide an incentive for
management employees to promote the success of the employer and its
stockholders. This section can be made more elaborate if there are particular
objectives the employer has in mind in creating a phantom stock plan.

*Explanation of
Phantom Stock
Plan*

Section 3: "Administration of the Plan"

The Plan is designed to be interpreted and administered by a Committee of
three or more individuals appointed by the governing body of the company.
The Committee is given broad powers to interpret the Plan. It would also be
possible to limit somewhat the powers of the Committee by providing more
interpretive rules in the body of the Plan and thus providing less discretion
to the Committee.

Section 4: "Eligibility"

The Plan is drafted only to apply to employees of the employer. It would
also be possible to include directors or independent contractors.

  One provision in the eligibility rules that should be observed carefully is
the requirement that the Plan qualify as a "Top Hat" Plan under ERISA. If
the Plan were to include a broader group of employees than "a select group
of management or highly compensated employees," then certain ERISA provisions would apply to the Plan, including reporting and disclosure requirements, fiduciary obligations and certain procedural requirements in the
Plan as specified in Title 4 of ERISA. A broad-based (i.e., non-"top hat")
phantom stock plan should expressly take these ERISA requirements into
account.

Section 5: "Shares of Phantom Stock"

Section 5.1: This section states the basic rule that shares of phantom stock
represent only the right to receive payments from the company in cash.

Section 5.2: This sets forth the total number of shares of phantom stock that may be granted under the Plan.

It is not necessary to establish a total number of shares of phantom stock that may be granted under the Plan. However, this is customary, in part so that the maximum payments that the employer might be called on to make can be established for financial reporting purposes. Also, for public companies, tax deductibility of the payments to certain employees may require such a cap. (See the discussion of Internal Revenue Code Section 162(m) under the discussion below of Plan Section 5.4.)

Section 5.3, *"Grant of Phantom Stock":* This section grants the Committee of the right to select, at its sole discretion, the employees who participate in the Plan.

Section 5.4, *"Vesting":* This section provides five-year level-graded vesting. It is also possible to provide for immediate vesting. Typically, the employer will take into account the anticipated period over which an employee's target for increasing stock value is to be measured and set the vesting period accordingly.

Section 162(m) of the Internal Revenue Code denies a tax deduction to publicly held employers for payments to the Corporation's chief executive officer or four other highest paid officers where the payments exceed $1 million, unless they are based on commissions or on attaining performance goals determined by a committee of two or more non-employee directors and approved by the corporation's stockholders. Before any payments can qualify as being made on the attainment of performance goals, the non-employee directors must certify that such goals have in fact been satisfied, except where: (1) the amount of compensation the employee may receive is based solely on an increase in value of stock and (2) the plan states the maximum number of shares that may be granted. An increase in value is measured from the stock value on the date of grant.

Explanation of Phantom Stock Plan

Section 6: "Exercise: Payments, Etc."

Section 6.1: The Plan is drafted to permit employees who have vested phantom shares to exercise them one year after they become fully vested, as provided in the definition of "Exercise Period," without having to wait for a termination of employment or other event.

Section 6.1(b) contains an optional provision that limits the amount payable with respect to phantom shares to a percentage of the employee's base compensation. This is designed to limit the cash flow impact of payment under the Plan. The percentage can be more or less than 100% of the Participant's base compensation. Ordinarily, the percentage would be determined based on how many employees are granted phantom stock and the total exposure of the employer to pay Plan-based compensation.

Section 6.2, *"Termination of Employment; Option of Employer to Purchase":* Section 6.2(a) gives the employer the right to redeem phantom stock upon an employee's termination of employment. Because an employee's right to exercise rights as to phantom stock can continue after the termination of employment, the employer is given a right to settle up its commitment by making payments with respect to an employee's phantom stock at the time of termination of employment.

Section 6.2(b) provides that if an employee is terminated for cause, he or she forfeits all vested shares and ceases any future vesting.

Section 6.2(c) provides an optional non-compete provision, so that exercise after termination of employment can be conditioned on the employee not having engaged in competitive activity between the time of termination and the time of exercise. As discussed in the definition of "Exercise Period," it is also possible to delay the start of the Exercise Period so that an employee is not able to exercise until six months after termination of employment. This kind of provision could be used to ensure that the company has an opportunity to prevent competitive activity following termination of employment.

Section 6.4, *"Source of Payments"*: To prevent "constructive receipt" of amounts that might be payable under the phantom stock Plan, Section 6.4 states that all payments under the Plan shall be made from the general assets of the employer and no separate fund shall be established.

Section 7: "Beneficiaries"

Explanation of Phantom Stock Plan

This section permits a Participant to designate a beneficiary who will be able to exercise rights with respect to the Participant's vested phantom shares following the Participant's death. Any exercise after an employee's death would be subject to the same provisions as exercised during life. It would also be possible to provide that if an employee dies while in employment, he or she would vest in all phantom shares then awarded

Section 8: "Changes in Capitalization"

Section 8(a) is included to prevent the dilution or enlargement of employee's rights under the Plan in the event the underlying equity of the employer is changed by a merger, reorganization, or similar event. These adjustments would be made by the Committee. The last sentence of Section 8(a) permits the Plan to set a cap on the net changes permitted in phantom shares pursuant to changes in the capital structure of the employer.

Section 8(b) provides that if there is a "Triggering Event," Participants must be given thirty (30) days' notice of the event by the employer unless the employer exercises the cancellation option provided in Section 8(c).

Under Section 8(c), the employer is given the power to cancel all unexercised shares of phantom stock in the case of a Triggering Event. To do this, the employer must pay the Plan Participants the value of the vested phantom stock at the time of the Triggering Event.

Section 8(d) provides that if the employer is liquidated, the employer shall give each employee thirty (30) days' notice and an opportunity to exercise his or her rights with respect to the phantom stock during that period.

Section 9: "Amendment and Termination of Plan"

This section provides a sunset date on the grant of shares under the Plan. It also provides that the Committee may amend the Plan so long as such amendments do not deprive any Participant of rights accrued under the Plan without the Participant's consent.

Section 10: "Miscellaneous Provisions"

- Section 10(a), *"Limitation of Rights":* This section provides that the Plan does not create an employment contract that otherwise would interfere with the employer's rights to discharge the Plan Participants.

- Section 10(b): This section simply provides that the Plan is not to be considered a trust.

- Section 10(c): This section provides that an award of phantom stock does not give an employee the right to receive actual stock of the employer.

- Section 10(d),*"Alienation of Benefits":* This section provides that Participants cannot assign their rights in the phantom stock Plan and that any rights are not subject to legal attachment of any sort by a Plan Participant's creditors.

- Section 10(e),*"Applicable State Law":* This section should be filled in to establish the law of the state in which the employer is situated, or the laws of whatever jurisdiction the employer wishes to have the Plan governed by.

*Explanation of
Phantom Stock
Plan*

*Explanation of
Phantom Stock
Plan*

Appendices

Appendix A: Files on the Accompanying Diskette

Files ending with an .RTF extension are Rich Text Format files. Files ending with a .TXT extension are plain text (ASCII) files. Almost any word processor should be able to open either type of file. The .TXT files, however, are not formatted, so you will want to use the .RTF files if possible.

Employee Stock Option Plans (OPTIONS directory)

Equity Incentive Plan
PLAN.RTF, PLAN.TXT

Incentive Stock Option Agreement
ISO.RTF, ISO.TXT

Nonqualified Stock Option Agreement
NSO.RTF, NSO.TXT

Restricted Stock Option Purchase Agreement
RESTRICT.RTF, RESTRICT.TXT

Action by Unanimous Written Consent
CONSENT.RTF, CONSENT.TXT

Summary Memorandum
SUM_MEM.RTF, SUM.MEM.TXT

Employee Stock Purchase Plan (423_PLAN directory)

Employee Stock Purchase Plan
423_PLAN.RTF, 423_PLAN.TXT

Stock Option Agreement Pursuant to the Employee Stock Purchase Plan
AGREEMT.RTF, AGREEMT.TXT

Action by Unanimous Written Consent of the Board
BOARD.RTF, BOARD.TXT

Action by Unanimous Written Consent of the Shareholders
SHAREHDR.RTF, SHAREHDR.TXT

Memorandum
MEMO.RTF, MEMO.TXT

Security Pledge Agreement
PLEDGE.RTF, PLEDGE.TXT

Promissory Note
PRO_NOTE.RTF, PRO_NOTE.TXT

Restricted Stock Purchase Agreement
RESTRICT.RTF, RESTRICT.TXT

Summary Memorandum
SUM_MEM.RTF, SUM.MEM.TXT

List of Financial Consultants
CONSULTS.RTF, CONSULTS.TXT

Phantom Stock Plan (PHANTOM directory)

Phantom Stock Plan
PHANTOM.RTF, PHANTOM.TXT

Letter to Participant in Phantom Stock Plan
LETTER.RTF, LETTER.TXT

*Files on the
Accompanying
Diskette*

Appendix B: About the NCEO and Our Other Publications

The NCEO

The National Center for Employee Ownership (NCEO) is widely considered to be the leading authority in employee ownership in the U.S. and the world. Established in 1981 as a nonprofit information and membership organization, it now has over 3,000 members, including companies, professionals, unions, government officials, academics, and interested individuals. It is funded entirely through the work it does. The staff includes people with backgrounds in academia, law, and business.

The NCEO's mission is to provide the most objective, reliable information possible about employee ownership at the most affordable price possible. As part of the NCEO's commitment to providing objective information, it does not lobby or provide ongoing consulting services. The NCEO publishes a variety of materials explaining how employee ownership plans work, describing how companies get employee owners more involved in making decisions about their work, and reviewing the research on employee ownership. In addition, the NCEO holds approximately 50 workshops and conferences on employee ownership annually. These include introductory workshops on ESOPs and stock options, meetings on employee participation, international programs, and a large annual conference.

The NCEO's work also includes extensive contacts with the media, both through articles written for trade and professional publications and through interviews with reporters. It maintains a Web site at *http://www.nceo.org* that has articles on employee ownership, regular columns, interactive training, a discussion forum, news on upcoming events, excerpts from publications, and more. Finally, the NCEO has written or edited five books for outside publishers during the 1980s and 1990s.

NCEO Membership Benefits Include:

- The bimonthly newsletter, *Employee Ownership Report*.

- The *Employee Ownership Resource Guide*, which lists over 150 members who are employee ownership consultants.

- Substantial discounts on publications and events produced by the NCEO (such as this book).

- The right to telephone the NCEO for answers to general or specific questions regarding employee ownership.

An introductory NCEO membership costs $70; see the order form at the end of this appendix.

Other Publications from the NCEO on Stock Options and Related Plans

The NCEO offers a variety of publications on all aspects of employee ownership and participation, from employee stock ownership plans (ESOPs) to open-book management. Listed below are our current publications relating to stock options and related plans (such as stock purchase and phantom stock plans):

- *The Stock Options Book* is a comprehensive resource covering the legal, tax, and design issues involved in implementing a broad-based stock option plan. It is our main book on the subject. ($25 for NCEO members, $35 for nonmembers)

- *Stock Options: Beyond the Basics* begins with a detailed overview of the field, followed by chapters on specialized topics such as repricing and evergreen options, and ends with a lengthy glossary. ($25 for NCEO members, $35 for nonmembers)

- This book, *Model Equity Compensation Plans*, provides sample plan documents for stock option, stock purchase, and phantom stock plans, along with brief explanations of the main plan documents. ($50 for NCEO members, $75 for nonmembers)

- *Equity-Based Compensation for Multinational Corporations* describes how companies can use stock options and other equity-based and equity-flavored programs across the world to reward a global work force. It includes general essays, a country-by-country summary of tax and legal consequences of stock plans, and case studies. ($25 for NCEO members, $35 for nonmembers)

- *Current Practices in Stock Option Plan Design* reports on our 1998 survey of companies with broad-based option plans. It includes a detailed examination of plan design, use, and experience broken down by industry, size, and other categories, as well as information on vesting, eligibility, allocation, repricing, and overhang practices. An appendix discusses the results of the 1999 Trinet/NCEO survey. ($50 for NCEO members, $75 for nonmembers)

- *Incentive Compensation and Employee Ownership* takes a broad look at how companies can use incentives, ranging from stock plans to cash bonuses to gainsharing, to motivate and reward employees. Includes both technical discussions and case studies. ($25 for NCEO members, $35 for nonmembers)

- *Communicating Stock Options* contains practical ideas and information about how to explain stock options to a broad group of employees. It includes the views of experienced practitioners as well as detailed examples of how companies communicate tax consequences, financial information, and other matters to employees. ($35 for NCEO members, $50 for nonmembers)

To obtain the most current information on what we have available, call us at 510-208-1300 or see our Web site at *www.nceo.org,* which also has a great deal of information on employee ownership and participation.

*About the
NCEO and
Our Other
Publications*

*About the
NCEO and
Our Other
Publications*

JavaScript Programming

Tim Poulsen

is a Senior Curriculum Developer
and Technical Writer for Element
K Content. He has been writing
courseware and providing
classroom instruction since 1990.
Prior to that, Tim worked as a
network consultant,
telecommunications technician,
WAN troubleshooter, and stocker
of grocery store shelves. He has
been published in PC Magazine
and even wrote a real bookstore-
type book. Tim's courses have
covered topics ranging from
Windows NT and NetWare
administration to Web site
development.

JavaScript Programming

Course Number: 077921
Course Edition: 4.0
For software version: 1.3

ACKNOWLEDGEMENTS

Project Team

Curriculum Developer and Technical Writer : Tim Poulsen • **Development Assistance** : Brian S. Wilson • **Senior Copy Editor** : Andrew LaPage • **Reviewing Editor** : Tom Elston • **Layout Technician** : Kristi Weese and Matthew Price • **Quality Assurance Analyst** : Jason Stinson • **Print Designer** : Carlo Atene

Project Support

Managing Editor, Internet & Programming : Carlene Jo Kline • **Managers of Instructor-Led Web Curriculum** : Jennifer Golden and Joy Morris • **Manager of Web Development** : Jeff Felice • **Publishing Technical Specialist** : Daniel L. Quackenbush • **Project Technical Support Specialist** : Michael Toscano • **Testing & Layout Technician** : Bonnie S. Watts

Administration

Senior Director of Content and Content Development: William O. Ingle • **Director of Certification:** Mike Grakowsky • **Director of Design and Web Development:** Joy Insinna • **Manager of Office Productivity and Applied Learning:** Cheryl Russo • **Manager of Databases, ERP, and Business Skills:** Mark Onisk • **Director of Business Development:** Kent Michels • **Instructional Design Manager:** Susan L. Reber • **Manager of Publishing Services:** Michael Hoyt

NOTICES

HELP US IMPROVE OUR COURSEWARE

Your comments are important to us. Please contact us at Element K Press LLC, 1-800-478-7788, 500 Canal View Boulevard, Rochester, NY 14623, Attention: Product Planning, or through our Web site at **http://support.elementkpress.com.**

JavaScript Programming

CONTENT OVERVIEW

CONTENTS

JavaScript Programming

Contents

Lesson 1: Getting Started

Lesson 2: JavaScript Building Blocks—Variables and Operators

Lesson 3: JavaScript Building Blocks—Control Statements

CONTENTS

CONTENTS

YOUR NOTES:

INTRODUCTION

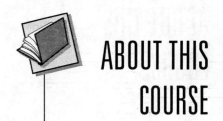

Welcome to the Element K Content training team.

Our goal is to provide you with the best computer training available and we know exactly what that takes. Our corporate heritage is based in training. In fact, we use our Student Manuals every day, in classes just like yours, so you can be confident that the material has been tested and proven to be effective.

If you have any suggestions on how we can improve our products or services, please contact us.

ABOUT THIS COURSE

JavaScript Programming is a hands-on instruction book that will teach you how to program using this powerful Internet-oriented programming language.

Course Prerequisites

We designed JavaScript Programming for the student who is an experienced developer of Web pages and who has had some exposure to JavaScript, probably through the use of scripts developed by others. If you are comfortable creating Web pages by writing HTML code, proficient with both Internet Explorer and Navigator, and have at least tried to use other peoples' scripts in your web pages, then you are well matched to the prerequisites for this course. This is a serious programming course. So, if you have programmed in another language, you will likely excel in this course.

To ensure your success, we recommend you first take the following Element K courses or have equivalent knowledge:

* *HTML Programming : Level 1*
* *Enhancing Web Pages with JavaScript*

Course Objectives

When you're done working your way through this book, you'll be able to:

* Describe the basics of the JavaScript programming language, write a simple script in a web page, and examine how the browsers handle and display error messages.

* List the JavaScript syntax rules, review language components, and evaluate some guidelines for good-coding practices.

* List the data types and variable types that JavaScript supports.

* Describe the detailed rules governing the creation, use, and manipulation of data types and variables.

* Use the operators to manipulate your data.

* Use the many control statements available in JavaScript

ABOUT THIS COURSE

- Create and use functions.
- Describe object characteristics, use objects, instantiate objects, and create custom objects.
- Describe the purpose of the Document object and its properties, methods, and event handlers.
- Use JavaScript statements to write to documents in the browser window.
- Create dynamic documents and briefly examine the incompatibilities issues facing dynamic HTML programmers.
- Review HTML frames and the methods for creating framed documents.
- Script with frames in mind.
- Describe the purpose of the Form object and its properties, methods, and event handlers.
- Read data from form elements using JavaScript.
- Choose a general process for validating user input into web forms.
- Test for required fields.
- Test for numeric data, including ensuring that the input is a number and that it is within a range of values you specify.
- Test for string data, including testing that it is not empty and that it is correctly formatted to represent the data type you specify.
- Describe the purpose of the Date object and its methods.
- Use and manipulate instances of the Date object to create clocks, countdown timers, and perform date math.
- Describe the purpose of the Math object and its constants and methods.
- Perform mathematical operations using the Math object's methods.
- Characterize the compatibility landscape and choose between the various techniques for dealing with potential incompatibilities.
- Detect browsers in order to create code that works around platform incompatibilities.

COURSE SETUP INFORMATION

Hardware and Software Requirements

To run this course, you will need:

- PC-compatible computer or Macintosh.
- Windows 9x, Windows NT, or MacOS.
- 32 MB RAM or greater.
- A monitor and video card capable of displaying at a resolution of 800x600 or greater.
- 200 MB disk space (to hold the browsers).
- Navigator 4.5x or newer and Internet Explorer 4.01 or newer.
- A connection to the Internet (optional, though recommended).
- A mouse or compatible tracking device.

Class Requirements

In order for the class to run properly, perform the procedures described below.

1. Configure your computer to display its output at 800x600 or greater resolution with at least 256 colors.

2. Prepare the computer for Internet access by configuring a dial-up connection or a direct connection (by setting a TCP/IP address). This does not have to be a working connection if you do not plan to access the Internet during class.

3. Install Netscape Navigator 4.5x or newer following the manufacturer's recommendations, performing all the configuration steps its set up program requires.

4. Install Internet Explorer 4.01 or newer following the manufacturer's recommendations, performing all the configuration steps its set up program requires. We recommend installing Navigator before Internet Explorer. If you do these steps in the other order, primary features of Internet Explorer, such as loading a page from a bookmark, are usurped by Navigator. For example, when you type an Internet address into Internet Explorer's Address text box, the page will be opened in Navigator instead of Internet Explorer.

5. Copy the data files for this course, including the Library sub-folder, to the hard disk. We recommend you name the folder Data or JSData.

6. If you plan to access the Internet during class, confirm that you have configured that access correctly by accessing some sites of your choice with both browsers.

7. If you plan to use the HomeSite HTML editor as the text editor for the course, install it from the HomeSite folder on the student data disc at this time.

   Configure the following settings in HomeSite: turn on line numbers in the gutter; turn off tag insight, tag completion, and tag validation; set the default file extension to be .html; configure HomeSite to treat tabs as spaces; configure the code templates so that the JavaScript code block is listed first (change its keyword name to "a script"); and configure the external browser list to recognize both Navigator and Internet Explorer as external browsers, set Navigator to be the primary external browser. Detailed instructions for performing these configuration steps are included in the config.html file in the HomeSite folder on the student data disc.

   Because this is a demonstration copy of the program, its license will expire after a period, forcing you to re-install the program. If you like the program and think it works well in class, please consider purchasing "live" copies from Allaire Corp. You can purchase HomeSite from Allaire's Web site, **http://www.allaire.com**.

ABOUT THIS COURSE

ABOUT THIS COURSE

HOW TO USE THIS BOOK

You can use this book as a learning guide, a review tool, and a reference.

As a Learning Guide

Each lesson covers one broad topic or set of related topics. Lessons are arranged in order of increasing proficiency with *JavaScript* ; skills you acquire in one lesson are used and developed in subsequent lessons. For this reason, you should work through the lessons in sequence.

We organized each lesson into explanatory topics and step-by-step activities. Topics provide the theory you need to master *JavaScript* , activities allow you to apply this theory to practical hands-on examples.

You get to try out each new skill on a specially prepared sample file. This saves you typing time and allows you to concentrate on the technique at hand. Through the use of sample files, hands-on activities, illustrations that give you feedback at crucial steps, and supporting background information, this book provides you with the foundation and structure to learn *JavaScript* quickly and easily.

As a Review Tool

Any method of instruction is only as effective as the time and effort you are willing to invest in it. For this reason, we encourage you to spend some time reviewing the book's more challenging topics and activities.

As a Reference

You can use the Concepts sections in this book as a first source for definitions of terms, background information on given topics, and summaries of procedures.

ICONS SERVE AS CUES:

Throughout the book, you will find icons in the margin representing various kinds of information. These icons serve as at-a-glance reminders of their associated text.

Topic:
Represents the beginning of a topic

Check Your Skills:
Represents a Check Your Skills practice

Task:
Represents the beginning of a task

Apply Your Knowledge:
Represents an Apply Your Knowledge activity

Student Note:
Highlights information for students

Glossary Term:
Represents a definition; this definition also appears in the glossary

Quick Tip:
Represents a tip, shortcut, or additional way to do something

Warning:
Represents a caution; this note typically provides a solution to a potential problem

Web Tip:
Refers you to a Web site where you might find additional information

Instructor Note:
In the Instructor's Edition, gives tips for teaching the class

Overhead:
In the Instructor's Edition, refers to a PPT slide that the instructor can use in the lesson

Additional Instructor Note:
In the Instructor's Edition, refers the instructor to more information in the back of the book

YOUR NOTES:

Getting Started

Overview

In this lesson, you will examine the basics of JavaScript, what it is and what it can do. You will examine the basic syntactical structure of the language, see how browsers handle errors, and review some coding best-practices.

This course assumes some basic familiarity with JavaScript. You should have at least tried to use someone else's script in one of your Web pages. If that's not the case with you, consider this lesson's materials carefully. If you've used JavaScript previously, you are encouraged to work through this lesson just the same. The review it will provide will ensure that subsequent lessons flow smoothly.

Objectives

To understand the basic operations of JavaScript and to begin the journey to proficiency, you will:

1A   Examine the basics of the JavaScript programming language.

You will write a simple script in a Web page and examine how the browsers handle and display error messages.

1B   Examine JavaScript syntax rules, review language components, and evaluate some guidelines for good coding practices.

You'll examine some scripts to see how JavaScript enforces its specific syntax rules. You'll examine a couple of options for putting scripts into your Web pages. And, you'll check out some suggestions for coding best-practices.

Data Files
blank.html
error.html
whitespace.html
lottery.html
mathpage.html

Lesson Time
45 minutes

 Topic 1A

JavaScript Overview

JavaScript is a widely adopted, powerful programming language developed by Netscape Communications Corp. It is designed to be used in Internet browsers, on Internet servers, and even in stand-alone configurations. Since its initial release in 1995, JavaScript has become one of the most widely used programming languages in the world.

JavaScript Is...

JavaScript is an interpreted language, meaning that you do not have to compile programs written with JavaScript before you can run them. JavaScript programs can be embedded into Web pages or saved in separate plain-text files. JavaScript is a powerful programming language that can be used to build very complex applications.

JavaScript Isn't...

JavaScript is not a simplified version of Java. Certainly the names sound similar. And both programming languages share a few basic syntax rules like case-sensitivity. But, the similarity ends there. Java is a full-fledged programming language from Sun Microsystems. JavaScript is an interpreted, moderately sized programming language from Netscape Communications.

JavaScript was originally called LiveScript. But the name was changed for marketing reasons just before its initial release.

JavaScript running on a user's computer cannot access local files or perform network operations, for example. Java, on the other hand, can perform such operations. JavaScript has very limited graphics capabilities. Java can fully manipulate the display, performing all sorts of graphical operations.

JavaScript Implementations

For better or worse, there are many implementations of JavaScript. Netscape and its licensees call their version of the language JavaScript. Microsoft, not an official language licensee, calls their version JScript. The European Computer Manufacturer's Association (ECMA) has standardized core features of the language. ECMA designated standard number 262 for their version of JavaScript. ECMA-262 is typically referred to as ECMAScript. Subtle differences exist between these versions. However, the number of versions attests to the popularity of the language.

JavaScript is more than just a browser macro language. The full specification for the language includes components and features that make it suitable for running on Internet servers or even in stand-alone configurations. Netscape and Microsoft both support server-side JavaScript coding in their Web server products. JavaScript has even been embedded into products such as Lotus Notes. The Windows Scripting Host, available with Windows 98 and Windows 2000, enables you to run JavaScript programs directly on your computer without the need for a browser.

For those reasons, you will see at least four terms describing JavaScript: core, client-side, server-side, and embedded.

Implementation	Description
Core	Core JavaScript is that central subset of JavaScript that is implemented no matter where the JavaScript interpreter is being implemented. This portion of the language defines the basic data handling and manipulation capabilities, syntactical specifications, and interpreter specifications of the language.
Client-side	Client-side JavaScript is that which runs in a Web browser. This portion of JavaScript defines how the language interacts with the browser, with data interpreted by the browser, and with the Internet environment (moving to a new URL, for example).
Server-side	Server-side JavaScript runs on a server, like a Web server or a Notes server. Serverside JavaScript can access files, databases, and other resources on the server enabling powerful applications.
Embedded	Applications other than Web browsers could certainly use JavaScript as their internal macro language. Such implementations would be described as embedded JavaScript implementations. The functionality of an embedded JavaScript implementtation would likely closely match that of client-side JavaScript. However, implementation-specific features could certainly be included.

This course is primarily concerned with core and client-side JavaScript. The techniques and knowledge you gain from this course will help you no matter what type of JavaScript programming you intend to do.

Why Multiple Browsers

The setup for this course specifies that you should have both Netscape Navigator and Microsoft Internet Explorer installed and available. You might think that an unnecessary and burdensome requirement. Unfortunately, each of the browser vendors have implemented JavaScript in a sometimes quirky and problematic way. Programs that run flawlessly in one browser will often fail miserably in another.

At the time of this writing, according to the Browserwatch Web site (**browserwatch.internet.com**), market share between Navigator and Internet Explorer is split nearly 50-50. Half of all users use Navigator, while the other half uses Internet Explorer. Hundreds of other browsers exist and are used in minimal proportions, though only a couple support any version of JavaScript. If your JavaScript programs are going to be used on the Internet, you will need to give equal consideration to Internet Explorer quirks as you do to Navigator quirks. That means running and testing your scripts in both browsers (and often in multiple versions of each of those browsers).

So, you say you're writing for an intranet and can specify which browsers users run? You should still take care to make your scripts as cross-browser compatible as you can. Browser preferences are often made for non-technical reasons, say a marketing agreement between companies. Users tend to be independent and use

Check out current browser usage statistics at **browserwatch.internet. com**.

whichever browser they want regardless of corporate standards. And, you might even change jobs and start working for a company that uses the other browser. For all these reasons, you should be prepared to understand the JavaScript implementations of both Internet Explorer and Navigator.

For all those reasons, this course specifies to use both Navigator and Internet Explorer for the exercises you will do. You should use a 4.x or 5.x version, unless you are specifically testing for backward compatibility, as that is what this course was developed for.

TASK 1A-1:

Creating some simple scripts

Objective: To create a few simple scripts (in order to review how to write scripts), embed scripts in a Web page, and to learn the operational conventions this course will use.

1. **Open Navigator or Internet Explorer.**

2. In the Location (or Address) text box, **type javascript: alert("Hello World"); and press [Enter].**

Depending on whether you chose to use Internet Explorer 5.0 or Navigator, you will get either the first or second alert box as shown above. Both of these browsers let you enter JavaScript commands in the URL entry text box. You can use this feature to test simple commands or enter short scripts. Separate multiple JavaScript statements with semi-colons in order to enter more than one statement at one time.

3. **Click OK** to dismiss the alert box.

4. **Open the text editor you will use to write the scripts for this course.**

5. **Open the Data folder and open the blank.html file that you will find in that folder.** Blank.html is a template file that you can use as a starting point for the scripts that you will write during this course. It contains the basic HTML elements that comprise a typical Web page. It also contains two empty JavaScript script blocks—one in the <HEAD> section of the document and another in the <BODY> section of the document.

6. Now, you will add a simple script in the <BODY> section of the document. **In the script block in the <BODY> section, type `alert("Hello World");`**

7. **Save the file as firstscript.html.**

8. **Switch to your browser, whichever you prefer to use, and load firstscript.html.** Your browser interprets the JavaScript statement you entered, and an alert box with your message appears.

9. **Click OK** to dismiss the dialog box.

10. **Switch to your editor and change the JavaScript statement to read**

    ```
    document.write("Hello World");
    ```

11. **Save your changes, switch to your browser, and click Reload or Refresh , depending on your browser.** This is the general procdure you will use going forward in this course. You will write your scripts in your editor, switch to your browser, and load or reload the file to see your scripts in action.

    The change you made to the script causes the "Hello World" message to be written to the Web page rather than being displayed in an alert box.

12. **Switch to your editor and close firstscript.html.** You are done with it.

Script Errors

Browsers handle errors in scripts in different ways. Internet Explorer prior to version 5.0 and Navigator prior to the 4.06 release display a dialog box noting the error and giving "helpful" information about it. Newer versions of Navigator and Internet Explorer suppress error messages, hiding them from the average user who probably knows nothing about JavaScript. Navigator displays error messages in the *JavaScript Console* window, which is normally not visible.

Internet Explorer 5.0 also hides JavaScript error messages, displaying only a small indicator icon at the left end of the status bar.

 Done, but with errors on page.

Figure 1-1: *The indicator of a script error in Internet Explorer 5.0.*

If you double-click on that icon, the error dialog box is opened. Click the Show Details button to see the details of the script error. You can check an option in that dialog box so that error message dialog boxes will always be displayed. This is a useful option to set, so that you can detect errors in the scripts you write.

A demonstration version of Allaire's HomeSite HTML editing tool is included on the CD-ROM that accompanies this course. If you are using a Windows-platform computer, we highly recommend you install HomeSite and use it as the editor for this course. We have also provided a quick overview of using HomeSite in the HomeSite folder on the disc.

The scripts you wrote here are obviously simplistic. Our main point here was to get used to the scripting procedures you will use going forward.

JavaScript Console: *A window, available in Navigator, that lists JavaScript errors and in which you can enter and execute JavaScript statements.*

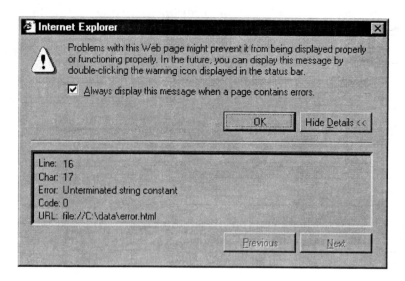

Figure 1-2: *Internet Explorer 5.0's script error dialog box after the Show Details button is clicked.*

Navigator is supposed to display a message in the status bar informing users that a JavaScript error has occurred. The message, when it appears, tells users to open the console window and instructs them how to do so. Unfortunately, Navigator is not very consistent in displaying such a message. As a developer, you will probably find this erratic behavior confusing and unhelpful. Quite possibly the only indication that a script error has occurred might be a blank window or incomplete page. Worse yet will be no visible indication that your script has failed.

JavaScript error: Type 'javascript:' into Location for details

Figure 1-3: *Navigator's unlikely-to-be-displayed indicator that a script error has occurred.*

To display Navigator error messages, type `javascript:` (make sure to include that full colon) into the Location box and press [Enter]. The JavaScript Console window will open. It shows not only the errors on the current page but any other errors that have occurred on any of the pages you have visited since you last cleared the window. The most recent errors are shown at the bottom of the list. Click the Clear button or close and re-open Navigator to clear the history of error messages.

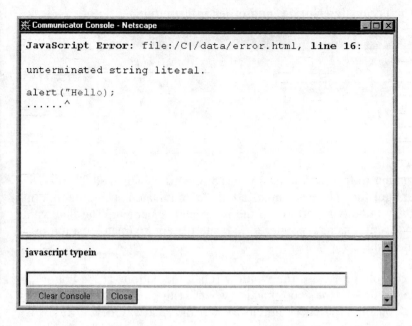

Figure 1-4: *The JavaScript Console window of Navigator 4.06 and newer.*

Both Microsoft and Netscape have released JavaScript debuggers—applications designed to help programmers write error-free code. You can download these applications for free from the vendors' Web sites:

- Netscape's JSDebug Java-based application is available at
  **http://developer.netscape.com/tech/javascript/index.html?content=
  /software/jsdebug.html**.

- Microsoft's Script Debugger Windows-based application is available at
  http://msdn.microsoft.com/scripting/default.htm?/scripting/debugger.

TASK 1A-2:

Examining script errors with Navigator and Internet Explorer

1. **Open error.html in Navigator.** The script on this page includes an error that will enable you to see how each browser handles and displays script error information.

2. Navigator gives no indication that an error has occurred. **Open the JavaScript Console window by typing `javascript:` in the Location box and pressing [Enter].**

As soon as you begin typing into the Location box, its label changes to Go To.

3. **Observe the error, description, and other information.**

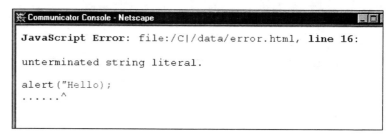

The information in the console tells you that the error happened on line 16 of the error.html file. The error involved an "unterminated string literal." In other words, a quote was left out of the `alert()` statement. The line with the dots and caret acts as a pointer to indicate the approximate position on the line where the error is located.

4. **Clear the console and close the window** (click the buttons at the bottom of the console window). It is good practice when writing and debugging scripts to clear the console after checking out each error. That way new errors will be obvious and clearly identifiable.

5. **Open error.html in Internet Explorer.**

6. **Double-click on the error indicator icon at the left end of the status bar** to open the error message dialog box. (The "Done, but with errors on page" message might be quickly replaced by a simple "Done" message. But, the exclamation point icon remains, telling that there truly was an error on the page.)

7. **Click Show Details** 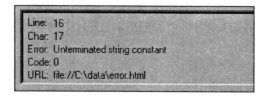. Then check out the dialog box and its line/column number

```
Line: 16
Char: 17
Error: Unterminated string constant
Code: 0
URL: file://C:\data\error.html
```

Internet Explorer gives you the same information as Navigator in regards to errors. Instead of graphically showing you where on the line the error is located, Internet Explorer tells you which character on the line is causing the error with the Char: # line. Internet Explorer does not include a sample of the line, as Navigator does.

8. **Check the Always Display This Message When A Page Contains Errors check box, then click OK.**

That way, the error message dialog box will be displayed automatically when script errors are encountered. This is a useful option for JavaScript programmers to enable.

When writing and debugging scripts, clear the console after checking out each error. That way new errors will be obvious.

We assume you are using Internet Explorer 5.0. If not, the error message dialog box will be opened automatically.

9. **Open error.html in your editor. Using the information provided by the browser error indicators, locate the error in the file.**

10. **In your opinion, which browser's error handling mechanism is better?**

11. **Correct the error in the error.html file and reload it in each browser.**

Topic 1B

JavaScript Programming Basics

Programming in any language involves writing statements that follow the language's *syntax* and that use the components available in the language. With JavaScript, you should follow the guidelines that dictate where you locate the code in the HTML that comprises the page. And, you should always follow the programming best-practices and the conventions of the language.

JavaScript Syntax

JavaScript is a case-sensitive programming language, much to the dismay of many who try to use it. Using `document.lastModified` will reference the date and time the Web page was last changed and saved; using `document.lastmodified` will get you a useless value of "undefined." If you're careful as you write your scripts to make the case match the language's specification, you'll be all set.

Fortunately, JavaScript is very forgiving with line breaks, line terminators, and white space. Not all languages are so forgiving. With JavaScript, you can break lines nearly anywhere, even in the middle of a statement! The language specification calls for each line to be terminated with a semicolon ";" but that is entirely optional. Some books, including this one, include the semicolon on every line. But, you can skip it if you want. Including the semicolon is good habit and will prepare you for other programming languages like Java that aren't so flexible. Finally, you can add white space (extra spaces and tabs) just about anywhere and JavaScript won't care.

Some JavaScript statements use brackets or parentheses to enclose *blocks of code*. You must use the specified type of bracket—the parentheses, square-bracket, or curly-bracket—when they are called for. And, you must use them in pairs. So, if you start enclosing a block of code with a curly-bracket "{" you must finish the block with another "}" or the JavaScript interpreter will report an error. You'll see how each of these brackets are used as you learn the features of the language. For now, just remember that they must be used in pairs.

syntax:
The rules that dictate how programming language statements are entered in order to create an error-free program.

code block:
A set of statements that are referenced as a unit.

Quotes are also used in matching pairs. If you start a string with a double-quote, you must finish with a double-quote. You can use either single- or double-quotes; just use them in matching pairs.

TASK 1B-1:

Examining JavaScript syntax and the forgiving nature of JavaScript

Objective: To see how you can break lines nearly wherever you want and still have your scripts run without a hitch.

1. **Open whitespace.html in your editor.** This sample file contains a script already completed for you. You will use this script to investigate JavaScript syntax and the forgiving nature of the language.

2. **Observe the use of line terminators.**

   ```
   var sadDay = new Date(1986, 0, 28);
   var today = new Date();
   var diff = today - sadDay
   var msPerDay = 1000 * 60 * 60 * 24
   diff = diff / msPerDay;
   diff = Math.round(diff);
   ```

   Demonstrating the language's forgiving nature, the first two lines of code have semicolon line terminators. The next two lines do not. JavaScript doesn't care.

3. **Open the file in your browser.** The script runs just fine, printing out a message noting the time since the Challenger space shuttle disaster

4. **Switch back to your editor. Add blank spaces and line breaks wherever you please. Save the file and reload it in your browser.** With only a few exceptions, you can add spaces and line breaks nearly anywhere in the file and the script will run without a hitch.

5. **What are a few locations where if you enter spaces or line breaks you will cause an error?**

6. **If necessary, switch to your editor. Look at the first line with the `document.write()` statement.** It outputs a message to the Web page.

   ```
   diff = Math.round(diff);
   document.write("<P>It has been " + diff + " days since the
   Space Shuttle Challenger exploded in flight.</P>");
   ```

   The text that is written to the page is enclosed in double quotes.

7. **Change the double quotes to single quotes throughout the `document.write()` statement** on line 18.

8. **Save your changes and reload the file in your browser.** It should still load without errors

9. Now, **switch back to your editor and change any one of the single quotes in the first `document.write()` statement to a double quote.** By doing so, you create a mismatched pair.

10. **Save your changes and reload the file in your browser.** The page should now generate an error. Depending on which browser you are using, you might get an error dialog box or just get an empty Web page.

11. You should fix your "mistake" before moving on. **Change the mismatched quotes back to a matching set. Save and test your changes.**

Language Components

The JavaScript language is made up of literals, identifiers, functions, objects, properties, methods, and event handlers.

Component	Definition
Literal	A Value, such as the number 43.5543, used in your code.
Identifier	A variable name (such as "x") that refers to some value, function, object, property, or method.
Function	A set of JavaScript statements collected into a group, given a name, and used elsewhere in the script. For example, you might write a function to calculate the wind chill based on wind speed and temperature. Then, as users enter data into a form, the wind chill gets calculated by your function. Your script defines the function in one place, but calls it (uses it) from someplace else.
Object	A compound data type that you could think of as a group of related variables and functions accumulated into a package with a distinct name. For example, the Window object, which represents the browser window, has variables (properties) that describe it, and functions (methods) that act on it.
Property	A variable associated with an object, akin to a characteristic of that object. The Document object, for example, has the `bgColor` property. That property desribes ans sets the background color of the document (Web page).
Method	An action that can be performed on or by an object. For example, the Document object has the `open()` method, which you can use to open new documents (Web pages).
Event handler	A function that gets invoked when a particular "event" happens. An event is something that happens, such as the user clicking a button or when a page finishes loading. For example, the Window object has an `onload` handler that gets called when the Web page finishes loading.

By putting these language components together into a combination that accomplishes some action, you create a JavaScript *statement* You could think of a statement as being a complete JavaScript command. Therefore, JavaScript programs are collections of statements.

Here is probably a good time to point out the print conventions this book uses to make clear the JavaScript and HTML components being described.

- JavaScript language components, HTML tags, variable names, and values are printed in a `monospaced` font to clearly differentiate them from the surrounding text.

- Blocks of sample JavaScript codes are shown in paragraphs like this:

```
<SCRIPT LANGUAGE="JavaScript">
alert("Hello");
</SCRIPT>
```

- In code listings, HTML tags are shown in all capital letters, except HTML event handler attributes, which are shown in mixed case. JavaScript statements are shown as appropriate for the language, which usually means in lowercase.

- Object names are expressed with a leading capital letter when the objects are referred to generically. For example, the Window object represents the browser window. When referring to a specific instance of an object, such as when referring to sample code, the case of object names match their programmatic use. For example, you can display an alert box using the `window.alert()` method.

Putting Code in Web Pages

The <SCRIPT> tag

JavaScript statements in a Web page must generally be enclosed within `<SCRIPT>` and `</SCRIPT>` tags, or they will be interpreted by the browser as text to be displayed the Web page. There are a couple of exceptions to that rule that we'll cover in a minute.

In its full specification, the opening tag includes additional information designed to tell the browser information about the script enclosed in the script block. The `LANGUAGE` attribute describes what scripting language the enclosed script uses.

Language attribute	Used to denote
JavaScript	A Script written in JavaScript.
JavaScript1.1	A script written in JavaScript version 1.1.
JavaScript1.2	A script written in JavaScript version 1.2.
JavaScript1.3	A script written in JavaScript version 1.3.
JavaScript1.4	A script written in JavaScript version 1.4.
VBScript	A script written in Micorsoft's VBScript scripting language.

The SRC attribute can be used to load an external JavaScript code file. The value of the SRC attribute is a filename and path to the file.

Finally, the TYPE attribute specifies the MIME type of the data enclosed between the script tags. For JavaScript, TYPE="text/javascript" is the appropriate attribute to use. This attribute is required for HTML 4.0 compliance but is optional with 3.2 and earlier. Whether you include or omit this attribute is up to you.

Location in the HTML Code

Script blocks can be put anywhere within a Web pages HTML coding. However, typically they are put in just a few spots. Script blocks that define code to be run as soon as the page starts loading or that define functions that are not used immediately are typically put between the <HEAD> and </HEAD> tags. Some programmers put these script blocks at the very beginning of the <BODY> section of the document.

Immediate scripts , those that should be executed as the page is loading, are put wherever they are needed in the HTML code. Scripts that depend on portions of the HTML content are often put at the very end of the Immediate scripts. Those that should be executed as the page is loading, however, are put wherever they are needed in the HTML code. Scripts that depend on portions of the HTML content are often put at the very end of the <BODY> section. Putting them there ensures that the HTML components exist before the script begins manipulating them. (An error might occur if you didn't take this sort of precaution.)

There are many ways to include JavaScript code in a Web page, but only two are widely used. The first is the script block described above. The other is to code into the event handler attribute for an HTML element. An HTML form button tag includes the onClick attribute, for example. You can enter JavaScript code as the value of that attribute and your code will be executed when the button is clicked. You will learn about these as you learn about forms, documents, and so forth throughout this course.

TASK 1B-2:

Examining how JavaScript code can be included in a sample file

1. **Open lottery.html in your browser.** This sample file generates lottery numbers within the range of numbers you specify.

2. **Click Generate Numbers** to see how numbers are generated and put into the output text boxes.

3. **Open lottery.html in your editor.**

Absent from this list are Microsoft's JScript and ECMA's ECMAScript. Those languages do not have their own language attribute values. Instead, both use the same language attribute values noted in this table.

deferred scripts:
Scripts that are interpreted, but not executed, as the page is loading.

immediate scripts:
Scripts that get executed as the page is loading.

4. **Observe the code block in the `<HEAD>` section.** This code is interpreted when the page loads. Because it defines a function, the code isn't executed then.

```
<HEAD>
     <TITLE>Random number generator</TITLE>
<SCRIPT LANGUAGE="JavaScript">
<!--

function lotto(frm)
  {
  var range = frm.range.value - 1;
  for(i=2; i<8; i++)
    {
    var lottoNum = Math.random()*range + 1;
    frm.elements[i].value=Math.round(lottoNum);
    }
  }
//-->
</SCRIPT>
</HEAD>
```

5. **Observe the code in the `onClick` attribute of the form button.** This code will be executed when the button is clicked.

```
<input type="button" value="Generate numbers" onClick="lotto(this.form);">
```

6. Finally, **observe the code in the `<BODY>` section.** It gets interpreted as the page is loaded and interpreted (parsed, in browser terms). It writes the date the file was last modified to the page.

```
<P></P>
<SCRIPT LANGUAGE="JavaScript" TYPE="text/javascript">
<!--
document.write("Last modified: " + document.lastModified);
//-->
</SCRIPT>

</BODY>
```

Coding Best-Practices

The JavaScript language specification gives you broad flexibility for how you write your script code. However, there are certain guidelines you should follow in order to make your code easy to read (by people), easy to write, easy to debug, and easy to maintain.

Comments

Comments are lines or statements in your JavaScript code that are not executed by the JavaScript interpreter. Nearly every programming language supports comments in one form or another. Their primary purpose is to give you a way to note the logic, purpose, or context of the code right in the code itself.

JavaScript supports two types of comments: the single line and the multiple line comment. Single line comments are useful for short notes or to explain single lines.

```
// single line comments start with the double slash
// everything to the end of the line is ignored
```

Multi-line comments are not used as often, though they are often useful for debugging.

```
/* Multi-line comments begin with the slash and asterisk and go
on until the closing asterisk and slash */
```

This form of comments is useful for long comments or to temporarily comment-out a problematic block of code.

In traditional languages, comments are stripped out of the code as the source code is compiled into executable form. JavaScript isn't compiled, so there isn't an automatic method for removing comments when they aren't needed. Comments in your JavaScript code can have a small but potentially noticeable impact on download time.

Thus, you should use single line comments to clearly annotate your code wherever such comments will make later reading and debugging easier. However, don't go overboard and comment every line or you could add noticeably to file size and download delay.

White Space and Consistent Indenting

White space is the extra spaces or line breaks that you add to make your code more readable. You should add white space liberally to your files, as it greatly enhances the readability of the files. Adding white space does not significantly increase the size of files. So, it has little downside other than being a tad bit more involved to write.

One way in which white space is used is to consistently indent blocks of code. Functions, if statements, and loops gather many lines of code into one block. Consistent use of white space, indents, and line breaks will make those blocks easier to identify, associate, and debug.

Case

Obviously, you must use the proper case of JavaScript language components. However, you do have quite a bit of flexibility with HTML tags. HTML is not case sensitive. Given that your scripts will be embedded within an HTML document in most situations, you can use uppercase or lowercase characters to make some aspects of your code stand out.

Generally, Web page authors and JavaScript programmers put HTML tag names and attribute names in all uppercase. Event handler attributes are almost universally noted in a mixed case format, where "on" is in lowercase, the next letter is capitalized, and the remainder is lowercase. For example, `onClick=""` is how the handler would be noted for a typical button element. Most JavaScript code needs to be in lowercase—with exceptions of course. Following the convention of all uppercase for HTML helps make clear what in the file is HTML and what is JavaScript code.

Variable and Function Name Choices

JavaScript lets you name your variables and functions just about any way you want, provided you start the name with a letter. So, you could name all your variables and functions with single letters. You'd hate yourself later for doing so. Just imagine trying to debug a 200 line script six months later that uses names like x, y, and z.

Instead, use meaningful yet short names. The purpose of a variable named `currentDate` is much easier to decipher than `dt`. The intention of a function named `calcSalary` is pretty clear, even out of context.

Many JavaScript programmers use a mixed-case format for variable and function names, generally believing them easier to type and read. So, instead of using `current_date`, you would typically see other programmers using `currentDate`. Choose a style that meets your needs, and then be consistent.

Line Terminators

You do not have to use, or even be consistent in using, line terminators (the semi-colon at the end of a line). However, you should adopt a style and stick with it. Line terminators are like periods at the ends of sentences. You can write without them, but they make for easier reading and more consistent style if you always include them (or always leave them out).

Hiding Your Code

Not everyone surfs the Web with Navigator or Internet Explorer. Almost none of the non-mainstream browsers, such as CyberDog or Mosaic, support JavaScript. Very old versions of the mainstream browsers also cannot handle JavaScript-laden Web pages without encountering errors.

Most browsers are built to ignore tags they don't recognize. Most every browser will ignore the `<SCRIPT>` and `</SCRIPT>` tags themselves. What comes between those tags is fair game, as far as most browsers are concerned.

Such non-JavaScript-enabled browsers will typically attempt to read your JavaScript code as if it were HTML text. Imagine getting a page of code when you expected some sort of readable text! While few people will actually be affected in this way, JavaScript programmers consider it good practice to hide their code from older browsers.

```
<SCRIPT LANGUAGE="JavaScript">
<!--
your code
// -->
</SCRIPT>
```

In the preceding code example, you can see the general procedure for hiding your code from older browsers. JavaScript recognizes the HTML start-of-comment tag as a single-line comment, as it is used in the second line of the preceding sample. The JavaScript interpreter will ignore that line, while non-JavaScript-compatible browsers will see it as the beginning of a block of HTML comments. Your code comes next, where it is accessible to the JavaScript interpreter yet hidden from browsers. To finish the comment block, as far as HTML is concerned, you need the —> closing tag. Unfortunately, JavaScript doesn't recognize that as a comment. So, you must precede it with the JavaScript single-line comment identifier. Thus, as far as the ancient browsers are concerned, the HTML comment block is closed.

TASK 1B-3:

Examining scripts that do and don't follow the coding best-practices guidelines

1. **Open mathpage.html in your browser.**

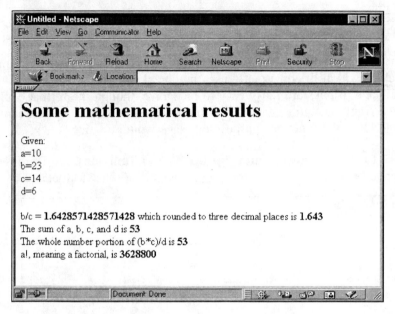

This page uses JavaScript to perform some mathematical calculations.

2. **View the source code for mathpage.html** (choose View→Source Code or View→Source, depending on your browser).

3. **Observe all the code in the `<HEAD>` section of the document.** It is all hidden from non-JavaScript-enabled browsers.

4. **Check out the first function, `r()`. Do you find this code easy to read and figure out?**

```
function r(v, p)
{ if(arguments.length != 2) {
alert("Requires two parameters."); return null; }
v = v * Math.pow(10,p);
v = Math.round(v);
v = v / Math.pow(10,p);
return v; }
```

5. **Identify some problems with this functions code.**

The name is not very descriptive: r-what? Similarly, the variable names within the function are equally cryptic. A comment or two might help make clear this functions purpose. No extra spacing is included to make the function readable. Finally, placement of the curly-brackets is not consistent, making it difficult to determine what code belongs with which block. Don't write your code this way.

> Netscape Navigator 4.6 seems to occasionally have troubles with scripts hidden in this way. It sometimes interprets the <!— sequence as <!C- and then reports a JavaScript error. Examination of the JavaScript code will convince you that there's no C in your code, but Navigator will fail anyway. Perhaps hiding code won't be the recommended practice going forward!

6. **Look at the `sum()` function.** What has been improved with this function and what could still be improved?

```
function sum() {
var add = 0;
for (i=0; i < arguments.length; i++) {
  add += arguments[i];
  }
return add;
}
```

The `sum()` function has a meaningful name and uses understandable names for variables within. It consistently uses line breaks to clearly place the curly-brackets. Blocks are fairly easy to recognize, though the format could be clearer. Some indenting is used, but more would be better. A short comment describing the functions purpose or usage would be nice.

7. **Compare the `wholenum()` and `factorial()` functions.** Do you notice a difference between them? Do you prefer one or the other format?

```
function wholenum(val)
{
    // returns the whole number portion of num
    if(arguments.length != 1)
    {
    alert("To use the wholenum() function, you must pass one value.");
    return null;
    }
    return val - (val % 1);
}
```

```
function factorial(val)
    {
    // computes the factorial of val (val times each of the numbers
    // smaller than it)
    if(arguments.length != 1)
        {
        alert("To use the factorial() function, you must pass one value.");
        return null;
        }
    if(val <= 1)
        {
        return 1;
        }
    return val * factorial(val - 1);
    }
```

The `wholenum()` and `factorial()` function are nearly identical, except that the indenting of code is exaggerated in the latter function. This makes code blocks very easy to recognize. Each is well-commented and named.

The coding format illustrated in the `factorial()` function is the style used in this course. We believe this is the most human-readable style of code formatting, even though it is admittedly non-standard. The format used in the `sum()` function is more typically used, yet we feel it is harder to read. For example, if you look at code samples provided by Netscape or other industry experts, you will encounter the format used in the `sum()` function. As teaching you JavaScript is our mission, we have chosen the format we feel best meets the needs of the learner. You can adopt whichever style you prefer, but we do recommend you stick to our style during the course.

8. **Close the source code window.**

Summary

In lesson 1, you looked at the basics of JavaScript. You learned about the different flavors of JavaScript. You examined the syntactical structure, JavaScript's rules. You checked out how the browsers handle and alert you to errors in scripts. And you reviewed some good coding practices. You should now have a solid foundation on which to build your JavaScript programming skills.

Apply Your Knowledge 1-1

Suggested Time:
10 minutes

In this activity, you will correct the poor coding practices in the mathpage.html file. Don't concern yourself with what is going on in the code. You'll learn plenty about how this code works during the rest of this course. Right now, you're concerned with form, not function.

1. Open mathpage.html in your editor.

2. Improve the readability and style of the `r()` function by adding line breaks and spaces. Line up the curly-brackets following the style of the `factorial()` function.

3. Add a comment noting that this function rounds a number to the precision specified.

4. Change the indenting and white space usage of `sum()` and `wholenum()` to match that of `factorial()`.

5. Add a comment to the `sum()` function stating that it adds up all the numbers provided

6. Save your changes and test for functionality by opening the page in your browser. Changing the white space, indenting, and adding comments to this code should not cause any changes in how it runs. If you now encounter errors, you might have changed something else in one of these blocks of code. Don't worry about fixing it at this point. You can do that some other time, when you're more comfortable with JavaScript programming.

Lesson Review

1A Describe how Internet Explorer and Navigator display error messages when JavaScript coding errors are encountered.

1B List the seven language components of JavaScript.

What is a statement in JavaScript?

JavaScript Building Blocks—Variables and Operators

Data Files
blank.html
object numerator.html
specialvars.html
varlimits.html
autocvt.html
tostring.html
average.html

Lesson Time
1 hour, 50 minutes

Overview

Variables represent your data, and like your data they can be simple or complex. We'll explore the types of variables available in JavaScript, how you can create them, use them, and, when necessary, destroy them.

To manipulate your data, you will need the JavaScript operators. JavaScript supports a wide range of operators, from simple addition to the complex assignment-with-operation operator. We'll examine the operators available and explore the order in which they are evaluated.

Objectives

In this lesson, you will:

2A **Examine the data types and variable types that JavaScript supports.**

You will use a few simple scripts to examine the data types that JavaScript supports.

2B **Explore the detailed rules governing the creation, use, and manipulation of data types and variables.**

With the scripts that you will write in this topic, you'll see how JavaScript handles variables, supports various data types, and how it automatically, or manually, converts between those data types.

2C **Explore the operators that let you manipulate your data.**

You'll examine the mathematical, string, and comparison operators that you can use to manipulate data in JavaScript.

Topic 2A

Variables and Data Types

JavaScript offers a wide range of data types to support your programming needs. You have probably used many of them in the scripts you have written or examined. This section carefully introduces each of the data types in order to give you both a broad overview of the types available as well as detailed information of the capabilities and limitations of each.

Primitive Data Types

Primitive data includes numbers, strings, booleans, and null values. These simple data types reference one data value at a time. For example, a number represents just one number. You'll see why we're making this distinction in a minute when we introduce the composite data types.

Numbers can have integer (whole numbers), floating-point (numbers with fractional components), octal (base-8 numbers), and hexadecimal (base-16 numbers) values. Strings are zero or more characters enclosed in quotes. Booleans are true-false values. And `null` is a non-value, one that is empty of all value.

You can use any of these primitives as literal values in your programs. The following code snippets are all legal uses of primitives.

```
alert(4 + 3);          // displays 7 in an alert box
alert(true);           // displays true in an alert box
alert("my message");      // displays the string in an alert box
```

You will certainly find uses for literals in your programs. But to make these data types more useful, you can store these values in *variables* . Variables are placeholders that represent the data you put in them. Variables can contain any of the primitive data types. Check out these code fragments.

```
var x = 4;          // create the variable x and assign
                    // a value to it
alert(x);           // displays 4 in an alert box
x = x + 2;
alert(x);           // displays 6 in a dialog box
```

To create a variable, you declare it; that's what's happening in line 1 of the code above. The var keyword informs the JavaScript interpreter that you are declaring a variable. x is the variable name. It's only natural to read the line as if it were saying "set x equal to 4." More precisely, this should be read "put the value 4 into the variable x." Why this matters might become clearer with another example.

```
var x = 4;       // declare the variable x and assign a value
var y;           // declare y but don't assign a value
y = x;           // put the value of x into y
x = 6;           // change the value for x
alert(y);        // displays 4
```

In line 3, y is assigned whatever the value x has at that point in the program. Changing x later doesn't change y—y isn't equal to x. The value of x was "put into" y at line 3. Of course, most people still use the "equal to" phrase when they read such code.

TASK 2A-1:

Using variables and simple data types

1. **Open blank.html in your editor** . This is a template file that you can use for your programming tests. It contains two empty script blocks, one in the <HEAD> section and one in the <BODY>.

2. **In the <BODY> section of the document, enter the following code into the empty code block:**

```
var pi = 3.141529;
var radius = 4;
var area = "<P>The area is ";
var circum =""<P>The circumference is ";
area = area + (pi * radius * radius);
circum = circum + (pi * radius * 2);
document.write(area + circum);
```

There is a built-in value for pi. It is a constant of the Math object. For simplicity's sake, we aren't using it here.

3. **Save the file as var.html.**

4. This program declares some variables of different types.

   Identify the variables that hold the floating-point, integer, and string values.

5. **Open var.html in your browser.** The variables in the script are declared, then manipulated (new values are calculated), and the results are displayed in your browser.

6. **In your editor, close var.html.**

Composite Data Types

In the examples above, each of the variables held just one value. The variable x held the value 4 until it was changed. x couldn't hold more than one value. Primitive variables like that store just one value. JavaScript supports two types of variables that can hold more than one value: arrays and objects.

composite data type: *Data types that reference more than one value.*

Arrays

Arrays are collections of values referenced with one name. You could think of arrays being like cars in a train. A train can have more than one car. Some cars in a train might be tank cars; others might be boxcars. Old fashioned trains even pulled a caboose. The collection of cars makes up the train, which for scheduling purposes might get a number. When referring to an arrival schedule, passengers would refer to the whole train using its number.

In the JavaScript world, an array also gets a single name (not a number) and can hold many values. You use a special notation to create arrays, populate them with values, and access the individual values in the array.

```
var myArray = new Array();        // create the array
myArray[0] = 1;            // populate it
myArray[1] = "some cute message";
myArray[2] = true;
alert(myArray[1]);          // displays "some cute message"
```

The code above shows the standard method for declaring and populating an array (there are other methods). You use the special keyword new with the `Array()` object to create the array. Then, you populate each member of the array with simple assignments. The number within the brackets designates which of the arrays elements to manipulate. The tricky part is that array elements are numbered using zero-based numerals; thus, the first element in an array is numbered 0.

ordinal numbering:
Sequences of numbers that begin with zero. For example, arrays use ordinal numbering to address the members of the array: the first element of an array is numbered 0.

Arrays are useful in many situations. They are typically used when you have related data to store. For example, if you had a Web form that asked users to list their favorite three movies, you could use three separate variables to store the results. Or, you could use a single array to store the same information.

```
var favMovies = new Array();
favMovie[0] = "The Shining""";
favMovie[1] = "Platoon";
favMovie[2] = "Monty Python: Search for the Holy Grail";
```

JavaScript provides many built-in arrays that you will find very useful. For example, each of the images on a Web page is automatically stored in an array. You can use JavaScript to manipulate those images by accessing them in the `images[ ]` array. Remember the ordinal numbering system for accessing elements of an array—the first image on the page is `images[0]` not `images[1]`.

TASK 2A-2:

Exploring arrays

1. **Open blank.html in your editor.**

2. **In the script block in the `<BODY>` section of the document, enter the following code:**

    ```
    var beatles = new Array();
    beatles[0] = "John";
    beatles[1] = "Paul";
    beatles[2] = "George";
    beatles[3] = "Ringo";
    document.write(beatles);
    ```

3. **Save the file as arraytest.html.**

4. **What is the value of the third element of the `beatles[]` array and what is its number?**

5. **Load the page in your browser to run the script. How is the data output?**

Objects

Objects are a composite data type like an array. Objects form the underpinnings of JavaScript, as it is an object-oriented programming language. Like arrays, objects reference a collection of values with a single name. However, objects have some additional features that arrays cannot match. Objects can do things, and objects can react to events.

Objects have three characteristic components: properties, methods, and event handlers. You might see these referred to as the PMEs of the object. *Properties* are like variables. They hold values related to the object. An object can have one or many properties, and not all its properties have to be of the same type. Objects have *methods,* which are basically functions associated with the object. Methods let the object do something. Finally, objects can react to things that happen, like the user performing some action. You define event handlers, which are functions to be run when the associated event occurs.

You can compare objects to real world items. A cat could be considered an object. A cat has properties, like the color and length of its fur. Cats can do things, like meow, scratch the furniture, and run around maniacally with no provocation. And, cats can react to events, like appearing from nowhere at the sound of the can opener.

Let's see how to use objects and their PMEs, for many useful objects are built in to the JavaScript environment. Objects have names, like `window`, `document`, and `form`. To access a property, you write the name of the object, a dot (period), and the name of the property. For example, to access the property that stores the background color for the HTML document that contains the script, you must access the `bgColor` property of the `document` object, like this:

```
currColor = document.bgColor;      // puts current value of
                // bgColor into currColor
document.bgColor = "000000";       // sets black background
document.bgColor = currColor;      // resets color
```

You use the same technique with methods, except that method names always end with open and close parentheses.

```
document.write("Hello");      // writes hello to current document
document.write(document.lastModified);
                    // writes the date
                    // that the document
                    // was last modified
```

Notice in the second line of the code above, we write the value of a property of the `document` object to the Web page using a method of the `document` object. Pretty nifty.

object:
A composite data type with three characteristics: properties, methods, and event handlers.

property:
A characteristic of an object, akin to a variable. Properties store values related to the object.

method:
A characteristic of an object, akin to a function. Objects can be manipulated or can manipulate other data via their methods.

event handler:
A characteristic of an object, a function to be called when a particular event occurs.

event:
An action that happens, like a user clicking a button or a page finishing loading.

Event handlers are like a method-in-waiting. You define some operation that the object should do when a particular event occurs. *Events* are actions that happen—some are user-generated, like when a user clicks on a button in a form, while others are system-generated, like the `onload` event that is "fired" when the document finishes loading.

The variety of events that an object can react to are predefined by the creators of JavaScript. So, you have limited options for event handlers that you can define for each object. To assign an action to an object's event handler, you again use the dotted notation. Note that event handlers all begin with "on."

```
window.onload = alert("Done loading. Enjoy my page.");
```

In this case, when the document is fully loaded, an `onload` event is passed to the `window` object. The line above tells the window object what to do when it receives this event. In this case, display an alert dialog box with a superfluous name.

TASK 2A-3:

Exploring objects

1. **Consider how each of these real world objects can be thought of as objects. List a couple of their properties, and methods, and the events they would react to:**

    A golf ball, a telephone, and a baby.

2. **Open object enumerator.html in either browser.** This Web page presents three buttons, one each for the Window, Document, and Form objects that are built into JavaScript.

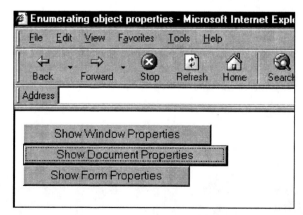

3. **Click on Show Window Properties.** The many properties of the Window object are written to the Web page by the script in this file.

4. **Check out a few of the properties.** Mainly, just observe that there are lots of properties for this built-in object. You don't need to be concerned with what they are or what they do.

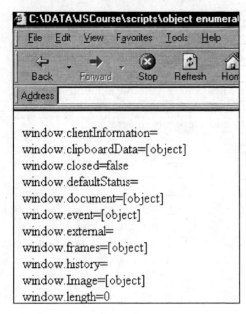

```
C:\DATA\JSCourse\scripts\object enumera
File   Edit   View   Favorites   Tools   Help

  ⇦          ➡          ⊗          🗘          🏠
 Back      Forward      Stop     Refresh     Hom
Address

window.clientInformation=
window.clipboardData=[object]
window.closed=false
window.defaultStatus=
window.document=[object]
window.event=[object]
window.external=
window.frames=[object]
window.history=
window.Image=[object]
window.length=0
```

5. **Click your browser's Back button.**

6. **Explore the many properties of either the Document or Form object. Click Back again when you're done.**

7. **Finally, if you used Navigator to perform these steps, repeat the steps with Internet Explorer. Or, use Navigator if you used Internet Explorer.** Each browser has its own selection of properties, which is made obvious by the script on this page.

Topic 2B

Using Variables and Literals

Declaring Variables

Let's circle back and talk about variables some more. We only briefly introduced variable *declaration* because our purpose was to lay the foundation for understanding what types of data JavaScript could support. Let's delve into the nitty gritty of variables and how you must deal with them in JavaScript.

When it comes to variables, arrays, and objects, JavaScript is a "helpful" language, much more so than languages like C++ or Java. If you forget to do something, JavaScript tries to help, often by doing it for you. Specifically, if you do not declare a variable, JavaScript doesn't care. It just creates the variable for you. The same holds true for object properties or array elements.

declare:
The process of creating a variable.

Let's see an example. As you know, JavaScript is a case-sensitive programming language. This and JavaScript's helpfulness can bite you.

```
var myVar;          // declare a variable but don't set it
myvar = 10;         // oops, now we have two variables
alert(myVar);       // gives a perhaps unexpected result
```

myVar and myvar are not the same in case-sensitive JavaScript. In some languages, line 2 would cause an error. We are using a variable without declaring it. JavaScript, on the other hand, simply creates a new variable for you. Line 3 displays an alert box with the word "undefined" as its contents. The same action would happen with properties of objects and elements of arrays.

Naming Variables

While we are talking about declaring variables, let's talk about how you should name them. There are certain rules and guidelines you must follow. Variable names must begin with an ASCII letter, an underscore, or a dollar sign (not supported in JavaScript 1.0). Subsequent characters in the name can be any of these items, plus numbers. Even though JavaScript 1.2 and ECMAScript support Unicode, you cannot use Unicode characters in your variable names. These rules also apply to function, object, array, and label names.

So, enough of the rules. How should you name your variables? It's up to you, but we would recommend you use logical and appropriate words or abbreviations for your variable names rather than single letters. The exception to this is variables used in loops or for simple counters. By convention, the letters i, j, k, w, x, y, and z are most frequently used as counter variables. If your variable names use more than one word or parts of words, mix case rather than using underscores. For example, use `dayOfWeek` rather than `day_of_week` for a variable used to hold a day of the week value. Mixed-case variable names are easier to type. Some think they are easier to pick out from a lot of code than are names built with underscores. The goal is to make your life easier when you have to debug or modify your code later on, so choose your variable names with care.

Undeclared, Undefined, and Not Defined

JavaScript makes a distinction between undeclared and undefined variables. An undeclared variable is one that you have not yet created. As explained above, if you attempt to set a value for an undeclared variable, JavaScript simply declares the variable for you.

If you declare a variable but don't give it a value and then try to read a value from that variable, JavaScript will return the special value of undefined. Such a variable is declared but `undefined`. Problematically, JavaScript does not consider this to be an error—an error message will not be generated. For this reason, you should always give a value to your variables when you declare them.

If you don't declare a variable but attempt to use its value, you will get an error. This is the case of the not defined variable.

TASK 2B-1:

Exploring undeclared, undefined, and not defined variables

1. **Open blank.html in your editor.**

2. **In the script block in the `<BODY>` section of the document, enter the following code:**

```
var x;
alert(x);
```

3. **Save the file as declare.html.**

4. **Open it in your browser.**

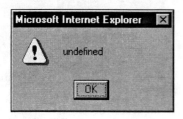

The dialog box contains the word "undefined." You declared but did not define the variable.

5. **Click OK.**

6. **Switch to your editor and change the code to read:**

```
var x = "";
alert(x);
```

7. **Save your changes and reload the page in your browser.**

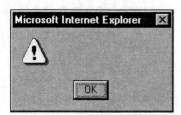

This time, the dialog box displays the empty string, though it probably just looks empty to you. You declared and defined a value for the variable.

8. **Click OK, and then switch to your editor and change the code to read:**

```
var x = 1;
alert(X);
```

Variable names must begin with an ASCII letter, an underscore, or a dollar sign (not supported in JavaScript 1.0). Subsequent characters in the name can be any of these items, plus numbers.

9. Save your changes and reload the page in your browser.

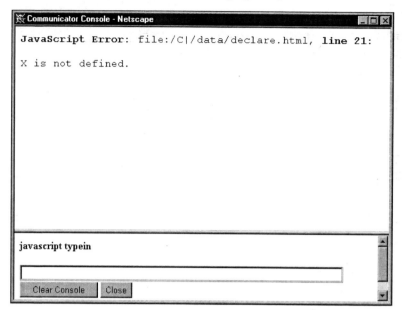

This time, the script generates an error. You declared and defined x, but are attempting to use the "not defined" variable X. The JavaScript interpreter considers this to be serious enough to generate an error message.

10. In your editor, close the file.

Special Data Values

NaN:
A special JavaScript data value that means "not a number."

JavaScript includes support for a few other special data values besides undefined. Chief among these is NaN, which stands for not a number. Case matters, and this value is *NaN* , not nan or NAN. The language specification says you should get this value if you divide a number by zero, for example (you don't, though). You will get this value returned if you try to perform math using a variable that doesn't have a numeric value (or one that can't be converted to a numeric value) in it.

```
var x = 1;
var y = "Hello";
var z = 0;
var x = x/z;        // NaN should be put into x, Infinity is
var w = x/y;        // NaN is put into w
```

The NaN value is supposed to be assigned to a variable when an illegal mathematical operation is used to set the value, as in the divide by zero operation in the code above. In some versions of JavaScript though, another special value, Infinity (case matters, here too), is assigned. Infinity represents a number greater than any number you can imagine. JavaScript has one more basic special value, that of -Infinity. As you would expect, -Infinity represents a number more negative than any number you can come up with (isn't the concept of infinity cool?).

TASK 2B-2:

Testing how JavaScript handles special variable conditions

1. **Open specialvars.html in your editor and observe the code.**

```
// declare our starting variables
var A;          // declare but don't assign a value
a = 10;         // assign a value
b = 0;          // assign a value

// display our starting variable conditions
document.write("<B>A = " + A + " ");
document.write("a = " + a + " ");
document.write("b = " + b + "</B><HR>");

// now, do the math to create the special variable conditions
document.write("A/a = " + A + "/" + a + " = " + A/a + "<BR>");
document.write("a/A = " + a + "/" + A + " = " + a/A + "<BR>");
document.write("a/b = " + a + "/" + b + " = " + a/b + "<BR>");
document.write("A/b = " + A + "/" + b + " = " + A/b + "<BR>");
document.write("b/a = " + b + "/" + a + " = " + b/a + "<BR>");
document.write("b/A = " + b + "/" + A + " = " + b/A + "<BR>");
```

This code defines three variables, A, a, and b, and then uses them in various combinations. The results of the mathematical operations with these three variables are written to the Web page with the `document.write()` method.

2. **Which, if any, of the lines of code do you think will cause a JavaScript error?**

3. **Open specialvars.html in either browser.**

A = undefined a = 10 b = 0
A/a = undefined/10 = NaN
a/A = 10/undefined = NaN
a/b = 10/0 = Infinity
A/b = undefined/0 = NaN
b/a = 0/10 = 0
b/A = 0/undefined = NaN

The results are displayed. Did they match your expectations?

Data Types and Converting Between Them

JavaScript supports a wide variety of data types that you can use in variables. These were introduced at the beginning of this topic, but we didn't go into too much depth at that point. Now, you'll get a chance to look at these variable types in more detail. JavaScript supports numbers, which include integer, floating-point, octal, and hexadecimal numbers; strings; Booleans; arrays; and objects. Each of these is described in more detail in the following sections.

Numbers

JavaScript represents all numbers in memory as 8-byte (IEEE standard) floating-point numbers. So, while you can make a distinction between integers and floating-point numbers, JavaScript essentially does not. JavaScript supports the following types of numeric data, with the range of values as noted.

integer:
A whole number, without a fractional component.

- *Integers* —whole numbers, without fractional components or a leading zero. Theoretically, they can range from -2^{53} (-9007199254740992) to 2^{53} (9007199254740992) . However, most integer operations are performed with 32-bit (four byte) numbers, making the reasonable range from -2^{31} to $2^{31}-1$.

  - If you use numbers outside of this smaller range, you might lose some precision in the right-most places. Valid integers include:

    4

    123

    9872345987

floating point number:
A real number that can have a fractional component.

- *Floating-point* —real numbers that can have fractional components. In JavaScript, these numbers can have positive or negative values from 5×10^{-324} to $1.7976931348623157\times10^{308}$. You can represent these numbers in your programs using the standard notation (digits, decimal point, then more digits) or in scientific notation, using an uppercase or lowercase E. Valid floating-point numbers include:

  5.123

  4.223e+23 (the plus sign is optional with positive exponents)

  -8.114E-12

octal number:
A whole number in the base-8 numbering system.

- *Octal* —base-8 numbers. In JavaScript, octals begin with a leading zero and can have one or more additional digits in the range of 0 - 7. In fact, JavaScript will interpret any number you enter with a leading zero as an octal number. Valid octal numbers include:

  01 (= 1 in base-10)

  027 (= 23 in base-10)

  0377 (= 255 in base-10)

hexadecimal number:
A whole number in the base-16 numbering system.

- *Hexadecimal* —base-16 numbers that begin with 0x or 0X and have one or more digits in the range of 0 though 9 and A through F (upper or lower case), which represent the base-10 numbers ten through fifteen. Valid hexadecimal numbers include:

  0x4 (= 4 in base-10)

  0xFF (= 255 in base-10)

  0Xcc99ff (= 13408767 in base-10)

Strings

Strings are letters, numbers, or spaces enclosed within quotes (either single or double, though they have to match). You can even create an empty string with " " (an empty pair of quotes). The ECMA specification calls for support of *Unicode* characters in strings. However, only IE 4.x and newer is compliant with this part of the specification. Navigator 4.x supports the Latin-1 subset of Unicode. Earlier browsers support either this subset or the ANSI/ASCII characters. So, you would be wise to stick with this limited subset of valid characters in your strings unless you can be sure of the browsers your users will be running.

You can include quoted substrings as long as you mix quotes. For example, "he said 'good day' to all those present" would be a valid JavaScript string. You can use additional special characters with escape sequences. Escape sequences are representations of characters that cannot otherwise be included in a string.

The following table lists the escape sequences supported by Javascript.

To represent	Use this escape sequence
Backspace	\b
Form feed	\f
New line	\n
Carriage return	\r
Tab	\t
Apostrophe (single quote)	\'
Double quote	\"
Backslash	\\
Latin-1 encoded character specified with octal digits (0–377)	\###, where # is an octal digit
Latin-1 encoded character specified with hexadecimal digits (00–FF)	\xx, where x is a hexadecimal digit
Unicode character specified with four hexadecimal digits 0000–FFFF (not supported in most browsers)	\xxxx, where x is a hexadecimal digit

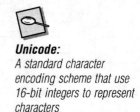

Unicode:
A standard character encoding scheme that use 16-bit integers to represent characters

Boolean Values

Boolean values are `true` and `false` values that you can use with the conditional statements. In some languages, you can use 1 or 0 to represent true and false. JavaScript is not one of those languages. However, see the section that follows on type declaration and conversion to see how JavaScript can in some ways support such a feature.

Arrays

JavaScript supports arrays whose members can be numbers, strings, booleans, objects, arrays, or a mix of any of these.

Objects

JavaScript supports built-in and custom objects, whose properties can contain values of any of the valid JavaScript data types.

TASK 2B-3:

Considering how JavaScript handles data types

1.   **Open varlimits.html in your editor.**

2.   **Examine the section of code that follows the comment "Integer handling."**

```
// Integer handling
document.write("<b>Integers</b>");
var i = 0;
for(pwr=52; pwr < 55; pwr++)
  {
  i = Math.pow(2,pwr);
  document.write("<BR>i = " + i + "  (which is 2<sup>" + pwr + "</sup>)");
  }
```

This code creates a loop. Each time through the loop, JavaScript calculates 2 raised to some power using the `Math.pow()` built-in function. The loop is set to calculate the values of 2^{52} through 2^{54}, which represent one order of magnitude smaller to one larger than the theoretical limit for JavaScript integers.

3.   **Open varlimits.html in your browser.**

4.   **Compare the output of the integer code to the limits given in the preceding text. Do integer limits really matter?**

Do not use HomeSite's internal browser (the Browse tab) to view this file. Doing so will crash HomeSite.

5.   **Switch back to your editor and examine the section of code that follows the comment "Floating-point handling."**

```
// Floating-point handling
document.write("<P><b>Floating-point numbers</b>");
var a = 1.7976931348623157e307;
document.write("<BR>a = " + a);
a = a*10;
document.write("<BR>a = " + a);
a = a*10;
document.write("<BR>a = " + a);
a = a/10;
document.write("<BR>a = " + a);
```

This code sets a value for a that is one order of magnitude smaller than the JavaScript limit for floating point numbers. Then, it multiplies the value by

10, displays the results, does so again, displays the result, and then divides by 10 and displays the results.

6. **Switch to your browser and compare the output of the floating point code to the values given in the preceding text. Do floating point limits really matter?**

7. **If you added the following code to the end of the floating point section of code, what do you think its results would be? Implement it and find out.**

```
a = a/a;
document.write("<BR>a = " + a);
```

CHECK YOUR SKILLS 2-1

Suggested Time:
5 minutes or less

Using blank.html as a starting point, write a script that would display the following message in an alert box. Make sure the quotes appear as shown here and that your message is formatted with an extra line between the lines of text. Refer to the proceeding table of escape codes, if necessary. Save your file as escapes.html and test it with either browser.

See xescapes.html for one possible script that would accomplish this objective.

Today's quote of the day is:

"On the Internet, nobody knows you're a dog."

Type Declaration and Conversion

As with variable declaration, JavaScript is very forgiving when it comes to the type of data you store in your variables. In some programming languages, you must not only declare that a variable exists but also assign a type to that variable before you can use it. Furthermore, with those languages, you cannot easily change the type of a variable (if at all) once it has been set. And, if you use a variable incorrectly, an error is generated.

JavaScript on the other hand doesn't seem to care—it is an untyped language. You might have noticed that you do not have to specify a type for your variables when you declare them. JavaScript has no such constructs. All you need to do is declare a variable and start using it (actually, all you need to do is start using the variable and JavaScript will create it for you).

It is completely legal in JavaScript to use a variable to hold numbers for part of your program then use it to hold a Boolean or string value in other parts. Of course, you might get confused when you try to later debug or modify your program. So, we don't suggest you do so.

JavaScript will also helpfully attempt to convert between data types if you use your variables in different ways. For example, if you have a variable that holds a number and you add it to a variable that holds a string, JavaScript will convert the number to a string and concatenate the two strings. This type of operation would simply cause an error in another programming language.

The following table shows the default actions JavaScript will take when attempting to convert variables.

If you use a	As a String	As a number	As a Boolean
String (non-emtpy)	the value of the string	Numeric value of string if possible or NaN	true
String (empty)	the value of the string	0	false
true	"true"	1	true
false	"false"	0	false
0	"0"	0	false
1 or any other number	the number enclosed in quotes	the number's values	true
NaN	"NaN"	NaN	false
null	"null"	0	false
Infinity	"Infinity"	"Infinity"	true
-Infinity	"-Infinity"	"-Infinity"	true
Array	Comma-separated list of array members	Non-convertible	Non-convertible
Object	Whatever is defined by the object's toString ( ) or functions or an error	Whatever is defined by the object's toString ( ) or toValue ( ) functions or an error	true

Of course, JavaScript can't convert between every combination of data types. For example, if you have a string with a value of "12 in a dozen", JavaScript will not be able to convert it to a number, even though it includes a number. With automatic string-to-number conversion, the string must contain only a number (no other characters). If your string starts with a number but includes extra characters, like our example above, you can use the parseInt() or parseFloat() functions to extract the number from the beginning of the string.

```
var w = "12 months in a year";
var x = "365.25 days in a year";
var y = parseInt(w);        // y equals 12
var z = parseFloat(x);      // z equals 365.25
var d = z/y;                // avg. days per mo. = 30.4375
```

If parseInt() and parseFloat() cannot convert the string to a number, these functions return the value NaN.

Mentioned in the preceding table is the toString() method. This is a method of all variables, objects, and arrays in JavaScript. It returns a string value for the item. Sometimes it can be a useful method. Sometimes, it's nearly useless. One useful purpose of this method is to force a number to be treated like a string. Then again, using it with an object typically produces a useless value like [object Object].

TASK 2B-4:

Converting between data types

Setup: Examine each of the following code blocks.

1. **What would be the value for z for each script?**

Example A:

```
var x = 2;
var y = "4";
var z = x * y;
```

Example B:

```
var x = 2;
var y = "4";
var z = x + y;
```

Example C:

```
var x = "2";
var y = "4";
var z = x + y;
```

Example D:

```
var x = true;
var y = "4";
var z = x + y;
```

Example E:

```
var x = true;
var y = 4;
var z = x + y;
```

2. **Open autocvt.html in your browser to see if you were right.** This sample file implements the code blocks from step 1.

3. **How might you override the default conversions that JavaScript makes?**

4. **Open tostring.html in your editor.**

5. **Check out the code in this file.** It declares four variables: an array, an object, a string variable, and a numeric variable. Then, using the `toString()` method, it displays the variables string equivalent.

6. **Open tostring.html in your browser.** The string value of each variable is written to the Web page. Using the method with an array produces a comma-separated list of the members of the array. Using it with an object produces a useless result. The string value of a string is obviously a string, so that's how it's used. And, the number, used as a string looks just as if it were a number.

Converting Numbers Between Bases

You can use the `parseInt()` and `toString()` methods to convert numbers with different bases. Each of these functions includes supports for a radix (base) parameter, as in `x.toString(radix)` and `parseInt(x, radix)`, where `x` is the number to be converted to a string and `radix` is the base by which to convert.

To convert from	to	Function (where x is the number to be converted)
Decimal	Octal	`y = x.toString(8);`
Decimal	Hexadecimal	`y = x.toString(16);`
Octal	Decimal	`y = parseInt(x, 8);`
Hexadecimal	Decimal	`y = parseInt(x, 16);`

Suggested Time:

20 minutes

Apply Your Knowledge 2-1

In this activity, you will write scripts that convert numbers between different numbering systems (bases).

1. In your editor, open the blank.html template file.

2. In the script block in the `<BODY>` section of the file, add a script that will convert the "normal" numbers 80, 255, and 32 to hexadecimal and convert the strings "FF", "CC", and "3A" (representing hexadecimal numbers) to "normal" numbers. Use the `document.write()` method to output your results to the Web page. Make sure your output notes the value before and after conversion, as in "80 is ## in hexadecimal."

3. Save your file as convert.html.

See xconvert.html for one possible script that would accomplish this objective.

4. Open it in either browser. If you encounter any coding errors, correct them and reload the file in your browser.

5. Modify your script to convert each of those numbers to binary. You'll need to convert the hexadecimal numbers to decimal, then to binary using two steps. You can't do it in one step. Save your file as binary.html and test it in your browser. A hint is provided in the answer section, if you are unsure of the method to use here.

See xbinary.html for one possible script that would accomplish this objective.

A Couple Extras

Garbage Collection

There is no way in JavaScript to destroy a variable. You can set its value to `null`, but the variable will still exist. This brings up the question of whether you need to worry about getting rid of old and unneeded variables? The answer is no. Unlike with other programming languages, JavaScript does *garbage collection* for you automatically. This means the JavaScript interpreter will detect when a variable, object, or array is no longer going to be used and will automatically free the memory associated with that item.

garbage collection:
The automatic process of detecting and destroying unused variables. Garbage collection is done for you by the JavaScript interpreter.

Reserved Words and Keywords

JavaScript reserves certain words that you cannot use for variable, function, or object names. These words are either keywords (names of JavaScript commands, functions, or objects) or *reserved words* (typically reserved for future use by the JavaScript designers).

reserved word:
Words designated as not to be used by JavaScript programmers. Reserved words will likely be used in future versions of JavaScript. Using them in your programs could cause compatibility problems with future versions of the language.

Actually, you can use the words that define the built-in JavaScript objects, properties, and methods for your variable and function names. However, in doing so you replace the built-in functionality with whatever you specify. This is a technique best left to very advanced JavaScript programmers who know exactly what they are doing in re-programming JavaScript itself.

JScript, Microsoft's JavaScript-clone, defines its own set of keywords and reserved words. For example, the word item is a keyword in JScript. The JScript keywords and reserved words are not included in this table.

abstract	alert	arguments	Array	blur
boolean	Boolean	break	byte	calle
caller	captureEvents	case	catch	char
class	clearInterval	clearTimeout	close	closed
confirm	const	constructor	continue	Date
debugger	default	defaultStatus	delete	do
document	doubl	else	enum	escape
eval	export	extends	false	final
finally	find	float	focus	for
frames	function	Function	goto	history
home	if	implements	import	in
Infinity	innerHeight	innerWidth	instanceof	int
interface	isFinite	isNaN	java	length
location	locationbar	long	Math	menubar
moveBy	moveTo	name	NaN	native
netscape	new	null	Number	Object
open	opener	outerHeight	outerWidth	package
Packages	pageXOffset	pageYOffset	parent	parseFloat
parseInt	personalbar	print	private	prompt
protected	prototype	public	RegExp	releaseEvents
resizeBy	resizeTo	return	routeEvent	scroll
scrollbars	scrollBy	scrollTo	self	setInterval
setTimeout	short	static	status	statusbar
stop	String	super	switch	synchronized
this	throw	throws	toolbar	top
toString	transient	true	try	typeof
unescape	unwatch	valueOf	var	void
watch	while	window	with	

Topic 2C

Operators

Operators let you manipulate your data. You can add, subtract, multiply, concatenate, and more with the JavaScript operators. JavaScript operators can be divided into three categories or types: unary, binary, and ternary. Unary operators work with one operand. For example, (-) is the unary operator to make a number or variable negative.

```
var x = -4;          // declare x as  negative number
                     // using unary negation
```

Binary operators work with two operands. Adding (+), subtracting (-), and modulus (%) are all binary operators. JavaScript supports a single ternary operator, the conditional statement. Ternary operators take three operands.

This table describes some of the JavaScript operators (yes, there are more than this), their type, and a description of the operation they perform.

operator:
Manipulators of data, noted with mathematical or punctuation symbols.

keyword:
The name of a JavaScript command, method, or object

Operator	Type	Description
.	Unary	Accesses an object's properties, methods, or event handlers.
++	Unary	Increment—adds one to the variable or value to which it is applied.
- -	Unary	Decrement—subtracts one from the variable or value to which it is applied.
-	Unary	Negation—makes a number or variable negative.
!	Unary	Logical complement—essentially a "not" as in != (not equal to) or !< (not less than).
*	Binary	Multiplication—multiplies two numbers or variables.
/	Binary	Division—divides two numbers or variables.
%	Binary	Modulus—calculates the remainder of the division of two numbers or variables.
+	Binary	Concatenation—concatenates two strings or variables that can be treated as strings.
+	Binary	Addition—adds two numbers or variables.
-	Binary	Subtraction—subtracts two numbers or variables.
&&	Binary	Logical AND—used in conditional statements to test for more than one criterion. For example if (x>0 && y < 100) ... (if x is greater than zero AND y is less than one hundred).
||	Binary	Logical OR—used in conditional statements to test for more than one criterion. For example if (x>0 || y< 100) ... (if x is greater than zero or y is less than one hundred).

Operator	Type	Description
? :	Ternary	Conditional operator—used to make a compact `if...then...else` statement.

The increment and decrement operators need a little clarification, for depending on how you use them you can get different results. If you place these operators before a number or variable, the variable is incremented, then used in whatever other operations. If you place these operators after a number or variable, the variable is used, then incremented or decremented. This is most often useful in a loop.

TASK 2C-1:

Using and evaluating the operators

1. Examine this code. What will be the value displayed for **x**?

    ```
    var x = 10;
    alert(x++);
    ```

2. Using blank.html as a template, enter the preceding code and save it to a file name of your choice. Load the file in your browser to test it. Were you right?

3. Modify the code so that line three reads `alert(++x);`. Now what is the value displayed for **x**?

CHECK YOUR SKILLS 2-2

1. Modify the code above to use the decrement operator (- -) proceeding the variable x. Test your changes. Then use it following the variable.

2. Create and test a short script that uses the modulus operator (%) with two numbers of your choice.

Suggested Time:
5 minutes or less

This lesson does not include the many bitwise operators that JavaScript supports.

Assignment Operators

JavaScript supports a variety of assignment operators, one of which you are sure to be familiar with. The standard assignment operator, =, assigns the value of the expression to the right of the equals sign to the variable to the left of the equals sign. Additionally, JavaScript supports assignment with operation operators that are handy shortcuts.

The following table lists some of the assignment operators supported by JavaScript.

Operator	Type	Description
=	Binary	Assignment
*=	Binary	Assignment with multiplication
/=	Binary	Assignment with division
%=	Binary	Assignment with modulus
+=	Binary	Assignment with addition
-=	Binary	Assignment with subtraction

Applications for the assignment with operation operators might not be intuitively clear. As an example, the following two lines of code are equivalent. The first line shows the notation you might be used to using to add 4 to the variable x and put the result back into x. The second line uses the assignment with addition operator to perform the equivalent operation.

```
x = x + 4;
x += 4;
```

TASK 2C-2:

Working with the assignment with operation operators

1. **Why would you use the assignment with operation operators?**

2. **Given a value of 23 for x, what would x equal after the following line was executed?**

```
x += 23;
```

3. **Given a value of 23 for x and 5 for y what would x equal after the following line was executed?**

```
x += y;
```

4. With the following block of code.

   What would be the displayed value of msg?

```
var msg = "forwards ";
msg += "backwards ";
alert(msg)
```

5. With the following block of code.

What would be the displayed value of msg?

```
var msg = "forwards ";
msg =+ " backwards ";
alert(msg);
```

Operator Precedence

If you use more than one operator within one statement, you will need to take heed of how JavaScript prioritizes the operations. Some operations are more "important" than others, thus are done first even if listed last. Consider this code:

```
var x = 1 + 2 * 3 - 4;
```

JavaScript does not simply evaluate from left to right. If it did, it would try to evaluate the = (assignment) operator before it did any of the math. Instead, first 2 and 3 are multiplied. Then, that result is added to 1. Finally, 4 is subtracted from the result.

Some operators share the same level of precedence. Adding and subtracting are considered to have the same level of importance. In this particular case, the operations are interpreted from left to right. This is called *associativity* and operators can be left-to-right associative or right-to-left associative.

The following table lists the common JavaScript operators, their precedence, and their associativity. The precedence column lists the order in which the operators are evaluated, so those listed with a 1 are evaluated first, before those listed with a 2 in that column. Those that have a matching precedence number are considered to be of equal priority. For those, consider the associativity column, which describes the order in which they will be evaluated.

Operator	Precedence	Associativity	Performs
.	1	Left-to-right	Property access
++	2	Right-to-left	Increment
--	2	Right-to-left	Decrement
-	2	Right-to-left	Negation
!	2	Right-to-left	Logical complement
*	3	Left-to-right	Multiplication
/	3	Left-to-right	Division
%	3	Left-to-right	Modulus
+	4	Left-to-right	Concatenation
+	4	Left-to-right	Addition
-	4	Left-to-right	Subtraction
&&	5	Left-to-right	Logical AND
||	6	Left-to-right	Logical OR
?:	7	Right-to-left	Conditional operator
=	8	Right-to-left	Assignment
*=	9	Right-to-left	Assignment with multiplication
/=	9	Right-to-left	Assignment with division
%=	9	Right-to-left	Assignment with modulus

Operator	Precedence	Associativity	Performs
+=	9	Right-to-left	Assignment with addition
- =	9	Right-to-left	Assignment with subtraction

Overriding Precedence and Associativity

Of course, you can override the default precedence and associativity using parentheses in your code. For example:

```
var x = (1 + 2) * (3 - 4);
```

This code overrides the defaults, forces JavaScript to add 1 and 2, subtract 4 from 3, and then multiply the results of those interim calculations.

The javascript: Pseudo-URL

Navigator and Internet Explorer 5.0 let you evaluate JavaScript statements that you enter into the Location (Address) field. To "tell" the browser that what you are entering is JavaScript code and not a URL, you must precede the statements with the `javascript:` identifier. This identifier is called the JavaScript pseudo-URL, as it is not a real URL. Separate multiple statements with semi-colons and press Enter when you're done to cause the browser to interpret your code. You'll have to use standard JavaScript output techniques, like writing to an alert box, in order to see the results of most operations, as the results won't be automatically written to the browser window.

TASK 2C-3:

A quick test of precedence

1. **Implement this script fragment using the Navigator or Internet Explorer javascript: pseudo-URL. Display the results of the calculation in an alert box.** (Enter the code into the Location / Address field, separate statements with semicolons, and press [Enter] to evaluate the code.)

    ```
    var x = 1 + 2 * 3 - 4; alert(x);
    ```

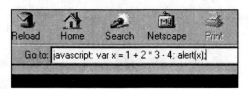

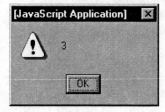

Figure 2-1: *The results of the calculation performed in step 1.*

See xaverage.html for one possible script that would accomplish this objective.

2. **Open average.html in your editor.**

3. **Complete the script that has been started for you to calculate the average of the test scores.** You should calculate the averages as percentage values (not fractions). Use the concatenation operator to include a percent sign in your output. You will need to use the JavaScript operators, consider operator precedence, and override the default precedence in order to perform this calculation. You should be able to use only one line of code to compute the averages of all the scores.

Special Operators

JavaScript supports a handful of additional, "special" operators. These are the `delete`, `typeof`, `void`, `new`, and `comma` operators, as described in the following table.

Operator	Type	Description
delete	Unary	Deletes object properties and array elements. With JavaScript 1.2, `delete` makes their value `undefined`. With prior versions, `delete` makes their values equal `null`. This operator is designed to be used with objects and arrays you create, not with the built-in objects. It has either no effect or unexpected effects with variables, especially those explicitly declared with `var`.
typeof	Unary	Determines the data type of its operand. Returns the following values for each of the items listed: • string-`"string"` • number-`"number"` • Boolean-`"boolean"` • object-`"object"` • function-`"function"`
void	Unary	Discards its operator value and returns `undefined`. One occasion when you might use this is if you want to test to see if a value is `undefined`. You would use `void` like this to accomplish that goal:`if(var== void(0) )` ...The `void (0)` returns `undefined` making the statement essentially, `if(var==undefined)`. The `0` in void `(0)` could be anything, as `void` simply discards the actual value of its operand.
new	Unary	Invokes the constructor function of the object, in other words, creates an instance of an object.
,	—	The comma operator lets you put multiple statements on a single line in a place in your JavaScript code that normally requires a single statement. For example, the `for` loop structure requires individual statements in its syntax. You could use the comma operator to bypass this limitation and execute multiple statements.

Summary

In lesson 2, you examined JavaScript's support for different types of data. You looked at how you can create and use the many types of variables supported by the language. And, you looked at the rich assortment of operators that you can use to manipulate your data.

Lesson Review

2A **List the six variable (data) types that JavaScript supports.**

2B **What keyword do you use to declare variables.**

Do you need to use that keyword?

2C **What is the difference between operator precedence and operator associativity?**

What does the += operator do?

JavaScript Building Blocks—Control Statements

Data Files
ifscript1.html
ifscript2.html
ifscript3.html
ifscript4.html
digiclock.html
forloop1.html
forloop2.html
forin.html
isNaN.html

Lesson Time
90 minutes

Overview

Control statements give you control over the flow of your programs. You can create loops or conditional statements, compare the values of variables, and enumerate the properties of objects using the JavaScript control statements. You'll learn about these language components in this lesson.

Objectives

To add logic and design to your programs, you will:

3A **Use the many control statements available in JavaScript.**

Without control statements, like the if, if-else, and switch statements, your programs would have to be very simplistic. In this lesson, you'll learn how you can control program flow using those and other related statements.

Topic 3A

Controlling the Flow—JavaScript Control Statements

control statements:
They let you control the flow
of your programs to create
loops, conditional
statements, compare the
values of variables, and
enumerate the properties of
objects.

Control statements do just that, control the flow of your programs. You may have encountered a few of these statements in your JavaScript explorations. Statements like if, for, and while are just some of the control statements supported by JavaScript.

Conditional Branching

Of the control statements, if is probably the most commonly used. This statement tests for criteria you specify and branches accordingly. The basic form of the statement is:

```
if(condition)
  {
  statements to do if condition is true;
  }
```

If only one statement is to be executed when condition is true, you can shorten this notation to fit on one line.

```
if(condition) statement;
```

The key to understanding how if works is to recognize that when condition evaluates to true, the statements will be evaluated. So, the code you use for condition can be anything that will evaluate to true or false, including those expressions that can be automatically converted to Boolean values.

Comparison Operators

The if statement (and the other conditional statements for that matter) rely on the comparison operators. These are:

Operator	Name	Description
==	Equal to	Tests that operand 1 equals operand 2; will perform automatic data conversion if necessary. See Identity.
!=	Not equal to	Tests that operand 1 does not equal operand 2; will perform automatic data conversion if necessary. See Non-identity.
>	Greater than	Tests that operand 1 is greater than operand 2.
>=	Greater than	Tests that operand 1 is greater than or equal to or equal to operand 2.
<	Less than	Tests that operand 1 is less than operand 2.
<=	Less than	Tests that operand 1 is less than or equal to or equal to operand 2.
===	Identity	Tests that operator 1 and 2 are identical, that is equal in value and of the same type—automatic data conversion will not be performed. Supported in Internet Explorer 4.0 and greater and Navigator 4.06 and greater.

Operator	Name	Description
! ==	Non-identity	Tests that operator 1 and 2 are not identical, that is either not equal in value or not of the same type—automatic data conversion will not be performed. Supported in Internet Explorer 4.0 and greater and Navigator 4.06 and greater.

TASK 3A-1:

Using the if statement

Setup: To explore the syntax of and use the if statement.

1. **Open ifscript1.html in your editor.**

2. **Read and evaluate the script. Will the alert statement be processed?**

3. **Change the ifscript1.html file to test that x is equal to y. Test your changes (save and load in your browser). What change did you make?**

4. **Modify ifscript1.html; this time change the value of y to "10" (a string value, so you will need the quotes) and test that x equals y.** Your if statement should read if(x==y).

5. **Open the page in your browser. Does your browser show the alert?**

6. **Change your script to test with the identity operators.** Your if statement should read if(x===y).

7. **Reload the script in your browser (you'll need to use Internet Explorer 4.0 or Navigator 4.06 or newer). Does your browser show the alert message?**

Logical Operators

Logical operators let you test for multiple criteria. You could, for example, test that a number is both greater than a certain value and not equal to another value. Or, you could test that one variable equals a certain value or a different variable equals a different value.

Operator	Name	Description
&&	And	Returns `true` only if both conditions are met.
||	Or	Returns `true` if either condition is met.
!	Not	Inverts the return value of a conditional statement. Thus, if the condition were to return `true`, with the Not operator it would return `false`.

TASK 3A-2:

Using the logical operators in if statements

1. **Open ifscript2.html in your editor.**

2. **Read and evaluate the script. Will the alert statement be processed?**

3. **Open ifscript2.html in your browser to check your answers to step 2.**

4. **Open ifscript3.html in your editor.**

5. **Complete the script so as to test for the condition of x being greater than y or y being less than z. If the conditions are met, display an alert message showing the value of x.**

6. **Save your changes and run your script to test its functionality.**

7. **Modify the script you created in the previous step to use the Not operator to test for x being not greater than y and y being less than z. Run your script to test its functionality.**

if...else and if-else-if

The `if` statement goes further than allowing a single test. You can use the else keyword to provide an alternate branch for your code to follow.

```
if(condition)
   {
   code to do if condition is true
   }
else
{
   code to do if condition is false
   }
```

You can even nest if statements—as many layers as you care to manage—with the `if-else-if` construct.

```
if(condition)
   {
code to do if condition is true
   }
else if(condition2)
   {
code to do if condition2 is true
   }
else
   {
code to do if both conditions are false
   }
```

TASK 3A-3:

Using the if-else-if statement

1. **Using ifscript4.html as a starting point, write a script that determines which of the three variables, x, y, or z, has the greatest value. If none of the variables has the greatest value, for example if two or more are equal, display a message stating that "None is the largest."** Your script should use an alert box to display a message describing which variable is the largest. Write your script using `if-else-if` statements.

See xifscript4.html for one possible script that would accomplish this objective.

2. **Save your script and load it in your browser. Does your script work?** If not, correct it and reload it.

3. **Test your logic by changing the values of x, y, and z in the source code and reloading in your browser.**

The switch Statement

A more compact version of the `if-else-if` statement is the switch statement. This statement is supported in JavaScript 1.2 and newer, so use it with care if you must support pre-4.x browsers. switch provides you with an easy way to build a complex if statement supporting many logic branches.

The general syntax of `switch` is:

```
switch(expression)
   {
   case value:

code to execute if expression equals value
      break;
   case value2:
      code to execute if expression equals value2
      break;
   default:
      default code to execute if expression never equals value
      break;
   }
```

With `switch`, you put the expression or variable whose value you are testing within the parentheses on the first line. Following each instance of the case keyword is the value you are testing for. The code to execute if the expression equals the value is placed next, followed by the break keyword. break stops the execution of the `switch` statement; without it, after the value was matched and the code executed, the remainder of your switch statement lines would be interpreted. The `default` block is optional and provides a chunk of code to execute if the expression doesn't equal any of the cases you provide. (This block would always be executed if you didn't use break to stop execution of a case block.)

The `switch` statement might be made clearer with an example. Here we are testing for the value of x and providing multiple branches depending on the actual value.

```
switch(x)
   {
   case 1:
      // if x == 1, do the next line of code then break
      alert(x + " is the loneliest number");
      break;
   case "Greetings":
      // if x == "Greetings", do the next line of code then break
      alert(x + " and Salutations!");
   break;
   default:
   // x doesn't match any of the cases
   alert("x = " + x);
   break;
   }
```

The first case block is executed if x equals 1 (a numeric value). The second case gets executed if x equals "Greetings" (a string value—you can mix your tests in a `switch` statement). And finally, if x doesn't equal either of those values, the code in the `default` block is executed. The above switch statement is equivalent to this `if-else-if` statement.

```
if(x == 1)
  {
  // if x == 1, do the next line of code then break
  alert(x + " is the loneliest number");
  }
else if(x == "Greetings")
  {
  // if x == "Greetings", do the next line of code then break
  alert(x + " and Salutations!");
  }
else
  {
  // x doesn't match any of the cases
  alert("x = " + x);
  }
```

TASK 3A-4:

Using the switch statement

1. **Open ifscript5.html in your editor.** The script in this file uses the if-else-if construct to perform conditional branching.

2. **Convert this script to use the switch statement instead.**

3. **Test your script using your browser.**

See xifscript5.html for one possible script that would accomplish this objective.

The Conditional Operator

Finally, JavaScript has one more conditional statement, usually called the conditional operator, that comes in handy in a few situations. The conditional operator is a very compact if...else statement with the following syntax.

```
condition  ? expression if true : expression if false
```

Thus, if you wanted to take one action if x were equal to 100 and another if it were not equal to, you could write:

```
x == 100 ? alert("x is 100") : alert("x is not 100");
```

The conditional operator is not particularly readable. Its syntax can be a bit too cryptic for some programmers' tastes. However, it is compact and efficient.

The conditional operator is the only ternary operator in JavaScript, that is, it is the only operator that takes three operands. Because of this, the conditional operator is sometimes called the ternary operator.

TASK 3A-5:

Using the conditional operator

1. **Open digiclock.html in your browser.**

Current Time: 16:13:16

2. **Open it in your editor. This script displays a digital clock in a form field.**

3. **Find the conditional operator in this script. What is its function in this script?**

4. **Describe a reason why you might use the conditional operator in a script like this rather than an if statement.**

Looping

Loops let you repeat blocks of code and are a common programming construct. JavaScript supports a few different looping commands, including `for`, `while`, `do/while`, and `for/in`.

for Loops

The most common and basic of the loop structures is the for loop. These loops repeat a block of statements until a condition you specify is no longer met.

```
for( start_condition;  continue_condition; increment)
  {
  statements
  }
```

When the loop starts, the `start_condition` is initialized with a variable assignment like `i = 0`. The key to understanding for loops is that they repeat until the `continue_condition` is `false`. So, you use something that will evaluate to `true` when you want to continue looping and evaluate to `false` when you want to stop the loop. The `increment` is a statement that modifies the value you set in the `start_condition` statement so that your loop won't continue forever.

Consider this example:

```
for(i = 0; i < 10; i++)
  {
  document.write("<BR>i = " + i);
}
```

To start, the variable `i` is set to `0` and the associated block of code is run. Then, using the increment operator, one is added to `i`. The `continue_criteria` condition is evaluated. If `i` is still less than `10`, then the loop repeats. With for loops, it might be convenient to read them something like "for i equals zero to ten," but this would be incorrect. Better would be to think of for loops as "for i equals zero until i is no longer less than ten."

With any of the JavaScript loop statements, simple variable names are most typically used for the counter variables. Variables like `i`, `j`, and `k` are often used. You can choose any variable name you would like, though.

Programming languages like BASIC repeat loops until a condition you specify is true—whereas JavaScript does the exact opposite. For example, in BASIC you would write for x = 1 to 10 to start a loop. Each time through the loop, x would be compared to 10. Until it equaled that value, the result would be false and the loop would continue.

TASK 3A-6:

Looping with for

Objective: To consider how for loops work and how you can use them.

1. **Open forloop1.html in your editor. How many times will this loop be performed and what will be the value of x when the loop last runs?**

2. **Load forloop1.html in your browser and run the script. Were your answers to question 1 correct?**

3. **Using forloop2.html as a starting point, write a script that loops twelve times using x as the counter variable.** The `document.write()` statement currently in that file should be executed in each iteration of the loop.

xforloop2.html is an example of one script that would meet this objective.

while Loops

Another type of loop supported by JavaScript is the `while` loop. These loops repeat as long as a condition is `true` rather than `false`, as is the case with the `for` loop. With `while`, before the loop statements are executed, condition is evaluated. If it is `true`, the statements are executed. If not (condition is `false`), then the statements are skipped. Assuredly, the statements in your while loop should modify the condition in some way. If not, your `while` loop would run forever.

```
while(condition)
  {
  statements
  }
```

In the example that follows, the while loop will repeat as long as x is greater than 100. Each time through the loop, 100 is subtracted from x. Eventually, x will no longer be greater than 100 (assuming it ever was) and the loop will stop.

```
while(x>100)
  {
  x = x - 100;
  }
```

TASK 3A-7:

Using the while loop

Objective: To convert the for loop you wrote in the previous task into a while loop.

1. **If it is not already open, open forloop2.html in your editor.**

2. **Convert the `for` loop to a `while` loop.** The functionality of the script should not change, just the loop statement you are using to accomplish that objective.

xwhileloop.html is an example of one script that meets this objective.

3. **Save the file as whileloop.html and test it by opening it in your browser.**

do/while Loops

The do/while is similar to the while loop except that the statements of the loop are always executed at least once. The do/while loop uses this syntax:

```
do
  {
  statements
  }
while(condition);
```

In this loop style, the statements of the loop are executed. Then, condition is evaluated, and if it is true, the loop is repeated. Otherwise, the loop stops and execution continues with whatever that follows this set of statements. This type of loop is not commonly used as it is a rare situation that requires the loop to always execute at least once. The do/while loop is new to JavaScript 1.2, so it is not supported by pre-4.x browsers.

for/in Loops

The for/in is another of the rarely used JavaScript loop statements. This loop structure is specifically designed to enable you to enumerate—that is, list the values or names of properties of objects. A for/in loop uses the syntax:

```
for(variable in object)
    {
statements
    }
```

In this statement, `variable` can be any variable name of your choice; `object` is the name of the object whose properties you wish to enumerate.

TASK 3A-8:

Enumerating object properties with a for/in loop

Objective: To see how you can use the for/in loop to enumerate the properties of an object.

1. **Open forin.html in your editor.**

2. **Check out the for/in loop statement;** it will enumerate the properties of the Window object.

```
for(var i in window)
    {
    document.write("<BR>window." + i + "=" + window[i]);
    }
```

3. **Open forin.html in both Navigator and Internet Explorer.** Not only does the loop enumerate the properties of the Window object, it shows that Navigator and Internet Explorer support a different set of those properties in their implementations of the Window object!

CHECK YOUR SKILLS 3-1

1. Change the script in forin.html to enumerate the properties of the Document object by changing the word window in the script to document. Make sure to change the output lines as well.

2. Run the script in Navigator or Internet Explorer 4.x.

Control Statement Extras

Even though `goto` is a reserved keyword in JavaScript, as of version 1.3 of the language you cannot jump to a labeled spot in code as you can in some languages. For that functionality, you will have to use functions or one of the other loop commands that JavaScript does support.

Suggested Time:
5 minutes

Internet Explorer 5.0 has a bug that will prevent this script from working. Look at the code in object enumerator.html if you are interested in seeing a workaround for the problem.

One final control statement to consider is the `isNaN()` built-in conditional function. You might recall the `NaN` value that means "not a number." Variables can have this value assigned when you attempt to perform mathematical operations with non-numeric variables, such as dividing a number by a string. The `NaN` value is special; it doesn't equal anything, including itself. This means you can't do a test like `if(some_number == "NaN")` or `if(some_number == NaN)`. For that, you'll need `isNaN()`.

TASK 3A-9:

Using isNaN()

> **Objective:** To determine how to test for NaN values using the isNaN() function.

1. **Open isnan.html in your editor.**

2. **Check out the script. It erroneously tries to divide 20 by the string "ten". Which of the statements do you think will detect the condition and display the alert box?**

3. **Open isnan.html in your browser. Were you correct in your assessment in step 1?**

Summary

In lesson 3, you used the control statements, like `if()` and `for()`, to create conditional and looping statements in your programs. You use these elements to add complex logic to your programs.

Lesson Review

3A **How many times will the `document.write()` statement in the following code sample be executed?**

```
for(x=12; x<24; x++)
    {
    document.write(x + "<BR>");
    }
```

Why would you use a `while` loop instead of a `for` loop?

JavaScript Building Blocks—Functions and Objects

Data Files
Function1.html
Function2.html
Function3.html
arguments.html
multireturns.html
Function4.html
Library\mathlib.js
blank.html
Function5.html
global.html
planet.html

Lesson Time
2 hours

Overview

Functions and objects are critical to all but the simplest of JavaScript programs. In this lesson, you'll carefully examine how to create and use functions, how to pass data to them for manipulation, and how to receive data back from them after processing. You'll investigate objects and their characteristics, how to use them, how to instantiate them, and even how to create custom objects.

Objectives

In this lesson, you will:

4A   Create and use functions.

Functions are deferred-action code, portions of your program that might get called repeatedly or only in certain situations. Functions are a powerful programming tool. You'll create and use functions in this topic, and examine how to pass data to and receive data from your functions.

4B   Examine object characteristics, use objects, instantiate objects, and create custom objects.

Object-oriented programming is now the norm, and JavaScript is no exception. In this topic, you'll examine how to use JavaScript's built-in objects, see which ones are available, and take a peek at how to create your own custom objects.

Topic 4A

Functions

Functions are deferred-action code. They are blocks of code that you define but that are not run right away. Instead, the functions are run later when you call them (using a function is referred to as "calling" it). Functions are useful for many reasons, but chiefly they improve code readability and help you streamline your program development practices.

Repetitive functionality that you would normally have to include throughout your program can be placed in a function and called when needed. This reduces program clutter, which improves readability. Functions that you develop might be useful in many different programs. To make your life easier, you can develop a function once, store it in a convenient file, and then copy and paste it into those scripts where you need its functionality.

You create functions using the function keyword as shown in the following syntax.

```
function myFunc(var1, var2, …)
  {
  statements
  }
```

Functions must be named; for example, myFunc above. Data that is sent to the function for processing is said to be passed to the function. The name or names of the variables, arrays, or objects passed to a function are included within parentheses following the functions name. The statements that make up the function are enclosed within the usual curly-brackets.

To call a function later in your program, simply use its name followed by parentheses. If you are passing data to the function, include that data within the parentheses. (Actually, you can omit the parentheses when calling a function, provided you aren't passing any data to it. However, including the parentheses makes it clear that you are calling a function and not using a JavaScript keyword. So, most programmers include the parentheses.)

TASK 4A-1:

Examining a function

1. **Open function1.html in your editor.**

2. **Examine the function definition in the `<HEAD>` section of the document.**

```
function say(msg)
  {
  alert(msg);
  }
```

This is a very simple function that displays an alert box showing the value of whatever data was passed to it. Of course, in a real program, you wouldn't write a function just to display an alert box—you'd just call the alert() method directly. This function is intended to illustrate how to define a function, call it, and pass data to it.

3. **Observe how the function is called in the <BODY> section of the document.**

```
say("Hello");
```

The message to be displayed is included within the parentheses. Because it is a string, the message is enclosed in quotes.

4. **Open function1.html in your browser.** An alert box with the message "Hello" is displayed.

5. **Click OK.**

CHECK YOUR SKILLS 4-1

With your editor, change the message that is displayed by the say function to a message of your choice. Reload the page in your browser to display that new message.

Suggested Time:
5 minutes or less

Passing Data

When you define a function, you can specify that it will receive *arguments* (passed data). You place variable names within the parentheses of the function definition block to define names for the arguments. The argument names you specify in the function definition are used within the function to represent the passed data. The first piece of data passed to the function when it is called is placed into the first variable name specified in the function definition line; the second piece is placed into the second variable, and so on.

argument:
A piece of data passed to a function.

Argument Names

The variable names you use in the script that calls your functions and the argument names within the functions do not have to match. To avoid confusion and potential bugs, the function names you use within a function probably should not match those in the script that calls the function.

For your sanity, however, the names should be similar. You could adopt the practice of adding an identifier to the beginning of passed variables so that, for example, a variable named time that gets passed to a function could be referred to within the function as fTime or f_time. Or, you could just come up with similar names, as long as it is clear to you and others who must read your code.

By Value or By Reference

When you pass data to a function, you can do so by value or by reference. When you pass data by value, you pass the actual data. In the simplistic function you used in the previous task, the message to be displayed was passed as a string value to the function. Instead, you could have put the string value into a variable and passed the variable to the function. Furthermore, you can use an expression, such as a calculation, within the function call—the resultant value of the expression is what is actually passed to the function.

Passing Differing Types of Data

You can pass any of the supported data types to a function. Simply pass that data by value or reference. Of course, your function must be able to handle the data type you pass it. JavaScript does not automatically check that the correct type of data has been passed. Your function script must do that if it is important to you and the correct operation of your function. You could use the `typeof` operator, for example, to make sure that the passed data is of the correct type.

TASK 4A-2:

Modifying the simple function

Objective: To explore how data can be passed to the function.

1. **In your editor, change the script in the `<BODY>` section of the document (the script that calls, not defines, the function) to read.**

    ```
    var myMsg = "Hello";
    say(myMsg);
    ```

    With this change, you have put the message to be displayed into a variable. Then, you pass the variable to the function. You'll notice that the variable name used when calling the function does not match the name used within the function itself. These variable names do not have to, and generally don't, match.

2. **Save your changes and reload the script in your browser.** Is your message displayed as you intended? It should be.

3. **Modify the page again so that the script in the `<BODY>` section of the document reads:**

    ```
    var myMsg = new Date();
    say(myMsg);
    ```

    With this change, you have set the variable `myMsg` to be a Date object and then have passed that object to the function. Of course, the function does not check data types and simply displays the variable passed to it.

4. **Run the script to see how the date is output.**

Passing Multiple Values

You can pass more than one value to a function. Simply separate the values (and the arguments in the function definition) with commas. Generally, your function must be written to accept each of the parameters you pass (though there is a way around that). JavaScript does not check to see that the function has been passed the correct number of arguments. If it's important to your needs, you must take care of that functionality.

One way that you could test to see if the correct number of parameters were passed would be to test each passed variable to see if it exists. You can compare the variable's value to `null`; if it matches `null` then the variable does not exist and thus was not passed. Of course, if `null` were a valid value for the arguments you'll be passing to your function, this method wouldn't work for you.

Another more powerful way is to use the Arguments object. An Arguments object is created automatically for each function as the function is initialized. The Arguments object represents an array of arguments that are passed to the function. A key point: a particular Arguments object exists only inside the function for which it was created.

You can use the `arguments.length` property to determine how many arguments were passed. You can check how many arguments were expected to be passed (the number defined in the function) using the `function_name.length` property, where `function_name` is the name of the function.

What makes this technique more powerful is that with the Arguments object you can access any and all passed arguments regardless of whether your function definition includes names for them. Simply access each argument as an element of the `arguments[]` array.

TASK 4A-3:

Writing functions that have multiple arguments

Objective: To examine how you can define and pass multiple arguments in function and test for their existence.

1. **Open function2.html in your editor.**

2. **Examine the function definition in the `<HEAD>` section of the document.**

```
function say(msg1, msg2)
  {
  alert(msg1 + " and " + msg2);
  }
```

This is a very simple function that displays an alert box showing the value of the two arguments that were passed to it with the word "and" between them.

3. **Run the script to see its output.** It displays an alert box with a message "Hello and Goodbye" built from the two arguments passed to the function.

4. **In your editor, change the function-definition script to read:**

```
function say(msg1, msg2)
  {
  if(msg2 != null)
    {
    msg1 = msg1 + " and " + msg2;
    }
  alert(msg1);
  }
```

5. **Further modify the page so that the script in the `<BODY>` section reads:**

```
say("Hello");
```

   With this change, you've added a testing capability to your function that more intelligently builds the output string to be displayed with `alert()`. And, you have changed the way the script was called so that only one argument is passed.

6. **Run the script.** Assuming no typos, the message "Hello" should be displayed.

7. **What other change might you want to make to the function definition to better handle all possibilities?**

8. **Change the call to the function to pass two parameters of your choice as arguments to the function. Test your changes by reloading the page.** Assuming that your second argument is not a `null` value, the two arguments should be concatenated with the word "and" in between them.

9. **Modify the `if()` statement in the function definition script to use the `arguments.length` property to determine if the correct number of arguments have been passed. Your script should test to see if two parameters were passed, and if so, create the concatenated string. Otherwise, your function should display just the first argument in the alert box. Test your changes by passing one and two arguments.**

Returning Values

The functions results can be returned to the place in the program where the function was called. This is the more common way to use functions. Typically, a function might calculate some value, format a string for output or some similar task, and then return the processed data to the calling script.

To return data from a function to the calling script, use the `return` keyword followed by the value to be returned. You can return any of the data types supported by JavaScript, including numbers, strings, Booleans, arrays, and objects.

TASK 4A-4:

Using functions that return values

Objective: To examine a function that returns a value in order to see how they are created and used.

1.   **Open function3.html in your editor.**

2.   **Examine the function definition in the `<HEAD>` section of the document.**

```
function square(x)
  {
  var result = x * x;
  }
```

This simple function computes the square of the number passed to it. But then it doesn't do anything with the calculated answer.

3.   **Examine the calling script in the `<BODY>` section of the document.**

```
for(i=0; i<11; i++)
  {
  document.write("<BR>The square of " + i);
  document.write(" is " + square(i));
  }
```

The script uses a loop that is intended to calculate the squares of all the numbers from zero to ten. The script calls the `square()` function.

4.   **Open function3.html in your browser.** Since the `square()` function doesn't return a result, the word "undefined" is printed out each time through the loop.

5.   **Change the function definition script in the `<HEAD>` section of the document to read:**

```
function square(x)
  {
  var result = x * x;
  return result;
  }
```

The new line you are adding sends the calculated square back to the script that called this function. The returned value will replace the call to the function, the `square(i)`, wherever it is used in the calling script.

6.   **Save your changes.**

7.   **Open function3.html in your browser and examine the results.** As the loop progresses, each value of the loop counter is passed to the function. The function computes the square of the counter variable and returns the results for output. The returned value replaces the `square(i)` notation in the script so that the value is written to the page.

8.   **Open arguments.html in your editor.**

9. **Examine how this function sums the arguments passed to it.** It does not used named arguments. Instead, it uses the Arguments object within a loop to sum all of the arguments, no matter how many arguments are passed. This function supports a variable number of arguments and returns a single result.

10. **Open arguments.html in your browser** to see the results. As it is written, the calling script "asks" the sum() function to add the numbers one through ten.

11. **Open multireturns.html in your editor.**

12. **Examine how this function sums and subtracts the arguments passed to it.** It places those results in an array and returns the array. The script in the body of the document also creates an array, this one storing the returned calculated results. Then, the body script outputs the results to the browser. By returning arrays or objects, you can return multiple values from a function.

13. **Open multireturns.html in your browser** to see the results. As it is written, the calling scripts "asks" the sumdiff() function to add 34 and 12, subtract 12 from 34, subtract 34 from 12, and then return all the results.

Function Libraries

You will probably create many useful JavaScript functions. To make your job easier and to save time, you can place those functions into separate files and use them in subsequent Web pages. You can "include" a JavaScript source file, typically named with the .js extension, using an attribute of the <SCRIPT> tag.

```
<SCRIPT LANGUAGE = "JavaScript" SRC="filename.js"></SCRIPT>
```

The content of the JavaScript source file is simply JavaScript code. You do not include the <SCRIPT> tag in that source file. Instead, that tag goes in the Web page that will be including the source file. The closing script tag, </SCRIPT> is required. It too is put in the Web page including the source file and not in the source file. And, if the JavaScript source file is not in the same place as the Web page, you can use either a file system path or URL path in the SRC parameter.

You might even consider placing multiple functions in a single source file to create a library of related routines. For example, if you regularly need a set of custom math routines, you could place them in a math.js file and include it when necessary.

TASK 4A-5:

Using functions from an included JavaScript source file

1. **Open function4.html in your editor.**

2. **Observe the script in the Observe the script in the <BODY> section of the document.** The script uses functions that are not defined in this document. They are defined for you in the mathlib.js file, which you must include in this file.

3. **In the `<HEAD>` section of the document, add this line:**

```
<SCRIPT LANGUAGE = "JavaScript" SRC="library/mathlib.js">
</SCRIPT>
```

The mathlib.js file is in the Library folder under the folder where this Web page is stored.

4. **Save your changes.**

5. **Open function4.html in your browser. Do the function calls work?**

6. **Open mathlib.js from the Library folder.** This JavaScript source file includes mathematical functions not included with JavaScript itself. It represents a library of functions that you might use on many different Web pages. Each script is commented to reflect its function. And, each script includes an `if()` statement that checks for the correct usage of the function. If you create libraries of your own functions, you should take care to include appropriate comment and also check for proper usage.

7. **Observe the `factorial()` function.** It uses a technique called recursion to calculate the factorial of a number. The factorial of a number is that number times each of the whole numbers smaller than itself. So, to calculate this value, the function calls itself as needed to calculate the factorial of the next smaller number, and so on, to reach the final result. Then, it returns that result.

Variable Scope

Where you define and use variables can affect where else you can use those variables. The concept of *scope* essentially describes where a variable exists. Variables you define outside of functions are called *global variables*. You can use these anywhere in your program. However, variables you define within a function are considered *local variables* and exist only within that function. Variables defined within a function nested inside another function are also local, yet exist only in the nested function.

scope:
The area of a program in which a variable is defined.

global variables:
Variables that are available anywhere within your program. These variables are defined outside of functions.

local variables:
Variables defined within a function and available only within that function.

The *scope chain* describes how and where JavaScript will search for variables you attempt to use in your programs. If you attempt to use a variable within a function, JavaScript will first look within that function for the variable. If it does not find it, JavaScript will look for a matching global variable. In a function nested inside another function, JavaScript will first look for a variable defined locally to the nested function. If it cannot find one, JavaScript will search upward to the function that contains the nested function. If it finds a matching variable defined there, it uses it. If not, JavaScript searches for global variables that match.

JavaScript searches the scope chain from most local to less local to global. In other words, it searches up the chain. It does not search in the other direction (down). If you attempt to use a local variable from a global context, your command will fail with an error.

TASK 4A-6:

Testing variable scope

1. **Examine the following code sample.** This code creates global and local variables, some in functions nested within other functions.

    ```
    var x = 100;
    function a()           // define function a()
      {
      var y = 200;
      alert(y/x);
      function b()           // define function b()
        {
        var z = 300;
        alert(z/y);
        }
      b();               // call function b()
      }
    a();               // call function a()
    alert(x/z);
    ```

2. **Which are the global and local variables?**

3. **Open blank.html in your editor.**

4. **Enter the program listed in step 1 the `<SCRIPT>` block in the `<BODY>` section and save the file as local global.html.**

5. **Open local global.html in your browser.** Due to its testing of local and global variables, the script will cause an error.

6. **Where did the errors occur and what were they? Were there no errors where you expected some to be?**

Code Interpretation

You should know how functions are interpreted and invoked on a page so that you are prepared when you experience unexpected results. When a browser receives a Web page, it begins at the top of the document and reads sequentially through the pages data in order to render the page. The document definitions contained in the <HEAD> section are interpreted and rendered before the <BODY> contents. When the browser first encounters a <SCRIPT> block, the JavaScript interpreter is initialized and the global, environment-provided components (like the standard set of objects) are created.

Because the <HEAD> section is interpreted first, you should typically place scripts that define functions in that section of the page. That way, the functions will be available when they are used later by scripts in the <BODY> section.

The 4.x versions of Navigator contain a bug in which multiple <SCRIPT> blocks in the <HEAD> can cause problems. Navigator will recognize only the first in some situations, ignoring the existence of the rest. Make sure that you use only one <SCRIPT> block in the <HEAD> of your pages for this reason. And because of this bug, some JavaScript programmers do not put <SCRIPT> blocks in the <HEAD> section, instead opting to put them as the first content in the <BODY> section. The choice is up to you.

Actually, functions receive special treatment by the JavaScript interpreter. When interpreting the script within a <SCRIPT> block, the first part of the script to be read and interpreted is function definitions—even if they do not come first in the script! This behavior applies to a single block of JavaScript code; that is, everything that resides between the opening <SCRIPT> tag and the closing <SCRIPT> tag. Separate script blocks are interpreted sequentially.

So, if you use a function before you define it within a single script block, you shouldn't receive any errors. Of course, relying on a quirk of the interpreter is not as reliable a coding technique as is putting function definitions into a script block in the <HEAD> of your document.

Finally, when the page is completely loaded, the browser fires the onLoad event for the page. If you have a script that is defined to handle such an event, it starts when this onLoad event occurs. Otherwise, the event goes unnoticed and the user does what he or she will with the page.

TASK 4A-7:

Evaluating how script in a page gets interpreted

Objective: To observe how different parts of the scripts you write are interpreted at different times during the page load process.

1. **Open function5.html in your editor and observe its script.**

```
var results = sum(1, 2, 3, 4);
alert(results);

function sum()
  {
  // sums as many arguments as it is passed
  if(arguments.length == 0)
    {
    alert("To use the sum() function, you must pass it at least one value.");
    return null;
    }
  var add = 0;
  for (i=0; i < arguments.length; i++)
    {
    add += arguments[i];
    }
  return add;
  }
```

This script uses a function before it has been defined!

2. **Open function5.html in your browser. Does the script work or does it generate an error?**

3. **Use your editor to modify the script to divide it into two `<SCRIPT>` blocks so that it looks like this.**

```
<SCRIPT LANGUAGE="JavaScript" TYPE="text/javascript">
<!--
var results = sum(1, 2, 3, 4);
alert(results);
// -->
</SCRIPT>


 <SCRIPT LANGUAGE="JavaScript" TYPE="text/javascript">
<!--
function sum()
```

```
      {
      // sums as many arguments as it is passed
      var add = 0;
  for (i=0; i < arguments.length; i++)
      {
      add += arguments[i];
      }
      return add;
      }
  // -->
  </SCRIPT>
```

4. **Then, save and reload the page in your browser. Now does the script work?**

5. **Move the script block that defines the function to the <HEAD> section of the document.**

6. **Save and reload the page in your browser. Does the script work now?**

Topic 4B

Objects

Objects are a compound data type that collect an assortment of variables, methods, and event handlers into a package accessed with a single name. Objects are very useful, and as you will see, nearly all-pervasive in JavaScript.

Object Basics

Objects have properties, which are like variables, that can store values. Each property has a name (just like a variable name) that you access with the dot syntax.

```
object_name.property_name
```

Objects have methods, which are actions that the object can take. Methods are actually just functions that are stored in a property of the object. Some methods are pre-defined by the creators of JavaScript, but you can create your own. To add your own method, you would simply assign a function to a property of the object. You access methods with the dot syntax as well.

Many objects have event handlers, which are functions that are called automatically when a particular situation occurs. Events are actions that happen—some being user generated while others are system generated. You generally cannot change which events an object will react to. Instead, you are limited to defining what an object will do when one of the events it supports happens. To set an event handler, you assign a function or statement to be executed to the event name. For example, to define a handler for the onload event of the Window object, you would write:

```
window.onload = myFunc();
```

Instances

Most JavaScript objects you simply use. A few, however, must be instantiated before you can use them. Date is one such object. You cannot write a working line of code using an expression like date.something. Instead, you must create an *instance*, that is, a copy of the object class. The instance contains current system information; the object prototype is like an empty shell that has no current information.

For example, the Date object supports the `getHour()` method, which extracts the current hour from the object. Until you instantiate a Date object, however, there is no current time information from which to extract the hour. Here's how you would *instantiate* a Date object and use the resulting object.

```
var today = new Date();
alert(today.getHour());
```

The first line creates a new object named today, which is an instance of the Date object. This instance contains the current system time information as of when it was instantiated. The second line simply displays an alert box with the hour information extracted from the `today` object.

Date, Array, and Object are the primary examples of objects that must be used through instantiation. Typically, to create a new array, you use a syntax similar to that shown for Date above. The same is true for Object.

```
var myArray = new Array();
myArray[0] = "some string";
myArray[1] = 12;
```

Some interesting techniques are possible by creating an instance of the Image object. You can pre-load images (download them to the browser without displaying them) to create roll-over and animation effects with this technique. Image handling techniques are covered in the Element K Content's Advanced JavaScript Programming course.

Destroying Instances

Once you create an instance, you cannot delete it. In fact, there is little reason for you to do so. Remember, JavaScript takes care of garbage collection for you automatically.

Event handlers in HTML are written with mixed case, like onLoad. Those in JavaScript are all lowercase, as in onload.

instance:
A working copy of an object class.

instantiate:
To create an instance of an object class.

class:
A prototype of an object, sort of like a category of objects. Date is a class, whereas a specific instance of that class would be the object that you would use in your code.

You don't need to destroy an instance of a Date object, for example, to update the current date and time in that object. Just re-declare the object instead. If you want to, you can assign the value `null` to the instance. This would accomplish the effect of destroying the object provided your script checked to see if the object equaled `null` before working with it.

TASK 4B-1:

Instantiating the Date object

1. **Open blank.html in your editor.**

2. **In the script block in the `<Body>` section of the document, enter the following code:**

    ```
    var today = new Date();
    alert(today);
    ```

3. **Save the file as instance.html.**

4. **Open instance.html in your browser.** The current date and time are shown in an alert box.

5. **Click OK** to close the alert box.

6. **Switch to your editor and change the code to read:**

    ```
    var today = new Date();
    alert(today);
    setTimeout("var today = new Date(); alert(today);", 3000);
    ```
    The `setTimeout()` command executes the code you put for the first parameter after a delay specified by the second parameter (in milliseconds). Your command or commands must be enclosed within quotes.

7. **Save your changes and reload the page in your browser.** An alert box with the current time is displayed.

8. **Click OK.** After three seconds, another alert box is shown with an updated time displayed in it. The first instance of today was overwritten by the second instance, created after a delay of three seconds.

Built-in Objects

The objects available in JavaScript can be divided into two broad categories and arranged in a logical order. Objects are either core objects, those objects provided by the JavaScript environment itself, or are client-side objects as determined by the Web document in which the script is defined. There is actually a third cat-

client-side objects:
Those objects provided by the browser environment in which client-side JavaScript runs. Examples include Window, Document, and Form.

core objects:
Those objects and classes common to all implementations of JavaScript (core, client-side, server-side, and embedded). Examples include Date, Math, and String.

The server-side JavaScript objects are also arranged into a hierarchy, the server-side JavaScript Object Model. However, those objects are not covered in this course.

egory, server-side objects, which are present in place of the *client-side objects* if your JavaScript code is running on the Web server rather than in the browser. However, as this course does not cover server-side JavaScript scripting, we can safely ignore their existence.

Core objects include the Array, Boolean, Date, Math, Number, Object, RegExp, Screen, and String objects, all of which are provided by the JavaScript environment. Client-side objects include the Anchor, Applet, Document, Form, Image, Layer, Link, Navigator, Style, and Window objects, which are all based on the document loaded in the browser. These do not represent complete lists of the JavaScript objects, by the way.

The client-side objects are arranged into a hierarchy starting with the Window object. You could think of these objects as all part of the same family tree with the Window object being the matriarch or patriarch of the extended family. This hierarchy is shown in the following figure.

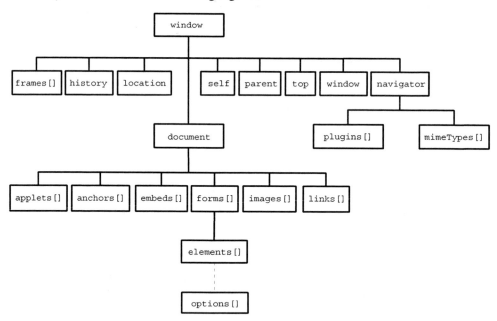

Figure 4-1: *The client-side JavaScript Object Model hierarchy.*

As you can see, the Window object is the root of the client-side JavaScript Object Model tree. The objects immediately below it in the tree are stored as properties of the Window object. Objects below each of those subordinate objects are stored as properties of the parent object. Due to the prominence of the Window object, you can use a shorthand notation when referring to its properties, methods, and event handlers. For example, window.status is a property that holds a message that is displayed in the status bar of the browser. You can leave off the "window." portion of that property name because the browser "assumes" that part. With other objects, you cannot use such a shortcut. You must note both the object name and its property, method, or event handler when you use those elements.

The following table lists the most common client-side objects supported by JavaScript up to version 1.3 and the ECMA-262 standard. The platform column lists the version of JavaScript in which the object was introduced. In the case of proprietary objects supported by only one of the browsers, that browser is listed instead.

Object name	Represents	Platform
Anchor	The target of a hypertext link.	JavaScript 1.2
Applet	A Java applet embedded in the page.	Navigator 4.x
Area	An image map link in the Web page. Essentially identical to the Link object.	JavaScript 1.0
Document	The Web page.	JavaScript 1.0
Form	A form on the Web page.	JavaScript 1.0
History	The history list maintained by the browser (the list of links that have been visited by the user).	JavaScript 1.0
htmlElement	A pseudo-object that describes any and all HTML elements defined on theWeb page. This object is intended to enable dynamic HTML functionality.	JavaScript 1.2 [1]
Image	An image on the Web page.	Navigator 4.x
Layer	A layer in the Web page.	JavaScript 1.0
Link	A link in the Web page.	JavaScript 1.0
Location	The browser location (currently loaded URL).	JavaScript 1.0
Navigator	Information about the browser that is being used by the user.	JavaScript 1.0
Style	Cascading Style Sheet attributes set for the Web page.	JavaScript 1.2 [2]
Window	The browser window or a frame.	JavaScript 1.0

[1] The htmlElement pseudo-object might be available in both 4.x browsers, but it is essentially useless in Navigator. Really, only Internet Explorer supports this object to any usable extent.

[2] While both major browsers support the Style object, they do so in radically different ways. This makes creating dynamic HTML Web pages a difficult and problematic exercise for Web page authors.

The following table lists the most common core objects provided by JavaScript up to version 1.3. Again, the platform column lists the version of JavaScript in which the object was introduced. In the case of proprietary objects supported by only one of the browsers, that browser is listed instead.

Object name	Represents	Platform
Arguments	The arguments passed to a function. This object is available only within a function	JavaScript 1.1 ECMA-262

Object name	Represents	Platform
Array	An array as well as properties and methods available for manipulating them.	JavaScript 1.1 ECMA-262
Boolean	A boolean data value as well as properties and methods available for manipulating them.	JavaScript 1.1 ECMA-262
clientInformation	A duplicate of the Navigator object.	Internet Explorer 4.x
Crypto	Cryptography resources provided by the browser	Navigator 4.04
Date	The system date and time as well as properties and methods available for manipulating them.	JavaScript 1.0 ECMA-262
Event	Events that happen or can happen.	ECMA-262 [1]
External	Access to Windows system functions.	Internet Explorer 4.x
Function	A JavaScript function as well as properties and methods available for manipulating them.	JavaScript 1.0
Math	Mathematical functions and constants.	JavaScript 1.0 ECMA-262
mimeType	MIME data types and functions supported by the browser.	Navigator 3.x [2]
Number	Numeric constants and functions.	JavaScript 1.1 ECMA-262
Object	An object as well as properties and methods available for manipulating them.	JavaScript 1.0 ECMA-262
Global	A psuedo-object that contains universal properties and methods.	ECMA-262 [3]
plugin	An installed plug-in as well as properties and methods availablefor manipulating them.	Navigator 3.x
RegExp	Regular expression methods.	JavaScript 1.2
Screen	Information about the display system (monitor and video adapter settings) on the user's system.	JavaScript 1.2

Object name	Represents	Platform
String	A string as well as properties and methods available for manipulating them.	JavaScript 1.0 ECMA-262

[1] While both major browsers support the Event object, they do so in radically different ways. This makes using this object (or handling events in general) a difficult and problematic exercise for Web page authors.

[2] The mimeType object actually exists in Internet Explorer. However, it is an empty object with no properties, methods, or event handlers.

[3] See the next subtopic for further discussion of this quasi-object.

The Global Object

The ECMA specification and the various vendor implementations of JavaScript define a "global" object as if there were an object in the JavaScript Object Model hierarchy above the Window object. Such an object only "sort of" exists. The global object, also called the top-level object, serves as a repository for global variables and functions that you create, plus built-in functions, object class definitions, and other characteristics of JavaScript that are not attributable to any of the other objects. For example, the parseInt() method, which extracts an integer value from the beginning of a string, is a method of this global object.

Navigator and Internet Explorer implement this global object in different ways. In Navigator and its version of client-side JavaScript, the Window object plays the role of global object. Global variables you create, functions you define, and custom objects you create are all stored as properties of the Window object. (In server-side JavaScript, a different object plays the role of global object, but that is another story.) With Internet Explorer, a hidden, non-modifiable Global object exists—you cannot manipulate, instantiate, or modify Internet Explorers global object directly. Global variables and functions you create are stored as properties of this Global object, yet it is the system that takes care of modifying Global for you.

The following table lists the properties and methods of the global object as of JavaScript 1.3.

Element	Type	Description
escape()	Method	Performs hexadecimal encoding of an argument (must be in the ISO Latin-1 character set). Typically, this is used to create valid strings to be used in a URL
eval()	Method	Evaluates a string of JavaScript code.
Infinity	Property	A numeric value representing infinity.
isFinite()	Method	Determine whether an argument is a finite number.
isNaN()	Method	Determines whether an argument is not a number.
NaN	Property	A value representing "Not a Number."
Number()	Method	Converts an object to a number.

Element	Type	Description
parseFloat()	Method	Parses a string and returns a floating-point number, provided the string begins with the numeric characters.
parseInt()	Method	Parses a string argument and returns an integer, provided the string begins with the numeric characters.
toString()	Method	Converts an object to a string.
taint()	Method	Adds tainting, a scripting security concept, to a data element or script.
undefined	Property	The value undefined.
unescape()	Method	The opposite of escape, returns the ASCII string value from a hexadecimal encoded argument.
untaint()	Method	Removes tainting from a data element or script.

TASK 4B-2:

Exploring the role of the global object with Navigator

Objective: To confirm that in Navigator, the Window object plays the role of the global (top-level) object.

1. **Open global.html in your editor.** This page has two scripts. The first is in the `<HEAD>` section and defines a global variable and a function, which enumerates object properties. The second is in the `<BODY>` section and simply displays the value of the global variable.

2. **Record the name and value of the variable and the name of the function here:**

    Global variable name: _____

    Global variable value: _____

    Function name: _____

3. **Open global.html in Navigator.**

4. **Click on the Show Window Properties button.** The many properties of the Window object are displayed.

5. **Scroll to the bottom of the page and look at the last two properties in the list.**

```
window.myGlobalVar=This variable, myGlobalVar, is a global variable, created outside of any functions.
window.showProps= function showProps(obj, objName) { var out = ""; for (var i in obj) { if (i == "domain") { continue; } out +=
(objName + "." + i + "=" + obj[i] + "
"); } document.write(out); document.close(); }
```

The second-to-last property is `window.myGlobalVar`, which is the global variable created in the script on the page. The last property is `window.showProps`, which is the function that enumerates the properties of the Window object. Its value is pretty ugly—it's the text of the function without any of the spacing that was used when the function was written. In Navigator, global variables and functions are stored as properties of the Window object.

6. **Open global.html in Internet Explorer and click on the button** to show the properties of the Window object.

7. **Do the variable and function show up as properties of the Window object here in Internet Explorer?**

Custom Objects

Creating objects (rather than instances of object classes) is covered in detail in the *Element K Advanced JavaScript Programming* course and not in this course. However, this section would be incomplete without at least a cursory look at how you can create your own objects. To create your own custom objects, use the new operator with the Object class.

```
var planet = new Object();
```

To create properties for your new object, simply set values for those properties. Defining methods for your objects, creating objects with object literals, object prototypes, and additional object topics are covered in the Advanced JavaScript Course.

TASK 4B-3:

Creating a custom object

Objective: To write a script that creates a custom object.

1. **Open planet.html in your editor.** This is a partially completed file to which you will add some more JavaScript code. The file contains a series of `document.write()` statements that output properties of a planet object. You will create that object.

2. **Following the comment line that says "add your script here," enter the following code:**

```
var planet = new Object();
planet.name = "Earth";
planet.radius = 6371;        // radius in kilometers
planet.mass = 5.974e24;       // mass in kilograms
```

3. **Save your changes and run the script by opening it in your browser.** The simple output script writes the properties of your custom object to the Web page. A completed version of this file is available as xplanet.html.

Summary

In lesson 4, you saw how functions and objects are critical to most interesting JavaScript programs. You learned how to create and call functions, send data to functions, and retrieve processed data back from them. You examined the wide variety of objects available in core and client-side JavaScript. And, you saw how to use, instantiate, and create objects.

Lesson Review

4A **What is the general syntax for creating a function?**

Where should you define functions and why?

4B **Define "instance" and "instantiating," and name one object that must be used this way.**

List three core objects and three client-side objects.

The Window Object

Overview

The Window object forms the underpinnings of client-side JavaScript. Opening and closing browser windows, displaying dialog boxes, setting status bar messages, and accessing frames and their contents are just a few of the tasks that you can perform using the Window object's features. This lesson serves as an overview of the Window object and its many uses.

Objectives

In this lesson, you will:

5A **Examine the Window object and its properties, methods, and event handlers.**

In this topic, you'll see how the Window object fits into the hierarchy of JavaScript objects. And, you'll take a quick look at some of its most important properties, methods, and event handlers.

5B **Create alert, prompt, and confirm dialog boxes using JavaScript.**

You'll see how you can use these dialog boxes to send informational messages to, and solicit input from users.

5C **Display and manipulate status bar messages.**

Displaying messages in the browser status bar is a popular trick. You'll examine a few techniques, ranging from simple static messages to scrolling messages, in this topic.

5D **Manipulate browser windows, including opening and closing them, with JavaScript.**

In this topic, you'll learn how to programmatically navigate to new URLs, open and close windows, and create new pages on the fly in those windows.

Data Files
object enumerator.html
alert.html
confirm.html
confirm2.html
prompt.html
status.html
scrollingstatus.html
scrollingleft.html
stopscrolling.html
ad.html
windoc.html

Lesson Time
2 hours, 15 minutes

Topic 5A

The Window Object

Window:
The object representing the browser window.

The Window object represents the browser window—every browser *window* has an associated Window object (and vice versa). If a user opens two windows (or your script does), then two Window objects are available for manipulation.

The Object Hierarchy

The Window object serves as the top of the client-side JavaScript object hierarchy. All of the client-side JavaScript objects exist as properties of the Window object. (Core and server-side objects are not part of the Window hierarchy.) The JavaScript Object Model hierarchy is shown in Figure 5-1.

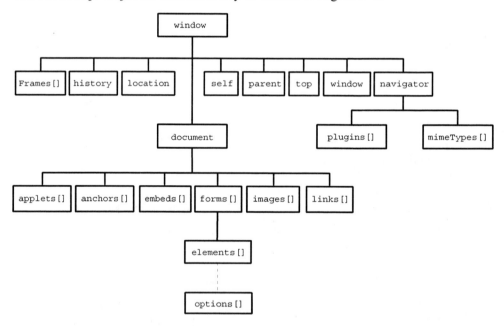

Figure 5-1: *The JavaScript Object Model.*

Because the Window object is of such importance to client-side JavaScript, you can use a shorthand notation to access its properties, methods, and event handlers. Normally, to represent a property of an object, you would need to use a dotted notation reference such as *object.property*. However, with the Window object you (and your scripts) can "assume" the `window.` portion of the notation. Thus, `window.status` and `status` are equivalent.

Browser windows normally have Web pages loaded in them. These pages are represented by their own object, the Document object. Of course, you could have a blank (empty) window that has no associated document. In that case, you could use the `location` property of the Window object to load a Web page and thus create a Document object.

You might guess then that in a Web page with frames, each frame is represented by a separate Document object. Actually, Window objects serve as the basis for frames. Each frame has its own Window object, each of which would have its own Document object (assuming it is not an empty frame) representing the document loaded in that frame.

TASK 5A-1:

Viewing the properties of the Window object

Objective: To take a quick view of the properties of the Window object (you'll be learning more about the individual properties and how to use them in the remainder of this lesson).

1. **Open object enumerator.html in both Internet Explorer and Navigator.**

2. **In either browser, click the Show Window Properties button.**

3. **Check out all properties that exist for the Window object on your computer.** You'll probably find many of these properties are cryptic or have little meaning. Take window.frames for instance. It is a property whose value is [object Window] in Navigator or [object] in Internet Explorer. What this means is that another object, in this case the Frames object, is stored within the window.frames property.

4. **Switch to the other browser and click the Show Window Properties button.** Each browser has its own set of properties. Fortunately, they share a large common set. Otherwise, programming with JavaScript would be impossible!

5. **If necessary, switch to Navigator.**

6. **Record the values for the OuterWidth and OuterHeight properties here** (these properties are not available with Internet Explorer):

   OuterWidth: _____

   OuterHeight: _____

7. **Resize your browser window and then click on your browser's Back button.**

8. **Click Show Window Properties again.**

   Did the OuterWidth and OuterHeight properties change?

9. **If you would like, resize your browser window to its former size.**

The objective here is only to see the many properties of the Window object. Don't worry if you don't understand their purpose. You'll get to that as you work through this lesson.

Properties, Methods, Event handlers (PMEs)

The Window object has quite a few properties, methods, and event handlers (PMEs). Some of the more commonly used PMEs of the Window object are listed in the following tables (these are all common to both Navigator and Internet Explorer, though not all are available in all versions of those browsers). The version column lists the version of JavaScript in which the feature was introduced. (The JavaScript version does not necessarily correspond to the release of a particular browser.)

Properties	Description	Version
closed	A read-only boolean value that is set to `true` if the window is closed.	1.1
defaultStatus	A read/write string that specifies the default message to be displayed in the browser's status bar.	1.0
frames[]	An array of frames (Window objects) contained within the window.	1.0
location	A read/write value that equals the URL of the document currently loaded.	1.0
name	The name of the Window, which is set by script or an HTML `<FRAME NAME=name>` tag.	1.0
parent	A reference to the window that contains this window (valid in a frameset).	1.0
self	A reference to the current window.	1.0
status	A read/write string that specifies a transient message displayed in the browser's status bar.	1.0
top	A reference to the top window of a frameset.	1.0

Methods	Description	Version
alert()	Displays an alert box (a dialog box with a text message and OK button).	1.0
clearInterval()	Stops periodically executing code that was started with `setInterval()`.	1.2
clearTimeout()	Stops executing deferred code that was started with `setTimeout()`.	1.0
close()	Closes the current window. For security and good-behavior reasons, you can close only windows you open with your scripts (not the user's main window).	1.0
confirm()	Displays an confirm box (a dialog box with a text message and OK and Cancelbuttons). Returns true when user clicks on OK and false when the user clicks on Cancel.	1.0
moveBy()	Moves the window by the amounts you specify.	1.2
moveTo()	Moves the window to the screen coordinates you specify.	1.2
open()	Opens a new window.	1.0
prompt()	Displays an prompt box (a dialog box with a text message, a text entry box, and OK and Cancel buttons). Returns the string the user enters when the user clicks OK and `false` when the user clicks on Cancel.	1.0
resizeBy()	Resizes the window by the amount you specify.	1.2
resizeTo()	Resizes the window to the size you specify.	1.2
scrollBy()	Scrolls the window by an amount (in pixels) you specify.	1.2
scrollTo()	Scrolls the window to a point you specify (by specifying coordinates of the point that will moved to the upper-left corner of the browser window).	1.2
setInterval()	Periodically executes the code you specify.	1.2

Methods	Description	Version
setTimeout()	Defers the execution of code by an amount of time you specify.	1.0

Event handlers	The handler invoked when	Version
onblur	The window loses focus (i.e., when another window is made active).	1.1
onerror	A JavaScript error occurs.	1.1
onfocus	The window is made the active window.	1.1
onload	The document in the window is fully loaded.	1.0
onresize	The window is resized. A bug with this handler sometimes causes the onload handler to be inappropriately invoked when the window is redrawn after being resized.	1.2
onunload	The document within the window is unloaded (i.e., the browser leaves the page). However, this handler is somewhat problematic and should probably be avoided.	1.0

Topic 5B

Dialog Boxes

JavaScript includes three basic Window methods for creating and displaying dialog boxes. These are alert(), confirm(), and prompt(). As you'll see in Topic D of this lesson, you can also create your own pseudo-dialog boxes by opening new windows.

Alert

The alert dialog box, more simply called an alert box, gives you a way to provide an informational message to users. This dialog box contains a text (not HTML) message that you provide and a single OK button.

Figure 5-2: *An alert box in Internet Explorer.*

To display an alert box, use the following syntax.

```
window.alert(message);
```

The window. portion is optional; thus, this is more commonly used as:

```
alert(message);
```

In either case, `message` is a string (including quotes) or a variable containing a string that is the message you want included in the alert box. You can use the escape sequence codes, for example `\n` for a newline character, to perform simple formatting. But you cannot use HTML formatting techniques with this message.

Most Web designers and users would consider it rude if you used an alert dialog box to delay users from leaving your site, for example by displaying an alert box with some message like "You're about to leave my cool Web site!" You should not use them in this way or you risk offending users and discouraging them from revisiting your site.

Security and Further Considerations

application-modal:
An action that stops processing for one application, permitting other applications to continue running unhindered. Displaying alert, confirm, and prompt boxes is an application-modal action.

Alert boxes are *application-modal;* that is, they stop the processing of the Web page until the user clicks OK. Some references say the same thing in a different way—they say alert boxes are "blocking in nature." In any case, make sure to consider this modal nature when designing your Web pages. The processing of your Web page stops as soon as an alert box is displayed.

Dialog boxes created with `alert()` contain a fixed title bar message. This is supposed to inform users which application created the dialog box. In Navigator, the title bar is fixed at [JavaScript Application]; with Internet Explorer it is Microsoft Internet Explorer. Navigator's title text is more explanatory in that it identifies the source of the dialog box as JavaScript. Internet Explorers alert boxes could be interpreted as being presented by Internet Explorer itself and not by a script in a Web page.

TASK 5B-1:

Displaying alerts

Objective: To create some alert boxes, use escape sequences to "format" the message text, and observe the modal nature and security features of these dialog boxes.

1. **Open alert.html in your editor.** This page has some basic HTML text, a script block, and some more HTML text.

2. **After the comment in the code, add the following code:**

```
alert("Hello fellow JavaScripter!");
```

The message to be displayed is a string of text. Notice that you must enclose it within quotes. If you had put this string into a variable (with a preceding statement), you would need to include just the variables name (and no quotes).

3. **Save the file and open it in your browser.**

4. Observe the alert dialog box.

Your message is displayed in the dialog box as plain text. Notice the title bar text. You cannot change this text, thus supposedly adding a measure of security to the browser.

5. Click OK.

6. In your editor, change the message displayed by alert to read as follows (the number of equals signs in your code is not critical, they're just included to produce some lines):

```
alert("============
\nHello\nfellow\nJavaScripter!\n===========");
```

7. Save your changes and reload the page in your browser. The alert box is now formatted differently.

8. Observe the page.

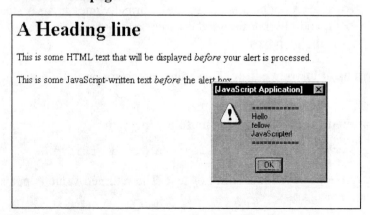

The HTML and JavaScript-written text that is defined before the alert box is shown. Then the alert box appears. The remaining text on the page is not yet shown.

9. **Click OK.** The remainder of the text on the page is displayed.

Confirm

The confirm box is similar to the alert box except that it has OK and Cancel buttons. This box is used to ask the user for yes/no or okay/not okay answers. As with alert, confirm is modal in nature. Thus this type of dialog box should be used only when necessary. In less-than-critical cases, HTML elements, like form buttons, should be used instead.

To display a confirm box, use the following syntax.

```
var answer = window.confirm(message);
```

The `window.` portion is optional; thus, this is more commonly used as:

```
var answer = confirm(message);
```

In either case, `message` is a variable or string (including quotes) that contains the message you want included in the confirm box. You can use the escape sequence codes, for example `\n` for a newline character, to perform simple formatting. But, you cannot use HTML formatting techniques with this message.

If users click OK in the confirm box, a `true` value is returned. If they click Cancel, `false` is returned. You can use an `if` statement to test for this return value.

Most Web designers and users would also consider it rude if you used a confirm dialog box to delay or prevent users from leaving your site; for example, by displaying a confirm box with some message like "Do you really want to leave my cool Web site?". You should not use them in this way or you will risk offending users and discouraging them from revisiting your site.

TASK 5B-2:

Displaying confirm boxes

Objective: To create a confirm box, use the returned values in an if statement, and observe the modal nature and security features of these dialog boxes.

1. **Open confirm.html in your editor.** This page contains a partially completed script.

2. **After the comment in the code, add the following code:**

```
var answer = confirm("Do you really want to do this?");
```

The message to be displayed is a string of text. The returned value is put into a variable named `answer`.

3. **Save the file and open it in your browser.**

4. Observe the confirm box.

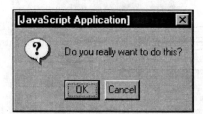

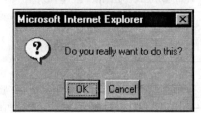

Your message is displayed in the dialog box as plain text with OK and Cancel buttons. As with `alert()`, you cannot change the title bar text.

5. Click OK. A message stating that confirm returned true is written to the Web page.

6. Reload the page. This time click Cancel. A message stating that confirm returned false is written to the Web page.

CHECK YOUR SKILLS 5-1

Suggested Time:
5 minutes or less

1. Open confirm2.html in your browser. Observe the modal nature of the confirm box. First, the HTML and JavaScript-written text that is defined before the confirm box is shown. Then the confirm box appears. The remaining text on the page is not yet shown.

2. Click OK and the remainder of the text on the page is displayed.

Prompt

The prompt box is used to display a dialog box with a message, text entry box, and OK and Cancel buttons. You use this sort of dialog box to get textual input from your users. As with alert and confirm, prompt is modal and should be used with restraint.

To display a prompt box, use the following syntax.

```
var userInput = window.prompt(messageToUser, defaultString);
```

As before, the `window.` portion is optional; thus, this is more commonly used as:

```
var userInput = prompt(messageToUser, defaultString);
```

In either case, `messageToUser` is a variable or string (including quotes) that contains the message you want included in the prompt box. As with alert and confirm, you can use the escape sequence codes to perform simple formatting of this message. `defaultString` is a variable or string that contains the default text to include in the text input box in the prompt box. If you don't include something for this parameter, the word "undefined" will be written to the text box.

If users click OK in the prompt box, the text they entered in the text box or the `defaultString` is returned. If they click on Cancel, a `null` value is supposed to be returned. However, in some especially old browsers, the string "null" is returned instead. You can use an `if` statement to test for this return value, but make sure to test for both cases to ensure the widest compatibility.

As with alert and confirm, most Web designers and users would also consider it rude if you used a prompt dialog box to delay or prevent users from leaving your site.

TASK 5B-3:

Displaying prompt boxes

> **Objective:** To create a prompt box and use the returned values in an if statement.

1. **Open prompt.html in your editor.** This page has some basic HTML text, a script block, and some more HTML text.

2. **After the comment in the code, add the following code:**

```
var name = prompt("What is your name?", "");
```

The message to be displayed is a string of text. The default text box string is simply an empty string. The returned value is put into a variable named name.

3. **Examine the rest of the code.**

```
if(name == null || name == "" || name == "null")
   {
   // if name is null, an empty string, or the string "null" write this message
   document.write("Hello there. I hope you're enjoying this class.");
   }
else
   {
   // otherwise, write this message
   document.write("Hello " + name + ". I hope you're enjoying this class.");
   }
```

The remainder of the code builds an output string using the data entered by the user. The code is contained in an `if` statement, so that if the user clicks on Cancel or doesn't enter anything in the text box and clicks OK then a default message is displayed. The `if` statement tests for name equaling a `null` value or the string "null" (to catch the case when the user clicks Cancel) or an empty string (for when the user enters nothing and clicks OK).

4. **Save the file and open it in your browser.**

5. **Observe the prompt box.**

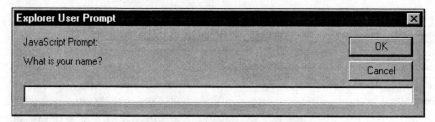

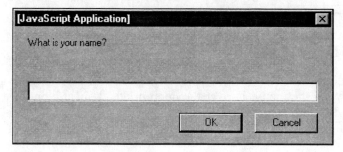

Your message is displayed in the dialog box as plain text with a blank text entry box and OK and Cancel buttons. As with `alert()`, you cannot change the title bar text.

6. **Enter your name and click OK.** A message containing your name is written to the Web page.

7. **Try reloading the page and either clicking Cancel or not entering a name and clicking OK.** The default message is displayed instead.

8. **In your editor, modify the prompt line so that it reads as follows:**

```
var name = prompt("What is your name?")
```

In this case, you are removing the default string that is shown in the text entry box.

9. **Reload the page.** The word "undefined" is displayed in the text box.

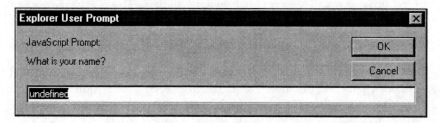

10. **Don't enter anything into the text box. Click OK.** The prompt box returns the word "undefined" and writes it as part of the string. For this reason, when you use prompt in your scripts make sure to always include a default string even if it is an empty string.

 Topic 5C

Status Bar Messages

One of the most popular uses of JavaScript is to put custom messages into the browser's status bar. Typically, these messages appear when a user points to a link, replacing the default message shown in the status bar, or they appear continuously. The continuous messages often scroll across the status bar. These scripts are built with the status and defaultStatus properties of the Window object.

Transient Status Bar Messages

To write a transient message to the status bar, you must consider three factors. You must determine when the mouse is over the appropriate element, you must write the message, and unfortunately, you have to deal with a handful of implementation-specific behaviors to make sure your message actually works as intended.

Capturing the Mouse Event

Transient status bar messages appear when users move their mouse pointer over a link (or selected other elements) in the Web page. To make such a message show up, you must be able to know when they are pointing at a link. In other words, you need to capture the mouse-over event for the link element. You do so by specifying an event handler for the mouse-over event. You can specify such an event using HTML or JavaScript, but doing so in HTML is by far the more common way.

Most JavaScript-enabled browsers support capturing the mouse-over event associated with hypertext links. Internet Explorer enables you to capture this event with images (Navigator 4.x does too, but not with all platforms). Navigator 4.x also captures the mouse-over event when the mouse pointer is over layers (a proprietary tag supported only by Navigator).

As mouse-over events with links are universally supported, we will use those elements for our examples here. But you can apply this technique to other elements if your users' browsers will support such event handlers. To specify the mouse-over event handler for a link using HTML, use this syntax:

```
<A HREF="http://somelink.com" onMouseOver="code">text</a>
```

In this sample, `http://somelink.com` is your URL and `text` is that text shown in the browser for this link. The `onMouseOver=""` parameter specifies some JavaScript code to be run when the mouse pointer is over this link. That code can be individual JavaScript statements or a function name.

Displaying the Message

Depending on the complexity of your code, you could write a function to display your status bar message. You would probably do this if you wanted to display something complicated, like a running clock, in the status bar. Or you might use a function to display the same message for many links—a function would save some repetition in your HTML. Most likely, though, you will simply put the statements right into the link tag.

To display the message, you will need to use the status property of the Window object as follows.

```
status = ">your message";
```

The message to be displayed must be a text string, thus it must be enclosed in quotes. So, in the HTML link tag, this would become:

```
<A
    HREF="http://somelink.com"
    onMouseOver="status='your message';"
>text</a>
```

This example looks a little different. But remember, HTML doesn't care about spacing or extra line breaks. So you can space out your code like this to make it more readable. Notice the use of quotes in the onMouseOver line. The value of an HTML attribute must be enclosed in quotes (if it contains spaces), and the text of your message must be enclosed in quotes. Thus, we have used two sets of nested matching quotes in this sample.

If you were using a function, simply replace status='your message'; with the name of your function.

Dealing With Real-World Issues

Ah, if life were that simple. Unfortunately, there are a few issues you must deal with to actually get your message to show up as you intend. First, the code that is run by the onMouseOver handler must return a true value. If it does not, your message might not be displayed at all or will be instantly replaced by the default status bar message text. So, to make it work, your code must be:

```
<A
    HREF="http://somelink.com"
    onMouseOver="status='your message'; return true;">text</a>
```

Both the status='your message' and return true statements must be enclosed within the quotes for the HTML attribute. Because there are two JavaScript statements in this attribute, they must be separated by a semi-colon. If you use a function in the onMouseOver handler, you must include a return true, as follows.

```
<A
    HREF="http://somelink.com"
    onMouseOver="myFunc(); return true;">text</a>
```

Most browsers don't automatically clear the transient message when the mouse pointer is no longer over the link (as they are supposed to). So, you should specify some reset code with the onMouseOut handler to clear your message when the mouse is no longer over the link.

```
<A
    HREF="http://somelink.com"
    onMouseOver="status='your message'; return true;"
    onMouseOut="status='';">
    text</a>
```

Consider your audience before using transient status bar messages in your Web pages. Some technical users like seeing URLs and browser messages. Less technically savvy users would probably prefer not to see such "techno-babble" and would appreciate your custom status bar messages.

TASK 5C-1:

Creating custom status bar messages

Objective: To create custom transient status bar messages that override those provided by the browser.

1. **Open status.html in your browser.** Point your mouse pointer at each of the links and observe the status bar. Some of the links are a bit complex and potentially confusing to novice users.

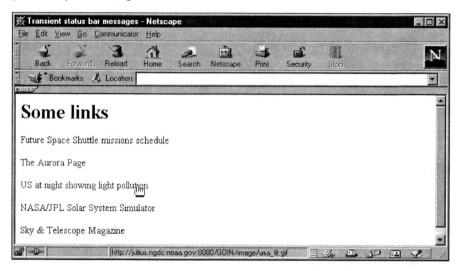

If you have Internet access, feel free to visit some of the sites (but don't get caught up with what's at those sites—you've got JavaScript to learn!). If you don't have Internet access now, the links, in order, would take you to a schedule of future NASA space shuttle missions, a page with information on auroras ("northern lights"), a satellite photo showing the US at night, a NASA solar system simulator Web site, and a popular astronomy magazine's Web site. (Sense a theme?)

2. **Open status.html in your editor.**

3. In the first link tag (the link for future space shuttle missions), **add the following to the <A HREF> tag:**

   ```
   onMouseOver="status='Shuttle flight schedule'"
   ```

   If the code would be clearer to you, add return characters and blank spaces within the <A HREF> tag. HTML doesn't care about extra spaces.

4. **Save the file and reload it in your browser.**

5. **Point to the last link and observe the status bar message.**

The normal URL message is shown in the status bar.

Check out the use of quotes in the onMouseOver line. The double quotes enclose the contents of the HTML attributes value. The single quotes enclose the status bar message text.

6. **Point to the first link and observe the status bar message.** f you are using Internet Explorer 4.0, your custom message is displayed. If you are using Navigator or Internet Explorer 5.0, it will not be shown.

7. **Move your mouse pointer off the link. Observe the message in the status bar.**

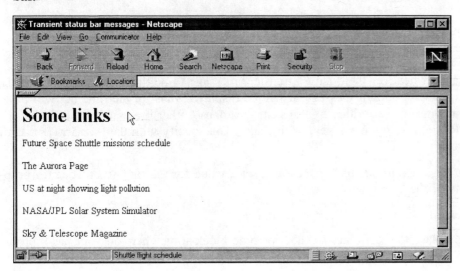

The custom message is now shown and remains visible until you point to another link. Then, the URL of that link is shown. Move off of that link and your custom message will return. You have more work to do to get this working correctly.

8. **Switch to your editor and change the `onMouseOver` code to read:**

   ```
   onMouseOver="status='Shuttle flight schedule'; return true;"
   ```

9. **Save your changes and reload the file in your browser.**

10. **Observe the behavior of the custom message as before.** As before, the status bar message remains after you remove your mouse from over the link. Hmm, still not working right; please continue.

11. **Switch to your editor and modify the `<A HREF>` tag to read** (the spacing is optional):

    ```
    <a
        href=
    "http://www-pao.ksc.nasa.gov/kscpao/schedule/schedule.htm"
        onMouseOver="status='Shuttle flight schedule'; return
    true;"
        onMouseOut="status='';"
    >Future Space Shuttle missions schedule</a><P>
    ```

12. **Save your changes and reload the file in your browser.** The transient message now works as intended.

Suggested Time:
5 minutes or less

CHECK YOUR SKILLS 5-2

Add custom messages to one or more of the other links in this file, as time permits. Test each change in both Internet Explorer and Navigator.

Default Status Bar Messages

You can also set default messages for the status bar. These messages are displayed whenever there isn't a transient message to be displayed. In other words, if you set a default message, it will be displayed most of the time but will be temporarily overwritten by transient messages (either browser-produced, like URLs and status messages, or messages you specify with the window.status property).

To set a default status bar message, set a value for the defaultStatus property of the Window object.

```
defaultStatus = "your message";
```

You place this code in a JavaScript code block somewhere on your page, probably in the <HEAD> section of the document.

TASK 5C-2:

Adding a default status bar message

1. **If necessary, open status.html in your editor.**

2. **In the script block in the <HEAD> section of the document, add the following code:**

    ```
    defaultStatus = "Check out some cool links!";
    ```

3. **Save your changes and reload the file in your browser.**

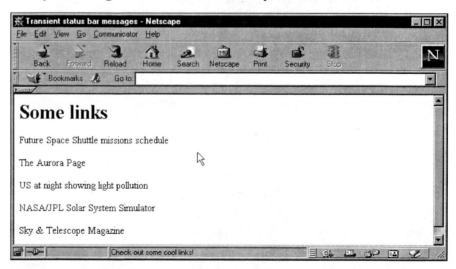

Whenever the mouse pointer isn't over another link, your default message is shown in the status bar. This file contains custom status bar messages. If it did not, the transient browser-generated status bar messages would still temporarily overwrite your default status bar message.

4. There's a harmless bug in Navigator and Internet Explorer 4.0 that might be interesting to explore. **If necessary, switch to Navigator** (we assume you are running Internet Explorer 5.0, which doesn't have this bug).

5. Move your mouse to a blank area of the Web page. Press [Ctrl] + R but do not move your mouse.

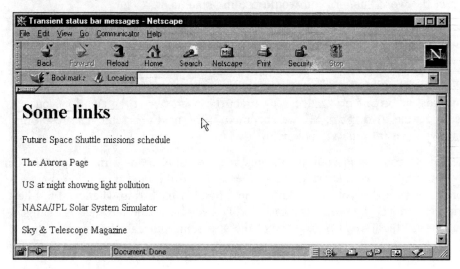

The default "Document: Done" message produced by your browser remains displayed.

6. Move the mouse just a little (not over a link though). The default status bar message you specified appears. It's a little quirk, but in Navigator the default status bar message doesn't overwrite that initial browser-generated message until the mouse is moved.

Scrolling Status Bar Messages

With a few extra tricks, you can make your status bar messages scroll to the left or right, flash, or build. These animation techniques rely on using the string manipulation functions to modify the message string and on adding timing to your scripts.

String Manipulations

To scroll a message across the status bar, you need a way of removing the first character of the string and putting it at the end of the string. Repeatedly modifying the string in this way and re-displaying it to the status bar will give the illusion of a smoothly scrolling message going from right to left. Of course, if you take the last character of the string, move it first, and re-display, you can create the illusion of the message scrolling to the right. Scrolling in that direction makes the message more difficult to read, however.

The key to string manipulation is the `substring()` method that can be used with any string. It extracts the characters from a string, starting and ending at the character position you specify. It is used in this way:

```
newString = string.substring(start_pos, end_pos);
```

Remember, substring uses zero-based (ordinal) numbering to reference characters in the string. Character number 3 is the fourth character in the string.

Where `string` is a variable containing your string, `substring` is the method name, `start_pos` is the zero-based numeric position of where to start, and `end_pos` is the position of where to stop. All the characters in between are extracted to form a new string (`newString`). The character at `start_pos` will be included in the new substring; the character at position `end_pos` will not. An example will surely make this clearer. Given the string "My name is Tim" to extract the word "name" you would use the statement:

```
var phrase = "My name is Tim";
newString = phrase.substring(3, 7);
```

The "n" in "name" is the fourth character in the string. With zero-based numbering it is in position 3. We want to include up to the "e" that is in position 6. However, `substring()` doesn't extract the character at the position you specify as the `end_pos`. So, we specified 7, the next character. The resulting string was put into the variable `newString`.

The strings you use in your Web pages will probably be of variable lengths. One day you might have a short scrolling message and the next might be a long wordy message. So you won't know the length of the string when writing the script, and since you won't want to modify every time the message is changed, you can use the `length` property of the string in your calculations like this:

```
strLength = msg.length
```

In this case, `msg` is the variable containing your message string. The result is the number of characters in the string. The length of a string will be one greater than the position number of the last character in the string. Position numbers are zero-based. The length, being a simple count, is "one-based."

TASK 5C-3:

Manipulating strings

Objective: To use the substring method to extract portions of strings. String manipulation is half the job of creating animated status bar messages.

1. **Open blank.html in your editor.**

2. **Enter the following code in the script block in the `<BODY>` section of that file, substituting your first name for "your_name."**

   ```
   phrase = "My name is your_name";
   newString = phrase.substring(3,7);
   alert(newString);
   ```

3. **Save the file as substring.html.**

4. **Open substring.html in your browser.**

5. **Did your code extract the word "name" from the string?**

   If not, correct your code and reload the file in your browser.

6. **Modify the substring statement to extract just your name from the string. Save your changes and reload in your browser.**

7. **What must you specify as the start and stop positions in order to extract your name from the string?**

8. **Open scrollingstatus.html in your editor.**

9. **Examine the `varmsg=` line in the code in that file.**

```
var msg = "Your thrilling message goes here . . . .";

function scrollStat()   // display scrolling text in status bar
  {
  status = msg;
  msg = msg.substring(1, msg.length) + msg.substring(0, 1);
  status = msg;
  }
```

    The `varmsg=` line sets a variable with the message string.

10. **Change this string to anything you choose and save the file.**

11. **Observe the `scrollStat()` function.** To start, it puts the msg into the status bar. Then it uses the string manipulation functions to extract parts of the string and put the resulting value back into the variable msg. It extracts the substring from the second character to the end. Remember, this method uses zero-based numbering, so the 1 really means the second character in the string. Then it takes the very first character and adds it to the end of the new string. The new value for msg is written to the status bar by the last line of the function. You could copy and paste these last two lines as many times as you wanted to cause the animation effect. You'll see a better way in just a minute.

12. **Observe the `<BODY>` tag.** The string manipulation is done inside a function, so you need to call the function by using the onLoad event handler in the `<BODY>` tag. This handler is invoked when the document is fully loaded.

    `<BODY onLoad="scrollStat();">`

13. **Open scrollingstatus.html in your browser. Observe the results.**

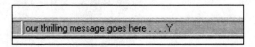
our thrilling message goes here . . . . Y

    The first character of the message is moved to the end of the string. The string appears shifted to the left by one character.

Code Timing

To create the animated scrolling effect, you need a way to repeatedly call the string manipulation function shown in the preceding task. You can use one of two methods to do that. The first is to use the setTimeout() method of the Window object. The second is to use the setInterval() method, also a method of the Window object. Since the latter method was introduced with JavaScript 1.2 (so it will work only in the 4.x browsers), you should use the `setTimeout()` method, which has been available since JavaScript 1.0.

The `setTimeout()` method schedules code to be run at a later time. You can use this to schedule the function to run itself again at a later time. Each time it runs, it will schedule itself to run again, thus creating the loop you want. The basic syntax of `setTimeout()` is:

```
setTimeout("code", ms);
```

In this example, `code` is the function or statement to be run, enclosed in quotes, and `ms` is the number of milliseconds from now in which to run the code. There are 1000 milliseconds in one second. So, you have fairly fine-grained control of when your function will run. To schedule the `scrollStat()` function to run in one-tenth of a second (100 milliseconds), you would write:

```
setTimeout("scrollStat()", 100);
```

If you put this line inside the `scrollStat()` function, it would schedule itself to run again every 100 milliseconds.

TASK 5C-4:

Using setTimeout()

Objective: To use the setTimeout() method to schedule the function to run itself again in 100 milliseconds.

1. The scrollingstatus.html file should be open in your browser and editor **Switch to your editor.**

2. **Change the function to read:**
   ```
   function scrollStat()
     {
     status = msg;
     msg = msg.substring(1, msg.length) + msg.substring(0, 1);
     setTimeout("scrollStat()", 100);
     }
   ```

   You are simply changing the second `status=msg;` line to be the `setTimeout()` statement. This new line will re-run the `scrollStat()` function in 100 milliseconds (one tenth of a second).

3. **Save your changes and reload the file in your browser.** The status bar message should be animated.

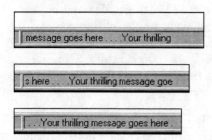

4. **In your editor, change the interval at which the scrollStat() function is called again to 125 milliseconds. Save your changes and reload the file in your browser. Do you notice a speed difference?**

5. **Try some other values until you see a noticeable change in the speed of the animation. Each time, save your changes and reload the file in your browser. When you are done, change the value back to 100 and save the file.**

6. **If you have been using Navigator, open scrollingstatus.html in Internet Explorer. If you've been using Internet Explorer, open it in Navigator.**

7. **Observe the status bars of each browser and how your message is displayed in them.**

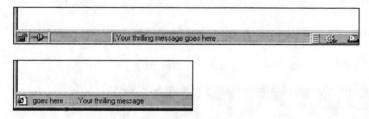

Both browsers use only that portion of the status bar necessary to show your message—your message seems to appear out of nowhere in the middle of the status bar.

8. **In both browsers, open scrollingleft.html.** Observe how this script shows the status bar message in a better way. It uses more of the status bar area in Navigator and the message isn't repeated immediately. There are many blank spaces between the repeated messages.

9. **Open scrollingleft.html in your editor and observe the code.** Before the function is run, a simple loop is used to add fifty blank spaces to the msg variable, effectively spacing it out. Then the scrolling function animates the combination of the message and blank spaces.

Clearing Scheduled Code

Code that you schedule to run with `setTimeout()` will run delayed by the number of milliseconds you specify. If you later want to cancel that code before it is run, you can use the `clearTimeout()` method of the Window object. To do so, you need to specify which scheduled code you are canceling. (In theory, you could have scheduled all sorts of different functions, and the interpreter needs to know which code to cancel.)

The `setTimeout()` method returns a value that serves as an identifier for the code being scheduled. To use `setTimeout()` in this way, you need to schedule the code using this notation.

```
id = setTimeout("code", ms);
```

In this syntax example, `setTimeout()` runs the code in ms milliseconds as before. The return value provided by `set-Timeout()` is put into the variable `id` (you can name this variable anything you want, `id` seems to be commonly used). This return value is said to be "opaque" in that you cannot manipulate it in any way. Its only purpose is for use in the `clearTimeout()` method.

TASK 5C-5:

Using clearTimeout() to cancel scheduled code

Objective: To observe how the clearTimeout() method of the Window object is used to cancel code that is already scheduled.

1. **Open stopscrolling.html in your browser.**

2. **Observe the status bar and two buttons on the page.**

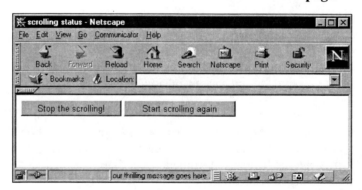

A scrolling message is displayed in the status bar. Two buttons are available: one to stop the scrolling and a second to start it again.

3. **Click the Stop The Scrolling! button.** The scrolling message stops wherever it was.

4. **Click the Start Scrolling Again button.** The message begins to scroll again, picking up where it left off.

5. Open stopscrolling.html in your editor and observe the function code.

```
function scrollStat(scroll)   // display scrolling text in status bar
   {
   if(scroll == "stop")
      {
      clearTimeout(id);
      return true;
      }
   status = msg;
   msg = msg.substring(1, msg.length) + msg.substring(0, 1);
   id = setTimeout("scrollStat()", 40);
   return true;
   }
```

The function works a bit differently than the simple scrolling scripts you used before. This function accepts a passed parameter. When the function is called, it checks to see if the passed value is equal to the string "stop." If so, the clearTimeout() method is called to clear any previously scheduled code. A return true; line breaks out of the function making sure it is not scheduled again. Unlike before, the value that setTimeout() returns is put into a variable. A return true; line is included for parallelism. The return values aren't used, so they could probably be anything you like. Navigator will often fail on scripts that return values only part of the time. So, we must include some sort of return even if that returned value is ignored.

6. Observe the <BODY> tag.

```
<BODY onLoad="scrollStat();">
```

As before, the onLoad handler is invoked once the document is fully loaded. It calls the function to start scrolling the message.

7. Observe the form code later in the document.

```
<form>
<input type=button value="Stop the scrolling!" onClick="scrollStat('stop');">
<input type=button value="Start scrolling again" onClick="scrollStat();">
</form>
```

A simple HTML form with two buttons is created. The first button is labeled "Stop The Scrolling!" and the second is labeled "Start Scrolling Again." Each of these buttons has an onClick event handler defined that is fired whenever a user clicks a button. In this file, when the onClick event occurs, the scrollStat() function is called with either a "stop" parameter passed or no parameter passed. Passing the parameter "stop" is what tells the function to stop the scrolling.

Topic 5D

Window Manipulations

One useful property of the Window object is the location property. It tells you the URL of the currently loaded document. You can also use it to navigate to a new URL.

This property is often used with forms to create custom navigation controls. You might have seen drop-down list boxes that point your browser to a new Web page after you make a choice from the list. That trick is done with window.location.

```
document.write("You are at " + window.location);
window.location = "http://some_url";
```

In the first line of the syntax example above, a message is written to the current document noting the current URL. In the second, by setting a new value for location, you cause the browser to load the document at the URL specified. As with other Window properties, you can leave off the `window.` portion.

 # TASK 5D-1:

Using window.location

Objective: To use the window.location property to write the current location (URL) of a page to the page, and to navigate to a new page by setting window.location.

1. **Open blank.html in your editor.**

2. **In the script block provided in the <BODY> section of the document, enter the following line of code.**

   ```
   document.write("Your current URL is " + window.location);
   ```

3. **Save the file as location.html and open it in your browser.**

The current URL—some ugly file path no doubt—is written to the page.

4. **Switch back to your editor and add the following new code in place of the previous line you entered.**

   ```
   url = prompt("Enter a URL to go to:", "");
   if(url != null && url != "null")
      {
      window.location=url;
      }
   ```

5.   Save the file and reload it in your browser.

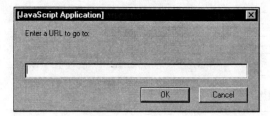

A prompt dialog box appears asking you to enter a URL.

6.   Enter the full URL of a site of your choice; make sure to include the http:// part of the URL (if you are connected to the Internet or enter scrollingleft.html). After you press [Enter] or click OK, the new page is loaded.

7.   Click Back.

8.   This time, don't enter a URL; just **click Cancel.** The prompt box goes away and just a blank white background is shown in your browser. Your script and page don't do anything if a URL isn't entered in the prompt box.

Opening Windows

The browser window is represented by the Window object. In fact, each browser window is represented by a separate Window object. You can use the `window.open()` method to open a new window and in the process create a new Window object.

```
var newWin = window.open();
```

The line above opens a new window, creates a new Window object, and puts a reference to that object in the variable `newWin`.

You can set a location (URL) for your new window by setting the new window's location property. Or you can open a window and set a location for it in one step using `window.open()`.

```
var newWin = window.open("url");
```

As with setting the `location` property, you must include the full URL specifier in this parameter, including the "http://" portion to load a page from someplace other than the current site.

You might want to check that your new window actually exists before manipulating it. For example, the user might close your new window before your script works with it. You can check the `closed` property of your new window object. It stores a Boolean value of `true` if the window is closed or `false` if it is open.

```
var newWin = window.open();
if(!newWin.closed) newWin.location = "http://someURL";
```

TASK 5D-2:

Opening new windows

Objective: To create a Web page that opens a new browser window.

1. **Open blank.html in your editor.**

2. **In the script block in the `<BODY>` section of the document, add this code:**

   ```
   var newWin = window.open();
   ```

3. **Save the file as window.html.**

4. **Resize your browser window so that it is not maximized** (does not take up the full size of your monitor).

5. **Load window.html.** A new blank window is opened. The new window inherits the size of your previous window. If your browser window was maximized, the new window would be too. The new window is blank (empty).

6. **Close the new window.**

7. **Switch to your editor and add a new line following the existing one.**

   ```
   newWin.location = "ad.html";
   ```

8. **Save your changes and reload the page in your browser.** This time, after the new window is opened, it loads the page you specified. You specify a Web page to load by setting the new window's `location` property equal to the full URL of the destination. The `newWin.` part of this syntax is equivalent to the `window.` you would use to set a location for the current window. However, you used the variable name referring to the new window's Window object. You cannot omit the `newWin.` portion of this notation as you can with `window.`, otherwise your script would set a new location for the current window (the one containing your script).

9. **Close the new window, which contains the ad.html page.**

10. **Switch to your editor. Remove the line that sets the location property for `newWin`.**

11. **Modify the window.open line to read:**

    ```
    var newWin = window.open("ad.html");
    ```

12. **Save your changes and reload the page in your browser.** The new window is opened at a location set for it in one step.

13. **Close the ad window.**

Window Features

You can set a name for your newly opened window. This name would be the equivalent of a frame name specified in a frameset document. You could subsequently use that name in a `TARGET` parameter of a link or in other ways that you would use a frame name. To specify a name, include it enclosed in quotes after the URL you want to load.

```
var newWin = window.open("ad.html", "adWin");
```

In this example, the new window loads the ad.html page and is named `adWin`.

You can set features (or decorations, as they are sometimes called) for your new windows using optional parameters of the `window.open()` method. In JavaScript parlance, window features are the buttons, toolbars, and even the dimensions of the window. When you open a window with `window.open()`, you can specify whatever features you would like.

Window feature	Specifies	Default
directories	Whether to display the Directory buttons (What's Cool, Search). Applicable only for Navigator 3.x and newer.	yes
height	The height of the document area of the window in pixels.	same dimensions as window that opens the new window
location	Whether to display the Location (Address) field, in which users can enter new URLs.	yes
menubar	Whether to display the menu bar.	yes
resizable	Whether to permit the user to resize the window. Even if you specify this parameter, users on some platforms will still be able to resize the window.	yes
scrollbars	Whether to display horizontal and vertical scroll bars when they are necessary.	yes
status	Whether to display the status bar	yes
toolbar	Whether to display the toolbar.	yes
width	The width of the document area of the window in pixels.	same dimensions as window that opens the new window

If you set any window features, only those you specify will be displayed. If you set even one feature, the remaining features will not be displayed. In other words, if you want to leave out only one feature (say the scroll bars), you need to specify to include all the rest of the features.

To set these window features, you include them as a third parameter to the `window.open()` method. All the features you want to set should be enclosed in one set of quotes and separated by commas. Do not include any spaces or Navigator won't show all the features you specify.

For example, to open a new window that is 400 pixels wide by 300 pixels high, without scroll bars, but with a menu bar, use the following line of code:

```
var newWin = window.open("ad.html", "", "width=400,height=
300,menubar=yes");
```

Opening a new window and displaying an ad in it is a common trick on shopping Web sites.

This example opens the window and loads ad.html into it. A name for the window is not set. However, that parameter is required otherwise the browser will interpret all those window features as the name of the window and generate an error. Following the empty name parameter are the features to include: a width, height, and menu bar.

TASK 5D-3:

Opening a new window and setting decorations for it

> **Objective:** To modify the window opened by window.html so that it contains only the decorations you specify.

1. **Switch to your editor;** window.html should still be open.

2. **Change the window.open() line to:**

   ```
   var newWin = window.open("ad.html", "", "width=300,height=
   300,menubar=yes");
   ```

Do not put any spaces inside the third parameter or Navigator will not show the features you specify. It will implement any features specified before the space, and then treat the space as if it were the end of the parameter. Internet Explorer is not so touchy.

3. **Save your changes and reload the page in your browser.**

The new window that gets opened is smaller and shows just the menubar.

4. **Close the ad window.**

5. **Switch to your editor and change the** `window.open()` **line to (still all on one line):**

   ```
   var newWin = window.open("ad.html", "","width=300,height=
   300,menubar=yes,status");
   ```

6. **What do you think will be shown now?**

7. **Save your changes and reload the page in your browser.**

The new window now contains the status bar. You can use this shorthand notation for the window features that don't require explicit parameters (like the height or width features).

8. Close the ad window.

CHECK YOUR SKILLS 5-3

Suggested Time:
5 minutes or less

1. Change the script so that the new window that is opened has no decorations other than height and width settings.

2. Save your changes and reload the page in your browser.

3. Close the ad window.

Closing windows

You can close windows with the `window.close()` method. This is useful for providing custom close buttons. Such a button might be nice with the ad window that was used in the script examples above. You would put this code into the `onClick` handler of a link or button in the HTML code. You must use a link because Navigator does not support capturing click events with images (which you would be using to create a custom button).

You can also close your new windows by using code in the window that opened them. For example, you could include the following code in window.html to close the ad window it opened after a three second delay:

```
setTimeout("newWin.close()", 3000);
```

Here, you schedule the window-closing code with the `setTimeout()` method to run after a three second (3000 milliseconds) delay.

JavaScript provides security to prevent you from closing the main browser window with the `close()` method. The main window is the one the user opened when they first launched their browser. It would be rude to close that window and JavaScript tries to keep you from doing it. If you call the `close()` method on the main browser window, the browser will display a confirmation message informing the user that you are trying to close their main window. They can cancel the operation at that point. The safeguard is not foolproof—sometimes you can close the main window without the user being prompted. However, you should not do so.

TASK 5D-4:

Closing windows with window.close()

Objective: To add code to ad.html and window.html that will close the ad window.

1. **Switch to your editor and open ad.html.**

2. The custom close button is included with a standard image tag. **Change the `<IMG>` tag to read** (enter this all on one line):

The ⇒ symbol denotes code that is too long to fit on one line in the book. Make sure to enter the code on one line in your editor.

```
<IMG SRC="close3.gif" WIDTH=50 HEIGHT=50 BORDER=0⇒
          onClick="window.close()">
```

To set the image to close the window when it gets clicked.

3. **Reload window.html in Internet Explorer.** The ad.html window is opened by the script in the window.html file.

4. **Click the custom close button. The window closes.**

5. **Reload window.html in Navigator.**

Don't use HomeSite's internal browser in place of Internet Explorer in this task. Doing so will cause HomeSite to crash.

6. **In the ad window, click the custom close button.** Navigator does not capture the click event with images, so nothing should happen.

7. **Switch to your editor. Remove the `onClick` handler from the `<IMG>` tag.**

8. **Change the `<A HREF>` tag to read as follows:**

```
<A HREF="#" onClick="window.close()">
```

Both Navigator and Internet Explorer support event handlers with hypertext links. By the way, the `HREF="#"` defines the link as connecting to a null location. Without the `href=` portion of the tag, Navigator will not recognize the tag as a hypertext link and the `onClick` handler won't work. You could actually put any URL in the link you wanted, as the `onClick` handler is evaluated first.

9. **Save the file and reload it in both browsers. The new window opens as before. Click the close button. Does the window close?**

10. **Switch to your editor and open window.html.**

11. **In the script block already there, add the following line after the existing code:**

```
setTimeout("newWin.close()", 3000);
```

12. **Save your changes and reload window.html in either browser.** After three seconds, the ad window closes automatically. Such an action might not be appropriate for an ad like this. But, it might be appropriate for a "splash screen" page that is opened when visitors first arrive at your Web site.

Creating New Pages in a New Window

Of course, you don't have to load an existing Web page into a new window. You can create a window with a brand new document and write your own custom information to it. This is a great way to enable dynamic content functionality on your Web site.

To write text or HTML to a new window, that window must have a document in it. While we won't go into too much detail here, to create that new document you will use the `document.open()` method. That method "opens an output stream" to the document and in doing so, creates a new Document object in your new window.

Once the document in the new window is created, you can write to it using the `document.write()` method. One catch: you need to identify which window's Document object you are writing to. Normally, you omit the `window.` portion of `document.write()`. That works fine if you're working with the current window's Document object. However, to work with a different window's Document object, you must include that extra notation. And, you must use the window's object reference name (in place of the generic "window"), as was done earlier in this lesson when closing windows with `setTimeout()`.

```
var newWin = window.open();
newWin.document.open();
newWin.document.write("Hello world.");
newWin.document.close();
```

In the preceding code, a new window is created and its object reference is put into the variable `newWin`. Line 2 opens a new document in that new window and line 3 writes some text to it. Both lines are using the new Window object's name to reference the correct window. Finally, the last line closes the document in the new window. If you did not include this last line, the document would remain open.

With some browsers, especially older ones, not closing the document would leave the "document loading" animation (the spinning logo or status-bar progress indicator) running, which users find annoying. You should always close your documents as a matter of consideration and best-practice. Sure, it doesn't really hurt anything and newer browsers handle an unclosed document more gracefully. But, why annoy users if you can avoid it?

TASK 5D-5:

Creating new pages with script

Objective: To examine a script that opens a new window, creates a document in it, and writes to the new document.

1. **Open windoc.html with your editor.**

2. **Observe the HTML portion of the document.**

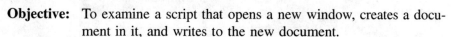

```
<H1>Parent window</H1>

<P>This is the parent window. It contains the document with the script
that opens the new window, opens a new document, and writes to it.</P>
```

This page has some very simple HTML that is designed to help you keep straight which window is which.

3. **Observe the script block.**

```
<script language="JavaScript">
<!--

// build an output string (in a variable)
var output = "<html>\n<head>\n<title>newWin - a new window</title>\n</head>\n<body>\n";
output += "<H1>Child window</H1>\n<P>This is the child window. ";
output += "It was opened by the parent window.</P>\n";
output += "<form>\n<input type=button value='Close this window' ";
output += "onClick='window.close()'>\n</form>\n";
output += "</body>\n</html>";

// enter your code here

// -->
</script>
```

To start with, a variable named `output` is created. Some HTML code is placed into that variable in a series of statements. Some new line escape sequences (\n) are included so the resulting code will be formatted nicely when it is written to the new document. This is the content that will be written to the new window. You will be adding the code to open the new window, open a document in it, and write the variable to the window.

4. **After the comment, enter this code:**

```
var newWin = window.open();
newWin.document.open();
newWin.document.write(output);
```

5. **Save your changes.**

6. **Switch to your browser, but don't load the file yet.**

7. **If your browser is maximized, shrink it to a smaller size.** (The new window that is opened inherits the size of the current window and we want to be able to see the new and old windows.)

8. **Load windoc.html in your browser.** A new window is immediately opened.

This new window contains some text and a button. This is all content that was defined in the script and put in the variable output. If you are using Navigator, you will notice that the status bar indicator (the bouncing gray bar) implies that the document is still downloading, though the "spinning logo" indicator in the upper right corner of the window has stopped animating. This is because you have not included the `document.close()` code yet.

9. You should be able to see the previous window behind the new window. If not, **move the top window.** The parent window contains some simple HTML text identifying it as the parent window.

10. **Click the Close This Window button.** The window closes.

11. **Switch to your editor and add the following line after the code you just added.**

```
newWin.document.close();
```

12. **Save your changes and reload the file in Navigator.** This time, when the new window is finished loading, the animated indicator in the status bar stops bouncing back and forth.

13. **Examine the JavaScript source code for the windoc.html file. Why does the Close This Window button work and where does its functionality come from?**

14. If you would like, **now would be a good time to maximize your browser window again.**

Apply Your Knowledge 5-1

Suggested Time:
15 minutes

In this activity, you will re-write the scrolling status bar message function in order to make the text scroll from left to right.

1. Open scrollingleft.html file in your editor.

2. Save the file as scrollright.html.

3. Modify the `scrollStat()` function to make the message scroll from the left to the right. Hint: You will need to use the `substring` method to extract the last character from the string and add it to the front of the remaining portion of the string.

4. Save your file and test it in both browsers.

The file xscrollright.html demostrates one possible way to accomplish this objective.

Summary

In lesson 5, you examined the Window object—the king of the hill, as far as JavaScript dialog boxes go. You displayed the various JavaScript dialog boxes and put messages in the status bar. You also used methods of the Window object to open nre windows and manipulate their content.

Suggested Time:

45 minutes

Apply Your Knowledge 5-2

Flashing status bar messages

In this optional activity, create a flashing status bar message function.

1. Open blank.html file in your editor

2. Save the file as flashstat.html.

3. In the script block in the <HEAD> section of the document, create a function that will display a message of your choosing on the status bar. Your function should display the message three times, clearing it between each time it is displayed. Each time the message is shown, it should remain visible fro 400 milliseconds and should remain invisible for 200 milliseconds. When the flashing is all done, the message should be visible in the status bar. The function should be called when the document is fully loaded

4. Save your file and test it in both browers.

Lesson Review

5A What is the purpose of the Window object and what place does it occupy in the JavaScript Object Model?

5B What buttons and text boxes are included with alert, confirm, and prompt boxes?

When using a confirm box, what value is returned if the user clicks Cancel?

5C Given the following code, what is missing that is required to display a transient status bar message?

```
<A HREF="http://someurl"
    onMouseOver="status='Some description';"
    onMouseOut="status=''"
>Link text</A>
```

5D If you opened a new browser window with the statement `newWin = window.open("", "myNewWin");` how would you later set a URL for that window?

YOUR NOTES:

The Document Object

Overview

The Document object represents the Web page loaded in a browser window. This object lets you do all sorts of fun things, like write to Web pages, create new Web pages, and manipulate the contents of existing pages. This lesson will get you started on creating dynamic Web pages through manipulation of the Document object and its properties.

Objectives

In this lesson, you will:

6A   Explore the Document object and its properties, methods, and event handlers.

In this topic, you'll see how the Document object fits into the hierarchy of JavaScript objects. And, you'll take a quick look at some of its most important properties, methods, and event handlers.

6B   Use JavaScript statements to write to documents in the browser window.

You'll use two different methods of the Document object to write to Web pages as they are loading and once they have fully loaded.

6C   Create dynamic documents and briefly examine the incompatibilities issues facing dynamic HTML programmers.

Dynamic HTML is a topic beyond the scope of this coure. Just the same, you'll take a peek at how you can create HTML documents with JavaScript and manipulate those already loaded in the browser. And, you'll create one of the more popular dynamic effects, the rollover image change.

Data Files
object enumerator.html
docwrite.html
docwritein.html
inertext.html
blank.html
clock.html
rollover.html
docfooter.html

Lesson Time
1 hour, 40 minutes

Topic 6A

Document object:
Represents the page in a browser window.

The Document Object

The Document object represents the page in the browser window. Each window has a *Document object,* unless it is a blank (empty) window. The Document object has many properties that describe the currently loaded page.

TASK 6A-1:

Viewing the properties of the Document object

Objective: To take a quick view of the properties of the Document object (you'll be learning more about the individual properties and how to use them in the remainder of this lesson).

1. **Open object enumerator.html in Navigator.** You'll start by loading this page in Navigator because Navigator supports fewer Document properties. So the output will be simpler and clearer.

2. **Click the Show Document Properties button.**

3. **Check out all properties that exist for the Document object on your computer.** You'll probably find many of these properties are cryptic or have little meaning. Take document.forms, for instance. It is a property whose value is [object FormArray] (in Navigator) or [object] (in Internet Explorer). What this means is that another object, in this case the Forms object, is stored within the document.forms property.

4. **Record the current value for the background color (document.bgColor) and last-modified date (document.lastModified):**

   bgColor: _____

   lastModified: _____

5. **Open object enumerator.html in your editor.**

6. **Change the <BODY> tag to read as follows:**

   ```
   <BODY BGCOLOR="#cc9999">
   ```

7. **Save your changes and reload the file in your browser.** (You will need to either press [Ctrl] [Shift] and reload or click Back ⬚ The background color of the document is now a dusty rose color.

8. **Click on Show Document Properties again.**

Did the `bgColor` and `lastModified` properties change?

CHECK YOUR SKILLS 6-1

Suggested Time:
5 minutes or less

1. Open object enumerator.html in Internet Explorer. Click the Show Document Properties button. You will notice that in IE, the Document object has many more properties than it does in Navigator. Support differs greatly between the browsers, with Internet Explorer being far more powerful and capable with respect to the ways you can manipulate the currently loaded document (via the Document object).

2. Click Back ![Back] to reload the object enumerator page and re-display the buttons of its initial screen.

Properties, Methods, Event handlers (PMEs)

The Document object is different in Internet Explorer and Navigator. However, the Document objects in these two browsers do share some common features. The following tables list the PMEs of the Document object that are common to both browsers.

Properties	Description	Version
alinkColor	A read/write value noting the color of the active link (a link as it is being clicked on). Must be set in the `<HEAD>` section of the document in Navigator.	1.0
bgColor	A read/write value noting the color of the page background. Can be dynamically set in both browsers.	1.0
cookie	A read/write string representing cookies (information saved on the client's computer) for the page.	1.0
domain	A read/write string noting the hostname from which the page was loaded.	1.1
fgColor	A read/write value noting the color of the foreground text. Must be set in the `<HEAD>` section of the document in Navigator.	1.0
images[]	A read/write array of images on the page. Images are added to the array in source order using ordinal numbering	1.1
lastModified	A read-only string noting the time and date the page was last modified. The information is read from the time stamp on the file, as provided by the operating system.	1.0

Internet Explorer 5.0 seems to have trouble with the domain property. Reading from it or writing to it simply produces an error in our testing.

deprecated:
Replaced by a newer object, property, method, or event handler. Deprecated elements miht not be included with future versions of JavaScript. so, you should not use deprecated features if you can avoid it.

Properties	Description	Version
linkColor	A read/write value noting the color of inks. Must be set in the section of the document in Navigator.	1.0
links[]	A read/write array of links on the page. Links are added to the array in source order using ordinal numbering.	1.0
location	A reference to the window.location property. This property *deprecated* in favor of the document.URL property.	1.0
referrer	The URL of the previous document. This property will conatin data only if the user clicked on a link to reach the current page. If the user accessed the page by choosing a bookmark or typing the URL, this property will be empty.	
title	The title of the page (as set with the <TITLE> HTML tag).	1.0
URL	A read-only reference to the URL of the current document. The document.URL property always contains the URL of the currently loaded document and may be different than the window.location property. The window.location property stores the URL that was requested by the user. If they were redirected to another page, the document.URL will contain the new page's address.	1.1
vlinkColor	A read/write value noting the color of visited links. Must be set in the <HEAD> section of the document in Navigator.	1.0

Methods	Description	Version
clear ()	Clears the current page. This property is deprecated. To clear a document, simply open a new one with document.open ().	1.0
close ()	Writes any information to the page that has been written but not yet displayed; then closes the current document. Use this method after you have finished writing all your content to a dynamically generated Web page to stop the "document loading" animation.	1.0
open ()	Open an output stream to a document. Doing so automatically clears the current document. The document.open() method accepts an optional MIME type parameter. Use the method in the format document. open(mimetype) where mimetype is a MIME type, such as text/plain, image/jpeg, and so forth. The default MIME type is text/html, which is the appropriate value for HTML pages.	1.0

Navigator has a bug associated with the document.open() method. If you specify a text/plain MIME type, when users resize their browser window after your text document is loaded, the document will convert to the text/html format. Spacing and line breaks you specified for text output will be lost, as HTML doesn't care about text-specified formatting.

Methods	Description	Version
write ()	Writes text to the document. If you write to a closed document, a new one is automatically opened. That means that the currently loaded page is cleared in preparation for your new content. By opening a document first, with `document.open()`, you can use a series of `document.write()` output statements without clearing the current contents. When you are finished, close the document with `document.close()` .	1.0
writeln ()	Almost identical to `document.write()` except that this method includes an ASCII new line character automatically. It is equivalent to `document.write(yourData +` `"\n")`.	1.0

Event handlers	The handler is invoked when	Version
onClick	The user clicks on the document (Web page).	1.0
onDblClick	The user double-clicks on the document.	1.2
onKeyDown	The user presses a key (on the keyboard) down.	1.2
onKeyPress	The user presses a key (on the keyboard) down or holds the key down. The difference between this event and a KeyDown event is that the KeyDown event happens first and only once. This event happens next and can repeat for as long as the user holds the key.	1.2
onKeyUp	The user releases a key that has been pressed or held.	1.2
onMouseDown	The user presses down the primary mouse button.	1.2
onMouseUp	The user releases the primary mouse button that has been pressed or held.	1.2

The onBlur, onFocus, onLoad, and onUnload event handlers that you define in the <BODY> tag are actually properties of the Window object. This might be counter-intuitive given that the Document object corresponds to the HTML page. JavaScript is not always intuitive.

Topic 6B

Writing to Documents

Even if you've worked with JavaScript for just a short time, you've probably used document.write() a million times. It's the method that you use to write text to a document. Just to re-cap, document.write() sends a text stream to the current document (or another if you provide a Window object reference). You can "turn it into" an HTML stream by simply embedding HTML tags in whatever you write to the document.

Very often the `document.write()` method is used to include system-type information in your Web pages. The classic examples are including the date and time the document was last modified and including the document's URL in the Web page. You could code these by hand with HTML, but you would have to remember to update them every time their values changed. Or you could use JavaScript.

TASK 6B-1:

Writing property values to the document

Objective: To review how the document.write() method lets you write text and system information (JavaScript object properties, like the URL) to the current document.

1. **Open docwrite.html in your editor.** This file is basically a shell of a Web page with just one output: an <H1> title line and an empty JavaScript code block.

2. **In the code block, enter the following code:**

    ```
    document.write("<H2>JavaScript rules!</H2>");
    ```

    This line writes some text information to the document. It is "turned into" HTML by including the HTML tags. Notice that everything that is written is enclosed within quotes. This is a requirement when writing a text string with `document.write()`.

3. **Add the following line to the script block.**

    ```
    document.write("<P>This page is located at:" + document.URL + "</P>");
    ```

    This line writes some text information and a property of the Document object to the document. This line will write the text message and the URL of the page. The text information is again enclosed within quotes. The property value is not. The two values are concatenated using the + operator. You could have written these two items with separate `document.write()` statements and then not included the concatenation.

4. **Add the following line to the script block:**

    ```
    document.write("<P>This page last modified:"
    document.lastModified + "</P>");
    ```

This line writes another combination of text and property value.

5.   **Save the file and open it in your browser.** The lines of JavaScript are interpreted as the file is loaded and the resulting text is written to the page.

Writing to a Fully Loaded Document

In the preceding example, `document.write()` was used to write output to the page as it was being loaded. This is the most common use of the method. As the page is parsed by the browser, JavaScript code is interpreted and any `document.write()` statements are processed.

In most cases, once the document is fully loaded (once the parser reaches the `</BODY>` tag), you cannot write to it again—at least not how you would expect. Using `document.write()` after the document is fully loaded will clear the current contents of the document and replace them with your newly specified content.

A more technical explanation is that using the `document.write()` method on a closed document implies the `document.open()` method. The `document.open()` creates an output "channel" to the document so that the document can accept information to be written. The `document.open()` method implies the `document.clear()` method, which has the effect of clearing the current contents of the document. So, simply calling `document.write()` starts a number of actions.

You can write to form fields after the document is fully loaded (using a different technique than that used here). And, with dynamic HTML techniques, you can write to a fully loaded document without clearing the current contents.

TASK 6B-2:

Writing to a fully loaded document

   Objective: To see how document.write() clears the current document, including its properties.

1.   **Open object enumerator.html in your editor.**

2. Examine the function in the `<HEAD>` section of the document.

```
function showProps(obj, objName)
  {
  var out = "";
  for(var i in obj)
    {
    if(i=="domain") continue;  // this line works around a troublesome IE5.0 bug!
    out += (objName + "." + i + "=" + obj[i] + "<BR>");
    }
  document.write(out);
  document.close();
  }
```

This function is called when you click on one of the three buttons that this page contains. Notice that the function calls the `document.write()` method to output the values of all the properties contained in the specified object. It is writing to the current document.

3. Open object enumerator.html in your browser.

4. Click any of the buttons. The page is cleared and the properties are written to the page. Notice that the background color changes. (You set it to be `#cc9999` in the `<BODY>` tag earlier in this lesson.) That's because the contents of the current document are being replaced by the text written with the `document.write()` call.

5. Switch to your editor. Before the `document.close()` line, add this new line:

```
document.bgColor="#cc9999";
```

This line writes a property value to the document. It comes after a `document.write()` call, which means it will be setting the color on the newly created document.

6. Save your changes and reload the page in your browser (or click Back).

7. Click any of the three buttons. The background color now stays the same. Actually, when `document.write()` clears the current page, the background color is reset to the default. Then, your new code line sets it back. You might notice a brief white flash as the new text is written to the window.

document.writeln()

Another output method that is available to you is `document.writeln()`. This method is very similar to `document.write()` with the difference that a carriage return is automatically included with `document.writeln()`.

This method has limited usefulness when you consider that Web browsers ignore carriage returns in HTML files. You would probably use `document.writeln()` instead of `document.write()` in only a few cases, such as:

- When you write to a plain text document. You create such a document with an optional parameter of `document.open()`.

- When you write to a preformatted text (`<PRE>`) portion of a Web page.

- When you want to create more readable source code in a dynamically created Web page. You can accomplish the same goal by using the \n escape sequence in your `document.write()` statements. However, `document.writeln()` might be easier to code and maintain.

TASK 6B-3:

Using document.writeln()

Objective: To observe how document.writeln() can be useful when writing some types of output to a document.

1. **Open docwrite.html in your editor.** This is the file you created with multiple `document.write()` statements. (If you did not complete that exercise successfully, open xdocwrite.html instead.)

2. **Open docwrite.html (or xdocwrite.html) in Navigator.**

3. **View the source code for the page (choose View→Page Source).**

```
<BODY>

<H1>Welcome to my home page</H1>

<P>This page is located at: file:///C|/data/docwrite.html</P><P>This p

</BODY>
</HTML>
```

Even though each of the `document.write()` statements is on a separate line in the source file, the output they produce is put on one line in the resulting HTML data.

4. **Close the source code window.**

5. **Open docwriteln.html in your editor.** This file matches what you created in docwrite.html except that it uses the `document.writeln()` method rather than `document.write()`. Again, each of the JavaScript statements is on its own line.

6. **Open docwriteln.html in Navigator.** The generated page appears identical in the browser to docwrite.html.

7. **View the source code for the page (choose View→Page Source).**

```
<BODY>
<h1>Welcome to my home page</h1>

<H2>JavaScript rules!</H2>
<P>This page is located at: file:///C|/data/docwriteln.html
<P>This page last modified: Thursday, April 01, 1999 16:56:04
```

This time the resulting code is more readable because each of the output lines is on its own line. This code is more readable and the resulting Web page is the same. This file illustrates one of the good uses of `document.writeln()`.

8. Close the source code window.

Topic 6C

Dynamic Documents

The Document object enables dynamic documents by letting you write to existing documents or even create entirely new documents. Unfortunately, the ways in which browser vendors have implemented their products have made dynamic content a difficult and frustrating adventure.

Dynamic HTML offers great promise for improved online experiences. DHTML is not so much a stand-alone technology as a combination of technologies. Most people regard DHTML to be a combination of standard HTML, JavaScript, Cascading Style Sheets, and vendor-specific technologies (scriptlets, behaviors, etc.).

Dynamic HTML:
The combined use of HTML, JavaScript, Cascading Style Sheets, and vendor-specific technologies to enable dynamic content in Web pages.

Dueling DOMs

The key to making a Web page dynamic is to access its existing contents (so that you can change them). You do so through the Document Object Model (DOM). The *DOM* describes how the components of a document are arranged in a hierarchical order. It further specifies how you will access each of the objects in the hierarchy. Unfortunately, the 4.x versions of Navigator and Internet Explorer implement different DOMs. The World Wide Web Consortium's (W3C) new standardized DOM, which both vendors helped to define, is different yet. (Both vendors have promised to support the new standardized DOM in future browser versions.)

DOM (Document Object Model):
The hierarchical arrangement of component objects (text, image, form, and other elements) in a document.

Internet Explorer

Internet Explorers DOM is closest to the W3C's specification. It enables you to access nearly every component of a Web page through the all collection. The all collection is an array of all of the objects on a page. It is stored as a property of the Document object.

For example, suppose you enclosed some text inside a `<DIV ID= "myText">` container. You could reference that `<DIV>` container with this JavaScript syntax:

```
window.document.all["myText"]
```

And, you could change the text inside that `<DIV>` with this syntax:

```
window.document.all["myText"].innerText = "new text";
```

Or, for a shorter version of the same, you could use:

```
myText.innerText = "new text";
```

Furthermore, and this is perhaps one of the best features of Internet Explorer, once you change the contents of an existing page element, the browser redraws the page. The page is said to *reflow*, meaning that your new content and resulting layout will be displayed correctly (and immediately) to the user.

reflow:
A feature of Internet Explorer in which the page is automatically refreshed to reflect newly added dynamic content.

TASK 6C-1:

Dynamic content in Internet Explorer

Objective: To see how you can dynamically change page contents in Internet Explorer.

1. **Open innertext.html in Internet Explorer.** This page contains a running clock (shown in yellow to make it more obvious). As the time changes, the display is automatically updated.

2. **Open innertext.html in your editor.**

3. **Observe the function in the <HEAD> section of the document.**

```
function clock()
 {
  time = new Date();
  var hour = time.getHours();
  if(hour > 12) hour -= 12;
  var mins = time.getMinutes();
  var sec = time.getSeconds();
  var temp = hour;
  temp += ((mins < 10) ? ":0" : ":") + mins;
  temp += ((sec < 10) ? ":0" : ":") + sec;

  currTime.innerText = temp;
  // could also use the full notation of
  // window.document.all["currTime"].innerText = temp;
  id = setTimeout("clock()", 1000);
 }
```

The clock() function calculates the current time, formats the results for output, then writes the time to the page. Don't worry too much about how the function works.

4. **Observe the `currTime.innerText = temp;` statement.** This is the statement that outputs the current time to the page. It sets the `innerText` property of the `currTime` page element to the current time.

5. **Look for the <SPAN> tag in the body of the document.**

```
<P>The current time is <span id=currTime class=clk>00:00:00</span></P>
```

This container has an `id` of `currTime`. It is the container that will be updated with the current time. When the page first loads, it contains some placeholder text of 00:00:00.

6. **Open innertext.html in Navigator. What happens?**

Navigator

Navigator uses a more proprietary DOM based on layers. A layer is somewhat like a frame except that it is shown without borders or (in most cases) scrollbars. Layers are shown within the current document, not in a separate window-like area as frames are shown. Like frames, a layer corresponds roughly to a window. Thus, a Layer object has a `document` property, which has methods like `write()` and so forth.

You create layer in an HTML document with the `<LAYER>` tag. Some "normal" text and a layer are shown in the HTML fragment that follows:

```
<H1>This is a heading</H1>
This is normal text in the document.<P>
<LAYER>This is text in a layer.</LAYER>
This is more text in the document.<P>
```

Layers are drawn in the flow of the document; however, they don't affect the flow. To position layers, you will need to resort to using Cascading Style Sheets Positioning (CSS-P) techniques.

TASK 6C-2:

Layers in Navigator

Objective: To see how layers are created in Navigator and how they affect (or don't affect) page layout.

1. **Open blank.html in your editor.**

2. **Enter the following HTML code in the `<BODY>` section of the document:**

```
<H1>This is a heading</H1>
<P>This is normal text inthe document.</P>
<LAYER>This is text in a layer.</LAYER>
<P>This is more text in the document</P>
```

3. **Save the file as layertest.html and open that file in Navigator.**

The text of the layer is drawn right on top of the last line of text of the document. This is because the layer, while displayed in the place where it is defined in the HTML, does not affect the flow of the document. Subsequent text is displayed as if the layer were not there.

4. **Open layertest.html in Internet Explorer.**

   Internet Explorer ignores the `<LAYER>` tags, which it doesn't support. The text that is supposed to be in the layer is shown as if it were a normal paragraph of HTML text.

5. **Switch to your editor and change the `<LAYER>` tag to read:**

   ```
   <LAYER STYLE="position: relative; top: 50px; left: 100px;">
   ```

6. **Save your changes and reload the document in Navigator.**

   You have used a Cascading Style Sheets style statement to move the layer down 50 pixels and to the right 100 pixels. It no longer overlaps the standard HTML text.

7. **Reload layertest.html in Internet Explorer. Does it honor the positioning style information you added to the layer tag?**

Dynamic Layers

In Navigator, you can move and modify layers after the document is fully loaded. Unlike Internet Explorer, however, Navigator does not automatically reflow the document. After all, layers exist "outside" of the document layout, as you saw in the previous task.

To reference with JavaScript a layer in a document that you created with the `<LAYER>` tag container, you would use this JavaScript syntax:

```
window.document.layers[#]
```

Where # is a zero-based number referencing the layers in the order in which they are created in the source HTML document. You can name layers by using the `<LAYER NAME="myLayer">` notation. In that case, you would refer to the layer with either of these equivalent statements.

```
window.document.layers["myLayer"];
window.document.myLayer;
```

And you could change the text inside that layer with these statements.

```
window.document.myLayer.document.write("new text");
window.document.myLayer.close();
```

You must close a layer after you have written to it or your new text will not be displayed!

Dynamic HTML

To create truly dynamic documents, in which elements move and change or respond to user actions, you must write scripts that take into consideration the DOM differences of the two browsers. You will need to have a full understanding of Cascading Style Sheets, JavaScript events (and the two browsers' different event handling models), and browser detection techniques.

Creating Dynamic HTML documents is not an impossible task, though it isn't trivial either. It is beyond the scope of this course.

Level 0 DOM

All is not lost. Both browsers support a core set of objects that has been called the Level 0 Document Object Model. Writing scripts that manipulate the *Level 0 DOM* is the way most people currently implement cross-browser dynamic HTML. The options this DOM gives you are to write to documents as they are being parsed and to create complete new documents using the `document.write()` method. Both browsers enable you to change the form and image elements.

You will commonly see form text boxes used as output lines for "dynamic" documents. An object representing each form in an HTML document is stored in the `forms[]` array, which is stored as a property of the Document object. You can refer to these forms by their position in the array (which corresponds to their position in the HTML code):

```
document.forms[0] // refers to the first form in a page
```

You can name forms when you create them by adding a NAME="name" parameter to the <FORM> tag. If you do so, you can use the name to refer to the form:

```
document.entryForm  // refers to a form named entryForm
```

Elements within the form are stored in arrays within the Form object. You could again access them through their positions within those arrays. However, it is far easier to name each elements, again with the NAME="name" parameter, and use that name in your script. For example, suppose you created a form with this HTML:

```
<FORM NAME="entryForm">
<INPUT TYPE=text NAME=txtBox1 VALUE="Enter your name">
<INPUT TYPE=button VALUE="OK">
</FORM>
```

You could later refer to the text box named txtBox1 with this JavaScript.

```
document.entryForm.txtBox1       // refers to txtBox1 in
entryForm
```

And, to read its value (or set it) you would use this syntax:

```
document.entryForm.txtBox1.value    // refers to value of txtBox1
```

TASK 6C-3:

Creating a dynamic form

> **Objective:** To use JavaScript and the Level 0 DOM to create a dynamic form button that changes text when you click it.

1. **Open blank.html in your editor.**

2. **In script block in the <HEAD> section of the document, enter:**

```
function updForm()
   {
   document.forms[0].btn.value= "Ouch!";
   setTimeout("document.forms[0].btn.value= 'Click me'", 1000);
   }
```

3. In the `<BODY>` section of the document, enter the following HTML.

```
<form>
<input type=button name=btn value= "Click me" onClick=⇒
"updForm()">
</form>
```

4. Save the file as dynaform.html and load it in your browser.

5. Click the "Click Me" button. After you click the button, the text changes. Approximately one second later, it changes back.

6. Open clock.html in your browser.

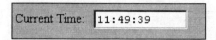

This page uses a form to display a running clock.

7. View the source code for the page. JavaScript is used to calculate the clock output. The resulting time is written to the value property of the form text box every second.

8. Close the source code window.

Cross-Browser Image Rollovers

One of the most popular dynamic HTML techniques is the image rollover. Image rollovers cause images to change when your mouse pointer is over them. You might have seen buttons or links that "light up" when you point at them. Or, this technique is sometimes used to build custom pop-out menus.

You can use many techniques, some of them quite involved, to produce rollovers. However, you can use features available with the Level 0 DOM to create the same effect. An object representing each image in an HTML document is stored in the images [] array, which is stored as a property of the Document object. You can refer to these forms by their position in the array (which correspond to their position in the HTML code):

```
document.images[0]
// refers to the first image
// in a page
```

You can name images when you create them by adding a NAME="name" parameter to the <IMG> tag. If you do so, you can use the name to refer to the form:

```
document.logo
// refers to an image named logo
```

One of the properties of interest of each of these image objects is its SCR property. The SRC property defines the URL of the image to be displayed. For example, to read the URL of the first image in a document, you could use this syntax:

```
imgURL = document.images[0].src;
```

This would be only a curiosity if this were all you could do. Fortunately, both browsers let you set the SRC property, and when you do so, they change the image that is shown. So, to make a rollover, you need only to determine when the mouse pointer is over an image, and when it is, change that image to something different.

Internet Explorer supports events with images. In other words, you could add an onMouseover="" event handler parameter to an <IMG> tag in Internet Explorer, and your code would be executed. Unfortunately, Navigator does not support events with images. Both browsers do support events with links, however. That's okay, because most often rollover images are used as navigation buttons.

TASK 6C-4:

Creating an image rollover effect with the Level 0 DOM

Objective: To write a script that creates a rollover effect so that images change when users move their mouse pointer over an image.

1. **Open rollover.html in your browser and put your mouse pointer over the image.** Of course, nothing happens. You'll be adding the necessary code to make the image change when the mouse pointer is over it.

2. **Open rollover.html in your editor.**

3. **Observe the existing link and image tag.**

   ```
   <A HREF="home.htm">
     <IMG SRC="img-off.gif" WIDTH=132 HEIGHT=44 BORDER=0 ALT="">
   </A>
   ```

   There is nothing special about these tags. The link tag simply links to a (non-existent) new page and the image tag puts an image on your page.

4. **Change the <IMG> tag so that it reads.**

   ```
   <IMG SRC="img-off.gif" WIDTH=132 HEIGHT=44 BORDER=0 ALT=
   ""NAME="img1">
   ```

   You have now named the image so that you can easily refer to it in script.

5. **Change the <A> tag so that it reads:**

   ```
   <A HREF="home.htm" onMouseover="document.img1.src=
   'imgon.gif';">
   ```

   You have specified some JavaScript code to run when the mouse pointer is over the image. This code changes the SRC property of the image named img1. The new image will be displayed when you point at the image. Remember to be careful with your quotes—they must be used in matched pairs.

6. **Save your changes and reload the file in your browser.**

7. **Put your mouse pointer over the image.** It might take a second, but the new image is displayed.

8. **Move your mouse pointer away from the image. What happens?**

9. **Switch to your editor.**

10. Following the format of the code above, **add an onMouseout handler that resets the image to img-off.gif** when the mouse pointer no longer points at the link. Your <A> tag should now read:

```
<A HREF= "home.htm" onMouseover= "document.img1.src=
'img-on.gif';" onMouseout= "document.img1.src='img-off.gif';">
```

11. **Save your changes and test your solution.**

A finished version of the file is available as xrollover.html.

CHECK YOUR SKILLS 6-2

Suggested Time:
5 minutes or less

If you used Navigator for the task, open rollover.html in Internet Explorer or vice versa. The rollover effect should work just fine in both browsers.

Apply Your Knowledge 6-1

Suggested Time:
less than 5 minutes

In this activity, you will use the properties and methods of the Document object to output some standardized information to a page.

1. Open docfooter.html in your browser. This file contains some simple HTML content. You will be adding a footer section to the page to note the date and time the file was last modified and to note the files URL.

2. Open docfooter.html in your editor.

3. So that it is displayed after the horizontal rule, add the code to display the URL of the page. Include a text label such as "This page is at:" so users will understand the purpose of the URL. Format the text and URL output as font size "-1" so that it appears smaller than the rest of the text on the page.

4. Following the code you just entered, add the code necessary to output the date and time the file was last modified. Include appropriate label text. Format the text as font size "-1" so that it appears smaller than the rest of the text on the page.

5. Save the file and reload it in your browser. The new coding should work without error to output the URL, the date and time the file was last modified, and your label text. If not, correct your mistakes, save, and reload.

Summary

In lesson 6, you saw how the many properties of the Document object can be used to add system information to the current document, how you can write to the current document or to a new one, and how you can use Level 0 DOM techniques to make your pages dynamic. You will probably use the properties and methods of the Document object more often than those of nearly any other object.

Lesson Review

6A List three commonly used properties or methods of the Document object and note their purpose.

6B Why might you use document.writeln() rather than document.write()?

6C What property of an image can you modify after the page is loaded to produce a dynamic page effect?

Working With Frames

Overview

Frames are a convenient and powerful HTML technique for creating complex layouts for Web pages. You can further use JavaScript to access and manipulate the contents of frames. You can even use some simple scripting to prevent your pages from being loaded into someone else's frames. This lesson starts with a review of HTML frames. Then, it covers what you need to know to work with frames through JavaScript.

Objectives

In this lesson, you will:

7A   Review HTML frames and the methods for creating framed documents.

You should be familiar with frames from the pre-requisites for this course. However, a little review never hurts. In this topic, you'll briefly review how to create frames in your Web pages using HTML.

7B   Script with frames in mind.

You will examine how to write scripts that interact with framed documents. You'll also explore a couple of techniques for preventing your Web pages from being loaded into someone else's frames.

Data Files

frameset1.html
main.html
frameinframe.html
sub2.html
sub3.html
frameset2.html
main2.html
frameset3.html
main3.html
leftbar2.html
framed.html
framebusters1.html
framebusters2.html
left.html

Lesson Time
1 hour, 15 minutes

Topic 7A

HTML Frames Review

Frames provide sub-windows within the browser window. They are a commonly used feature of HTML—one you have probably implemented many times yourself.

Creating a Frameset

frame:
A sub-window within a Web page. Used for creating complex layouts for Web pages.

frameset, also frameset document:
The Web page document that describes the frames to be created. Uses the <FRAMESET>, </FRAMESET>, and <FRAME> HTML tags to define the frame structure of the page.

Framesets define the structure of the *frames* on your "page. " A *frameset document* uses the <FRAMESET></FRAMESET> HTML tags rather than <BODY></BODY> tags. The frameset tags define how many frames you will create, their geometry, and other parameters.

```
<FRAMESET ROWS="20%,*">
  <FRAME SRC="topbar.html">
  <FRAMESET cols="20%,*">
      <FRAME SRC="leftbar.html">
      <FRAME SRC="main.html">
  </FRAMESET>
</FRAMESET>
```

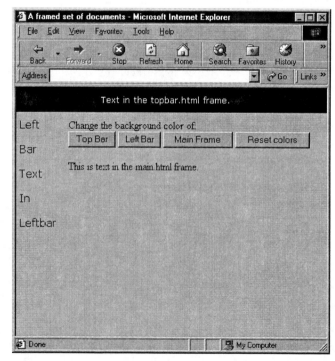

Figure 7-1: *The resulting framed document.*

Typically, you name your frames so that you can control where subsequent Web pages are loaded. Adding the TARGET="name" to a link will cause the linked-to Web page to be loaded into the named frame rather than the frame containing the link. The preceding code could be rewritten as:

```
<FRAMESET ROWS="20%,*">
   <FRAME NAME="topbar" SRC="topbar.html">
   <FRAMESET COLS="20%,*">
      <FRAME NAME="leftbar" SRC="leftbar.html">
      <FRAME NAME="main" SRC="main.html">
   </FRAMESET>
</FRAMESET>
```

In this example, the frame names correspond to the HTML documents initially loaded into the frames. You can use any names you wish, but using easily remembered names like these will help you in maintaining your Web site.

For more complete information on creating frames, visit the Netscape HTML Frames documentation page at: developer.netscape.com/docs/manuals/htmlguid/tags11.htm.

Topic 7B

Scripting for Frames

Many Web sites, perhaps including yours, use frames to lay out content in the Web browser. JavaScript includes strong support for manipulating multi-frame Web sites. JavaScript treats each frame like a separate window, making the techniques for accessing framed data familiar for those comfortable with working with multiple windows.

Every Window object has a few properties that are related to frames, as detailed in the following table.

People often build calculators in frames. The left frame is typically used to enter the values and the right frame displays the calculated results.

Property	Comments
Frames []	An array of frame (window) objects stored as a property of the Window object. This property exists for all windows, even if they do not have sub-frames.
frames.length	The number of frames contained in the `frames []` array. For documents without frames, this value is set to 0 (zero).
parent	A reference to the window that contains the window. In a page with one level of frames)the frameset document defines frames that contain only documents, not sub-frames), this refers to the frameset document. In pages with nested frames, this property refers to the document one level above the current page.
top	No matter how deeply nested frames, each frame has a property, `top`, that refers to the topmost document in the hierarchy.
self	A synonym for `window`, representing the current Window. Sometimes this property is useful to avoid confusion as to which Window you are referring.

You can use these properties to refer to sibling frames for the purposes of accessing their properties or writing to those frames. For example, in a frameset with two frames, there will be three Window objects: top, representing the frameset document, and `frames[0]` and `frames[1]` representing the pages loaded into each of the two frames.

To access one frame from the other frame, you must create a notation that points up either to the top of the hierarchy or to a parent level over both frames. So, in the example preceding, a script in the first frame (`frames[0]`) could refer to the second frame as `top.frames[1]` or `parent.frames[1]`. In this case, top and parent are synonyms. That would not be the case with nested frames.

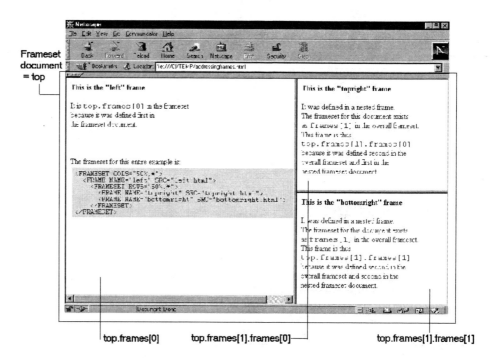

Figure 7-2: *How frames are noted within a frameset.*

You could think of the `top.frames[]` notation the same way you might think about a family's hierarchy. In a family, you could think of yourself as Grandpa. Dad.me (or Grandma.Mom.me, if you prefer), noting your lineage from the head of your family. Assuming you're the first-born, your siblings could be Grandpa. Dad.child[1] and Grandpa.Dad.child[2]. Or, you could refer to them as Dad. child[1] and so forth, noting the lineage starting at the common parent. Frames are accessed through the same type of hierarchical notation. The top is the patriarch (or matriarch) of the family. Frames at the next level down are like children of top. Furthermore, they can be `parent` to frames nested within themselves.

TASK 7B-1:

Accessing other frames

Objective: To observe a script that accesses the properties of another frame and writes content to sibling frames.

1. **Open frameset1.html in your browser.** This file is a frameset file that opens three frames: topbar.html, leftbar.html, and main.html. This file creates a framed document that looks like this:

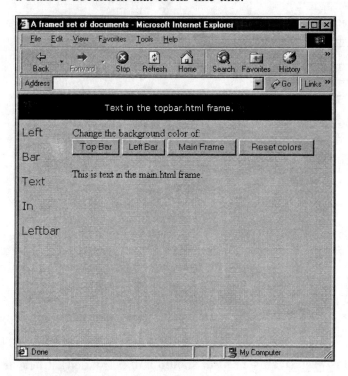

2. **Open frameset1.html in your editor.** For appearance's sake, many tag parameters have been used. Many of these are, of course, optional.

```
<HTML>
<HEAD>
  <TITLE>A framed set of documents</TITLE>
</HEAD>

<FRAMESET ROWS="10%,*" FRAMESPACING="0" FRAMEBORDER="0" FRAMEMARGIN="no" BORDER="none">
    <FRAME SRC="topbar.html" FRAMEBORDER="No" SCROLLING="No"  FRAMESPACING="0">
    <FRAMESET COLS="15%, *" FRAMESPACING="0" FRAMEBORDER="0">
        <FRAME SRC="leftbar.html" FRAMEBORDER="No" SCROLLING="No" FRAMESPACING="0">
        <FRAME SRC="main.html" FRAMEBORDER="No" SCROLLING="Auto" FRAMESPACING="0">
    </FRAMESET>
</FRAMESET>

</HTML>
```

3. **Open main.html in your editor.** This page creates four buttons that you can click to change the background colors of each of the frames. The onClick handler for each of the buttons has been assigned a script that sets the bgColor (background color) property of the Document object in each of the frames. Observe the frame notations used in the onClick handlers for each button:

```
<INPUT TYPE="button"
       VALUE="Top Bar"
       onClick="top.frames[0].document.bgColor='white'">

<INPUT TYPE="button"
       VALUE="Left Bar"
       onClick="parent.frames[1].document.bgColor='white'">

<INPUT TYPE="button"
       VALUE="Main Frame"
       onClick="self.document.bgColor='white'">

<INPUT TYPE="button"
       onClick="top.frames[0].document.bgColor='black';
                parent.frames[1].document.bgColor='#cccc99';
                self.document.bgColor='#cccc99'"
       VALUE="Reset colors"
       >
```

The top bar frame is referred to as `top.frames[0]`, which reflects its status as the first frame defined in the frameset. The left bar is created next in the frameset. Using the `parent notation`, this frame would be called `parent.frames[1]`. Equivalently, we could have referred to this as `top.frames[1]`. Finally, the frame containing main.html is referred to using the `self` synonym for `window`. We could have referred to this frame with the top notation also (`top.frames[2]`), or as `window`.

4. **Switch to your browser (framset1.html should still be loaded). Click any or all of the three buttons, and then click Reset Colors.** The background of each frame in turn is changed to white and then reset to its original color.

5. Consider a frameset that loads three files, topbar.html, leftbar.html, and mainframe.html. In this case, mainframe.html is also a frameset document, which opens sub1.html, sub2.html and sub3.html. None of the frames are named in the frameset documents. If you had a script in the sub2.html document.

   How would you refer to a property of the documents loaded in leftbar. html and sub3.html?

It might help to draw a sketch of what this frameset might look like in order to answer this question.

6. Open frameinframe.html in your browser.

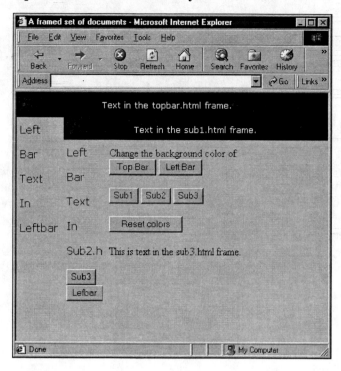

7. Click each of the buttons to change the colors. Buttons in the frames set the colors of the other frames.

8. Open sub2.html in your editor. Observe the `onClick` handlers. Was your speculation in step 5 correct?

9. Open sub3.html in your editor. This page can set colors for any of the frames. Observe the notation used. It uses the top notation to access the subframes by starting at the top of the frames hierarchy. So, you'll see notations like `top.frames[2].frames[1].document.bgColor='white'` to access the nested frames.

Naming Frames

Rather than refer to frames using the `frames[]` array, which can quickly get confusing, you can refer to frames by their names. You name the frames in the frameset document.

```
<FRAMESET ROWS="20%,*">
   <FRAME NAME="topbar" SRC="topbar.html">
   <FRAMESET COLS="20%,*">
      <FRAME NAME="leftbar" SRC="leftbar.html">
           <FRAME NAME="main" SRC="main.html">
   </FRAMESET>
</FRAMESET>
```

In the preceding example, three frames are created and each is named. As you have seen, you could refer to these frames as `top.frames[0]`, `top.frames[1]`, and `top.frames[2]`. Better yet, you can use their names; `top.banner`, `top.leftbar`, and `top.main`.

TASK 7B-2:

Using frame names in your script

Objective: To observe a script that accesses the properties of another frame via the frame names rather than the frames[] array.

1. **Open frameset2.html in your editor.** This file is a frameset file that opens three frames: topbar.html, leftbar.html, and main2.html. This file creates a framed document that looks just like the one created by frameset1.html.

2. **Open main2.html in your editor.** This page also creates four buttons that you can click to change the background colors of each of the frames. However, in this document, the scripts in the `onClick` handlers use the frame names to refer to each of the frames.

```
<FORM>Change the background color of:<BR>
    <INPUT TYPE="button"
        VALUE="Top Bar"
        onClick="top.topbar.document.bgColor='white'">
    <INPUT TYPE="button"
        VALUE="Left Bar"
        onClick="top.leftbar.document.bgColor='white'">
    <INPUT TYPE="button"
        VALUE="Main Frame"
        onClick="top.main.document.bgColor='white'">
    <INPUT TYPE="button"
        VALUE="Reset colors"
        onClick="top.topbar.document.bgColor='black';
                top.leftbar.document.bgColor='#cccc99';
                top.main.document.bgColor='#cccc99'"
        >
</FORM><P>This is text in the main2.html frame.</P>
```

The top bar frame is referred to as top.topbar, the left bar is referred to as `top.leftbar`, and the third frame is referred to as `top.main`. Using frame names is probably easier for most scripters.

3. **Open frameset2.html in your browser. Click any or all of the three buttons, and then click Reset Colors.** The background of each frame in turn is changed to white and then reset to its original color.

Cross-frame Scripting

Variables, functions, and objects that you create with JavaScript are stored as properties of the Window object. That fact doesn't change when you add frames to the picture, except that frames are treated like Window objects. So, to access a variable's value, a function, or object from one frame that has been created in another frame, you simply need to use the standard frame notation to refer to the appropriate frame. You can read and write to variables, functions, and objects in another frame.

Functions are executed in the scope in which they are defined. If you define a function in one frame and call it from another, it executes in the scope of the first frame. This can have an impact on which global variables and object properties are available for the script to use. Keep that in mind if you use functions across frames.

TASK 7B-3:

Examining cross-frame scripting

Objective: To modify a sample page to read and write values of variables in another frame.

1. **Open frameset3.html in your editor and examine the HTML code.** This frameset document creates a page with three frames.

2. **Open frameset3.html in your browser.**

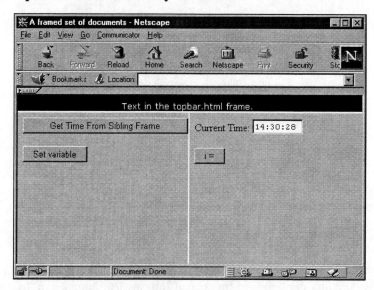

The top frame contains only text. The left frame contains two buttons, which you will make access values set in the main frame. The main frame contains a running clock and a single button.

3. **Click the i=**  **button.**

An alert box is displayed showing the current value of the variable `i`.

4. **Click OK then click the other buttons** (in the left frame). They do nothing at this point as you haven't added the code to make them work yet.

5. **Open main3.html in your editor.** This is the file that is loaded into the right frame.

6. **Examine the script in this file,** some of which is shown in this screen capture.

```
var i = 100;                     // declare a global variable i

// === create a running clock =====================================
var now;                         // declare now as global variable
function clock()
  {
  var time = new Date();         // create date object
  var hour = time.getHours();    // extract hours
  var min = time.getMinutes();   // extract minutes
  var sec = time.getSeconds();   // extract seconds
  now = hour;                    // begin building the output string

  // if minutes less than 10, append colon and zero then minutes
  // otherwise append colon and minutes
  if(min < 10)
    {
    now += ":0" + min;
    }
  else
    {
    now += ":" + min;
    }

  // repeat same for seconds
  if(sec < 10)
```

First, the code declares and sets a global variable i, which has the value 100. Next, the code creates a clock: a global variable, now, is created to hold the value produced by the clock() function. The onLoad handler of the <BODY> tag starts the clock. You won't be modifying any of this code.

7. **Open leftbar2.html in your editor.** This is the page that is loaded into the left frame. It contains the two non-functional buttons. An empty onClick handler has been added to each of the buttons created on this page.

8. For the first button, you will add the code necessary to display an alert box showing the current time as calculated in the main3.html frame. **Add the following code to the first button's event handler.**

```
onClick = "alert(top.main.now);"
```

The current time is stored in the variable now by the function in the right frame (named "main"). This notation is how you would read the value of that variable from another frame in the frameset.

9. **Save your changes and reload the frameset in your browser.** (If you are using Navigator, you will need to hold down [Ctrl]+ [Shift] and click Reload to force the frames to reload.)

10. **Does the button work? If not, correct your code and retry this step.**

11. **Switch to your editor and add the following code to the second button's event handler.**

```
onClick = "top.main.i='Hello';"
```

The value of the variable i was set by the script in the right frame (named "main"). This notation is how you would write a new value to that variable from another frame in the frameset.

12. **Save your changes, and reload the frameset in your browser.** (Don't forget to do a [Ctrl] + [Shift] + Reload with Navigator.)

13. **Click the i=** i = **button.** The alert box is displayed showing a value of 100.

14. **Click the Set Variable** Set variable **button, and then click on the i=** i = **button.** The alert box should now display a value for i equal to "Hello." If it does not, correct your code and retry these steps.

Sample working code answering both steps 7 and 9 is provided in the xleftbar2.html file. You will need to modify frameset3.html to load that file instead of leftbar2.html if you want to see it in action.

Detecting Frames and Breaking Out

It is rude, and even a violation of copyright laws, to include someone else's Web site within a frame on your site. Of course, you wouldn't be so inconsiderate. But there are those on the net who might put one of your pages into their frameset. You can use some simple JavaScript to make sure your pages are not loaded into someone else's frames.

Every Window object has `parent`, and `self` properties. In the case of a document without frames, each of those objects simply refers to the current window. However, when a document is part of a frameset, those properties do take on unique values. For example, `top.frames.length` is zero when frames don't exist and non-zero when they do. In a framed document, `parent` and `self` refer to different objects. You can use either of these facts to create a "frame busting" script.

TASK 7B-4:

Examining two frame-busting scripts

Objective: To examine two scripts that can be used to make sure your Web page is not loaded into somebody else's frameset.

1. **Open framed.html in your browser.**

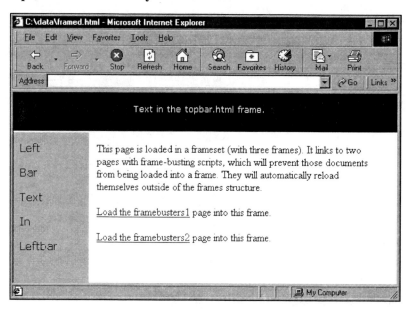

This page is a frameset that defines three frames. The top frame and left frame are simply fillers to show you the structure of the frameset. The right frame contains links to two pages, each with a different frame-busting script in it.

2. **Click on the Load The Framebusters1 link and watch what happens.** For a quick moment, the framebusters1.html page is loaded into the right frame. Then, it reloads itself outside of the frame structure.

3. **Click Back** ⬅️ **.**

4. **Click on the Load The Framebusters2 link and watch what happens.** Just like the first sample, the framebusters2.html page is loaded into the right frame. Then it reloads itself outside of the frame structure.

5. **Open framebusters1.html in your editor.** This is the first document that busted out of the frames.

6. **Examine the code block in the `<HEAD>` section of the document.**

```
if(top.frames.length != 0)
  {
  top.location = self.location
  }
```

Whether you choose to use method one or two as shown in these samples is up to you. Both are effective and cross-browser and cross-version compatible.

Do not use a frame-busting script like this in a frameset document. Doing so will most likely crash your browser (or those of the people visiting your Web site).

This script tests for a non-zero length to the `top.frames[]` array. If it is non-zero, then frames must exist and the page must have been loaded into a frameset. In that case, the `location` property for the top window is set to the value as the current (`self`) window. This effectively reloads the page, opening only the framebusters1.html page outside of the frameset.

7.   **Open framebusters2.html in your editor.**

8.   **Examine the code block in the `<HEAD>` section of the document.**

```
if(self != parent)
   {
   top.location = self.location
   }
```

This code might not be as intuitively clear. It tests to see if the `self` object is the same as the `parent` object. These objects would be different objects if the page has been loaded into a frameset. In the case they aren't equal, the `location` property for the `top` window is set to that of the current window—again, effectively reloading the page, this time framebusters2.html, outside of the frameset.

Summary

In lesson 7, you reviewed how to create frames with HTML. Then, you looked at some of the issues of accessing and manipulating framed documents and their contents. You even saw two methods for keeping your pages from being loaded into someone else's frameset.

Apply Your Knowledge 7-1

Suggested Time:
15 minutes

In this activity, you will create a frameset document and use it and its sub-documents to practice cross-frame scripting.

1.   Use your editor to create a frameset document that creates two frames. The frames should divide the browser window into two columns, each taking up 50% of the window area. Name the frames leftbar and body. Specify to load the documents left.html and body.html into those frames, respectively. Blank HTML documents of those names are included with the rest of the data files. Save the file as myframe.html.

2.   Open left.html in your editor. Create a form with one button with the label text "Navigate". Add an `onClick` handler to the button so when the button is clicked, the file clock.html is loaded into the right frame.

3.   Save your changes and load your frameset into your browser. Click on your button. The clock.html file should be loaded into the right frame. If it is not, correct your code and try again.

4. Switch to your editor. Add a new button to the left frame with the label "Write Text". Add an `onClick` handler that uses the `document.write()` method to the button so that when the button is clicked, the text "Hello body frame, this is the leftbar frame speaking" is written to the right frame.

5. Save your changes and load your frameset into your browser. Click your new button. The text should be written into the right frame. If it is not, correct your code and try again.

Lesson Review

7A What is the purpose of the `<FRAMESET>` and `<FRAME>` tags of HTML?

7B Given a document with three frames named `left`, `righttop`, and `rightbottom` and loaded in that order in the frameset document, how would a script in the `righttop` frame access a variable named `currDate` in the left frame?

Working with Forms and Forms-Based Data

Data Files
object enumerator.html
form elements.html
formleft.html
formright.html
writeform.html
select.html
changeoption.html
radio.html
formnav.html

Lesson Time
2 hours

Overview

Forms are everywhere on the net. JavaScript is a great tool for working with HTML forms. You can read data users enter into your forms. You can write to form fields—even creating dynamic page elements like clocks in them. Once you have mastered those techniques, you can use JavaScript to validate the data users enter into forms. Though, that's not the focus of this lesson.

Objectives

In this lesson, you will:

8A   **Explore the Form object and its properties, methods, and event handlers.**

In this topic, you'll see how the Form object fits into the hierarchy of JavaScript objects. And, you'll take a quick look at some of its most important properties, methods, and event handlers.

8B   **Read data from and write data to form elements using JavaScript.**

Often, form processing is performed with server-side programming. However, you can use JavaScript to access and modify the data users enter into forms. You'll examine those techniques in this topic.

Topic 8A

The Form Object

The Form object represents HTML forms on the page. One Form object exists for each HTML form on the page. Form objects have properties that represent the elements of the form (text boxes, check boxes, and so forth), some of which are also objects with properties.

form element:
The various text boxes, check boxes, buttons, and so forth that make up an HTML form.

The Form object on its own isn't very interesting. Sure, the Form object has a couple of methods that are designed to simulate the user clicking buttons on the form. It also has a few event handlers that are triggered when the user enters data in the form, submits it, or resets the form. Those are commonly used for form-data validation. But in most cases the real interest lies in the elements of the form—those objects representing the buttons, text boxes, and so forth on the form.

TASK 8A-1:

Viewing the properties of the Form object

Objective: To take a quick view of the properties of the Form object.

1. **Open object enumerator.html in Navigator.** This page contains three buttons, which when clicked show the properties of certain JavaScript objects.

2. **Click the Show Form Properties button.** The buttons on the Object Enumerator page are created with a simple HTML form. The object enumerator script reads and displays the properties of that form. Because of its simplicity in this example, only a few properties of the Form object are available.

3. **What do you think the method, action, encoding, and target properties refer to?**

4. **What do you think the first three properties (form.0, form.1, and form.2) represent?**

5. **Open object enumerator.html in Internet Explorer and click the Show Form Properties button.** Internet Explorer supports a much larger set of properties for the Form object. Thus, the resulting set is much larger than with Navigator. If you are programming for an all-Internet Explorer environment, feel free to learn about and use these properties. Otherwise, stick to those supported by Navigator because Internet Explorer supports that subset of properties too.

Accessing Forms

Form objects are stored in the document.forms[] array in the order in which they are created on the page. So, if your Web page has two forms, the first will be `document.forms[0]` and the second will be `document.forms[1]`. Elements of each form are stored within that Form object. So, the first element of the first form would be `document.forms[0].elements[0]` and the first element of the second form would be `document.forms[1].elements[0]`.

To access forms within the document and elements within the forms, you use a similar hierarchical notation that you use for frames. In this case, you are accessing a hierarchy of items within a single document rather than accessing a hierarchy of documents.

To make your JavaScript programming life easier, you can name your forms and their elements. Then, you can use a much more intuitive means to access those items. You'll still use a hierarchical notation. But, the names will make the items more easily recognizable.

Consider the case where you have created a form with the `<FORM NAME="signupForm">` tag. Your JavaScript code could refer to that form as document.signupForm regardless of whether it was the first or fiftieth form on the page. In the same manner, now imagine that our example form has a text box that was created with the `<INPUT TYPE="text" NAME="firstName">` tag. In your scripts, you could refer to that text box as `document.signupForm.firstName`.

You will notice that buttons appear in the listing of form properties. That's to be expected. The properties actually contain HTML codes. When the browser reads the data to be displayed, it finds those codes and interprets them in the same way it would interpret any other codes in a Web page.

TASK 8A-2:

Naming a form

Objective: To name an HTML form and view the Form object's name property.

1. **Open object enumerator.html in your editor.**

2. **Locate the `<FORM>` tag. Change the tag to read:**

   ```
   <FORM NAME="showObjProps">
   ```

3. **Save your changes and reload the page in your browser.** We suggest you use Navigator, because its set of form properties is smaller. Thus, the changes you are making might be clearer.

4. **Click the Show Form Properties button.** Look for the `form.name=` line. Your new form name is shown.

5. **Switch back to your editor. Locate the following code:**

```
<INPUT
    TYPE="button"
    VALUE="Show Form Properties"
    onClick="showProps(forms[0], 'form');
>
<BR>
```

This block of code, like the others within the form, creates a button that when clicked on calls the `showProps()` function. Two parameters are passed to the function: the first is an object reference and the second is a string representing the name of the object, which will be used in the output of the function. The Form object is passed to the function as part of the function call. You'll learn more about that a little later in this lesson.

6. **Copy that block of code and paste a new copy immediately following the existing copy.**

7. **Change the VALUE parameter for the new button you have created to:**

    `VALUE="Show Named Form Properties"`

8. **Cahnge the `onClick`hander to read:**

    `onClick="showProps(document.showObjProps, 'form');"`

9. **Save your changes and reload the page in your browser. You should now have** You should now have a new button on your form. If not, correct your HTML and repeat this step.

10. **Click your new button.** You should get the same results as you did in step 4. You have accessed the same object using a different notation—by using its name rather than its ordinal position within the `forms[]` array. Using the form's name is useful and convenient, especially if you have more than one form on a page.

Properties, Methods, Event Handlers (PMEs)

The Form object contains the following PMEs.

Properties	Description	Version
`action`	A read/write string that stores the URL to which the form's contents will be submitted.	1.0
`elements[]`	An array of elements on the form, in ordinal order. One entry is added to the array for every element (button, text box, etc.) on the form.	1.0
`encoding`	A read/write string that stores the encoding method used toformat.	1.0
`length`	The number of elements on the form. This is the same as `form.elements.length`.	1.0
`method`	A read/write string that stores the name of the form.	1.0
`name`	A read/write string that stores the name of the frame in which the returned results from this form should be displayed.	1.0

9. **Add the following line to the addItem() function:**

```
frm.changeMe.options[frm.changeMe.length] =⇒
new Option(frm.addTo.value);
```

Make sure to enter all that on just one line. This code creates a new option, reading the text for that option from the addTo field on the form. The remainder of the new Option() constructor's parameters are optional and not specified in this code.

10. **Scroll to the HTML portion of the document and add this handler to the Add It To The List button:**

```
onClick="addItem(this.form)"
```

Without this change, you could click the Add It To The List button until you were blue in the face, but the select lists contents would never change! Here, you are calling the addItem() function and passing it the form you want it to manipulate.

11. **Save your changes and reload the page in your browser.**

12. **Test your function by adding a new item to the select list.** (Enter text in the text box, then click Add It To The List.) Your new item shows up immediately in the select list box.

13. **Click the Show Select List Contents button.** Your new item is included in the list.

14. **Click OK.**

Removing Items From a Select List

Removing items from a select list is a bit easier. Just set the option equal to null and it will be removed from the list. The list will automatically collapse so that there isn't a "hole" in it where your option used to be. In the following statement, i is the option's ordinal position number in the array.

```
document.myForm.mySel.options[i] = null;
```

TASK 8B-6:

Removing items from a select list

> **Objective:** To add the coding necessary to remove selected options from a select list after the page has been fully loaded.

1. **Switch to your editor.**

2. **Observe the remItem() function code.** It's an empty function. This function is going to have to determine which option is selected, then delete it.

3. **Add this line to the remItem() function:**

```
frm.changeMe.options[frm.changeMe.selectedIndex] = null;
```

This code determines which is the selected option with `frm.changeMe.selectedIndex` and uses that to note which option to work with in the `frm.changeMe.options[]` part of the statement. Then it sets that option equal to `null`, removing it from the select list. If no options are selected, your function should do nothing.

4. **Scroll to the HTML portion of the document and add this handler to the Remove It button:**

```
onClick="remItem(this.form)"
```

5. **Save your changes and reload the page in your browser.**

6. **Test your function by removing an item from the select list.** (Select an item in the list and click the Remove It button.) The selected option disappears from the list immediately.

7. **Click the Show Select List Contents button.** The item you deleted is no longer included in the list.

8. **Click OK.**

Radio Buttons and Check Boxes

Radio buttons and check boxes present users with items to choose from. Radio buttons allow an exclusive choice: only one radio button from a set can be selected at any one time. Check boxes allow multiple simultaneous selections.

The following tables list the PMEs for radio buttons and check boxes.

Properties	Description
checked	A read/write Boolean that indicates whether the element is checked or not.
defaultChecked	A read-only Boolean that indicates whether the element is checked when the form is first loaded or after being reset.
form	A reference to the form that contains the element.
name	A read/write string that stores the name of the set of radio buttons or check boxes. All of the check boxes or radio buttons in a set have the same value for this property—that's what defines them as a set.
name[]	A read-only string that specifies the elements type.
type	A read-only string that specifies the elements type.
value	A string that stores the text that will be submitted to the server when the form is submitted. By default, the value equals on. This property does not indicate whether the element is checked or not. This string is not the text that shows up alongside the radio button or check box.

Methods	Description
blur()	Removes focus from the element.
click()	Simulates a mouse click on the element.
focus()	Gives focus to the element.

Event handlers	The handler invoked when
onblur	Focus is taken away from the element.
onclick	The element is clicked on.
onfocus	The element receives focus.

Checking Out Radio Buttons and Check Boxes

Radio button and check box sets work much like select- multiple lists in that there is no single property that you can read to determine which button is checked. You have to loop through the items in the set, looking at the checked property for each to determine which one the user has checked.

Radio buttons and check boxes are built as sets that share a common name. Each button or box is stored as an element in an array named after the set's name. For example, if you produced a radio button set with code like this:

```
<FORM NAME="simpleFrm">
Yes: <INPUT TYPE="radio" NAME="rad" CHECKED>
No: <INPUT TYPE="radio" NAME="rad">
Maybe: <INPUT TYPE="radio" NAME="rad">
<BR><BR>
<INPUT TYPE="button" VALUE="Which radio button is checked?"⇒
     onClick="whichIsIt(this.form)">
</FORM>
```

You could determine which radio button was checked with JavaScript code like this:

```
for(i=0; i<document.simpleFrm.rad.length; i++)
   {
   if(document.simpleFrm.rad[i].checked == true)
      {
      alert("Radio button " + i + " is checked.");
      }
   }
```

You will notice that the array of radio buttons is accessed through its name, as assigned in HTML. So the array is called `rad[]`, the number of elements in the array is rad.length, and an individual radio button is `rad[i]`.

The code for check boxes would work just like the preceding sample except that it would have to accommodate the fact that multiple check boxes in a set can be checked at once.

TASK 8B-7:

Determining which radio buttons are checked

1. **Open radio.html in your editor.** This simple page contains a form with three radio buttons and one button. The button has an `onClick` handler that calls the `whichIsIt()` function, which right now is empty.

2. The code for this sample will be slightly different than that shown in the preceding concepts. That code read the form directly from the page via the `document.forms[]` array. Your code here will use a form object that you pass to the `whichIsIt()` function. So, **add this JavaScript code to the `whichIsIt()` function to display an alert box that states which radio button is checked.**

```
for(i=0; i<frm.rad.length; i++)
   {
   if(frm.rad[i].checked == true)
     {
     alert("Radio button " + i + " is checked.");
     }
   }
```

3. **Save your changes.**

4. **Open radio.html in either browser.**

5. **Select any one of the radio buttons and click Which Is Checked to test your code.** If necessary, correct any errors and re-test.

Apply Your Knowledge 8-1

Reading from check boxes

In this activity, you will modify your code in the radio.html page so that the form displays check boxes and your JavaScript determines which check boxes are checked.

1. If necessary, open radio.html in your editor.

2. Modify the HTML form so that it displays three check boxes instead of three radio buttons. (Change the type to checkbox for each of the elements in the set.)

3. Change the name of the set of check boxes to `check` (it's `rad` right now, which doesn't seem to apply anymore).

A finished version of the file is avaible as xradio.html

Suggested Time:
15 minutes

4. Modify the `whichIsIt()` function so that it determines which check boxes are checked and displays an appropriate message. Don't forget that more than one check box can be checked at one time. So, you will need to build a list of check boxes that are checked as the loop progresses. You will probably need to declare an output variable before the loop begins and then append to it within the loop. Finally, display the results when the loop is complete.

5. Save the file as checkbox.html. Load it in your browser to test your coding. Correct any errors and re-test.

A finished version of the file is avaible as xcheckbox.html

Buttons

This category of form elements include buttons in their various forms. HTML lets you create generic buttons with the `<INPUT TYPE="button">` tag. Or, you can create buttons with a purpose with either the `<INPUT TYPE="submit">` or `<INPUT TYPE="reset">` tags.

The following tables list the PMEs for the button elements.

Properties	Description
form	A reference to the form that contains the element.
name	A read/write string that stores the name of the element.
type	A read-only string that specifies the elements type.
value	A read/write string that stores the text shown on the button. While this is a read/write string, not all platforms will display the new text, should you write to this property. Make sure that any new text you write to this property doesn't increase the size of the button. Not all platforms accommodate reflowing the page to reflect new content.

Methods	Description
blur()	Removes focus from the element.
click()	Simulates a mouse click on the element.
focus()	Gives focus to the element.

Event handlers	The handler invoked when
onblur	Focus is taken away from the element. In reality, there is probably little use for this event handler with a button.
onclick	The element is clicked on.
onfocus	The element receives focus. This event handler can be dangerous with a button if the handler does not load a different page or change focus to another element. By default, the button regains the focus after calling whatever function is defined in the `onfocus` handler. That means, the handler function will be called again immediately, creating an endless loop.

Buttons are used to kick off processing of your forms. So, most typically you will define a function that processes the data in your form in some way. Then, you will call that function with a button. Typically, you would do processing that doesn't submit the form to a Web server using a generic button and its `onclick` handler function. In fact, the preceding examples in this lesson already used this technique.

Data in forms that are submitted to a Web server are typically processed in a different way. In those cases, you will typically be validating the data in the form. The most common technique is to use a standard Submit type button and define an `onsubmit` handler for the form itself. With this technique, if the handler function returns a true value, the form's data is submitted to the server. If the function returns false, the data is not submitted.

Summary

In lesson 8, you saw how you can use JavaScript to access and modify HTML forms. You were able read data users entered into those forms. And you modified the contents of the forms using JavaScript. One of JavaScript's greatest benefits is its ability to manipulate forms and their data. You will probably use this capability frequently.

Suggested Time:
15 minutes

Apply Your Knowledge 8-2

Creating a forms-based navigation tool

In this activity, you will write the scripts necessary to make a select box become a navigation tool. You might have seen such a tool on other Web pages. When you choose an item from the list, you are immediately taken to that page. The HTML form has been created for you; all you need to do is add the code.

1. Starting with the formnav.html page, add the JavaScript code necessary to activate this navigation list. Your code should meet these objectives:

    •   There isn't a "go to the site" button on the page. So, navigation should happen as soon as the user chooses an item from the list. Pick the appropriate event handler and this should be a snap.

    •   To make the page easily maintainable, your code should not include the URLs. Instead, you should read the URLs directly from the select list options. In this way, adding a new option to the select list won't require any code modification.

    •   Make your code as simple as possible. You should be able to accomplish this entire task with a single line of code in the event handler attribute of a single element on the page.

    •   Remember that you need to set the value of the `window.location` property to navigate to a new Web page.

2. Save your changes and test your solution in both browsers.

3. Add a new Web site to the select list. If you have coded correctly, adding a new element to this list should not require you to modify your JavaScript code. Save and test your changes.

4. Compare your code to that included in the xformnav.html file, located with the rest of the course data files.

Lesson Review

8A **Describe the purpose of the Form object. Is it the object you use most frequently when manipulating HTML form contents?**

8B **How would you describe to a colleague the process of determining which check boxes are checked (in other words, describe the process, don't give code).**

Determining which check boxes are checked is very similar to determining which options are selected from a _____.

Validating Form Data

Overview

Users can enter all sorts of junk in your forms. You really need to check what they enter or you're bound to live the credo "garbage in, garbage out" once that data reaches your server or wherever you'll be using it. This lesson will show you some generic techniques and one specific approach for validating form data. As with any task in programming, there are many possible ways to accomplish a task. You might or might not adopt the methods shown here. But, in any case, the information in this lesson will certainly help you develop your own routines.

Data Files
validtest.html
statecodes.txt
validform.html
Myecement.html

Lesson Time
3 hours

Objectives

In this lesson, you will:

9A   Examine a general process for validating user input into Web forms.

The techniques for validating form data is as varied as the programmers who invent such schemes. In this topic, you'll examine the technique that we have chosen as one of the most powerful and re-usable methods available.

9B   Test for required fields.

You'll implement a technique for testing that data has been entered into required fields.

9C   Test for numeric data.

Not only will you test that numeric data has been entered, when that's required, but you'll also see how to ensure that the input data is within a range of values that you specify.

9D   Test for string data.

You'll test that a field marked as requiring text input is not empty and that it is correctly formatted to represent the data type you specify.

 Topic 9A

The General Approach

Validating the data users enter into a form is an important task, one that JavaScript is well suited to handle. In fact, one of the most common uses of JavaScript in the "real world" is to validate or pre-process form data.

Many variations on the validation theme exist. The method you choose is up to you. Generally, every validation process follows something like the following steps.

1. Calling the validation function with the `onSubmit()` handler of the Form object.

2. Accessing the form's data and looping through the contents of the form.

3. Testing each field for valid data.

4. Building an error report and presenting it to the user.

That is the approach that will be used in this lesson.

The General Methodology

Calling the Function

Calling the validation function—the first step—is most often accomplished by adding an `onSubmit()` handler function to your form. When the user clicks the Submit button, the function is called. If the code in the `onSubmit()` handler returns a true value, the form is submitted. If it returns `false`, the form is not submitted.

You could also use an `onClick()` handler on the Submit button. As with `onSubmit()`, if the code in the `onClick()` handler returns a true value, the form is submitted. If it returns `false`, the form is not submitted. Given that form validation is the reason for the existence of the `onSubmit()` handler on the Form object, that method, not this `onClick()` method, is used in this lesson.

Another way in which data could be validated would be to add `onBlur()` or `onChange()` handlers to each field that needs to be validated. After the user enters data into the field and moves to a new field the handler function would get called. With this technique, your function must test the data, and if invalid, alert the user and move focus back to the field in error. This technique has the advantage of providing immediate feedback to the user. However, nothing prevents the user from submitting an empty form or skipping over required fields. This is not the technique used in this lesson.

Accessing the Data

Your handler function must access the form's data and can do so in one of two ways. The first is to directly access the form on the page using a notation like `document.myForm.field1`. The problem with this method is the handler function isn't generic and will require modification every time you use it.

The second, and preferred method is to pass the form to the handler function as part of the function call statement. Then, using the elements[] array, you can loop through the fields of the form. In this way, the validation function can be used on many different pages. All you have to do is pass it a different form and it's off to work validating the data.

Testing the Data and Building a Report

Your handler function will need to test fields for any criteria you specify. For example, you might mark some fields as required, others as numeric fields, and so forth. If there is data in any field that does not meet your criteria, you will need to build and display some sort of message.

You could display an "error" message each time your function encounters some inappropriate data. This could end up creating many messages for your users to endure. Better yet is to build up all the messages and display one big report at the end.

The Specifics Steps

The form validation function of this lesson follows the general approach just described. Specifically, here is how it implements those general steps to produce a generic, easily re-usable validation function.

1. The function is called with the onSubmit() handler of the Form object. The Form object is passed to the function as part of that call. Additionally, each field to be validated is marked as such within the html code of the onSubmit() handler.

2. Global variables are used to store routine-specific error messages. For example, one variable will store all the messages regarding required fields that are missing. Another will note all the fields that are supposed to contain numeric data but do not. To begin with, these variables are all declared and assigned null values.

3. A "master" validation function loops through all the fields on the form, using the elements[] array, validating any fields that are marked as needing validation. Sub-functions are called to perform the actual field-level validation.

4. Each sub-function is named like "isEmpty" to convey the value it will return. If a field "is empty" then the function returns true. The sub-functions in our sample all return true if the field's data is somehow inappropriate.

5. For each field that does not meet its specified criteria, an error message is appended to the global variable for that category of errors.

6. An error report is built by checking each of the global error variables. For each that is not null, its contents are appended to the final output message. That message is displayed.

7. Finally, each of the global error variables is reset to null so that the user can re-enter data and resubmit the form without reloading the page.

Returning true for inappropriate data seems backwards. But, it leads to more readable code.

TASK 9A-1:

Seeing the form validator function in action

Objective: To see the validation function that you will build during this lesson so that you can get a feel for how it will work.

1. **Open validtest.html in your browser.** This file contains a form that will be validated by the sample function. The finished script is included in the page.

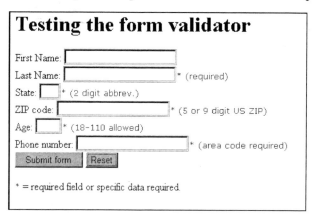

2. **Don't enter any data into the form, but click Submit Form (insert gif).**

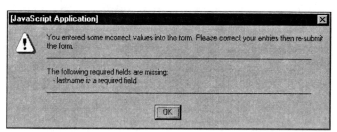

The function determines that you didn't enter anything into a required field and displays an appropriate message. You'll notice that the other fields, which do require specific formats, are not included in this list of missing fields. The functions are built such that you can require a specific format for data, yet still allow it to be an optional field.

3. **Click OK.**

4. **Enter the following data into the form:**

```
Last name: your last name
State: N
Zip code: 123
Age: 1
Phone number: 555-1212
```

Click Submit Form.

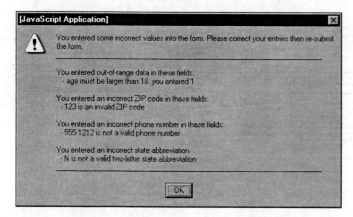

The validation function lists all the errors encountered. While only Last Name is required, the others all have specific data requirements, which were not met with this data.

5. **Click OK.**

6. **Open validtest.html in your editor.**

7. **Scroll down past all the JavaScript code to find the HTML form tag.**

```
<FORM onSubmit="
    this.lastname.required=true;
    this.age.numeric=true;
    this.age.minVal = 18;
    this.age.maxVal = 110;
    this.zipcode.zip = true;
    this.phonenumber.phone = true;
    this.state.state = true;
    return validate(this);
">
```

A property is added to each field to be validated, using the `this.fieldname.propertyname` syntax. You can add properties to any object by just assigning a value to a new property's name in this way. Finally, the `validate()` function is called with the form passed to it. The function returns either a `true` or `false`, noting whether the form should be submitted or not submitted, respectively. The `return validate(this)` syntax takes care of passing the returned `true` or `false` to the handler so that submission will happen (or not) as desired.

8. **Observe the tags that build the fields in the form.** You'll find nothing special or different about them. All the work of marking fields to be validated is done in the `onSubmit()` handler code.

Don't get bogged down in the details of how the code works at this stage. Right now, you are looking at the overall logic and flow of the function. Later in the lesson you'll delve into the nitty-gritty details.

This and the other forms used in this lesson don't really submit their data to a server. Notice that there are not ACTION attributes on the <FORM> tags. Don't worry about entering data into the forms. It never leaves your computer.

9. Scroll to the top of the file and observe the beginning of the validation code.

```
<SCRIPT LANGUAGE="JavaScript" TYPE="text/javascript"><!--

/* ***********************************************************
 * set some global variables that will be checked later      *
 ***********************************************************/
var msg = "";                 // an output message
var missing = "";             // for missing required fields
var invNum = "";              // for invalid numeric fields
var outOfRange = "";          // less than min or more than max
var invZIP = "";              // for invalid zip codes
var invPhone = "";            // for invalid phone numbers
var invState = "";            // for invalid state fields
```

10. Observe the beginning of the `validate()` function.

```
/* ***********************************************************
 * The main validation function, calls other sub-functions   *
 ***********************************************************/
function validate(frm)
  {
  for(i=0; i<frm.elements.length; i++)        // loop through form elements
    {
    var el = frm.elements[i];
    if(el.required)                           // if element has required property
      {                                       // test to see if field is empty
      if(isEmpty(el))
        {
        missing += "\n  - " + el.name + " is a required field";
        }
      }
```

The function loops through all the fields on the form using the `elements[]` array. Within each iteration of the loop, a shortcut variable is declared to represent the field being tested. That will save some typing later. Then, a series of `if()` statements test for the presence the various validation properties on the field. Those properties will exist only if they were added by the `onSubmit()` code; they are not standard properties. If those properties are present, the sub-validation function is called. If the sub-validation function returns `true`, then the field is invalid and a message is appended to the appropriate variable.

11. Scroll down in the code to find the `// build output message` comment.

```
// build output message
if(missing.length !=0 || invNum.length != 0 || outOfRange.length != 0 || invZIP.len
  {
  if(missing.length !=0)
    {
    msg += "\n\nThe following required fields are missing:";
    msg += missing;
    }
```

The length of each of the global error message variables is tested for a non-zero length. If one of them has a non-zero length, then an error must have been encountered somewhere on the form. That variable is appended to the final output message variable.

12. Scroll down in the code to find the `errMsg(msg)` line.

```
errMsg(msg);           // call the output function
msg = ""; missing = ""; invNum = ""; invZIP = ""; invPhone = ""; invS
return false;
}
else
  {
  return true;
  }
}
```

The final output message is passed to the `errMsg()` function, which takes care of formatting it and displaying it to the user. Then, each of the individual error message variables is reset. This is so that the user can correct their errors and resubmit the form without reloading the page. If you didn't include this, the error messages would remain even after they corrected their mistakes. The function finally returns either `false` or `true` depending on whether there have been errors or not. That return value will be used to cancel or enable the final submission.

Apply Your Knowledge 9-1

Suggested Time:
15 minutes

Creating a generic reporting function

In this activity, you will create the generic error reporting function that you will use with your validation routines.

1. Switch to your browser. The validtest.html page should still be loaded. Reset the form. Don't enter anything and click Submit Form. Check out the resulting alert box.

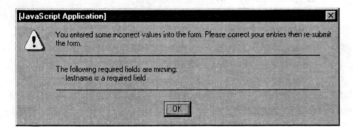

Figure 9-1: *The error message box of the validtest.html page.*

The alert box message contains some generic message text, some formatting characters (a line), the specifics of the error message, and finally another line. This surrounding text is created by the `errMsg()` function.

2. Switch to your editor. Close the validtest.html page.

3. Open validform.html. This page has the same form as validtest.html, but none of the JavaScript. You will be adding that throughout the rest of the lesson.

4. In the <HEAD> section of the document, add a JavaScript script block. Create an `errMsg()` function to display the final output message in an alert box.

    Your error messages could be output to a new browser window, to the existing window, to the status bar, or to an alert box. Opening new windows consumes a fair amount of resources and could take a noticeable time on slower computers. For that reason, you might want to avoid the new browser window technique. Writing to the current window will clear the current contents, including the data users have entered, which would be inconvenient to users and inconsiderate on your part. Messages in the status bar can be easily overlooked. Users might sit and wonder why the data they entered is still sitting there in the form after they clicked Submit, not noticing your error message in the status bar. Alert boxes are quickly displayed, use few system resources, and can't easily be missed.

5. Write the `errMsg()` function so that it meets the following criteria:
    *   Your function should accept one parameter, a string variable that will contain the details of the data entry errors in the form.
    *   Your function should be generic so that it is useable in many situations (validating many different forms).
    *   Your function should display some standard error message text that will appear in the dialog box before the detailed error information. The output your function displays should be clear and nicely formatted. Use the escape codes, underscores, or other characters to make a clear and pleasing output format. Refer to figure 9-1 if you would like.

6. To test your new function, add the following line after the function code:

    ```
    errMsg("\nThis is a test");
    ```

7. Save your changes and load the file in your browser.

8. An alert box with the test message should be displayed. If any JavaScript error messages are encountered, correct your function code. Reload the page to re-test.

9. When you are sure the `errMsg()` function is working the way you want it to, delete the `errMsg("\nThis is a test");` line and save the file.

Calling the Function

The form validation function is typically called by the `onSubmit()` handler of the Form object. That technique is handy, because if the code in that handler returns a `true` value, the form will be submitted. If it returns a `false` value, the submission will be canceled. Your validation function will return such values for that reason. Additionally, you will add statements in that handler to set properties on fields that must be validated in some way.

TASK 9A-2:

Calling the validation function

Objective: To add the necessary code to call the form validation function when the form is submitted.

1. **Switch to your browser.** 1The validform.html page should still be loaded.

2. **What fields on this form do you think should be validated and what criteria should be tested for?**

3. **Switch to your editor.** The validform.html page should still be loaded.

4. **Change the** `<FORM>` **tag to read:**

```
<FORM onSubmit = "
  return validate(this);
">
```

With this step, you've set an `onSubmit()` handler for the form. The `validate()` function, which you will write, will return a `true` or `false` value depending on whether the data in the fields is valid or not. The code in the `onSubmit()` handler must return `true` or `false` to either submit or not submit the form's data.

Remember, you can add as many spaces and line breaks to your HTML code as you like. Doing so makes the HTML more readable.

5. **Save your changes.**

Topic 9B

Testing for Required Fields

Some forms have data that must be included; otherwise, processing the remainder of the data would be a wasted effort. For example, you might require users to enter their names or account numbers so you can identify them. You might require a quantity number so that users order the correct amount of merchandise. Even if you're doing a simple calculator with your form, you could require certain fields so that you prevent problems like divide-by-zero errors, which could be caused by missing data.

Testing for a required field means simply testing that the field is not empty. You should test to see if the contents of the field equal a `null` value, a single space, or if the field is all spaces.

charAt()

The charAt(i) string function extracts the character at position i in the string. This is a useful function when testing form fields because it lets you examine individual characters within the data users enter into the form. Use it like this:

```
var theCharacter = str.charAt(i);
```

TASK 9B-1:

Testing for required fields

Objective: To write a function that will test data entered into required fields to make sure data was entered. The function will be named isEmpty() and will return a true value if the field "is empty." This fits the plan for the validate() function that you will write next.

Make sure there is not a space between the quotes in the if(str == "") statement. Make sure there is a space between the quotes in the if(str.charAt(j) != " ") statement.

1. If necessary, open validform.html in your editor.

2. Enter the following code after the existing code in the file.

```
function isEmpty(field)
  {
  str = field.value;
  if(str == "")
    {
    return true;
    }
  else
    {
    for(j=0; j     for(j=0; j++)
      {
      if(str.charAt(j) != " ")
        {
        return false;
        }
      }
    }
  return true;
  }
```

This function tests to see if the field passed to it is empty or filled with spaces. It starts by creating a shortcut variable, str, to save some typing. Then, it tests to see if it is an empty string. If so, it returns true—the field "is empty." Otherwise, it loops through each of the characters in the string and tests them with the charAt(i) string function. If any of the characters does not equal a space, then false is returned. Otherwise, at the end of the function true is returned—the field "is empty."

This is a generic function that will be called by a function named validate(), which is called by your form's onSubmit() handler.

3. Save the file.

The validate() function

The `validate()` function will be the core of your validation routine. It will call the other sub-functions, which you will write throughout the rest of this lesson, as needed.

TASK 9B-2:

Creating and using the validate() function

Objective: To begin the validate() function, which you will modify throughout the rest of the lesson. This is the main validation function, which calls all the other sub-functions as needed.

1. At the very beginning of the script block in the validform.html file, **add this code** .

```
var msg = "";
var missing = "";
```

These variables will hold the final output message and a message noting any missing required fields, respectively.

2. **Following the lines you just added, add this code.**

```
function validate(frm)
  {
  for(i=0; i<frm.elements.length; i++)
    {
    var el = frm.elements[i];
```

You've now started the `validate()` function. It will be passed a Form object to test. Within the function, that form will be referred to as `frm`. Next, you loop through all the elements on the form with a `for()` loop. Within each iteration of the loop, you create a shortcut variable `el`, which will represent the field to be tested during that iteration, in order to save lots of typing.

3. Next comes the first test within the function. If the field has a required property, then it has been marked as a required field and should be tested by the `isEmpty()` function. So, **add this code** .

```
    if(el.required)
      {
      if(isEmpty(el))
        {
        missing += "\n   - " + el.name + " is a required
field";
        }
      }
    }
```

The preceding code tests the field with `isEmpty()` and appends an error message to the missing variable if that function returns a true value. All those brackets close the `if()` statements and the loop. So, when the above code is done executing, all the fields on the form will have been tested.

In the real-world application of this sort of script, you should add comments within all your code. It has been purposely left out here to save typing during class and to make the code more readable in the printed book. The completed version of this file, validtest.html, includes comments.

4. Now, you need to build the final output message, reset the `missing` variable, and return the appropriate values to the `onSubmit()` handler. So, **add this code** .

```
// build output message
if(missing.length !=0)
  {
  msg += "\n\nThe following required fields are missing:";
  msg += missing;
  errMsg(msg);
  msg = ""; missing = "";
  return false;
  }
else
  {
  return true;
  }
}
```

You have now completed the main validation function. It will call the other sub-functions as needed and ultimately return a `true` or `false` value to the `onSubmit()` handler.

5. You've entered a lot of code, so **save the file** , just be on the safe side.

6. Change the `<FORM>` tag code to read:

```
<FORM onSubmit = "
    this.lastname.required=true;
    return validate(this);
">
```

You're just adding that second line. With it, you specify that last name is a required field by adding a property to the element's object. As you entered above, the `validate()` function will look for this property, and if it exists test to see if the field is empty. The nice thing about this technique is that it is easy to mark a form field as required. You won't have to change your validation code or your form to mark a new or different field required.

The `this` keyword can be confusing. It is a reference to the current object, which in this case is the form (because this code is within the `<FORM>` definition tag). So, `validate(this)` calls the function, passing it the current form object.

7. Save your changes.

8. Switch to your browser and reload the page.

9. Do not enter any data into the form and click on Submit. You should get an error message (in an alert box) informing you that lastname is a required field.

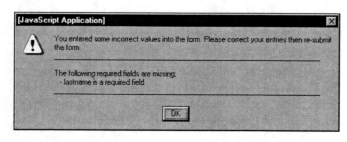

Make sure you enter the comment "// build output message" as noted at the top of this block. You will use that comment in subsequent tasks to re-locate this section of the code.

We highly recommend using Navigator to do all your form testing. It does not clear the data you have entered into a form when you reload a page. So, you can change the JavaScript coding on the page and reload it without losing the test data you entered into the form.

10. **Click OK.**

11. **Enter your last name into the lastname field and click on Submit.** The form should be submitted. As this form data isn't really being submitted to a server, the data is simply cleared from the form and the page remains visible.

Topic 9C

Validating Numeric Data

Validating numeric data involves checking that the user has entered only numbers, not letters or punctuation symbols. The case is fairly easy if you consider only positive integers. You can use a test like the following one to make sure users have entered only digits. This simple test would not account for negative or real numbers (those with decimal places).

```
if(char >= 0 && char <= 9) ...
```

You would use such a statement within a loop that extracts the character at each position in the string entered by the user. The situation becomes a more difficult test if you need to consider the entry of negative or real numbers. You will have to test for the possibility of the characters in the string being a decimal point or minus sign. You can have only one of each of those in a valid number. A decimal point can be located anywhere in the number, but the minus sign can be only at the beginning of a valid number.

Validating numeric data can also involve checking that those numbers are within a specific range of value. The functions you will build here will accomplish all those goals.

TASK 9C-1:

Creating a numeric validation functions

Objective: You will create a function that determines if the form field contains a number or not. Your function will consider negative numbers and those with decimal places as valid numbers. The function will be named notNumeric() and will return a true value if the field is "not numeric."

1. **If necessary, open validform.html in your editor.**

2. Within the existing JavaScript code block, **after the existing code, add this new code:**

```
function notNumeric(field)
  {
  var errCount = 0;
    var numdecs = 0;
  for(j=0;j<field.value.length;j++)
    {
    c = field.value.charAt(j);
```

We highly recommend using Navigator to do all your form testing. It does not clear the data you have entered into a form when you reload a page. So, you can change the JavaScript coding on the page and reload it without losing the test data you entered into the form.

This code begins the `notNumeric()` function, which will be passed a form field to be named field within the function. Two variables are set: `errCount`, which will be an error counter, and numdecs, the number of decimal points in the data. Next, you start looping through the characters in the field, creating a shortcut variable for that character within each iteration of the loop.

3. After that code, enter this code.

```
if((c >= 0 && c <= 9) || c== "." || (j==0 && c == "-"))
    {
    if(c== ".")
       {
       numdecs++;
       }
    }
  else
    {
    errCount++;
    break;
    }
 }
```

This is the code that will be evaluated during each iteration of the loop. It tests to see if the character is greater than zero and less than nine, a decimal point, or a minus sign at position 0 in the string. If any of these are true, another test is done to see if the character is a decimal point. (If so, the numdecs counter is incremented. There can be only one decimal point, but it could be located anywhere within the number.) If any of those conditions are not true, the `errCount` variable is incremented and the loop is stopped with the `break` statement. There is no need to continue looping once you know that the data isn't a number.

4. Now that you have written the testing portion of the function, you need to create the return value portion of the function and finish it all up. So, **enter this code:**

```
if(errCount > 0 || numdecs > 1)
   {
   return true;
   }
 return false;
 }
```

This code tests to see if `errCount` is greater than zero or numdecs is greater than one. Either of these conditions being true would indicate that the field does not contain a valid number. So, `true` would be returned, the field is "not numeric." Otherwise, `false` is returned.

5. Now, you need to update the rest of the code in the file. **Scroll to the top of the file. After the existing variable declarations, add this new variable declaration** (it will become the third declaration of the code in this file).

```
var invNum = "";
```

This variable will hold the output message for fields that do not pass your numeric test function.

6. Next, you need to modify the `validate()` function to call the new sub-function and deal with its return value. You need to **add the following code within the `for()` loop of the `validate()` function, but after the existing `if()` test block.** That way it will get called each time through the loop.

```
if(el.numeric)
   {
   if(notNumeric(el))
      {
      invNum += "\n    - "" + el.name + " must be a number";
      }
   }
```

This code checks for the `numeric` property of the field. If it is `true`, then the field is tested with the `notNumeric()` function. The `notNumeric()` function that you wrote returns a `true` if the field is not numeric. So, if the field is "not numeric," an output message is created.

7. Next, you need to update the output message section of the `validate()` function. Because this portion of the code is going to get a bit more complex, **replace the existing code, starting with the comment `// build output message` to the end of the function with this code.**

```
       // build output message
    if(missing.length !=0 || invNum.length != 0)
    {
    if(missing.length !=0)
       msg += "\n\nThe following required fields are
missing:";
       msg +=    missing;
    }
  if(invNum.length !=0)
{
     msg += "\n\nYou entered incorrect numeric data in these
fields:";
     msg += invNum;
     }
   errMsg(msg);
   msg = ""; missing = ""; invNum = "";
   return false;
   }
 else
   {
   return true;
   }
```

You could create the msg variables all on one line. Those statements just don't fit well in the printed book. So, multiple lines were used for each.

With this new output-building code, the output message will contain only the appropriate messages, including a heading line for each category of data entry errors. The error message variables are reset, so that the user can correct their errors and resubmit the form without reloading the page. And, the final return values for the `validate()` function are constructed.

8. Phew! That's a lot of typing. **Save the file** just to be on the safe side.

Marking a field as numeric

To use the numeric input-validation routine, you need to mark a form field as requiring numeric input. You do so in the HTML code defining the form. Consider a form with a field named `someField`. To mark that field as requiring numeric data, change the <FORM> tag to read:

```
<FORM onSubmit = "
    this.someField.numeric=true;
">
```

TASK 9C-2:

Marking a field as numeric

Objective: To mark one of the fields in the form as requiring numeric data, and to test your work.

1. Now, you need to indicate which field must be a numeric field. **Scroll to the section of the page that defines the form.**

2. **Change the `<FORM>` tag to read:**

```
<FORM onSubmit = "
    this.lastname.required=true;
    this.age.numeric=true;
    return validate(this);
">
```

You're adding the third line as shown above. With this change, you have marked that users must enter only numbers into the age field.

3. **Save your changes.**

4. **Reload the page in your browser. Do not enter anything into the last name field, but enter "xx" into the age field. Click Submit.**

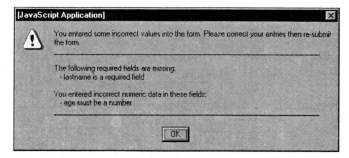

The error message indicates that `lastname` is required and `age` must be a number. Your code compiles all the error messages into one output message and categorizes those messages.

5. **Enter a last name and then try each of these values and a few others of your choosing for the age field: 3x, -23, 6.43, 275.** Some are valid numbers, others are not. (You might need to re-enter the last name occasionally, as some of those are valid numbers.)

6. Do you see a problem with the form validation logic that should be fixed?

7. Enter a last name, don't enter anything into the age field, and click Submit. What happens? Is that okay?

Range Checking

Sometimes, you will want to check numbers to make sure they are within a specified range of values. With an age field, for example, you might want to set a lower-limit of 18 and consider values over 110 to be so unlikely as to be invalid.

TASK 9C-3:

Adding a numeric range-checking function

> **Objective:** To add a numeric range-checking function to the validate() function.

1. Switch to your editor; validform.html should still be open.

2. Following the other variable declarations at the beginning of the file, add this new declaration statement.

```
var outOfRange = "";
```

This variable will hold an output message if any fields are less than the minimum value or more than the maximum value.

3. The test for being within range is simple enough that the code will be put right into the loop within `validate()` rather than in a sub-function. Within the `for()` loop, after the other `if()` tests currently there, add the following code.

```
if(el.minVal)
   {
   if(parseFloat(el.value) <= el.minVal)
     {
     outOfRange += "\n    - " + el.name + " must be larger
than";
     outOfRange += el.minVal + ", you entered" + el.value;
     }
   }
```

This `if()` test starts by checking for the existence of the `minVal` property on the field. If it exists, it then uses `parseFloat()` to extract a real number from the field and tests it for being less than the value of `minVal`. If it is less than `minVal`, a message is appended to `outOfRange`.

You could create the outOfRange variable all on one line. It just doesn't fit well in the printed book, so two lines were used here.

4. That takes care of checking for a minimum value. Now you'll write a parallel test to make sure the data isn't too large. **After the code you just entered, add:**

```
if(el.maxVal)
   {
   if(parseFloat(el.value) >= el.maxVal)
     {
     outOfRange += "\n   -" + el.name + " must be smaller
than";
     outOfRange += el.maxVal + ", you entered" + el.value;
     }
   }
```

5. Next, you need to modify the output section of the `validate()` function. Find the `// build output message` comment and **add another or clause (with ‖) to the existing `if()` statement so that it reads:**

```
if(missing.length !=0 || invNum.length != 0 ||⇒
outOfRange.length != 0)
```

This new clause tests the length of the `outOfRange` variable. If it is not zero, as would be the case if an out-of-range entry had been encountered, then the code within the `if()` block will execute.

6. Within that `if()` statement, **immediately preceding the `errMsg(msg)` line, add this code:**

```
     if(outOfRange.length !=0)
        {
        msg += "\n\nYou entered out-of-range data in these
fields:";
        msg += outOfRange;
        }
```

This code adds to the output message variable the contents of the outOfRange variable.

7. One last change is needed. After the **errMsg(msg)** line, you reset the value of all the error message variables to null strings. Now that you have added a new variable, you need to reset its value as well. **Change the line after the errMsg(msg) line to read:**

```
msg = ""; missing = ""; invNum = ""; invZIP = "";
outOfRange = "";
```

8. **Save your changes.**

Enforcing numeric ranges

To use the range limits input-validation routine, you need to mark a form field as requiring numeric input, plus you need to note the minimum and maximum values for the field's data. You do so in the HTML code defining the form. Consider a form with a field named `someField`. To mark that field as requiring numeric data within a certain range, change the `<FORM>` tag to read:

```
<FORM onSubmit = "
     this.someField.numeric=true;
     this.someField.minVal = minimumValue;
     this.someField.maxVal = maximumValue;
">
```

TASK 9C-4:

Marking a field with range limits

Objective: To mark one of the fields in the form as requiring data to fall within a range of values. And, to test your work.

1. Now, you need to indicate which field must be within a range. **Scroll to the section of the page that defines the form.**

2. **Change the `<FORM>` tag to read:**

```
<FORM onSubmit = "
     this.lastname.required=true;
     this.age.numeric=true;
     this.age.minVal = 18;
     this.age.maxVal = 110;
     return validate(this);
">
```

To set a minimum age of 18 and a maximum age of 110. You already set a requirement that the age field be numeric. So, you do not need to worry about the potential failings of the `parseFloat()` function, which is used in the range-checking code. Anything that would slip by `parseFloat()` will be caught by `notNumeric()`.

3. **Save your changes and reload the file in your browser.**

4. **Test your changes by entering an age less than 18 and clicking Submit.**

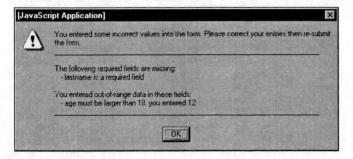

The parseFloat() function can be fooled by some entries. For example, 123.456.789 isn't a number. But, parseFloat() would extract 123.456 from it anyway. That is why we did not use it to test for fields that must contain numeric data. For that reason, you should check that fields with minVal and maxVal requirements are also numeric.

5. **Click OK then test again, this time entering an age greater than 110.**

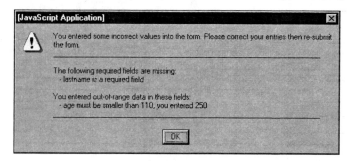

6. Finally, **test again with an age within the range and a last name (a required field)** . The form is submitted.

Topic 9D

Validating String Data

String input includes data like names, addresses, phone numbers, state or country names, and so forth. These types of data might include digits, but also include characters. This topic will investigate three string validation routines:

- A US zip code validator that will check the fields by their lengths looking for either five- or nine-digit strings of digits. It assumes those are zip codes.

- A phone number validator that will accommodate the entry of long distance prefixes and allow for either dashes, parentheses, or periods to separate the area code, exchange, and station number. The test assumes that strings of digits of certain lengths are valid phone numbers.

- A state name validator, that you could modify to use for country name validation or any other similar data. The test checks for the existence of the entered string within a list of valid state abbreviations.

TASK 9D-1:

Reviewing the functionality of the completed file

Objective: To review how the zip code, phone number, and state name validation functions are supposed to work before you begin re-creating them.

1. **Open validtest.html in your browser.** This is the completed version of validform.html. The state, zip code, and phone number fields have been marked as requiring data of a certain format to be entered. They are all optional fields, however.

2. **Enter "New York" into the state field and click Submit Form.** Don't worry that it doesn't fit well into the form.

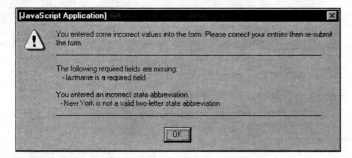

You're told that New York isn't a valid two-letter state abbreviation.

3. **Click OK, and then try entering just "N" in the state field.** You should get the same type of error message.

4. **Try entering "NY" (or "ny") into the state field and clicking Submit Form.** You'll still get an error message noting that last name is required. But, because you don't get a message about the state being invalid, you can tell that it passed the test.

5. **Reset the form.**

6. **Enter 123456 into the zip code field.** This number is too long to be a valid zip code. **Submit the form.**

7. **Click OK and then try 12345-6789.** It should work (the last name error will still be present), as it fits the format for US 9-digit zip codes (ZIP+4). You could also use 12345, as it is fits the criteria for a valid five-digit zip.

8. **Reset the form.**

9. **Enter 123 into the phone number field and click Submit Form.** This isn't a valid phone number, so you get an error message.

10. **Click OK** and then try 555-1212. It should generate an error because it does not include an area code.

11. **Reset the form and try 716-555-1212.** This should also work fine.

Zip Code Validator

US zip codes are either five-digit or nine-digit numbers. With nine-digit zip codes, the first five characters are typically separated from the last four by either a space or a dash. Here's the logic of a function you could use to validate zip codes.

1. Determine the length of the entered data.

2. If it is five or nine characters long, strip any non-digit characters, and then test the remaining string's length. If it still equals its starting length, you can assume that the data is a valid zip code.

3. If the entered data is ten digits long, the user might have separated the first five and last four digits by a dash or space. So you'll have to test the sixth character to see if it's one of those characters. If so, create a new string from the first five and last four characters of the string (omitting that separator character). Then, strip the non-digit characters from the resulting string. Finally, test the length of the new string to make sure it equals nine. If so, you can assume it's a valid zip code.

Of course, this type of function does not compare the resulting code with the city to check for a correct correspondence. Nor does it determine if the resulting number is really a valid zip code as defined by the US Postal Service. Such a function would not be appropriate for client-side JavaScript, as it would need to access a large database of codes and locations.

TASK 9D-2:

Creating the stripNonDigits() function

Objective: To create a function that will remove any non-digit characters from a string. You will need this to validate zip codes.

1. **If necessary, open validform.html in your editor.**

2. In the existing script block, **after all the existing code, add this function:**

The example and code in this example are based on U.S. zip codes but could be adapted to support other postal code systems. The logic of the test would probably change considerably, though. As you examine the code in this section, consider how it could be adapted to other postal code validation needs. For example, Canada uses a six character postal code, which includes numbers and letters.

```
function stripNonDigits(str)
  {
  newStr = "";
  for(j=0; j<str.length; j++)
    {
    c = str.charAt(j);
    if(c >= "0" && c <= "9")
      {
      newStr += c;
      }
    }
  return newStr;
  }
```

This function simply loops through the string, testing each character along the way. If the character is a digit, it is appended to a new string variable. Finally, the new string is returned. Any non-digits encountered are simply discarded by this function.

3. **Save your changes.**

Zip code validation

The zip code validator will be implemented in the invalidZip() function, which will return a true value if the field contains an invalid zip code or false if it's a valid zip code.

TASK 9D-3:

Creating the zip code validator function

1. After the function you just added, **add this function code to the file** .

```
function invalidZIP(field)
  {
  var zipcode = field.value;
  if(zipcode.length == 5 || zipcode.length == 9)
    {
    var subZip = stripNonDigits(zipcode);
    if(subZip.length == zipcode.length)
      {
      return false;
      }
    else
      {
      return true;
      }
    }
  else if(zipcode.length == 10 && (zipcode.charAt(5) ⇒
== "-" || zipcode.charAt(5) == " "))
    {
    subZip = zipcode.substring(0,5) + zipcode.substring(6,10);
    subZip = stripNonDigits(subZip);
    if(subZip.length == 9)
      {
      return false;
      }
    else
      {
      return true;
      }
    }
  return true;
  }
```

Make sure to enter the else if() line (shown here on two lines) as just one line. Otherwise, the script might fail.

This is a pretty long, though pretty simple function. It creates the variable `zipcode` as a shortcut to the field's value. Then, it tests for a length of either five or nine characters. In cases when that is true, it uses the `stripNonDigits()` function to remove any non-digits. After it does so, if `zipcode` is still the same length (meaning there were no non-digit characters in it), then the function assumes that it is a valid zip code.

The second part of the test checks for zip code strings with a length of ten. These might be ZIP+4 codes, in which the sixth character is the space or dash separator. It creates a new string out of the first five digits and the last four digits, leaving off the sixth character. Then, as before, it uses `stripNonDigits()` and compares the before and after length to determine the zip code's validity.

If any invalid characters are found, the function returns `true`, as the zip code "is invalid."

2. **Save your changes.**

Modifying the validate() function to support the zip code validator

You have to make a few changes to `validate()` to support the new zip code validator. Chief among these changes is changing the error message portions of the function to handle the case of invalid zip codes being detected.

TASK 9D-4:

Implementing the zip code validator function

Objective: To add the necessary code to the validate() function and to modify the form so as to activate the zip code validator.

1. **Scroll to the top of the file.**

2. After the other variable declaration statements, **add this new line** .

```
var invZIP = "";
```

As before, this variable will hold any messages describing invalid entries and is empty to start.

3. **Within the `for()` loop of the `validate()` function, after all of the other `if()` statement blocks already present, add this code:**

```
if(el.zip && el.value.length !=0)
   {
   if(invalidZIP(el))
      {
      invZIP += "\n  - " + el.value + " is not a valid zip
code";
      }
   }
```

This `if()` block determines if the `zip` property has been added to the form field and if the length of the data entered into that field is not zero (in other words, something has been entered). If so, it sends the field to the `invalidZIP()` function. If the field is an invalid zip code, an error message is appended to the `invZIP` variable.

4. **Scroll to find the output section of the validate() function. Change the `if()` statement there to read**

```
if(missing.length !=0 || invNum.length != 0 ||⇒
 outOfRange.length != 0 || invZIP.length != 0)
```

Of course, you should enter this statement all on one line. What it does is add another or condition to the statement. This time, if the `invZIP` variable does not have zero length, the contents of the `if()` block is executed.

5. Scroll down to after the other `if()` statements within, and right before the `errMsg(msg)` line, **add this new block of code.**

```
if(invZIP.length !=0)
   {
   msg += "\n\nYou entered an incorrect zip code";
   msg += invZIP;
   }
```

You could create the msg variable all on one line. It just doesn't fit well in the printed book. So, two lines were used here.

As with the other blocks, this one adds to the final output message variable a string and the contents of the invZIP variable.

6. One last change is needed. After the `errMsg(msg)` line, you reset the value of all the variables to null. Now that you have added a new variable, you need to reset its value as well. **Change the line after the errMsg(msg) line to read:**

```
msg = ""; missing = ""; invNum = ""; outOfRange = "";
invZIP = "";
```

7. **Save your changes.**

Marking a field as requiring a valid zip code

To use the zip code input-validation routine, you need to mark a form field as requiring a zip code string input. You do so in the HTML code defining the form. Consider a form with a field named `someField`. To mark that field as requiring a valid zip code, change the `<FORM>` tag to read:

```
<FORM onSubmit = "
     this.someField.zipcode=true;
">
```

TASK 9D-5:

Marking a field to be validated as a zip code

Objective: To mark one of the fields in the form as being a zip code and needing to be validated as such. And, to test your work.

1. Now, you need to indicate which field is the zip code. **Scroll to the section of the page that defines the form.**

2. **Change the `<FORM>` tag to read:**

```
<FORM onSubmit = "
     this.lastname.required=true;
     this.age.numeric=true;
     this.age.minVal = 18;
     this.age.maxVal = 110;
     this.zipcode.zip = true;
     return validate(this);
">
```

3. **Save your changes.**

4. Reload the page in your browser.

5. Test your changes by entering 1234567 in the zip code field. This is an invalid entry and should generate an error message.

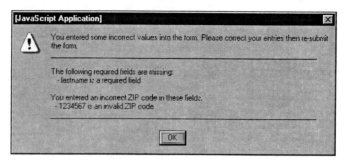

> **[JavaScript Application]**
>
> ⚠ You entered some incorrect values into the form. Please correct your entries then re-submit the form.
>
> The following required fields are missing:
>   - lastname is a required field
>
> You entered an incorrect ZIP code in these fields:
>   - 1234567 is an invalid ZIP code
>
> [OK]

6. Click OK.

7. Repeat your testing with 12345 and 12345-6789. Both are examples meet the criteria for valid zip codes and should not generate an error. Unless you include a last name, which is a required field, the form will still not be submitted.

Phone Number Validator

The routine presented here is designed to check for the presence of a ten-digit phone number. That number of digits is what is required for a US phone number that includes the area code. You could easily modify the function to work with seven digit numbers (no area code) or larger numbers representing international numbers.

This function will use the `stripNonDigits()` function that you created for the zip code validator. It will simply strip all the non-digit characters from the input string and then test the length of the resulting string. If it is ten digits long, the string will be assumed to be a valid phone number. With this method, users could enter numbers as (716) 555-1234 or 716-555-1234 or even 716.555-1234, and the number would still be considered valid.

A potential failing of this technique is that users could enter a string of any characters that happened to have ten digits embedded in it, such as 1a2b3c4d5e6f7g8h9i0j. The `stripNonDigits()` function would simply remove all those other characters, leaving behind the ten digits. It is unlikely that users would go to that much trouble.

To work around this, you would need to use a technique similar to that used with the zip code validator. You would need to remove characters from selected positions within the string (those spots where you would expect a non-digit to be used as a separator). Then you could test the length of the remaining string. It would get very tricky when you consider the wide range of entry styles used nowadays for phone numbers. And the benefits would be marginal.

TASK 9D-6:

Creating the phone number validator function

1. **Switch to your editor,** validform.html should be open.

2. **After the other functions in the code block, add this new function.**

```
function invalidPhone(field)
   {
   newStr = stripNonDigits(field.value);
   if(newStr.length == 10)
      {
      return false;
      }
   return true;
   }
```

This function simply tests to see if the length of the string, after any non-digit characters have been removed, is ten characters long. If so, it assumes the field is a valid phone number.

This function could also be easily adapted to work for non-U.S. locations, to work for local areas (without requiring the area code), or for international calls, which require the inclusion of a country code. You might want to consider how you would modify the script to accommodate those needs.

Modifying the validate() function to support the phone number validator

You have to make a few changes to validate() to support the new phone number validator. Chief among these changes is changing the error message portions of the function to handle the case of invalid phone numbers being detected.

TASK 9D-7:

Implementing the phone number validator function

1. **Scroll to the top of the file.**

2. **After the other variable declaration statements, add this new line.**

```
var invPhone = "";
```

As before, this variable will hold any messages describing invalid entries and is empty to start.

3. **Within the `for()` loop of the `validate()` function, after all of the other `if()` statement blocks already present, add this code:**

```
if(el.phone && el.value.length !=0)
   {
   if(invalidPhone(el) || el.value.length > 14)
      {
      invPhone += "\n  - " + el.value + " is not a valid phone
number";
      }
   }
```

This `if()` block determines if the phone property has been added to the form field and data has been entered into the field. If so, it sends the field to the `invalidPhone()` function. If the field is an invalid phone number or is longer than 14 characters, an error message is appended to the `invPhone` variable. Fourteen characters would be the maximum reasonable size for a valid phone number such as (716) 555-1234 (counting spaces and delimiter characters).

4. **Scroll to find the output section of the `validate()` function. Change the if statement there to read**

```
if(missing.length !=0 || invNum.length != 0 ||⇒
 outOfRange.length != 0 || invZIP.length != 0 ||⇒
 invPhone.length != 0)
```

Of course, you should enter this statement all on one line. What it does is add another or condition to the statement. This time, if the `invPhone` variable does not have zero length, the contents of the `if()` block is executed.

5. **Scroll down to after the other `if()` statements within, and right before the `errMsg(msg)` line, add this new block of code.**

You could create the msg variable all on one line. It just doesn't fit well in the printed book. So, two lines were used here.

```
if(invPhone.length !=0)
  {
  msg += "\n\nYou entered an incorrect phone number";
  msg += invPhone;
  }
```

As with the other blocks, this one adds to the final output message variable a string and the contents of the invPhone variable.

6. One last change, after the `errMsg(msg)` line, you reset the value of all the error message variables to null strings. Now that you have added a new variable, you need to reset its value as well. **Change the line after the `errMsg(msg)` line to read:**

```
    msg = ""; missing = ""; invNum = ""; outOfRange = "";
invZIP = ""; invPhone = "";
```

Of course, you should enter it all on one line.

7. **Save your changes.**

Marking a field as requiring a valid phone number

To use the phone number input-validation routine, you need to mark a form field as requiring a phone number. You do so in the HTML code defining the form. Consider a form with a field named `someField`. To mark that field as requiring a valid phone number, change the `<FORM>` tag to read:

```
<FORM onSubmit = "
    this.someField.phone=true;
">
```

TASK 9D-8:

Marking a field to be validated as a phone number

Objective: To mark one of the fields in the form as being a phone number and needing to be validated as such. And, to test your work.

1. Now, you need to indicate which field is the phone number. **Scroll to the section of the page that defines the form.**

2. **Change the <FORM> tag to read:**

```
<FORM onSubmit = "
    this.lastname.required=true;
    this.age.numeric=true;
    this.age.minVal = 18;
    this.age.maxVal = 110;
    this.zipcode.zip = true;
    this.phonenumber.phone = true;
    return validate(this);
">
```

3. **Save your changes.**

4. **Reload the page in your browser.**

5. **Test your changes by entering invalid and valid phone numbers in the phone number field.** An invalid entry and should generate an error message like this.

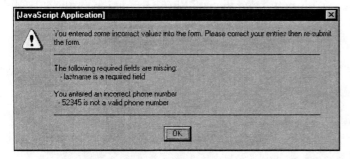

Unless you include a last name, which is a required field, the form will still not be submitted even if you enter a valid phone number.

A state-name validator

The function described in this section checks for two-letter state abbreviations. You could easily modify this function to check for other location abbreviations, including two-letter country codes, full province names, or any other subset of strings you would like.

More string functions

The state validator code used here relies on two more string manipulation functions: `toUpperCase()` and `indexOf()`. The `toUpperCase()` function simply converts a string to all upper case letters. Use it like this:

```
var capStr = str.toUpperCase();
```

The `indexOf()` function is a bit more complex. It looks within a string for whatever substring you specify and then returns the character position where that substring begins within the string. An example might help.

```
var str = "The quick brown fox jumps over the lazy dog";
var subPos = str.indexOf("fox");
var otherPos = str.indexOf("Hello");
```

The preceding code defines a string named `str`. It then uses `indexOf()` to search within that string for the string "fox" and puts the result into `subPos`. Because "fox" exists within `str`, the value of `subPos` will be 16. That's where the first character of "fox" is located within `str`. The value of `otherPos` will be -1, because that string does not exist within `str`.

TASK 9D-9:

Creating the state code validator function

1. **Open statecodes.txt in your editor.** This text file contains the shell of the function you will create. The reason for doing this is to save you from typing all the two-letter state abbreviations, which are stored in the variable `STATES`.

2. **Copy the entire contents of the file and then close the file.**

3. **If necessary, open validform.html in your editor.**

4. **After all of the other code in the script block, paste the text you copied from statecodes.txt.** You now have the shell of the function in this file.

5. **After the `STATES= "..."` line, enter the following code.**

```
var newStr = field.value.toUpperCase();
var newStr = field.value.toUpperCase();
if(STATES.indexOf(newStr) == -1 || newStr.indexOf("/") !=
-1 ||⇒
 newStr.length != 2)
    {
    return true;
    }
  return false;
  }
```

Make sure to enter the `if()` statement all on one line. The function starts by converting the contents of the field to upper case letters with the `toUpperCase()` function and puts the resulting string into the `newStr` variable.

Then, it uses the `indexOf()` string function to search within the string. In the first part of the `if()` statement, the code looks for the existence of the `newStr` string within the `STATES` string. If `newStr` is not found within `STATES`, the result is a value of -1. That result would mean that the user did not enter a valid state code. The `if()` statement also looks for the existence of the "/" character in the `newStr` string. That character is used in the `STATES` variable to divide all the state abbreviations. If a user were to enter a slash, the results of this `indexOf()` search would be some number other than `-1` and again it would be an invalid state abbreviation. Finally, it tests the length of what the user entered. If it's not two, then the user didn't enter a valid state code.

So, if any of those cases is met, the data is not a valid state code and `true` is returned. Otherwise, `false` is returned, indicating that the data is a valid state code.

6. **Save your changes.**

Modifying the validate() function to support the state code validator

You have to make a few changes to `validate()` to support the new state code validator. Chief among these changes is changing the error message portions of the function to handle the case of invalid state codes being detected.

TASK 9D-10:

Implementing the state code validator function

1. **Scroll to the top of the file.**

2. **After the other variable declaration statements, add this new line.**

```
var invState = "";
```

As before, this variable will hold any messages describing invalid entries and is empty to start.

3. **Within the `for()` loop of the `validate()` function, after all of the other `if()` statement blocks already present, add this code:**

```
if(el.state)
   {
   if(invalidState(el))
      {
      invState += "\n  - " + el.name + " is not a valid
two-letter";
      invState += " state abbreviation";
      }
   }
```

You could create the invState variable all on one line. It just doesn't fit well in the printed book. So, two lines were used here.

This `if()` block determines if the phone property has been added to the form field. If so, it sends the field to the `invalidState()` function. If the field is an invalid state code, an error message is appended to the `invState` variable.

4. **Scroll to find the output section of the `validate()` function. Change the `if()` statement there to read:**

```
if(missing.length !=0 || invNum.length != 0 ||⇒
   outOfRange.length != 0 || invZIP.length != 0 ||
   invPhone.length != 0 ||⇒
   invState.length != 0);
```

Of course, you should enter this statement all on one line. What it does is add another or condition to the statement. This time, if the `invState` variable does not have zero length, the contents of the `if()` block is executed.

5. **Scroll down to after the other `if()` statements within, and right before the `errMsg(msg)` line, add this new block of code.**

```
if(invState.length !=0)
   {
   msg += "\n\nYou entered an incorrect state abbreviation";
   msg += invState;
   }
```

As with the other blocks, this one adds to the output message variable a string and the contents of the `invState` variable.

6. **One last change, after the `errMsg(msg)` line, you reset the value of all the variables to `null`. Now that you have added a new variable, you need to reset its value as well. Change the line after the `errMsg(msg)` line to read:**

```
msg = ""; missing = ""; invNum = ""; invZIP = ""; invPhone =
"";  // reset all our variables
```

Of course, you should enter it all on one line.

7. **Save your changes.**

Marking a field as requiring a valid state code

To use the state code input-validation routine, you need to mark a form field as requiring a state code string input. You do so in the HTML code defining the form. Consider a form with a field named `someField`. To mark that field as requiring a valid state code, change the `<FORM>` tag to read:

```
<FORM onSubmit = "
     this.someField.state=true;
">
```

TASK 9D-11:

Marking a field to be validated as a state field

Objective: To mark one of the fields in the form as being a state field and needing to be validated as such. And, to test your work.

1. Now, you need to indicate which field is the state field. **Scroll to the section of the page that defines the form.**

2. **Change the <FORM> tag to read:**

```
<FORM onSubmit = "
    this.lastname.required=true;
    this.age.numeric=true;
    this.age.minVal = 18;
    this.age.maxVal = 110;
    this.zipcode.zip = true;
    this.phonenumber.phone = true;
    this.state.state = true;
    return validate(this);
">
```

3. **Save your changes.**

4. **Reload the page in your browser.**

5. **Test your changes by entering invalid and valid state abbreviations in the state field.** An invalid entry and should generate an error message like this.

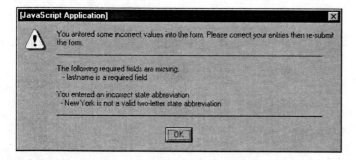

Unless you include a last name, which is a required field, the form will still not be submitted even if you enter a valid state.

Creating a library file

Complex functions, like those that make up the `validate()` function, are difficult to write. Once you have done so, you want to get as much mileage from them as you can. Putting all that code into the HTML file makes it inaccessible to other files that might need similar code. Better would be to put that code into a JavaScript source file and then include that file in each page that needs it.

A word of caution, though. Debugging scripts that are included into a Web page from a JavaScript source file can get tricky. The error messages you might receive will be difficult to decipher. The line numbers they report will be a combination of the lines in the HTML file and in the JavaScript source file.

For that reason, we recommend that when developing library functions, such as your validate() function, you should do so right in an HTML file. When you are sure it is working correctly, move all the code to a JavaScript source file. Then, simply add the include statement to use it within your HTML page.

TASK 9D-12:

Creating a JavaScript source file

Objective: To move all the code of the validate() function to a JavaScript source file to make it easily re-usable.

1. **Switch to your editor.**

2. **Scroll to the top of the validform.html file.**

3. **Select all of the code between the beginning and ending <SCRIPT> tags, but do not include those tags in your selection.**

4. **Cut the text.**

5. **Open a new file in your editor; save changes to validform.html if prompted.**

6. **Paste the code you cut from the validform.html file.**

7. **Save the file as formval.js.**

8. **Close the file and if necessary, re-open validform.html.**

9. The <SCRIPT> tags should be still be in this file. **Change them to read:**

```
<SCRIPT LANGUAGE="JavaScript" SRC="formval.js"></SCRIPT>
```

10. **Save the file.**

11. **Reload validform.html in your browser.**

12. **Test its functionality.** You shouldn't see any differences in the way the file works now. The code in formval.js is included into the validform.html file, even though it is a separate file.

Should you need it, the file xformval.js is a finished version of this JavaScript source file.

Should you need it, the file xvalidform.html is a finished version of this page, which includes the xformval.js JavaScript source file.

Apply Your Knowledge 9-2

Suggested Time:
15 minutes

Applying the validation library to another form

Objective: In this activity, you will re-use the form validation library function that you created in this lesson.

1. Open myecement.html in your browser. This page contains a form that requires data validation before users submit the form's contents to the server.

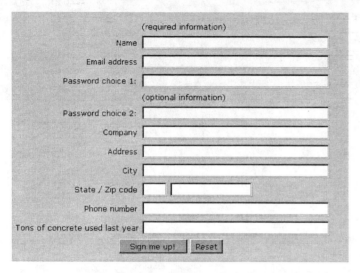

Figure 9-2: *The my eCement sign up form page.*

As you can see, the page indicates that some fields are required. Other fields are optional, but should be validated to make sure users enter correct data.

2. Open myecement.html in your editor.

The file xmyecement.html, which includes the xformval. js JavaScript source file, represents a finished version of this exercise.

3. Add the necessary `<SCRIPT>` tag to include the formval.js library function in this page. Add that statement before the `<STYLE>` block.

4. Using this table as a guide, mark the following fields with the appropriate parameters so that they are validated.

Field label	Field name	Validate as
Name	`name`	Required
Email address	`email`	Required
Password choice 1	`pwd1`	Required
State	`state`	State
Zip code	`zip`	Zip code
Phone number	`phone`	Phone number
Tons of concrete used last year	`tonnage`	Numeric

5. Save your changes.

6. Reload the file in your browser.

7. Test the validation features you specified by entering some incorrect data into the form. The validator routines should catch your errors and report on them.

8. Finally, enter some correct data. The form should submit without error. (The data doesn't go anywhere, as this form does not have an ACTION attribute.)

Summary

Phew! That was a long lesson. Form validation is an important topic, and it is a function you will often need to provide. In lesson 9, you saw a comprehensive approach to form data validation. And you created a validation code library that you can use with any other page that contains a form that needs to be validated.

Lesson Review

9A **Describe two general approaches to form field validation that you could use.**

9B **Describe how you can test that data has been entered into required fields.**

9C **What criteria must you consider when validating numeric data? Assume you will consider real numbers as passing your criteria.**

9D **List at least three string manipulation functions that you might use while validating string data.**

Dates and Math

Overview

Clocks, calendars, and calculators are some of the most popular JavaScript applications. As mundane as they might be, they're useful, well-liked by users, and not too difficult to program. In this lesson, you'll see how the Date and Math objects offer you many opportunities for temporal and analytical additions to your Web site.

Objectives

In this lesson, you will:

10A   Explore the Date object and its methods.

In this topic, you'll see how the Date object fits into the hierarchy of JavaScript objects. And, you'll take a quick look at some of its most important properties, methods, and event handlers.

10B   Use and manipulate instances of the Date object.

You'll use instances of the Date object to create clocks and count-down timers, and perform date math.

10C   Explore the Math object and its constants and methods.

In this topic, you'll see how the Math object fits into the hierarchy of JavaScript objects. And, you'll take a quick look at some of its most important properties, methods, and event handlers.

10D   Perform mathematical operations using the Math object's methods.

You'll see how to generate random numbers, round numbers to varying degrees of precision, and in the process create a page that generates lottery number picks for you.

Data Files
blank.html
datepage.html
datearrays.txt
basicclock.html
random.html
roundit.html
statclock.html

Lesson Time
1 hour, 45 minutes

Topic 10A

The Date Object

The Date object has no properties or event handlers, but it does have many useful methods. You use the "get" methods to extract date and time information from the Date object or use the "set" methods to change the date or time.

In most situations, you will not need to be concerned with this millisecond representation. Many useful methods are provided that extract date and time information that is easy to use in your programs. For example, you can easily extract the current day of the month from a date object with the `date.getDate()` method. You will not need to do any millisecond math to arrive at that value, either!

To create an instance of the Date object, use a statement like this.

```
var today = new Date();
```

You can choose any name you want for your date object; this code uses today. Once you have instantiated the object, you could use the variable today in your code. For example, to extract the time from today, you would use code like this.

```
var today = new Date();
var hours = today.getHours();
var mins = today.getMins();
var sec = today.getSeconds();
alert("It is now" + hours + ":" + mins + ":" + sec + "o'clock");
```

The first line instantiates the date object today. The next three lines extract the hour of the day, the minutes, and the seconds values respectively. The last line simply creates an output string and displays it in an alert box.

Date object instances are not dynamic. That means if later in your code you wanted to display the current time (rather than the time when the today object was created), you would need to re-create the today object or create another Date instance that then stores the current date and time.

This code needs some polishing before you would actually use it. For example, if the time were 10:09:08 pm, the code here would produce output of 20:9:8. You might want to use additional processing to add the zeros that are not automatically included with minutes and seconds less than ten and to convert the 24-hour clock time to the more familiar 12-hour time.

Properties, Methods, Event Handlers (PMEs)

The Date object has no properties or event handlers, but it does have many useful methods. You use the "get" methods to extract date and time information from the Date object or use the "set" methods to change the date or time.

"Get" Methods	Returns the following from the Date object	Version
getDate()	Day of the month	1.0
getDay()	Day of the week	1.0
getFullYear()	Full year-in other words, the four-digit representation of the year	1.2
getHours()	Hour value	1.0
getMinutes()	Minutes value	1.0

"Get" Methods	Returns the following from the Date object	Version
getMonth()	Month number, zero-based; January is represented by zero and December by eleven	1.0
getSeconds()	Seconds value	1.0
getTimezoneOffset()	Difference between local time and Greenwich Mean Time (also called Coordinated Universal Time-UTC) in minutes	1.0
getUTCDate()	The UTC day of the month	1.2
getUTCDay()	The UTC day of the week	1.2
getUTCFullYear()	The UTC full year	1.2
getUTCHours()	The UTC hour value	1.2
getUTCMinutes()	The UTC minutes value	1.2
getUTCMonth()	The UTC month, also zero-based	1.2
getUTCSeconds()	The UTC seconds value	1.2
getYear()	The two-digit year, when the date is within the 1990s (or more correctly, within the current century). A date of 1850 would return —50 and a date of 2050 would return 150 using this method. Deprecated in favor of getFullYear().	1.0

Some of the times are based on the user's local time zone (the user that loads your Web page) and others on Greenwich Mean Time. Those with *"UTC"* in their names are based on the time zone of Greenwich, England. The world's time zone system is based on Greenwich, which sits at a longitude of 0. All other time zones are defined by their offset from Greenwich. Approximately every 15 degrees east or west of Greenwich is a time zone and is one hour ahead or behind Greenwich time.

Greenwich Mean Time, or UTC, is useful because it is the same for everybody. If you were to include time information with a form that is submitted to you, for example, you should use the UTC time. If you don't, you won't know if the user's 3:00 p.m. is your 3:00 p.m. or 11:00 a.m. You can extract the user's time zone, but then you would have to include that information in later calculations to compare the user's time to yours. Why bother? Just use UTC.

Most of the "get" methods listed in the preceding table have a "set" counterpart that is listed in the next table. Rather than listing a description of what these methods are for, which should be obvious by looking at the "get" method counterpart, the syntax for using the method is listed.

UTC or Coordinated Universal Time:
A standardized reference time based on the time in Greenwich, England, which has a longitude of 0. Other times are offset from Greenwich, or UTC, time by approximately one hour for every 15 degrees of longitude (a time zone's "dimensions").

"Set" Methods	Syntax	Version
setDate()	date.setDate(day), where day is the numeric day of the month from 1 to 31.	1.0
setFullYear()	date.setFullYear(year), where year is the four-digit year.	1.2
setHours()	date.setHours(hour), where hour is an hour between 0 (midnight) and 23 (11:00 p.m.).	1.0
setMinutes()	date.setMinutes(min), where min is a minutes value between 0 and 59.	1.0

"Set" Methods	Syntax	Version
setMonth()	date.setMonth(month), where month is the numeric month from 0 (January) to 11 (December).	1.0
setSeconds()	date.setSeconds (sec), where sec is the seconds from 0 to 59, in universal time (UTC).	1.0
setUTCDate()	date.setUTCDate (day), where day is the numeric day of the month from 1 to 31, in universal time UTC).	1.2
setUTCFullYear()	date.setUTCFullYear(year), where year is the four-digit year, in universal time (UTC).	1.2
setUTCHours()	date.setUTCHours(hour), where hour is an hour between 0 (midnight) and 23 (11:00 p.m.), in universal time (UTC).	1.2
setUTCMinutes()	date.setUTCMinutes(min), where min is a minutes value between 0 and 59, in universal time (UTC).	1.2
setUTCMonth()	date.setUTCMonth(month), where month is the numeric month from 0 (January) to 11 (December), in universal time (UTC).	1.2
setUTCSeconds()	date.setUTCSeconds (sec), where sec is the seconds from 0 to 59, in universal time (UTC).	1.2
setYear()	date.setYear (year), where year is the two-digit or four-digit year. If you specify a two-digit year, JavaScript assumes you mean the year to be in the 1900s by using a four-digit year. Deprecated in favor of setFullYear().	1.0

Finally, the Date object has a few useful "to" methods. These, as listed in the next table, are used for extracting date information as formatted strings.

"To" Methods	Returns the following from the Date object	Version
toGMTString()	A String representation of the date, converted to Greenwich Mean Time. For example, Wed, 28 Apr 1999 10:22:25 GMT. Deprecated in favor of the toUTCString() method.	1.0
toLocaleString()	A string representation of the date that uses locale-specific formatting. The exact format will vary with operating system and location and is determined by settings in the user's operating system.	1.0
toString()	A string representation of the date in the local time zone. The format of the string is browser- and version dependent; however, it is not locale-specific.	1.0

"To" Methods	Returns the following from the Date object	Version
toUTCString()	A string representation of the date, converted to Greenwich Mean Time. This method returns the same information and format as toGMTString(). However, the name is supposed to more precisely describe the method's purpose; therefore, this is the preferred method.	1.2

TASK 10A-1:

Comparing the "standard" and full-year methods

1. The getYear() and getFullYear() methods are nearly identical, returning the two-digit and four-digit values of the year.

   What is one reason to use getYear() instead of getFullYear()?

2. Given the potential Year 2000 problems that can be associated with two-digit year values,

   could you use the getYear() method and still be Y2K-compliant?

3. **Could you forgo using the setFullYear() method and use setYear() exclusively?**

Topic 10B

Using and Manipulating Dates

The Date object is a class, or type, of objects. To use dates and times in your code, you create an instance of the Date object. Instantiating a Date object creates a new object that holds either the current date and time, as extracted from the operating system, or a date and time you specify.

Once you have instantiated a Date object, your new instance holds a static date. Its value does not change as your computer's time changes.

TASK 10B-1:

Instantiating a Date object

Objective: To create a simple script that instantiates a Date object, displays its value, and ten seconds later displays its value again.

1. **Open blank.html in your editor.**

2. **In the code block in the `<BODY>` section of the document, enter the following code:**

```
var now = new Date();
alert(now);
setTimeout("alert(now)", 10000);
```

This code creates an instance of Date named now. Conveniently, you can use a Date object as a string, as is done with the second line. The alert box will display the date and time information contained within the now object. Finally, the third line schedules the alert box to be displayed again in ten seconds, showing now at that time.

3. **Save the file as date.html.**

4. **Load date.html in your browser.** Record the minutes and seconds value of the time that is displayed.

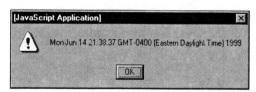

Minutes: _____ Seconds: _____

5. After ten seconds, another alert box is displayed.

Did the minutes or seconds values change?

Current Date and Time

Commonly, Web page authors will write the current date and time to a Web page as it loads. Sometimes this information is included at the end of the document, sort of as a footer. But most times, a formatted date string is written prominently to the page.

TASK 10B-2:

Writing a formatted date string to the page

1. **Open datepage.html in your browser.** This is a mock-up of a portal page. The black square at the top of the page is where you will display a formatted date string.

2. **Open datepage.html in your editor.** This is an example of a fictitious portal page, which has a placeholder for a JavaScript clock.

3. **Scroll to find the comment line that says "Date Code Goes Here." After that comment, add a JavaScript code block, and then enter this code.**

```
var today = new Date();
var wkDay = today.getDay();
var mon = today.getMonth();
var day = today.getDate();
var fyear = today.getFullYear();
var out = wkDay + ", " + mon + " " + day + " " + fyear;
document.write(out);
```

The code instantiates a Date object. Then, it extracts the day of the week, the month, the day of the month, and the full year. It concatenates those values along with some commas and spaces to build an output string. Then, using the `document.write()` method, it writes the string to the Web page.

4. **Save your changes and reload the page in your browser.**

5. **What is wrong with the code?**

6. **Open datearrays.txt in your editor.** This text file contains two array declarations, one for the names of the days and the second for the names of the months.

7. **Copy the entire contents of the datearrays.txt file. Close the file. If necessary, open datepage.html in your editor.**

8. **Preceding the code you entered earlier, paste the array declaration code into the script block.**

9. **Change the out variable declaration line to read as follows.**

```
var out = weekDays[wkDay] +"," + monthNames[mon] +" " + day
+" " + fyear;
```

Make sure to enter the code on one line. This new variable declaration line references the appropriate name within the date name arrays using the date numbers extracted from the `today` object.

10. **Save your changes and reload the file in your browser.**

The date is now automatically written to the page as it loads. The output uses the names of the days and months to produce a pleasing date format.

Clocks

Clocks are a popular feature of Web pages. They are relatively simple to construct, but can get quite fancy. You will need to instantiate a date object, build the desired output string (as the default string might not suit your fancy), and repeat the steps periodically to create a running clock effect.

To display the output, you can write the string to the status bar, to an empty frame, or as is most commonly done, to a form field. Form fields are dynamically updateable across most browsers. Writing dynamically to the current document is not possible with most browsers.

Since Date instances are static, to create a continually updating clock, you will need to periodically re-instantiate the Date object. The best method to do this is to put your date instantiation code, your string building code, and the output code into a function. Call the function when the page loads. Then, use the `setTimeout()` method within the function to periodically call the function again.

TASK 10B-3:

Creating a running clock

Objective: To create a running clock that displays its output in a form field.

1. **Open basicclock.html in your editor.** This is a shell of a very simple page. The page contains some label text and one form field, which you will use to display the clock's output. A script block and an empty function, `clock()`, is included in the `<HEAD>` section of the document.

2. **Begin your clock coding by adding the following code to the clock() function.**

```
var time = new Date();              // create date object
var hour = time.getHours();          // extract hours
var mins = time.getMinutes();        // extract minutes
var sec = time.getSeconds();         // extract seconds
var temp = hour + ":" + mins + ":" + sec;
```

This section of the code instantiates a Date object, extracts the hours, minutes, and seconds from it, and then builds the output string.

3. Next, you need to write the output string to the form field. The form on the page is named `clock` and the form field is named `time`. **So, add this line to your function.**

```
document.clock.time.value = temp;
```

4. To give the clock the appearance of running continuously, you will need to repeat the function every second. **So, add this line to your function.**

```
id = setTimeout("clock()", 1000);
```

This line uses the `setTimeout()` method to call the `clock()` function in 1000 milliseconds (one second).

5. Finally, you need to call the clock function when the page loads. **Add this onLoad handler parameter to the <BODY> tag.**

```
onLoad="clock();"
```

6. Save your changes and load the basicclock.html page in your browser.

Current Time: `22:57:15`

You should have a running clock that displays its output in the form field.

7. What problems can you identify with the script as it is written so far?

Apply Your Knowledge 10-1

Suggested Time:
10-15 minutes

In this activity, you will finish and polish the clock you started in the preceding task.

1. You should have a running clock page, basicclock.html, that displays its output in a form field. That page should be open in your editor. If you were unsuccessful with the previous task, you can open xbasic.html in your editor. It is completed as far as this stage. If necessary, switch to your editor.

2. Using either an *if...else* statement or a conditional operator statement, add the code necessary to add ":0" when the minutes are less than 10. Add just ":" when the minutes and seconds are greater than 10. Do the same for the seconds. You will need to change some existing lines in the script to accommodate your changes.

The conditional operator statements to perform these conditional tests are:

3. Save your changes and reload the file in your browser.

4. Modify the `clock()` function to account for hours greater than 12. In other words, make your clock display its output in a 12–hour clock format rather than a 24–hour format. You will need to add an am/pm indicator to the end of the clock output string, as appropriate.

5. Save your changes and reload the file in your browser.

Date Math

No, we don't mean counting the number of dates you've been on in the last year. By date math, we mean determining the time intervals between two dates, counting up or down to a specified date, or all sorts of other interesting applications of calendars and clocks.

JavaScript Date objects actually store a millisecond value—the number of milliseconds since midnight GMT (UTC) on January 1, 1970. So, if you subtract one Date from another Date, you are left with a number of milliseconds representing the difference. Remembering that a millisecond is one-thousandth of a second, converting to workable values, like hours or days, is simply a case of dividing.

Determining differences between dates often involves using two Date objects, one for the present and another for the future or past date of interest. The syntax for creating a Date to represent a non-current time is:

```
var notNow = new Date(year, month, day, hours, mins, secs, ms);
```

So, to create a Date object representing the day when NASA's Mars Pathfinder spacecraft landed on Mars, July 4, 1997, you could use a statement like:

```
var coolEvent = new Date(1997, 6, 4);
```

Remember, months in JavaScript are oh-so-intuitively zero-based. So, July, the seventh month is entered as 6 in our statement. Since the statement did not include any time information, midnight of the start of that day was assumed.

You can use the `new Date()` statement in two alternate forms. One alternate format uses milliseconds. This is useful for creating a new Date object after performing math on the milliseconds value of another Date object.

```
var someDate = new Date(milliseconds);
```

The other alternate format uses a date string, a string just like what would be written to the browser if you wrote a Date object as a string to the document.

```
var oneMoreDate = new Date("Friday July 06 00:00:00 1997");
```

You have quite a bit of flexibility when using the date string format of the new `Date()` constructor. You could abbreviate Friday or July with their three-letter abbreviations. You can leave out the time information and even put a comma between the day and month. JavaScript will figure it out.

TASK 10B-4:

Doing a little Date math

Objective: To instantiate some Date objects and perform some math with them, adding and subtracting some time intervals.

1. **Open blank.html in your editor.**

2. **In the JavaScript block in the <BODY> section of the document, enter this code:**

```
var coolEvent = new Date(1997, 6, 4);
alert(coolEvent);
```

3. **Save the file as datemath.html and load it in your browser.** You should see a dialog box like this one.

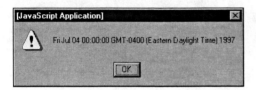

4. **Switch to your editor.**

5. **Using the milliseconds format of the new Date() constructor (new Date(milliseconds), create a Date object for some time today. Display your date in an alert box.** You could try to guess how many milliseconds have passed since the beginning of 1970. But using JavaScript to calculate that number would be a lot easier. As a guide, there are 1000 milliseconds in a second, 60 seconds in a minute, 60 minutes in an hour, and so forth.

   Check the answer key for some sample code to help you calculate this value.

6. **Save your changes and reload the file in your browser.** Your alert box should show a date and time value sometime during today. If not, adjust your millisecond value and try again.

7. **Switch to your editor. Remove the existing code and enter:**

```
var msPerDay = 1000 * 60 * 60 * 24;
var coolEvent = new Date(1997, 6, 4);
var now = new Date();
var temp = now - coolEvent;
temp = temp / msPerDay;
alert("It has been " + temp + " days since July 4, 1997");
```

To start, a variable noting the number of milliseconds per day is created. Then, a Date object called coolEvent is created with the date of July 4, 1997. Next, a Date object for the current date and time is created. The coolEvent object is subtracted from the now object, resulting in a value of some number of milliseconds. That number is stored in the variable temp. temp is divided by the number of milliseconds per day. Finally, an output string is displayed with an alert box.

8. **Save your changes and reload the file in your browser.**

The resulting number is a little ugly. Later in this lesson, you will see how to round numbers by using the Math object's methods.

Suggested Time:
15 minutes

Apply Your Knowledge 10-2

Counting down to an important date

In this activity, you will create a script that determines the number of days until an important date of your choice.

The xanniversary.html file included with the rest of the data files provides one possible solution to this lab.

1. Open blank.html in your editor.

2. Enter your code in the script block in the <BODY> section of the document. Add the JavaScript code necessary to create a Date object for an important date in the future. You could use a favorite holiday, like Christmas or Martin Luther King Day, or you could use an anniversary date, like your wedding anniversary. The date should be in the near future, preferably within one year of the current date.

   Create a Date object for the current date and time. Subtract the current date from the future date to determine the difference in milliseconds.

   Convert those milliseconds to days using the formula: msPerDay = 1000 * 60 * 60 * 24 (there are 1000 milliseconds in a second, 60 seconds in a minute, 60 minutes in an hour, and 24 hours in a day).

   Write a message to the page using document.write(), such as "There are ## days till (date)" using the value you calculated and your future-date object.

3. Save your script as anniversary.html. Load it in your browser to test it. Correct any errors and re-test until no further errors exist.

Topic 10C

The Math Object

Not everyone likes or wants to do mathematics, but if you do, JavaScript has a rich set of mathematical capabilities made possible by the Math object.

Basic mathematical operations, such as adding, subtracting, multiplying, and dividing, are provided by the basic JavaScript operators. The Math object makes available other capabilities, such as calculating the square root, logarithm, or sine of a number.

Math is a built-in object that you use directly. You don't need to create an instance of it as you do with the Date object. One fact to keep in mind, the Math object is named with an uppercase M. So, in your code, you must use it that way. For example, to use the random number generation method, you will need to spell Math with an uppercase M like this:

```
var rnd = Math.random();
```

Properties, Methods, Event Handlers (PMEs)

Math has no properties, per se. The Math object contains eight constants that at first glance would appear to be properties. However, an object enumeration script, such as that in object enumerator.html, will not display those properties or their values.

The Math object has many useful methods that let you perform all sorts of mathematical operations. Unlike the methods of other objects, those of the Math object do not operate on the Math object itself. Instead, they operate on numbers or values that you provide and return a result for your further use. Finally, the Math object has no event handlers.

Constants	Description
Math.E	The value of e, 2.718281828459045. Math.E is the base of the natural logarithm.
Math.LN10	The natural logarithm of 10, which equals 2.302585092994046.
Math.LN2	The natural logarithm of 2, which equals 0.6931471805599453.
Math.LOG10E	The base-10 logarithm of e, which equals 0.4342944819032518.
Math.LOG2E	The base-2 logarithm of e, which equals 1.4426950408889634.
Math.PI	The value of p (pi), which equals 3.141592653589793.
Math.SQRT1_2	One divided by the square root of 2, which equals 0.7071067811865476.
Math.SQRT2	The square root of 2, which equals 1.4142135623730951.

Methods	Computes	Version
Math.abs(x)	The absolute value of x.	1.0
Math.acos(x)	The arc cosine of x. The argument is the cosine of an angle. The result is an angle in radians.	1.0
Math.asin(x)	The arc sine of x. The argument is the sine of an angle. The result is an angle in radians.	1.0

If you will be using the Math object quite frequently in a script and you find lead-capping Math just too cumbersome, you can create a synonym for the Math object. Add the statement math = Math; to the beginning of your script. Then use math with a lowercase m throughout the remainder of your script.

Methods	Computes	Version
`Math.atan(x)`	The arc tangent of x. The argument is the tangent of an angle. The result is an angle in radians.	1.0
`Math.atan2(x,y)`	The counterclockwise angle between the X axis and a point defined by the coordinates x and y. The result is an angle in radians.	1.0
`Math.ceil(x)`	The ceiling of x, (the integer equal to or greater than x).In other words, `Math.ceil(x)` rounds x to an integer but always rounds up.	1.0
`Math.cos(x)`	The cosine of x. The argument is an angle in radians.	1.0
`Math.exp(x)`	The value of e raised to the power of x.	1.0
`Math.floor(x)`	The floor of x, (the integer equal to or less than x). In other words, `Math.floor(x)` rounds x to an integer but always rounds down.	1.0
`Math.log(x)`	The natural logarithm of x.	1.0
`Math.max(x, y)`	The greater of the two arguments, x and y.	1.0
`Math.min(x, y)`	The lesser of the two arguments, x and y.	1.0
`Math.pow(x, y)`	The value of x raised to the power of y.	1.0
`Math.random()`	A random number between 0 and 1.	1.0
`Math.round(x)`	The integer closest to x.	1.0
`Math.sin(x)`	The sine of x. The argument is an angle in radians.	1.0
`Math.sqrt(x)`	The square root of x. x must be greater than 1 or `Math.sqrt()` will return a NaN value.	1.0
`Math.tan(x)`	The tangent of x. The argument is an angle in radians.	1.0

Topic 10D

Doing Math with JavaScript

JavaScript has a rich set of mathematical functions provided by the Math object. Mathematics is typically a subtle component of most Web sites. Regardless, a few of the Math object's methods come in very handy. Generating random numbers and rounding numbers are two commonly used mathematical operations that will be explored here.

Random Numbers

JavaScript includes a random number generator function as a method of the Math object. Like all computer-based random number generators, this one is not 100% random. But, it's pretty good.

`Math.random()` generates a random number between 0 and 1, inclusive (the generated numbers could equal 0 or 1 or any real number in between). You can use it to generate a random number between any two numbers with just a little extra creativity. For example, to generate a random number between 0 and 100, inclusive, use this code:

```
var randNum = Math.random() * 100;
```

And, to generate a random number between 1 and 100, inclusive, use this code:

```
var randNum = Math.random() * 99 + 1;
```

TASK 10D-1:

Generating random numbers

Objective: To use the Math.random() method to generate random numbers.

1. **Open random.html in your browser.** This page will generate six random lottery numbers, ranging from 1 to the value you specify. Of course, the page doesn't work right now; you haven't added the script to it yet.

2. **Open random.html in your editor.**

3. **In the empty JavaScript code block, add this function.**

```
function lotto(frm)
    {
    range = frm.range.value - 1;
    for(x=2; x<8;  x++)
        {
        var lottoNum = (Math.random() * range) + 1;
        document.lottery.elements[x].value = lottoNum;
        }
    }
```

To start, this function determines the range of generated numbers by reading the upper limit from the range field on the form. Then, it uses a loop to generate six random numbers. The loop counts from two to seven, which might seem odd. You'll see why in a minute. In each iteration of the loop, `Math.random()` generates numbers from zero to one, which is multiplied by the range value, resulting in a random number from 0 to `range`. One is added to make the generated number be between 1 and `range`. Finally, the function writes the calculated number to the form field using the `elements[]` array notation and the loop counter x. Because the first two elements of the form are the button and the range value text box, the loop counts from 2 to 7, addressing the third through eighth form fields (the output boxes).

4. **Save your changes and reload the file in your browser.**

5. **Click Generate Numbers.** Random numbers between 1 and 54 are calculated.

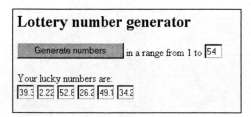

Lottery number generator

Generate numbers | in a range from 1 to 54

Your lucky numbers are:
39.3 | 2.22 | 52.8 | 26.2 | 49.1 | 34.2

6. **What problem do you notice with this function?**

7. **Change the range value and click Generate Numbers again.** A new set of numbers is calculated, this time within the range you specify.

Rounding Numbers

The `Math.round()` method rounds numbers to whole numbers (integers). This is fine for many applications, including the lottery number generator application you just created. Sometimes, the rounding that you need will be better performed by the `Math.ceil()` or `Math.floor()` methods. These force the rounding either up or down, respectively.

TASK 10D-2:

Rounding the numbers generated by the lottery page

1. **If necessary, open random.html in your editor.**

2. **Using the `Math.round()` method, round the numbers generated by the `lotto()` function so that only whole numbers are written to the form.**

xrandom.html is a finished version of the file after this task.

3. **Save your changes and reload the file in your browser.**

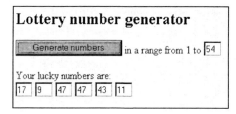

Lottery number generator

Generate numbers   in a range from 1 to 54

Your lucky numbers are:
17 9 47 47 43 11

4. **Generate some random lottery numbers.**

Rounding with Decimal Places

Sometimes, you will need to round numbers to include decimal places. The built in `Math.round()` method does not enable rounding to a specified number of decimal places. However, you can easily write your own rounding function to accomplish this goal.

Apply Your Knowledge 10-3

Suggested Time:
15 minutes

In this activity, you will write your own function to round numbers to a specified precision (number of decimal places).

1. Open roundit.html in your browser and click the Generate A Number button. The script on this page generates a random real number between 1 and 1000 and displays the results to a text field.

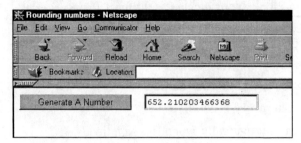

2. Open roundit.html in your editor. This page contains a simple form with two fields. The button's `onClick` handler calls the `gen()` function, which generates a random number between 1 and 1000 and writes it to the text field.

3. Add a new function named `myRound()` that accepts two parameters: a number to be rounded and the precision to which to round it. The precision value will be the number of decimal places to remain after rounding `myRound()` should return the rounded number. You will need the `Math.pow()` and `Math.round()` methods in your new function. Here's the logic you can use:

    *   Multiply the number to be rounded by 10 raised to the power of the precision value. For example, if you'll be rounding to a precision of two, multiply by 100 (10^2). Use the `Math.pow()` method to do this.

    *   Then, round the number with `Math.round()`.

    *   Finally, divide the result by 10 raised to the power of the precision value. Again, use `Math.pow()`.

4. Modify the `gen()` function so that it calls myRound() to round the generated number to two decimal places.

5. Save your changes and reload the page in your browser. Test your new function by repeatedly clicking the Generate A Number button. The displayed numbers should all have two decimal places.

xroundit.html is a finished version of the file after this activity.

6. Modify the code on the page to round the randomly generated number to three decimal places. This should only require a single change to the call to the `myRound()` function. Save and test your changes in your browser.

Apply Your Knowledge 10-4

In this activity, you will create a running clock that is displayed in the status bar.

1. Open statclock.html in your editor. You will add the code necessary to this file to create a running digital clock that is displayed in the status bar.

2. An empty `clock()` function has been provided for you. Add the necessary coding to create a running clock. Your clock should meet these criteria:

   * The clock should display its output as hh:mm:ss (make sure two digits are shown for the minutes and seconds) where hh is the hours in a 12-hour clock format.

   * Include an am/pm indicator with your output.

   * The clock should update every second.

   * The clock should start automatically when the page loads.

   * Use the `defaultStatus` property for writing the clock output to the status bar so that other status bar messages will still be shown.

3. Save the file and load it in your browser. The clock should show up in the status bar and run continuously. If not, correct your errors and reload the file.

xstatclock.html is a finished version of the file after this exercise.

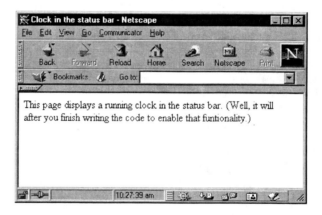

Figure 10-1: *The finished statclock.html page showing the clock in the status bar.* 9

Summary

In lesson 10, you created clocks, manipulated dates, and used a few of the methods of the Math object to perform mathematical operations. Manipulating dates and doing mathematics are very common tasks for which JavaScript is very capable.

Lesson Review

10A Describe the purpose of the "get" methods and the "set" methods of the Date class of objects.

Given that Date is a class of objects, how do you use them in your programs?

10B Describe the steps necessary to create a running clock. (Don't provide code; just describe how you would do this).

10C List one constant of the Math object.

Do you have to instantiate Math objects?

10D What syntax would you use to generate a random number between 28 and 4378, inclusive?

YOUR NOTES:

An Introduction to Cross-Browser Compatibility

Data Files
Navonly.html
ieonly.html
detectomatic.html
navprops.html
blank.html
Library\detecto.js
isobjprops.html

Lesson Time
2 hours, 15 minutes

Overview

Some programmers would rather swim shark-infested waters than attempt to write cross-browser compatible code. Okay, so it's not that bad. But you'll encounter many incompatibilities between the browsers' implementations of JavaScript. And, you'll find even greater challenges await you once you decide to take on the challenge of dynamic Web pages. This lesson will introduce a few of the pitfalls you'll encounter and provide a few strategies you can use to work around the fallout of the browser wars.

Objectives

In this lesson, you will:

11A   **Examine the compatibility landscape and examine techniques for dealing with potential incompatibilities.**

You'll take a look at the factors that affect compatibility, including varying browser and JavaScript versions.

11B   **Detect browsers in order to create code that works around platform incompatibilities.**

You'll examine a couple of techniques for determining which browser a user is running to view your Web pages. Then, you'll examine two pre-built detection libraries that you can use in your future scripting endeavors.

Topic 11A

Examining the Compatibility Landscape

The Web browser is a rapidly evolving beast, and vendors have different ideas of how their browsers should evolve. The capabilities and features of the 4.x and 5.x browsers are enormously more advanced than their 3.x predecessors.

The feature sets of Navigator, Internet Explorer, Lynx, Opera, CyberDog, and Mosaic, just to name a few of the hundreds of browsers available, are increasingly different. Only Navigator and Internet Explorer, and Opera to a lesser extent, support JavaScript. Of course, not everyone rushes right out to get the newest browsers when they are released. To top it off, the capabilities of a single browser will vary depending on which operating system it is run on!

This is the landscape in which your JavaScript programs will have to run. You will very often need to consider browser types, browser versions, and platforms on which they run, when writing your scripts. Each of these factors affects the subset of JavaScript language features you can use.

TASK 11A-1:

Exploring some cross-browser compatibility problems

Objective: To load some Web pages into Navigator and Internet Explorer to see how the JavaScript language offers different features in each of these browsers.

1. **Open navonly.html in Navigator.** The page contains a simple message describing the geometry of the browser window and the document it contains.

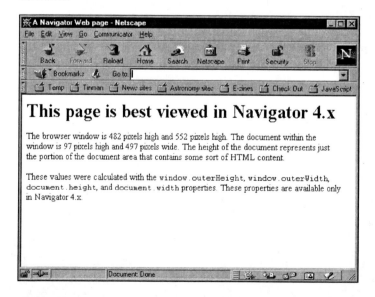

2. **Change the size of your browser window and reload the document.** The property values are updated.

3. **Open navonly.html in Internet Explorer. What happens?**

4. **Open ieonly.html in Internet Explorer.** The text moves back and forth across the page. The script randomly sets Cascading Style Sheets Positioning (CSS-P) information, which moves the text element.

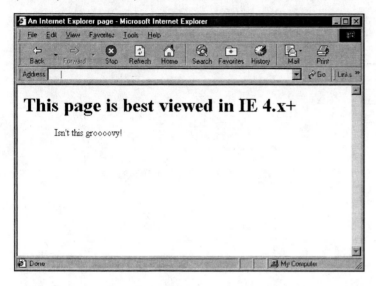

5. **Open ieonly.html in Navigator. What happens?**

Browser and JavaScript Versions

Browsers come in many varieties, though only a few are popular and widely used. Most people use either Netscape Navigator or Microsoft Internet Explorer. Of those browsers, multiple versions of each are in widespread use. As of this writing, the 5.0 version of Internet Explorer and the 4.6 version of Navigator are the most current browser versions. Even so, the 3.x versions of those browsers are still commonly used by many Web surfers.

Netscape seems to have finally synchronized the version number of Navigator and the Communicator suite, of which Navigator is a part. Both now have the version number 4.6. Prior to 4.6, Navigator had 4.0x version numbers corresponding to the Communicator 4.5x suite. For example, Navigator 4.08 was the browser component of the Communicator 4.51 suite.

As browsers have evolved, so has the version of JavaScript that each one has supported. The following table correlates the major browsers, versions, and the language levels each supports. JScript is Microsoft's implementation of JavaScript, which is compatible with but considerably extends standard JavaScript. ECMA-262 is the version of JavaScript as standardized by the European Computer Manufacturer's Association. That language is commonly known as ECMAScript. ECMAScript is roughly equivalent to JavaScript 1.2 with a few minor differences.

Throughout this book, the PME references for each object have noted the version of JavaScript in which they were first implemented. You can assume that unless otherwise noted, later versions of JavaScript support those PMEs. You can compare those notations with this table to determine which browsers support each of those PMEs.

| Browser | JavaScript Version | | | | JScript | ECMA-262 |
	1.0	1.1	1.2	1.3		
Navigator 2.x	X	–	–	–	–	–
Navigator 3.x	X	X	–	–	–	–
Navigator 4.0-4.05	X	X	X	–	–	X
Navigator 4.06-4.08	X	X	X	X	–	X
Navigator 4.6	X	X	X	X	–	X
Internet Explorer 3.0	X	–	X	X		–
Internet Explorer 4.0	X	X	X	–	X	X
Internet Explorer 5.0	X	X	X	X	X	X
Opera 3.x	X	X	–	–	–	–
Lynx	–	–	–	–	–	–

[1] The brower component of the Communicator suite is called Navigator. Communicator 4.51 includes Navigator 4.08. Communicator 4.6 includes Navigator 4.6.

[2] With a few minor deviations.

Many other browsers are available. However very few of them offer any JavaScript support. You might notice the omission of the browsers from the various Internet access providers, such as America Online, in the preceding table. In many cases, these access providers are simply distributing a browser from Microsoft or Netscape. Often, the provider will add custom logos, starting pages, and splash screens to "customize" the browsers. These cosmetic changes, however, do not affect the browser's implementation of JavaScript. In other cases, the providers offer their own proprietary browsers or provide "crippled" versions of a major vendor's browser. JavaScript support in those proprietary access programs is typically extremely limited.

Specifying the Language Version

JavaScript statements in a Web page are typically enclosed within `<SCRIPT>` and `</SCRIPT>` tags. The opening script tag typically includes additional information designed to tell the browser what language the script uses and other information about the script.

The `LANGUAGE` attribute describes what scripting language the enclosed script uses. In the case of JavaScript, the `LANGUAGE` tag can also denote the version of JavaScript the browser should use to interpret the enclosed code.

Language attribute	Used to denote a script written in
JavaScript	JavaScript
JavaScript1.1	JavaScript version 1.1
JavaScript1.2	JavaScript version 1.2
JavaScript1.3	JavaScript version 1.3
VBScript	Microsoft's VBScript scripting language

Specifying a version of JavaScript in the `<SCRIPT>` tag tells the browser to use the rules of that version of the language when interpreting the enclosed script. You do not need to specify a version of JavaScript in this way. In fact, in most cases you should not. Navigator, for example, has a few quirks that arise only when you specify the `LANGUAGE="JavaScript1.2"` attribute.

If you don't specify a version (you just use `LANGUAGE="JavaScript""`), the browser will use the rules of the latest version of the language it supports to interpret your script. Leaving it up to the browser like this works well in most situations.

One situation when you might want to specify the version is when you want certain blocks of code to run only on newer browsers, say the 4.x browser. You could put that code in a script block specified with the `LANGUAGE="JavaScript1.2"` attribute and it would run on only the 4.x and newer browsers. Perhaps you would use this technique to redirect newer browsers to other pages with enhanced code, for example.

TASK 11A-2:

Determining the version of JavaScript your browser supports

1. **Open detectomatic.html in both Navigator and Internet Explorer.**

2. **Compare the output of this pages scripts as produced by those two browsers.** The page reports the type of browser and version you are running. It also determines and displays a list of all of the versions of JavaScript that your browser supports. In Internet Explorer, it also reports that your browser supports JScript.

3. **View the source code for the page or open the file in your editor. How is the version of JavaScript support determined?**

4. **Close the source code window if you opened one.**

Compatibility Strategies

You have a few options for dealing with the inevitable problems: ignore the incompatibilities, program for the lowest common denominator, and code around incompatibilities.

As with anything in life, ignoring JavaScript compatibility problems won't make them go away. Your scripts might work fine on your system, but they are sure to break on someone else's. This is not a realistic way to write your scripts.

Programming for the lowest common denominator involves using only simple elements of the language, mostly those from the JavaScript 1.0 release. This technique greatly limits your options. Unless you are writing very simple scripts, programming for the lowest common denominator is not likely to be an option you can often use.

Your only true option then is to code with potential incompatibilities in mind. To do so, you must know what you're up against. You must know the limitations of the language so that you can know when techniques that you use have the potential to fail. You must detect browser and platform versions whenever you use language features that might not work universally. And you must provide a way to fail gracefully when you do use potentially incompatible techniques.

You can choose to detect the browser and provide multiple logic branches within the scripts on one page. Or once you have detected which browser is in use, you can redirect users to an appropriate page. Or you can build or buy a library of cross-browser compatible functions that mask browser incompatibilities. These three techniques could be described as:

code branching:
A cross-browser programming technique in which multiple logic branches are maintained within a single file and conditional statements are used to determine which blocks are executed.

page branching:
A cross-browser programming technique in which multiple logic branches are maintained within separate files and conditional statements are used to determine which files are loaded.

- *Code branching* —multiple logic branches are maintained within a single file. Conditional statements and browser detection control which functions or blocks of code are executed in a given instance.

- *Page branching* —multiple logic branches are maintained within separate files. Conditional statements and browser detection control which pages are loaded by particular users when they visit your site. Functions or blocks of code within each of the files are specific to browser type and version.

- Cross-browser library—also called the custom API (application programming interface) method. Libraries of functions that mask browser incompatibilities are used in place of native JavaScript commands. Typically, these library functions are built by an in-house programmer or a third party. The functions are typically quite complex, having to resort to complex code branching to achieve similar functionality whether they run in Navigator or Internet Explorer. However, to the programmer that uses them, they provide a simple unified outward appearance.

Some find that maintaining a single page, even a very complex page, is simpler than maintaining two pages. Others find the code complexity required with the code branching technique to be too cumbersome and feel separate pages are simpler to maintain. Proponents of using cross-browser libraries cite the advantage of "write-once and your code can run on both browsers." However, typically you have to learn all the syntax and capabilities of the library, which in many ways can be as complex (or more so) as learning how to write the cross-platform code yourself. Which method you choose is entirely up to you.

Topic 11B

Detecting Browsers and Platforms

There are probably as many techniques for detecting browsers as there are browsers. We'll stick to just two basic techniques: reading the properties of the Navigator object, and using the `if(object)` shortcut.

The Navigator Object

The *Navigator object*, supported since JavaScript 1.0, provides a set of properties that describe the browser that is being used by the user. The following table lists the most pertinent properties of the Navigator object.

Property	Description	Version
appCodeName	The code name of the browser. Both Navigator and Internet Explorer report the `appCodeName` property to be `Mozilla`.	1.0
appName	The name of the browser. Navigator reports `"Netscape"` and Internet Explorer reports `"Microsoft Internet Explorer"` with this property.	1.0
appVersion	The version number of the browser and browser-specific additional information.	1.0
platform	The operationing system the browser is running on. Some of the values are as follows: `Win32` = Windows 9x and Windows NT `Win16` = Windows 3.x and Windows or Workgroups `MacPPC` = Macintosh Power PC `SunOS5.5.1` = Sun Microsystems Ultra Sparc This same information is available in the `appVersion` property, which is a more widely supported property.	1.2
userAgent	Provides nearly the same information as the `appVersion` Property, but also includes the `appCodeName` information.	1.0

Internet Explorer also supports the `clientInformation` object, which is almost a clone of the Navigator object. It has a more vendor-neutral name; but, alas, only Internet Explorer supports it.

Mozilla was the name Netscape used for their cute little dragon mascot. That icon and name was dropped when the company changed their name from Mosaic Communications to Netscape. Their product went from Mosaic to Navigator at that time, too. The Mozilla icon is now sometimes used by the mozilla.org group, which is the open-source offshoot of Netscape.

TASK 11B-1:

Using the Navigator object to detect the browser

Objective: To examine a script that uses properties of the Navigator object to determine the browser version and platform.

1. **Open navprops.html in your editor.**

2. **Observe the code in the file.** This file contains HTML and JavaScript code. The code simply writes the values of the three primary Navigator object properties to the page. (The HTML makes it look pretty.)

3. **Load the file into both Navigator and Internet Explorer. Compare the results.** Each browser reports similar information, though the specifics are a bit different.

4. **If you have it available, open navprops.html in Internet Explorer 5.0 (or switch to it if it's already running).**

5. **Why do you think the appVersion property reports two different versions: 4.0 and MSIE 5.0?**

6. **How do you think you could use the navigator.appName property to detect browser type?**

7. **How could you use the navigator.appVersion property to detect browser version?**

8. **How could you use the navigator.platform property?**

String Functions

Here's a summary of the methods that are useful for manipulating the values of the various properties of the Navigator object.

Method	Description and syntax
`chartAt ()`	Extracts the character at the specified position in the string.`var x = string.charAt(pos);`
`indexOf()`	Searches within a string for a specified substring and returns the position where the first letter of the substring appears in the string (or -1 if substring isn't part of string).`var num = string.indexOf(subStr);`
`parseFloat()`	Extracts a floating point (real) number from the beginning of a string.`var num = parseFloat(string);`
`parseInt()`	Extracts an integer from the beginning of a string.`var num = parseInt(string);`
`toLowerCase()`	Converts the characters in the string to their lowercase equivalents.`var newString = string.toLowerCase();`
`toUpperCase()`	Converts the characters in the string to their uppercase equivalents.`var newString = string.toUpperCase();`

Apply Your Knowledge 11-1

Suggested Time:
45 minutes

Creating a browser detection script

In this activity, you will write a browser detection script that reads the properties of the Navigator object and takes different actions depending on which browser is detected.

1. Open blank.html in your editor.

2. Using the properties of the Navigator object, create a script as follows:

    *   Your script should detect and store the results in a series of global variables. The detection script should be placed in the `<HEAD>` section of the document so that it runs before the page is loaded.

    *   Your script should report the browser type as either "Netscape Navigator" or "Microsoft Internet Explorer" (not quite the information contained in the `navigator.appName` property).

    *   Your script should report the major-version number without any extra version information. In other words, for Navigator 4.6, Internet Explorer 4.x, or Internet Explorer 5.0, it should report 4. (Again, this is not exactly what is contained in the `navigator.appVersion` property.)

    *   Your script should report the platform on which the user is running his or her browser. Extract this information from the navigator.appVersion property. Report a human-readable operating system name, such as Windows 95, Windows 98, Windows NT, UNIX, and Macintosh. Look for the following substrings within the `navigator.appVersion` property to determine this information. (You will probably want to convert the appVersion value to all lowercase or uppercase to make searching easier.)

According to Netscape, Opera 3.0 reports "Windows 95/NT4" on all of the Win32 platforms. So you can't distinguish between those operating systems if the user is running Opera.

Platform	appVersion substrings
Windows 95	Win and 95
Windows 98	Win and 98
Windows NT	Win and NT
UNIX	X11
Macintosh	Mac

- Your output script should read the global variables you set. This script should be located in the <BODY> section of the document.

- If the browser in use is Navigator, display the above information in an alert box. If the browser in use is Internet Explorer, use the document.write() method to write the information to the page. (Using these different output methods is not meant to imply browser capabilities or best-practice techniques. It is only meant to show how your code can do different things depending on which browser is used to load the page.)

3. Save your page as detect.html.

4. Open your page in both browsers. The page should report the information as described above. Correct any errors and retest, if necessary.

The file xdetect.html located with the rest of the data files offers one possible solution to this exercise.

The if(object) Shortcut

JavaScript has a handy feature that provides a shortcut for browser detection. JavaScript converts data to different types depending on how it is used. This is something other programming languages do not do for you. In particular, if you use an object's property as a Boolean, it will be converted to true if it exists and false if it does not.

What this means is that you can use a statement like if(window.screen) in a detection script. You could read that statement something like "if the screen property of the Window object exists." The screen property, which provides information about the video capabilities of the user's computer, was added to the Window object in JavaScript 1.2. If the user is running a 4.x browser, that if() statement will evaluate to true. With older browsers, the property doesn't exist and the statement will evaluate to false.

This technique is inconvenient to use with properties of objects that have to be instantiated or created in some way. For example, the select.type property, added with JavaScript 1.1 exists only in association with a particular select list object as part of an HMTL form.

You cannot use this technique with objects, methods, event handlers, or properties whose contents are Boolean values. For example, the window.closed property stores a true or false value. You'd be testing its value not its existence if you use it in your test.

This technique works only with properties of objects that exist in all of the browsers. If you used the statement if(RegExp), trying to test for the existence of that object (introduced with JavaScript 1.2), you'd get an error with an older browser. Also, you cannot use properties of the global object, such as Infinity (added in JavaScript 1.3), as the browsers treat the global pseudo-object differently.

These limitations lessen the usability of this trick to detecting only certain versions of JavaScript or browsers, as described in the following table.

To detect this browser or version	Use this property
JavaScript 1.1 and higher	`document.images`
JavaScript 1.2 and higher	`window.screen`
JavaScript 1.3 and higher	No unique properties available for testing
Internet Explorer 3.x and higher	No unique properties available for testing
Internet Explorer 4.x and higher	`document.all`
Navigator 3.x and higher	No unique properties available for testing
Navigator 4.x and higher	`document.layers`

Of those, only two are widely used. If document.all exists, you can be sure that the user is running Internet Explorer 4.x or newer. If `document.layers` is present, the user is running Navigator 4.x or newer. These properties are used quite often when programming dynamic Web pages.

TASK 11B-2:

Using the object detection technique

1. **Open blank.html in your editor.**

2. **In the `<SCRIPT>` block in the `<BODY>` section of the document, enter the following code.**

```
if(document.all)
   {
   document.write("You're running Internet Explorer 4.x+");
   }
else if(document.layers)
   {
   document.write("You're running Navigator 4.x+");
   }
else
   {
   document.write("You're not running a 4.x browser");
   }
```

3. **Save the file as objdetect.html.**

4. **Open the file in each browser. If you have a 3.x browser available, test your script in that environment, too.**

Detection Script Techniques

So now that you know how to detect the browser, version, and platform, how should you use that knowledge to build an efficient browser detection script? Many JavaScript programmers create a detection function and put it in a JavaScript source code library file. Such a function should detect the browser information and create some standardized variables that can be tested for later.

You could write a script that creates a variable for each browser and platform for which you want to test. For example, your script could create an isNav4 variable that would be set to `true` when the script runs in a Navigator 4.x browser and `false` otherwise.

TASK 11B-3:

Examining and using a sample detection library function

1. **From the Library folder included with the data files, open detecto.js in your editor.**

2. **Examine the script.** This script detects the browser type, version, and platform and sets variables that can be used to branch accordingly. For example, if the browser type is Navigator, you could test for that later on the page by simply using a statement like `if (isNav)`.

3. **Open browsedetect.html in your editor.** This page uses the detecto.js library file to detect the browser type and version.

4. **Check out how the variables are used on the page to build simple and readable platform-specific branching with `if()` statements.**

5. **Open browsedetect.html in both Internet Explorer and Navigator.** You should get a customized message for each platform.

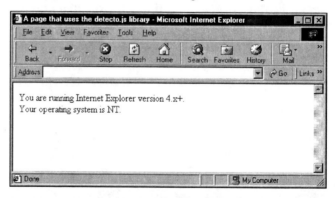

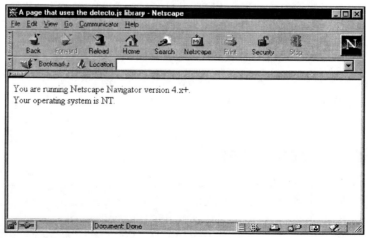

Apply Your Knowledge 11-2

In this activity, you will explore a browser detection script provided by Netscape Corporation.

Suggested Time:
30 minutes

1. If necessary, connect to the Internet.

2. Use your browser to connect to **http://developer.netscape.com/docs/examples/javascript/browser_type.html**. This page describes Netscape's "Ultimate client-side JavaScript client sniff" browser detection script. (A copy of the function presented on that page is included in the Library folder in the file is.js.)

3. Read the explanatory text that precedes the function. This text describes the purpose of the function and the set of "is" properties it creates (all the properties are named "is_something" such as `is_nav4up`).

4. Explore the workings of the function and the properties it creates. Similar to the script presented in this lesson, Netscape's function creates a series of properties with Boolean values that you can use with `if()` tests in your scripts. The properties define the browser type, version, and platform. This is a very comprehensive browser detection function.

5. Copy the function code from Netscape's page, paste it into a new blank file in your editor, and save it to a file called is.js to the same location as the rest of the data files for this course. (Or copy the is.js file from the Library folder to the current folder.)

6. Open isobjprops.html in your editor. This is a partially completed page that you can use to test the functionality of Netscape's browser detection script.

The file xobjdetect.html is a completed version of the file you create in this exercise.

7. Using a `<SCRIPT>` tag in the `<HEAD>` section of the document, include the is.js file into isobjprops.html. Save your changes.

8. Open isobject.html in both Internet Explorer and Navigator. The script detects your browser, platform, and other information and displays it to the page. The function is comprehensive, though perhaps a little overwhelming to use. Your code could get a bit cumbersome using Netscape's function. However, if you need comprehensive browser detection, this script should fit your needs.

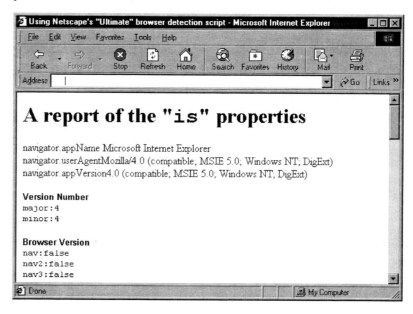

Figure 11-1: *The output of isobjprops.html when loaded in Internet Explorer 5.0.*

Summary

In lesson 11, you briefly examined the cross-browser compatibility landscape. You explored a number of techniques for detecting which browser a user is running and then reacting accordingly. You even wrote your own browser detection function. Unfortunately, these are skills that you will probably have to use frequently in your scripting careers.

Lesson Review

11A List the three strategies you can use to code with potential incompatibilities in mind.

246   *JavaScript Programming*

Which browser or browsers support JavaScript version 1.2? Which are completely ECMA-262 compliant?

11B List the object and its properties that you will most often use to detect browsers and versions.

YOUR NOTES:

LESSON 1

Task 1A-2 Page 7

10. In your opinion, which browser's error handling mechanism is better?

Both hide cryptic and confusing error messages from novice or average users. However, Internet Explorer is typically more useful for JavaScript programmers. It is more consistent at indicating that errors have been encountered. Also, it offers the option of displaying error messages in a dialog box to make them more immediately identifiable. Then again, some programmers prefer Navigator's 'graphical' method of indicating the location of the error within the line of code.

Task 1B-1 Page 10

5. What are a few locations where if you enter spaces or line breaks you will cause an error?

Of course, you cannot enter spaces or line breaks in the middle of words. You also cannot put them between the minus and equal signs on line 23 or between the two plus signs on line 24.

LESSON REVIEW 1

Topic 1-A

Describe how Internet Explorer and Navigator display error messages when JavaScript coding errors are encountered.

Internet Explorer 5.0 notes the fact that there is an error by writing the message "Done, but with errors on page" in the status bar. Double-clicking on the associated icon opens a dialog box that describes the error. Navigator is supposed to put a message about the error into the status bar but often does not. You can view JavaScript errors by opening the JavaScript console.

Topic 1-B

List the seven language components of JavaScript.

Literals, identifiers, functions, objects, properties, methods, and event handlers

What is a statement in JavaScript?

statement is like a complete JavaScript sentence. It is a combination of the language components that accomplishes an action.

LESSON 2

Task 2A-1 Page 23

4. Identify the variables that hold the floating-point, integer, and string values.

The variable pi stores a floating-point number (one with decimal places), radius stores an integer, and area and circum store a string.

Task 2A-2 Page 24

4. What is the value of the third element of the `beatles[]` array and what is its number?

The third element is "George" and is numbered 2.

5. Load the page in your browser to run the script. How is the data output?

When you use an array as it is in the `document.write()` statement, the elements of the array are output in a comma-separated list.

Task 2A-3 Page 26

1. A golf ball, a telephone, and a baby.

Golf ball—properties: color, insignia or label, number of dimples; methods: fly, bounce, roll; events: you hitting them.

Telephone—properties: color, shape, size of buttons; methods: ring; events: you pressing their buttons.

Baby—properties: weight, length, color of hair; methods: eat, sleep, and fill diapers; events: you picking them up.

Task 2B-2 Page 31

2. Which, if any, of the lines of code do you think will cause a JavaScript error?

If you are using a 4.x browser, none of the document.write lines will cause an error. (The lines using the variable A will produce an error in Navigator 3.x.) The lines that calculate using the variable A will all produce NaN outputs, whereas the line calculating a/b will produce the value of Infinity. This is a divide-by-zero operation, which in theory should also produce a NaN output. Only the b/a line will produce an actual number.

Task 2B-3 Page 34

4. **Compare the output of the integer code to the limits given in the preceding text. Do integer limits really matter?**

    Integer limits really have little bearing on reality. JavaScript works with floating point numbers pretty much exclusively. So, while the official specifications might call for an upper limit for integer values, as you can see, you can exceed those limits.

6. **Switch to your browser and compare the output of the floating point code to the values given in the preceding text. Do floating point limits really matter?**

    Yes. You can see that once the variable is raised above the floating point limit, its value becomes infinite. Subsequent operations on that value don't have an effect. An infinite value remains infinite even if you perform mathematical operations on it.

7. **If you added the following code to the end of the floating point section of code, what do you think its results would be? Implement it and find out.**

    ```
    a = a/a;
    document.write("<BR>a = " + a);
    ```

    The value of a would become NaN. As far as JavaScript is concerned, Infinity is essentially a non-numeric value.

Task 2B-4 Page 37

1. **Example A:**

    ```
    var x = 2;
    var y = "4";
    var z = x * y;
    ```

    z would equal 8 (the string is automatically converted to a number).

    Example B:

    ```
    var x = 2;
    var y = "4";
    var z = x + y;
    ```

    z would equal "24" (a string result, the + operator can either add numbers or concatenate strings and in this case, JavaScript converts x to a string rather than y to a number; thus the strings are concatenated).

    Example C:

    ```
    var x = "2";
    var y = "4";
    var z = x + y;
    ```

    z would equal "24" (a string).

    Example D:

    ```
    var x = true;
    var y = "4";
    var z = x + y;
    ```

    z would equal "true4" (the Boolean is converted to a string).

Example E:

```
var x = true;
var y = 4;
var z = x + y;
```

z would equal 5 (the Boolean is converted to a number).

3.   **How might you override the default conversions that JavaScript makes?**

You could use the `parseInt()`, `parseFloat()`, *and* `toString()` *functions to manually convert values.*

Apply Your Knowledge 2-1 Page 38

5.   **Modify your script to convert each of those numbers to binary. You'll need to convert the hexadecimal numbers to decimal, then to binary using two steps. You can't do it in one step. Save your file as binary.html and test it in your browser. A hint is provided in the answer section, if you are unsure of the method to use here.**

Binary numbers are base-2 numbers. You can use the `x.toString(2)` *function to convert to binary or* `parseInt(x, 2)` *function to convert from binary.*

Task 2C-1 Page 42

1.   **Examine this code. What will be the value displayed for x?**

```
var x = 10;
alert(x++);
```

The correct answer is 10. The variable x is incremented after it is used.

3.   **Modify the code so that line three reads `alert(++x);`. Now what is the value displayed for x?**

The correct answer is 11. The variable x is incremented before it is used.

Task 2C-2 Page 43

1.   **Why would you use the assignment with operation operators?**

Primarily, the benefit of the assignment with operation operators is their compactness. They require less typing than the standard form of these expressions.

2.   **Given a value of 23 for x, what would x equal after the following line was executed?**

```
x += 23;
```

46.

3.   **Given a value of 23 for x and 5 for y what would x equal after the following line was executed?**

```
x += y;
```

28.

4. What would be the displayed value of msg?

```
var msg = "forwards ";
msg += "backwards ";
alert(msg)
```

The message "forwards backwards " would be displayed.

5. What would be the displayed value of msg?

```
var msg = "forwards ";
msg =+ " backwards ";
alert(msg);
```

This would generate an error; it would not generate "backwards forwards" as you might have expected because =+ is not a valid operator.

LESSON REVIEW 2

Topic 2-A

List the six variable (data) types that JavaScript supports.

Numbers, strings, booleans, null, arrays, and objects.

Topic 2-B

What keyword do you use to declare variables.

var

Do you need to use that keyword?

No. If you assign a value to a variable that does not exist, JavaScript will simply create the variable for you.

Topic 2-C

What is the difference between operator precedence and operator associativity?

Operator precedence determines the order in which operators will be evaluated when more than one of a different type is used in one statement.

Operator associativity determines the order in which operators will be evaluated when more than one of the same type is used in one statement.

What does the += operator do?

The assignment with addition operator adds the value to its right to the variable on its left and puts the result back into the variable listed to its left.

LESSON 3

Task 3A-1 Page 51

2. Read and evaluate the script. Will the alert statement be processed?

No, x is not greater than y, so the condition returns false and the statement inside the block is not executed.

3. Change the ifscript1.html file to test that x is equal to y. Test your changes (save and load in your browser). What change did you make?

The first line of the if statement should now read `if (x==y)`*. The remaining lines stay the same. Did you remember to include the double equals sign? One of the most common if statement mistakes is to use the single equals sign, which assigns the value of y to x rather than comparing their values. If you made this mistake, make sure to fix the script before moving on.*

5. Open the page in your browser. Does your browser show the alert?

Yes, provided you used the `==` *operator for your equality test. The* `==` *operator will perform automatic data conversion before testing. So, the string value of "10" equals the numeric value of 10 once the string is automatically converted to a number.*

7. Reload the script in your browser (you'll need to use Internet Explorer 4.0 or Navigator 4.06 or newer). Does your browser show the alert message?

No. The identity operator does not perform automatic data conversion. So, the string value of "10" is not identical to the numeric value of 10.

Task 3A-2 Page 52

2. Read and evaluate the script. Will the alert statement be processed?

Yes. Both of the criteria evaluate to true, so the block of code within the if statement is executed.

6. Save your changes and run your script to test its functionality.

Your if statement should be `if (x > y || y < z)`*.*

7. Modify the script you created in the previous step to use the Not operator to test for x being not greater than y and y being less than z. Run your script to test its functionality.

Your if statement should be `if (!(x>y) && y < z)`*. You use the Not operator to invert the value of the greater than test. Given that* `!=` *is not equal to, you very well might have tried something like* `!>` *to test for not greater than. JavaScript is not always that logical!*

Task 3A-5 Page 56

3. Find the conditional operator in this script. What is its function in this script?

The conditional operator in this script adds either a colon or a zero and a colon depending on whether the minutes or seconds are less than or greater than 10. This makes the output of the clock more realistic.

4. **Describe a reason why you might use the conditional operator in a script like this rather than an if statement.**

Some programmers take great pride in writing very compact code, a task for which the conditional operator is well suited. Code that you will use repeatedly in many situations, such as clock-producing code, should probably be written in that manner.

Task 3A-6 Page 57

1. **Open forloop1.html in your editor. How many times will this loop be performed and what will be the value of x when the loop last runs?**

The loop will repeat ten times, and when it stops x will have the value of 12.

Task 3A-9 Page 60

2. **Check out the script. It erroneously tries to divide 20 by the string "ten". Which of the statements do you think will detect the condition and display the alert box?**

The `if(isNaN(z))` *block is executed.*

LESSON REVIEW 3

Topic 3-A

How many times will the `document.write()` statement in the following code sample be executed?

```
for(x=12; x<24; x++)
    {
    document.write(x + "<BR>");
    }
```

Twelve times.

Why would you use a `while` loop instead of a `for` loop?

The `while` *loop is most useful when you do not know ahead of time how many iterations of the loop might be required.*

LESSON 4

Task 4A-3 Page 65

7. What other change might you want to make to the function definition to better handle all possibilities?

You should also probably test to see if msg1 *is* null.

9. Modify the if() **statement in the function definition script to use the** arguments.length **property to determine if the correct number of arguments have been passed. Your script should test to see if two parameters were passed, and if so, create the concatenated string. Otherwise, your function should display just the first argument in the alert box. Test your changes by passing one and two arguments.**

This sounds challenging, but a simple change is all that is necessary. Change the if statement to read if(arguments.length == 2) *and leave the remainder of the function definition script the same.*

Task 4A-5 Page 68

5. Open function4.html in your browser. Do the function calls work?

Yes. The functions are defined in mathlib.js and are accessible to other scripts in the document now that you have included that file.

Task 4A-6 Page 70

2. Which are the global and local variables?

x is a global variable. y *and* z *are local variables, with* z *being local to the nested function.*

6. Where did the errors occur and what were they? Were there no errors where you expected some to be?

The use of z *in the final* alert(x/z) *line causes the error. That line uses the local variable* z *outside of its context. In the other cases, JavaScript searches up the scope chain to find the variables it needs.*

Task 4A-7 Page 72

2. Open function5.html in your browser. Does the script work or does it generate an error?

Perhaps surprisingly, the script works just fine even though the function is defined after it is used. This is because the JavaScript interpreter in your browser scans the whole script block first looking for function definitions before it executes any other code. So, even though the function definition code comes last in the script, that code is executed first.

4. Then, save and reload the page in your browser. Now does the script work?

No, with this modification the script will fail. Because the function definition is not within the same script block where the function is used, it is not automatically defined first.

6. Save and reload the page in your browser. Does the script work now?

Yes. Because the <HEAD> section is interpreted first, the function is defined by the time it is used. In general, you should put your function definitions in the <HEAD> section just to make sure they are defined when you call them in your subsequent scripts.

Task 4B-2 Page 80

7. Do the variable and function show up as properties of the Window object here in Internet Explorer?

No. With Internet Explorer, the Window object is not the global object, the inaccessible Global object is. Global stores global variables and functions in Internet Explorer.

LESSON REVIEW 4

Topic 4-A

What is the general syntax for creating a function?

```
function funcName(arg1, arg2, ...)
  {
  code
  return val
  }
```

Where should you define functions and why?

You should define your functions in a script block in the <HEAD> section of the document so that you are sure they are available when called by scripts elsewhere on your page.

Topic 4-B

Define "instance" and "instantiating," and name one object that must be used this way.

An instance is a "live" copy of an object class. Instantiating is the process of creating an instance. The Date class is one that must be used through instantiation.

List three core objects and three client-side objects.

Core: Array, Date, Math, and Screen, to name a few. Client-side: Window, Document, Form, and Image are a few examples.

LESSON 5

Task 5A-1 Page 85

8. Did the OuterWidth and OuterHeight properties change?

Yes. They reflect the new dimensions of your browser window. In fact, they represent the dimensions of the entire window, whereas the InnerWidth and InnerHeight measure the document area within the window (minus the window border).

Task 5C-3 Page 100

7. What must you specify as the start and stop positions in order to extract your name from the string?

The start position is 11. You must use a number one greater than the position number of the last character in the string in order to extract the last character of the string. You could use the phrase.length property to easily specify this number.

Task 5C-4 Page 102

4. In your editor, change the interval at which the scrollStat() function is called again to 125 milliseconds. Save your changes and reload the file in your browser. Do you notice a speed difference?

Probably not; 25 milliseconds is only one-fortieth of a second.

Task 5D-3 Page 110

6. What do you think will be shown now?

The status bar will now be shown with this change.

Task 5D-4 Page 112

9. Save the file and reload it in both browsers. The new window opens as before. Click the close button. Does the window close?

Yes. The onClick handler on the <A HREF> tag works in both browsers.

Task 5D-5 Page 113

13. Examine the JavaScript source code for the windoc.html file. Why does the Close This Window button work and where does its functionality come from?

Part of the HTML text put into the variable output is an HTML form. That form contains the button. An `onClick` *handler is defined for the button, which calls the* `window.close()` *method.*

LESSON REVIEW 5

Topic 5-A

What is the purpose of the Window object and what place does it occupy in the JavaScript Object Model?

The Window object represents the browser window and is the top of the JavaScript Object Model hierarchy.

Topic 5-B

What buttons and text boxes are included with alert, confirm, and prompt boxes?

The alert box contains a single OK button. The confirm box contains OK and Cancel buttons. The prompt box includes a text entry box, an OK, and a Cancel button.

When using a confirm box, what value is returned if the user clicks Cancel?

A false value is returned.

Topic 5-C

Given the following code, what is missing that is required to display a transient status bar message?

```
<A HREF="http://someurl"
   onMouseOver="status='Some description';"
   onMouseOut="status=''"
>Link text</A>
```

Transient status bar messages require a return `true` to be include in the `onMouseOver` code or the messages might not show up when and how you intend.

Topic 5-D

If you opened a new browser window with the statement `newWin = window.open("", "myNewWin");` how would you later set a URL for that window?

You could use the statement `newWin.location="yourURL";` to set a URL for that window.

LESSON 6

Task 6A-1 Page 120

8. Did the `bgColor` and `lastModified` properties change?

Yes, the `bgColor` property now reflects the background color you specified. The `lastModified` date reflects your system's current date and time and corresponds to the last time the document was modified and saved. You'll learn later why the background color changes to white after you click the button.

Task 6C-1 Page 129

6. Open innertext.html in Navigator. What happens?

A JavaScript error is reported. It reports that `currTime` is not defined. Navigator does not support the techniques used here to produce dynamic content.

Task 6C-2 Page 130

7. Reload layertest.html in Internet Explorer. Does it honor the positioning style information you added to the layer tag?

Internet Explorer ignores the `<LAYER>` tags, which it knows nothing about. Thus, it ignores the CSS positioning you specified within that tag, even though Internet Explorer has robust support for CSS.

Task 6C-4 Page 134

8. Move your mouse pointer away from the image. What happens?

The "on" image remains visible. You will need to add additional code to re-display the original image.

LESSON REVIEW 6

Topic 6-A

List three commonly used properties or methods of the Document object and note their purpose.

Answers might include:

`document.lastModified` — the last date and time the page's file was modified

`document.URL` — the URL of the currently loaded document

`document.write()` — opens as output stream to the document (creates a new document for writing)

Topic 6-B

Why might you use document.writeln() rather than document.write()?

The document.writeln() *method automatically includes a (text) carriage return, which makes it especially useful when writing to a text document, to a preformatted section of the document, or to produce dynamic code that is easily readable in the source code viewer window.*

Topic 6-C

What property of an image can you modify after the page is loaded to produce a dynamic page effect?

You can modify the SRC *(source) property to cause a new image to load. You can produce rollover effects, slide shows, and many other dramatic effects using this technique.*

LESSON 7

Task 7B-1 Page 141

5. How would you refer to a property of the documents loaded in leftbar.html and sub3.html?

From sub2.html, sub3.html is top.frames[2].frames[2] and leftbar.html is top.frames[1].

LESSON REVIEW 7

Topic 7-A

What is the purpose of the <FRAMESET> and <FRAME> tags of HTML?

The <FRAMESET> *tag describes the geometry or layout of the frames to be created. The* <FRAME> *tag describes the documents to load into those frames.*

Topic 7-B

Given a document with three frames named left, righttop, and rightbottom and loaded in that order in the frameset document, how would a script in the righttop frame access a variable named currDate in the left frame?

With either top.frames[0].currDate *or* top.left.currDate.

LESSON 8

Task 8A-1 Page 152

3.   What do you think the method, action, encoding, and target properties refer to?

These are the same properties as their HTML equivalents. Whatever parameters were set in the HTML code are reflected in these properties.

4.   What do you think the first three properties (form.0, form.1, and form.2) represent?

There are one each of these properties for the buttons on the form—that is what these properties represent. Notice that form.length equals 3, telling you how many elements are contained in the form.

Task 8A-3 Page 156

5.   What is the value of a radio button or check box that has been checked?

Radio buttons and check boxes that are checked have a value of "on."

6.   What is the value of a button?

Button values are the text that appears on them.

7.   Is the text you enter in the password box encrypted in any way?

The text you enter in a password box does not show up on the form but is clearly available as the value property (with no encryption of any sort) of the elements object.

Task 8B-1 Page 160

3.   What is the text box's name?

The text box is named "textbox1."

7.   In what situations is the `onBlur` handler called?

The onBlur handler is called when the focus is taken away from the field, in other words, when the insertion point leaves the field.

8.   What is the `onBlur` handler doing?

The code is calling the writeProps() function, passing the currently selected elements object using the very handy "this" keyword. The writeProps() function then enumerates the object's properties, displaying the results in the text area in the right frame.

11.   The statement you use to accomplish this task is included in the answer section for this lesson.

Your code should be: alert('Your password is' + this.value);

12. How might you use this fact in one of your forms?

If the value and defaultValue are the same, the user hasn't entered any text into the form. You could check this to make sure they weren't submitting inappropriate or useless data, but only if you specify a default value when creating the form.

Task 8B-2 Page 161

2. Record the following values:
- The form's name =
- The text area's name =

output

eleOut

4. Using the information you recorded in step 2 above, speculate on the purpose of the last line (`top.right.document.output.eleOut.value = prop;`) of the function.

The last line writes the contents of the variable prop to the value of the eleOut field in the output form in the document in the right frame, which is one level down from the top of the frames hierarchy. So, in the last line, top.right.document accesses the Document object of the right frame and output.eleOut accesses the field in the form on that page. Writing a string to the value of a text-style form element displays that string in the form field.

LESSON REVIEW 8

Topic 8-A

Describe the purpose of the Form object. Is it the object you use most frequently when manipulating HTML form contents?

The Form object represents HTML forms on the Web page. Most times, you manipulate the objects representing the elements within those forms, rather than using the Form object itself.

Topic 8-B

How would you describe to a colleague the process of determining which check boxes are checked (in other words, describe the process, don't give code).

1. First, you loop through the check boxes in the array of options.

2. Next, you see if each has its checked property set to true.

3. As you find elements that are checked, you note them in some variable so that you can retrieve the list after the loop is done.

4. Finally, when the loop is done, you do something with the information you gathered during the loop (display a message or use the facts in some other way elsewhere in your code).

Determining which check boxes are checked is very similar to determining which options are selected from a _____.

select-multiple list

LESSON 9

Task 9A-2 Page 185

2. **What fields on this form do you think should be validated and what criteria should be tested for?**

In the remainder of this lesson, you will be building validation code to test the following fields: lastname will be a required field, state must be a valid two-letter US state abbreviation, the zip code must be a 5 or 9 digit US Zip code, age must be a number and you will set a minimum and maximum value allowable, and the phone number must be a valid number with area code.

Task 9C-2 Page 192

6. **Do you see a problem with the form validation logic that should be fixed?**

Ages are never negative and are unlikely to be too much over 100. Also, you might want to set a lower limit on the age in some cases. You need to do range checking.

7. **Enter a last name, don't enter anything into the age field, and click Submit. What happens? Is that okay?**

The form is submitted. The logic of the validation function says that age, if entered, must be a number. It doesn't automatically make age a required field. This is so that you can make fields optional, but if data is entered into them, it must be numeric. You could simply add the required property to the age form field to make it be a required field.

LESSON REVIEW 9

Topic 9-A

Describe two general approaches to form field validation that you could use.

One method is to check all the fields, buiding an error report as you go, and then finally displaying the report to the user. Another method is to test the fields individually as users navigate the form, providing feedback on an as-needed basis.

Topic 9-B

Describe how you can test that data has been entered into required fields.

Test that the data in the field doesn't have zero length or that it is not all space characters.

Topic 9-C

What criteria must you consider when validating numeric data? Assume you will consider real numbers as passing your criteria.

You will have to make sure that every character in the data is a digit, minus sign, or decimal point. Additionally, you will have to make sure that the minus sign appears only as the first character and that only one decimal point is included.

Topic 9-D

List at least three string manipulation functions that you might use while validating string data.

Answers might include charAt(), toUpperCase(), substring(), and indexOf().

LESSON 10

Task 10A-1 Page 217

1. **What is one reason to use `getYear()` instead of `getFullYear()`?**

   The `getYear()` method was introduced with JavaScript 1.0, so it is universally supported. The `getFullYear()` method was introduced with JavaScript 1.2, which corresponds to the 4.x browser versions. It is less widely supported. For broadest compatibility, use `getYear()`.

2. **could you use the `getYear()` method and still be Y2K-compliant?**

   You could, but your programs would get a bit convoluted. The getYear() method returns "odd" values when the dates are outside of the current century. For example, if a date object has been set to the year 1850, getYear() would return -50. For a date of 2050, getYear() returns 150. Coding to support pre-1900 or post-2000 dates could get tricky, but it is possible. Obviously, using four digit dates and the getFullYear() method would be easier. But, remember you won't be able to use that method if you need to support pre-4.x browsers.

3. **Could you forgo using the `setFullYear()` method and use `setYear()` exclusively?**

   You could. With getYear(), if you supply a two-digit date, JavaScript assumes your date is in the 1900s (20th century). However, to set years outside of that century, simply use a four-digit year. getYear() is a JavaScript 1.0 method and is universally supported. getFullYear() is a JavaScript 1.2, method and is less widely supported. A caveat, as of JavaScript 1.2 setYear() has been deprecated in favor of setFullYear(). So, future browsers might not support it. In the meantime, it is the safer method to use.

Task 10B-1 Page 218

5. Did the minutes or seconds values change?

No. The information in the now variable is static and is not updated with the current date and time when it is used.

Task 10B-2 Page 219

5. What is wrong with the code?

The getDay() and getMonth() methods extract zero-based numeric references to the current dates. From the looks of the string, names would be better.

Task 10B-3 Page 220

7. What problems can you identify with the script as it is written so far?

When the minutes or seconds values are less than ten, the display needs to have an added zero (to display :01 rather than :1, for example). Also, the time is displayed in a 24-hour clock format.

Apply Your Knowledge 10-1 Page 221

2. The conditional operator statements to perform these conditional tests are:

```
(mins<10) ? (temp += ":0" + mins) : (temp += ":" + mins);
(sec<10) ? (temp += ":0" + sec) : (temp += ":" + sec);
```

Task 10B-4 Page 223

5. Check the answer key for some sample code to help you calculate this value.

You could calculate with lines like:

```
var msPerDay = 1000 * 60 * 60 * 24;
var msPerYear = msPerDay * 365.25;  // don't forget leap years!
```

Or, you could determine the milliseconds value for now with these two lines:

```
var now = new Date();
alert(now.valueOf());
```

Task 10D-1 Page 227

6. What problem do you notice with this function?

The numbers are real numbers, that is they have decimal components. This does not reflect the real-world application of lottery numbers.

LESSON REVIEW 10

Topic 10-A

Describe the purpose of the "get" methods and the "set" methods of the Date class of objects.

The "get" methods extract date and time values from Date objects. The "set" methods assign dates and times for those objects.

Given that Date is a class of objects, how do you use them in your programs?

You must instantiate Date objects using the new `Date()` *constructor before you can use them in your programs.*

Topic 10-B

Describe the steps necessary to create a running clock. (Don't provide code; just describe how you would do this).

1. *Instantiate a Date object.*
2. *Extract the hours, minutes, and seconds from that object.*
3. *Optionally, format the hours for a 12-hour clock.*
4. *Optionally, format the minutes and seconds to display as two-digit values even if they are less than 10.*

Topic 10-C

List one constant of the Math object.

Probably the most commonly used constant of the Math object would be Math.pi, which equals approximately 3.14159.

Do you have to instantiate Math objects?

No.

Topic 10-D

What syntax would you use to generate a random number between 28 and 4378, inclusive?

*var x = Math.random() * 4350 + 28;*

LESSON 11

Task 11A-1 Page 234

3. Open navonly.html in Internet Explorer. What happens?

The property values, rather than being calculated, are undefined. The word "undefined" is put in the document wherever the property values were supposed to be inserted.

5. Open ieonly.html in Navigator. What happens?

Navigator reports a script error (to the JavaScript console). Navigator does not support Internet Explorers object notation for referencing objects on a Web page.

Task 11A-2 Page 237

3. View the source code for the page or open the file in your editor. How is the version of JavaScript support determined?

Simply with a series of <SCRIPT> tags that specify particular JavaScript versions.

Task 11B-1 Page 240

5. Why do you think the appVersion property reports two different versions: 4.0 and MSIE 5.0?

Internet Explorer 5.0 is compatible with 4.0. So the first number is supposed to tell you. But it is actually version 5.0, and that fact is reported in the (somewhat buried) MSIE 5.0 notation. If you were writing a script specifically for Internet Explorer 5.0, you would have to test for the presence of the MSIE 5.0 string in the appVersion value.

6. How do you think you could use the navigator.appName property to detect browser type?

You could use an if() statement to determine the value of the property. If it equals "Netscape," the user is running Navigator. And if it equals "Microsoft Internet Explorer," that is what they are running. Your if() statement would then branch accordingly.

7. How could you use the navigator.appVersion property to detect browser version?

You could use the parseInt() method to extract an integer from the beginning of the string (the value of the property) and then test the result with an if statement. Or you could use the parseFloat() statement to extract a floating point number. The problem with that technique is that Internet Explorer does not report interim version information at the beginning of the appVersion string. So, you could use the indexOf() statement in a series of tests to determine a sub-version number (or to detect Internet Explorer 5.0).

8. How could you use the navigator.platform property?

First, you would have to test for JavaScript version support—the property only exists in JavaScript 1.2 and newer. Once you have done that, you can use an if() statement to determine which platform the user is running. However, the same information is available in the appVersion property. So, use it instead.

Lesson Review 11

Topic 11-A

List the three strategies you can use to code with potential incompatibilities in mind.

They are code branching, page branching, and using a cross-browser library.

Which browser or browsers support JavaScript version 1.2? Which are completely ECMA-262 compliant?

Navigator 4.x and newer and Internet Explorer 4.x and newer support JavaScript 1.2. Internet Explorer 4.x and newer and Navigator 4.6 are ECMA-262 compliant.

Topic 11-B

List the object and its properties that you will most often use to detect browsers and versions.

Perhaps this is a trick question, because your preferences for technique might play a role in determining the answer. Typically, programmers examine the appName and appVersion properties of the Navigator object or they use the if(object) shortcut and detect the presence of the document.all or document.layers objects.

application-modal

An action that stops processing for one application, permitting other applications to continue running unhindered. Displaying alert, confirm, and prompt boxes is an application-modal action.

argument

A piece of data passed to a function.

associativity

The characteristic of an operator that determines whether multiple instances of the operator in a statement are evaluated left to right or right to left.

class

A prototype of an object, sort of like a category of objects. Date is a class, whereas a specific instance of that class would be the object that you would use in your code.

client-side objects

Those objects provided by the browser environment in which client-side JavaScript runs. Examples include Window, Document, and Form.

code block

A set of statements that are referenced as a unit.

code branching

A cross-browser programming technique in which multiple logic branches are maintained within a single file and conditional statements are used to determine which blocks are executed.

composite data type

Data types that reference more than one value.

control statements

They let you control the flow of your programs to create loops, conditional statements, compare the values of variables, and enumerate the properties of objects.

core objects

Those objects and classes common to all implementations of JavaScript (core, client-side, server-side, and embedded). Examples include Date, Math, and String.

declare

The process of creating a variable.

deferred scripts

Scripts that are interpreted, but not executed, as the page is loading.

deprecated

Replaced by a newer object, property, method, or event handler. Deprecated elements miht not be included with future versions of JavaScript. so, you should not use deprecated features if you can avoid it.

Document object

Represents the page in a browser window.

DOM (Document Object Model)

The hierarchical arrangement of component objects (text, image, form, and other elements) in a document.

Dynamic HTML

The combined use of HTML, JavaScript, Cascading Style Sheets, and vendor-specific technologies to enable dynamic content in Web pages.

event

An action that happens, like a user clicking a button or a page finishing loading.

event handler

A characteristic of an object, a function to be called when a particular event occurs.

floating point number

A real number that can have a fractional component.

form element

The various text boxes, check boxes, buttons, and so forth that make up an HTML form.

GLOSSARY

frame
A sub-window within a Web page. Used for creating complex layouts for Web pages.

frameset, also frameset document
The Web page document that describes the frames to be created. Uses the <FRAMESET>, </FRAMESET>, and <FRAME> HTML tags to define the frame structure of the page.

function
A named block of code that is defined but not used immediately.

garbage collection
The automatic process of detecting and destroying unused variables. Garbage collection is done for you by the JavaScript interpreter.

global variables
Variables that are available anywhere within your program. These variables are defined outside of functions.

hexadecimal number
A whole number in the base-16 numbering system.

immediate scripts
Scripts that get executed as the page is loading.

instance
A working copy of an object class.

instantiate
To create an instance of an object class.

integer
A whole number, without a fractional component.

JavaScript Console
A window, available in Navigator, that lists JavaScript errors and in which you can enter and execute JavaScript statements.

keyword
The name of a JavaScript command, method, or object

Level 0 DOM
The subset of objects, properties, and methods that both browsers support and with which you can create dynamic Web pages.

local variables
Variables defined within a function and available only within that function.

method
A characteristic of an object, akin to a function. Objects can be manipulated or can manipulate other data via their methods.

NaN
A special JavaScript data value that means "not a number."

null
A non-value, one that is empty of all value.

object
A composite data type with three characteristics: properties, methods, and event handlers.

octal number
A whole number in the base-8 numbering system.

operator
Manipulators of data, noted with mathematical or punctuation symbols.

ordinal numbering
Sequences of numbers that begin with zero. For example, arrays use ordinal numbering to address the members of the array: the first element of an array is numbered 0.

page branching
A cross-browser programming technique in which multiple logic branches are maintained within separate files and conditional statements are used to determine which files are loaded.

precedence
The order in which operators are evaluated when more than one of a different type is used in a single statement.

primitive data type
Data types that reference one value. Numbers, strings, Booleans, and null are primitive data types.

property
A characteristic of an object, akin to a variable. Properties store values related to the object.

reflow
A feature of Internet Explorer in which the page is automatically refreshed to reflect newly added dynamic content.

reserved word
Words designated as not to be used by JavaScript programmers. Reserved words will likely be used in future versions of JavaScript. Using them in your programs could cause compatibility problems with future versions of the language.

scope
The area of a program in which a variable is defined.

scope chain
The hierarchy of areas of your program that the JavaScript interpreter will check when determining if a variable exists.

statement
A combination of language components, which follow the JavaScript syntax rules, that accomplish a single task.

syntax
The rules that dictate how programming language statements are entered in order to create an error-free program.

text-style elements
The author's category for text box, text area, password box, hidden field, and file upload box form elements. For the most part, these elements share a common set of PMEs.

Unicode
A standard character encoding scheme that use 16-bit integers to represent characters

UTC or Coordinated Universal Time
A standardized reference time based on the time in Greenwich, England, which has a longitude of 0. Other times are offset from Greenwich, or UTC, time by approximately one hour for every 15 degrees of longitude (a time zone's "dimensions").

variables
Variables are placeholders that represent the data you put in them.

Window
The object representing the browser window.

INDEX